P9-DEH-753

THE COLUMBIA UNIVERSITY
SCHOOL OF PUBLIC HEALTH

40+ GUIDE TO GOOD HEALTH

THE COLUMBIA UNIVERSITY
SCHOOL OF PUBLIC HEALTH

40+ GUIDE TO GOOD HEALTH

ROBERT J. WEISS, M.D.,

GENELL J. SUBAK-SHARPE, M.S.,

and the Editors of Consumer Reports Books

CONSUMER REPORTS BOOKS
A Division of Consumers Union
Yonkers, New York

Published by Consumers Union of United States, Inc., Yonkers, New York 10703.

Library of Congress Cataloging-in-Publication Data

The Columbia University School of Public Health 40+ guide to good health / Robert J. Weiss, Genell J. Subak-Sharpe, and the editors of Consumer Reports Books. — Rev. and updated.
p. cm.
"Originally published in 1988 by Times Books under the title 'The Columbia University School of Public Health complete guide to health and well-being after 50.'"
Includes bibliographical references and index.
ISBN 0-89043-541-3
1. Aged—Health and hygiene. 2. Middle-aged persons—Health and hygiene. 3. Aged—Mental health. 4. Middle-aged persons—Mental health. 5. Aged—Diseases—Prevention. 6. Middle-aged persons— Diseases—Prevention. I. Weiss, Robert J. II. Subak-Sharpe, Genell J. III. Columbia University. School of Public Health. IV. Consumer Reports Books. V. Title: 40+ guide to good health. VI. Title: Forty plus guide to good health. VII. Title: Columbia University School of Public Health complete guide to health and well-being after 50.
RA777.6.C65 1993
613'.0434—dc20
92-43953
CIP

ISBN 0-89043-541-3

Design by GDS / Jeffrey L. Ward
Drawings by Beth Anne Willert

Originally published in 1988 by Times Books under the title *The Columbia University School of Public Health Complete Guide to Health and Well-Being After 50.* This edition has been revised and updated.

"The Stresses of Life," page 112, is reprinted from "Epidemiological Studies of Life Change and Illness" by Richard Rahe, *International Journal of Psychiatry in Medicine* 6 (1975):133–46. Reprinted by permission.

"The Benson Relaxation Response," page 115, is adapted from *Beyond the Relaxation Response* by Herbert Benson and William Proctor, Times Books, 1984. Reprinted by permission of Times Books, a division of Random House, Inc.

"Your Medicare/Medical Insurance Claims Record," page 402, is reprinted from *Medicare/Medigap* by Carl Oshiro, Harry Snyder, and the Editors of Consumer Reports Books. Reprinted by permission of Consumer Reports Books, copyright © 1990 by Consumers Union of United States, Yonkers, New York 10703.

Second printing, July 1993
Manufactured in the United States of America

The Columbia University School of Public Health 40+ Guide to Good Health is a Consumer Reports Book published by Consumers Union, the nonprofit organization that publishes *Consumer Reports,* the monthly magazine of test reports, product Ratings, and buying guidance. Established in 1936, Consumers Union is chartered under the Not-For-Profit Corporation Law of the State of New York.

The purposes of Consumers Union, as stated in its charter, are to provide consumers with information and counsel on consumer goods and services, to give information on all matters relating to the expenditure of the family income, and to initiate and to cooperate with individual and group efforts seeking to create and maintain decent living standards.

Consumers Union derives its income solely from the sale of *Consumer Reports* and other publications. In addition, expenses of occasional public service efforts may be met, in part, by nonrestrictive, noncommercial contributions, grants, and fees. Consumers Union accepts no advertising or product samples and is not beholden in any way to any commercial interest. Its Ratings and reports are solely for the use of the readers of its publications. Neither the Ratings, nor the reports, nor any Consumers Union publication, including this book, may be used in advertising or for any commercial purpose. Consumers Union will take all steps open to it to prevent such uses of its material, its name, or the name of *Consumer Reports.*

 This book is printed on recycled paper.

Dedicated to the Columbia University
Division of Health Sciences
for its work in the forefront
of patient education

Contents

Foreword

Since its founding in 1921, the Columbia University School of Public Health has been widely recognized for its global as well as national and community health programs. The protection and improvement of health within specific community and population groups have always been the domain of public health. In our early days, the profession focused on sanitation and the spread of communicable diseases. Widespread immunization and pasteurization programs helped bring these scourges under control, at least in most of the industrialized world.

In recent decades the domain of public health has broadened to encompass virtually the entire spectrum of health care. Nutrition, environmental concerns, epidemiology of chronic diseases such as cancer and heart disease, cost-effective use of new technologies, delivery of high-quality health care to rural and urban poor, burgeoning population and disease in third world nations—these are but a few of the vital issues that we deal with every day.

At Columbia we have developed programs dealing with everything from teenage pregnancy to the myriad problems facing the aged. In looking ahead to the next century, it is obvious that our profession is going to be increasingly involved in the special problems of our "graying" population. Today the elderly make up 11 percent of our population, but the Bureau of the Census projects that this percentage will nearly double in the next four decades. By the year 2030 about 21 percent of all Americans—64.5 million in all—will be 65 or older.

It is hard to pick up a newspaper or turn on a television news program without encountering a reference to health-care costs and intimations of impending disaster in caring for our aging population. We in the public health field tend to take a more optimistic view. Thanks to new technological advances and increasing attention to preventive health care, an ever-growing number of Americans are reaching a healthy old age.

The Columbia University School of Public Health was one of the first to develop a specific division of geriatrics and gerontology. This book is a reflection of our optimism and concern. We are dedicated to educating both physicians and the general public in sound preventive health-care practices for all ages and walks of life. We know that each individual is his or her own best health-care provider. We firmly believe that knowledge is good medicine, and that a well-informed patient is a physician's best partner in total health care. This book is intended to provide that information, not only about specific diseases but also about the practical aspects of a healthful life-style.

Allan G. Rosenfield, M.D.
DeLamar Professor and Dean
Columbia University School of Public Health

Acknowledgments

The creation of any book inevitably involves many people, and this venture is no exception. Many dedicated physicians, writers, editors, researchers, illustrators, and others worked closely with us to bring this book to fruition. While it is not possible to name all of the people who have lent services and support, there are some whose outstanding contributions cannot be overlooked. Drs. Allan Rosenfield and Stephen Rosenberg have been particularly helpful in reviewing chapters and offering invaluable suggestions. Michael O'Connor has helped keep the project on track by coordinating efforts from the Columbia University School of Public Health. Catherine Caruthers, Emily Paulsen, and Jane Margaretten-Ohring have lent their considerable editorial and writing skills to help make the text readable. Janet Heath and Judith Wilmott both spent long hours researching and compiling material. Beth Anne Willert provided the original illustrations. David, Sarah, and Hope Subak-Sharpe helped with typing and numerous other details.

Minnie Weiss diligently pulled together masses of resources on educational opportunities for older students; Gerald Subak-Sharpe provided practical insight and suggestions. Julie Henderson and Sarah Uman, our editors at Consumer Reports Books, have done a masterly job in shaping the final manuscript, for which we are particularly grateful. Finally, we are especially appreciative of the many faculty members at the Columbia University School of Public Health who have contributed their particular insight and expertise; without them, this book could never have been produced.

Introduction

THE NEW PRIME OF LIFE

If you are approaching 50, you are entering into the new prime of life. At the turn of the century, the thirties were looked upon as the key decade during the adult years—the life stage when a person was expected to mark his or her major achievements and enjoy the best of health and wisdom. By the middle of the century, however, the forties became the prime decade. Today, thanks to the achievements of modern medicine and an unparalleled standard of living, we can expect our second 50 years to be as rich and full as the first. Of course, this does not mean that age does not bring changes, or that we can breeze through our mature years painlessly without any of the stresses and problems associated with aging. Nor does it change the fact that we live in a youth-oriented society. But today people in their fifties, sixties, seventies, or even older can—and do—run in the Boston Marathon, earn college degrees, start new businesses, travel throughout the world, and experience all of the enthusiasm and excitement of new ventures. In fact, it is now so commonplace for older people to participate in activities once considered the exclusive domain of youth that no one even questions our ability to do so.

Still, advancing years do bring inevitable changes: Children grow up, leave home, and establish families of their own; retirement from a lifelong career leaves us at loose ends; the body becomes more vulnerable to disease and requires more care, and we have to use common sense and pay more attention to preventive medicine; friends and loved ones move away or die. This book is intended to help you overcome inevitable hurdles and to put life changes in their proper perspective. You will learn how to avoid becoming one of the frail elderly, how to cope with losses, how to recognize medical warning signs and what to do about them. We also suggest resources for everything from adult education to medical insurance and entitlement programs for older Americans.

Throughout this book, you will be reminded repeatedly that an optimistic attitude and positive feelings of self-worth are vital assets in dealing with problems of getting older. It is often said that our middle years represent a time of personal stocktaking—of reevaluating goals, making adjustments, reaching a plateau in our professional lives, and seeking out new interests and activities. At some point in our second 50 years, most of us experience a feeling of coming to a dead end, of being overwhelmed by change and loss. Even the most Pollyannaish outlook cannot diminish the very real sense of loss that comes with the death of a loved one, or the feeling of diminished self-worth that comes with retiring from a career that has been a central focus of life for most of our adult years. It is important to realize that grief, anger, sadness, and fear are part of the human experience, and that all of us experience these feelings from time to time. How we deal with these negative feelings can be as important to overall health and well-being as daily exercise, proper nutrition, and other good health habits. In addition to providing practical health information, then, we also focus on realistic yet positive coping techniques that you can use in dealing with the emotional side of growing older.

IT'S NEVER TOO LATE

We have all heard the old saws: You can't teach an old dog new tricks. . . . Time takes its toll and there's nothing you can do about it. . . . There's no point in changing a bad habit after 40. . . . Of course, all are patently false, but it is surprising how often we hide behind these lame excuses to avoid making the effort to break a bad habit like smoking, for example. Frequently we hear people say: "I've smoked (not exercised, been overweight, etc.) for 40 years. . . . It's not going to do any good to change at this late date."

The fact is, numerous well-documented scientific studies clearly demonstrate that changing a bad habit, no matter what your age, is beneficial. For example, a long-term study by researchers at Harvard Medical School found that within two years of stopping smoking, the risk of a heart attack was about the same as for people who had never smoked. This was true regardless of age or how long a person had smoked. Obviously it would be better never to have smoked at all, but it is important for the millions of Americans who continue to use cigarettes to recognize that it is never too late to undo at least some of the damage. The same is true of lack of exercise, overweight, poor nutrition, alcohol or drug use, and other health-impairing habits. Throughout this book we offer practical guidance on how you can alter old habits and form new, more healthful ones.

In some ways, changing our psychological outlook may be even more difficult than breaking a bad physical habit, but it is not as hard as many people think, and the benefits may be even more rewarding. For example, learning to adopt a slower, less aggressive pace is not easy for the hard-driven Type A professional who is facing retirement, and all too many retired Type A executives live out their lives in frustration or turn to alcohol or other destructive outlets. Channeling that drive into community activities, learning a new skill, starting a new career, building stronger personal relationships, or any of a number of other stimulating and worthwhile activities can help a person retain his or her self-esteem and interest in life.

Even so, it would be a mistake to assume that the basic theses outlined in this book are the exclusive domain of older people. Looking ahead, realistic planning and commonsense approaches to health are important at any age. Nothing mysterious happens when you turn 50, 60, or even 80 or 90. The wise words of an 89-year-old friend provide an important lesson for all of us: "No matter what the age, we dream the same dreams, have the same hopes and aspirations. My joints may creak a bit, and I know I'm never going to climb Mount Everest or be elected President. But there are thousands of interesting things I can do, and I intend to try as many of them as I can before throwing in the towel." Our goal in creating this book has been to instill a similar outlook in our readers and to provide a realistic and practical guideline to make the second 50 years as—or even more—full and rewarding as the first.

Part I

Health and Fitness

1

Nutrition in the Later Years

"We are what we eat." The truth of this old adage is obvious, and it is truly amazing that nutrition has remained a largely neglected area of modern medicine until just recently. Most physicians in the United States have had little or no training in the effects of nutrition on health, and only now are we beginning to understand the relationship between nutrition and many of our most serious health problems, including heart disease and cancer.

Eating habits are formed early in life and influenced by many factors—cultural heritage, personal likes and dislikes, and finances, to name but a few. Because our eating habits are so firmly ingrained, they are perhaps the most difficult of all health practices to change. Still, as we emphasize throughout this book, it is never too late to change unhealthy behavior patterns, and this certainly applies to nutrition. Unfortunately, many people think that adopting more healthful eating habits means a total dietary overhaul, giving up everything they like and existing on a boring and expensive regimen of brown rice, seeds, blackstrap molasses, yogurt, and other "health store" specialties. Actually, what is needed in most instances is not a total change but, instead, relatively simple modifications to bring individual dietary patterns and eating habits in line with recommended nutritional guidelines. This may entail a refresher course in the principles of good nutrition and a close look at eating patterns, so let's start with the basics.

ESSENTIAL NUTRIENTS

All humans require some 40 essential nutrients to maintain life and health. Two of these—oxygen and water—are so commonplace that we don't even think of them as nutrients, yet they are the most essential of all. We can survive only a few minutes without oxygen and a few days without water; still, acquiring them requires little conscious effort. We take in oxygen with every breath, and water is readily available in everything we drink and in most foods. The other essential nutrients come from proteins, fats, carbohydrates, vitamins, and minerals.

PROTEIN

Protein, made up of chains of building blocks called amino acids, is used for building and maintaining body tissue, maintaining the balance of body fluids, and forming antibodies. Around 12 percent of total calories should come from protein. As the body ages, its need for protein decreases slightly; although it still has to maintain and repair existing tissue, the body is producing less new tissue. An older person, however, should not reduce the amount of protein in the diet. Since the body's ability to digest and absorb protein decreases with age, we may actually have to consume *more* protein just to meet the lowered requirement (see Table 1.1).

Even so, most of us do not have to worry about getting adequate protein; the typical American diet provides more than enough. Protein is found in both animal and plant products. Meat of all kinds, fish, poultry, milk and milk products, and eggs all are high in complete proteins, meaning these products contain all of the essential amino acids. Dried beans, peas and other legumes, grains, nuts, and seeds also are good

MATCHING PLANT FOODS TO MAKE COMPLETE PROTEINS

Combine	With
Legumes*	Grains or nuts and seeds
Nuts and seeds†	Legumes
Nuts, seeds, grains, or legumes	Dairy products

*Legumes include dried peas (black-eyed, chick, field, green), lentils, dried beans (adzuki, black, cranberry, fava, kidney, lima, marrow, mung, navy, pinto, soy), buckwheat groats, and peanuts.

†Nuts and seeds include almonds, beechnuts, Brazil nuts, cashews, filberts, pecans, pine nuts, walnuts, and pumpkin and sunflower seeds.

TABLE 1.1
Sources of Protein

To calculate your daily protein requirement in grams, multiply your ideal body weight by 0.36. Most healthy adults may reduce this amount by one-third without harmful effects.

Food	Portion size	Protein (grams)
ANIMAL SOURCES		
Beef, lean ground	3 oz	21
Cheddar cheese	1 oz	7
Chicken, dark w/o skin	3 oz	23
Chicken, light w/o skin	3 oz	26
Cottage cheese, low-fat	½ cup	16
Eggs	1 large	6
Flounder	3 oz	20
Ham, boneless	3 oz	19
Milk, skim	8 oz	8
Shrimp	3 oz	18
Tuna, white, canned	3 oz drained	23
Turkey, light w/o skin, roasted	3 oz	25
Turkey, dark w/o skin, roasted	3 oz	24
Yogurt, plain, low-fat	8 oz	12
VEGETABLE AND GRAIN SOURCES		
Beans, kidney	½ cup	8
Beans, lima	½ cup	6
Bread, whole wheat	1 slice	3
Lentils	½ cup	9
Muffin, corn	1 medium	3
Oatmeal	1 cup	6
Potato	½ cup	1
Rice, white	1 cup	4
Shredded wheat	2 biscuits	5
Spaghetti	1 cup	6
Tofu (soybean curd)	½ cup	10

Source: Adapted from Victor Herbert, M.D., F.A.C.P., and Genell J. Subak-Sharpe, M.S., *The Mount Sinai School of Medicine Complete Book of Nutrition* (New York: St. Martin's Press, 1990), 723–74.

sources of protein, but individually these items do not contain all of the essential amino acids and must be consumed in the right combination to make complete proteins.

The typical American diet is high in animal protein and relatively low in plant sources. Since a diet high in meat is also likely to be high in fat and cholesterol, most nutritionists urge a reduction in meat consumption and a corresponding increase in legumes and other plant proteins. This is important because myths abound concerning the value of protein. For example, many people are convinced that because protein helps build muscles, the more a person consumes, the more muscles they will build. This is not true, of course; once muscle tissue has reached its full size, it will not continue to grow, no matter how much protein is consumed. Muscle cells can be strengthened and enlarged by exercise, but consuming extra protein will not increase muscle mass. Instead, excess protein that is not used for repair, energy, and other body functions simply will be converted to fatty tissue and stored in the body. Also, there is some evidence that excessive protein intake may be a factor in Parkinson's disease and prostatic disorders.

CARBOHYDRATES

Carbohydrates are the body's major source of energy for all of its tissues and varied functions. There are two major types of carbohydrates: simple (sugars) and complex (starches). Simple carbohydrates are quickly converted to glucose or blood sugar, the body's major fuel. This is why a piece of candy, a high-sugar soft drink, a glass of orange juice, or other foods high in sugars or simple carbohydrates give a quick burst of energy. Starches are not as quickly metabolized to glucose and therefore produce a slower and steadier supply of energy.

Nutritionists recommend that carbohydrates make up about 55 to 58 percent of daily calories consumed, and that most of these calories should come from starches, the form of complex carbohydrates. Excellent sources of complex carbohydrates are whole-grain breads and cereals, pastas, potatoes, and other vegetables. Simple carbohydrates should come mostly from fruits, which provide important vitamins and minerals in addition to natural sugars, rather than from refined sugar, honey, corn syrups, and other sweets, which are essentially empty calories. Milk, which contains lactose (milk sugar), is another good source of simple carbohydrates.

Many people mistakenly assume that pasta, potatoes, and other starchy foods are more fattening than high-protein foods. In fact, both proteins and carbohydrates contain the same number of calories per gram. Since meats and other animal proteins usually contain large amounts of fat (and fat contains 9 calories per gram), a high-meat diet actually is much more fattening than a diet high in starches. In addition, many high-carbohydrate foods are also high in dietary fiber (roughage), which gives a feeling of fullness. This makes us less likely to overeat.

TABLE 1.2
Cutting Down on Fats

If you cut out	Times per day or week	Approximate reduction in fat consumption (grams)
1 oz light cream in coffee	5/day	200 grams/week
8 oz ice cream	3/week	48 grams/week
1 slice apple pie	3/week	53 grams/week
1 slice bread and butter	3/week	12 grams/week
10 french fries	3/week	20 grams/week
1 oz roasted peanuts	4/week	55 grams/week
10 potato chips	4/week	32 grams/week
1 slice cheese pizza	1/week	5 grams/week
1 tbsp French dressing	1/day	37 grams/week
3.5 oz ground sirloin steak	1/week	34 grams/week
3.5 oz lamb chop	1/week	26 grams/week
8 oz whole milk	1/day	63 grams/week
2 chocolate chip cookies	3/week	15 grams/week
1 oz Cheddar cheese	3/week	32 grams/week
2 slices bologna	2/week	32 grams/week
1 plain doughnut	3/week	20 grams/week
2 slices bacon	3/week	20 grams/week

Note: 1 gram of fat contains 9 calories.

FATS

Many people are surprised to learn that a certain amount of fat is essential to maintain health. However, most Americans consume too much fat, and we are constantly urged to cut down or eliminate it from our diet. Less than 30 percent of our total calories should come from fats (compared to the 40 percent in the average American diet). For example, a 52-year-old woman of average height and activity level who is not overweight requires 1,800 calories a day, of which a maximum of 540, or 60 grams, may be derived from fats.

That is not to say that the body needs this much fat. There is no RDA for fat, and often as little as a tablespoon a day is sufficient. People with other risk factors, or people who are trying to lose weight, may want to decrease the fat content of their diet to about 20 percent (see Table 1.2).

Most dietary fats are made up of three types of fatty acids: saturated, polyunsaturated, or monounsaturated. These fatty acids differ in the number of hydrogen atoms each molecule can carry. Saturated fats, which are found in most meats and in palm and coconut oils, tend to be hard at room temperature and carry the fewest hydrogen atoms, while polyunsaturated fats can carry the most. Monounsaturated fats fall in between. Vegetable fats—olive, peanut, corn, and safflower oils, for example—all are high in unsaturated fats of one kind or the other.

Saturated fats tend to raise the level of cholesterol in the blood, which increases the risk of heart disease. Daily intake of saturated fat should be limited to less than 10 percent of total calories. In addition, animal fats tend to contain large amounts of cholesterol themselves. In contrast, both mono- and polyunsaturated fats lower blood cholesterol, and, of course, vegetable fats do not contain any cholesterol.

It is important to distinguish between the dietary fat we consume and body fat, which is stored energy and can be made from excess dietary fats, proteins, or carbohydrates. To convert dietary fat into body fat, we need to consume a certain amount of linoleic acid, an essential fatty acid found in polyunsaturated fats. This is a substance that the body cannot manufacture itself. We can get all of the linoleic acid we need from only about a tablespoon of polyunsaturated fat each day.

Fats have a number of important functions: They make foods more palatable by adding flavor, aroma, and texture. They are needed for growth and for maintenance of healthy skin. Fats carry the fat-soluble vitamins A, D, E, and K, and are also essential

KINDS OF FATS

Mostly polyunsaturated	Mostly monounsaturated	Mostly saturated
Corn oil	Avocado	Butter
Cottonseed oil	Cashew	Cheese
Fish	Olives and olive oil	Chocolate
Margarine (especially if soft and/or made from corn, safflower, or sunflower oil)	Peanuts and peanut oil	Coconut and coconut oil
Safflower oil	Peanut butter	Egg yolk
Soybean oil	Poultry	Lard
Sunflower oil		Meat
		Palm oil
		Vegetable shortening

COOKING TIPS TO CUT DOWN ON FATS

- Use a broiler, wok, vegetable steamer, or nonstick pan instead of frying in fat.
- Use pan spray instead of fat.
- Switch to a polyunsaturated margarine. Liquid or soft margarines high in corn, safflower, or sunflower oil are the best choices.
- Use skim or low-fat milk.
- Buy lean grades of meat and trim away fat. Use smaller amounts of meat by making stir-fried vegetable and meat dishes.
- Increase use of fish, poultry, legumes, or pasta for main dishes.
- Use salad dressings made with small amounts of olive or polyunsaturated oil instead of creamed dressings.
- Use low-fat cream cheese or yogurt as a substitute for blue cheese and sour cream.
- Bake, broil, or roast meats using a rack.
- To reduce cholesterol from eggs, use an egg white plus a teaspoon of polyunsaturated oil instead of the whole egg in cooking. Discard every other egg yolk when making an omelette, scrambled eggs, or other egg dishes, and limit whole eggs to two or three per week.

for the body to absorb these vitamins. Stored fat provides a concentrated source of energy, and it is also essential to make certain hormones and other body chemicals. Body fat helps prevent heat loss and provides protection for internal organs.

VITAMINS

Vitamins are organic substances the body needs in very small quantities for such essential processes as metabolism and for the formation of blood cells, hormones, chemicals, and genetic materials. The fat-soluble vitamins (A, D, E, and K) can be stored in the body and therefore do not have to be consumed daily. Water-soluble vitamins (the B-complex vitamins and C) are not stored, so they should be consumed every day or so.

The U.S. Recommended Dietary Allowances (RDAs) serve as guidelines to how much of each vitamin or mineral we need each day (see Table 1.3). The best way to ensure adequate amounts of all vitamins is to eat a variety of foods from all food groups.

TABLE 1.3

Basic Facts About Vitamins

FAT-SOLUBLE VITAMINS

Nutrient (RDA for adults and children 11 and older)	What it does	Sources	Signs of deficiency	Signs of overdose
Vitamin A (1000 retinal equivalent for men; 800 for women.)	Helps to form and maintain healthy function of eyes, hair, teeth, gums, skin, nails, bones, mucous membranes, and various glands. It is also involved in fat metabolism. Helps ward off infection. Prevents night blindess.	Whole milk, butter, fortified margarine, eggs, green leafy or yellow vegetables and fruit, fish, liver and other organ meats.	Night blindness, growth reduction, impaired resistance, infection, rough skin, drying of the eyes.	Headaches, blurred vision, rashes, extreme fatigue, diarrhea, nausea, loss of appetite, hair loss, menstrual irregularities, liver damage, dry skin, itchiness.
Vitamin D (5 to 10 mcg)	Needed for the body to absorb calcium and phosphorus, which build strong bones and teeth.	Vitamin D–fortified milk, liver, oils, egg yolks, butter. Exposure to the sun's ultraviolet rays enables the body to produce its own.	*In children*: rickets. *In adults*: bone softening, thinning of the bones leading to spontaneous fractures; may play a role in osteoporosis.	Calcium deposits in kidneys and blood of infants and throughout the body in adults; nausea, loss of appetite, kidney stones, high blood pressure, high blood cholesterol, fragile bones.
Vitamin E (alpha tocopherol) (10 mg for men; 8 mg for women)	Helps form red blood cells, muscle and other tissues. Prevents fatty acid oxidation.	Wheat germ, vegetable oil, margarine, nuts, seeds, eggs, milk, whole-grain cereals, breads, poultry, seafood, cooked greens.	Unknown but rare.	Possible reduced sexual function.
Vitamin K* (45 to 80 mcg)	Needed for normal blood clotting and normal bone metabolism.	Green leafy vegetables, peas, cereals, grains, dairy products, liver, potatoes, cabbage. Also made by intestinal bacteria.	Bleeding problems and liver damage.	Jaundice in infants.

WATER-SOLUBLE VITAMINS

Vitamin B_1 (thiamine) (1.0 to 1.5 mg)	Helps get energy from food by promoting proper metabolism of sugars and starch; promotes normal appetite and digestion; needed for nerve function.	Pork, poultry, liver, pasta, wheat germ, whole-grain or enriched bread, lima beans, seafood.	Anxiety, hysteria, nausea, depression, muscular cramps, loss of appetite. Extreme deficiency leads to beriberi, peripheral paralysis, and heart failure. In United States, deficiency occurs mainly among alcoholics.	Unknown. However, due to the interdependency of the B-complex vitamins, an excess of one may cause a deficiency of another.
Vitamin B_2 (riboflavin) (1.2 to 1.8 mg)	Functions in the body's use of carbohydrates, proteins, and fats, particularly to release energy to cells; helps maintain good vision; needed to maintain mucous membranes and certain enzymes that help change food into energy.	Milk, eggs, dark-green leafy vegetables, liver, meat, whole-grain or enriched bread and cereals.	Lesions around the nose and eyes; soreness and burning of the lips, mouth, and tongue; difficulty eating and swallowing; visual problems; sensitivity to light.	See vitamin B_1.
Vitamin B_6 (pyridoxine) (1.7 to 2.0 mg for men; 1.4 to 1.6 mg for women)	Has essential role in both protein and carbohydrate metabolism. It also aids in the formation of red blood cells and proper functioning of the nervous system, including brain cells.	Green leafy vegetables, meat, fish, poultry, whole-grain cereal, liver, nuts, carrots, herring, bananas, avocados, potatoes, prunes, watermelon.	Depression, confusion, convulsions, inflammation of mucous membranes in the mouth, patches of itchy, scaly skin. Older people and alcoholics are more prone to a deficiency.	Overconsumption can lead to dependency and cause deficiency symptoms when reduced to normal levels. Also can cause loss of feeling in fingers, legs, etc., because of sensory nerve destruction.
Vitamin B_{12} (cobalamin) (2 mcg)	Helps to build vital genetic material (nucleic acids) for cell nuclei and to form red blood cells. Essential for normal functioning of all body cells, including brain nerve cells as well as tissues that make red cells.	Milk, saltwater fish, oysters, meat, liver, kidneys, eggs, poultry, other animal products.	Rare except in strict vegetarians, elderly people, and people with malabsorption disorders. Can cause blood and nerve damage.	See vitamin B_1.

TABLE 1.3
Basic Facts About Vitamins (*cont'd*)

WATER-SOLUBLE VITAMINS *(cont'd)*

Nutrient (RDA for adults and children 11 and older)	What it does	Sources	Signs of deficiency	Signs of overdose
Niacin (B_3, nicotinic acid) (15 to 20 mg for men; 13 to 15 mg for women)	Promotes normal appetite and digestion. Necessary for healthy nervous system. Needed in certain enzymes that help convert food into energy. Cholesterol-lowering agent in high doses.	Liver, meat, fish, poultry, green vegetables, nuts, whole-grain bread and cereal (except corn), enriched bread and cereal.	Pellagra, a disease in which the skin forms a reddish rash that turns dark and rough. Diarrhea.	Ulcers, liver disorders, high blood sugar, high uric acid, hot flashes, cardiac arrhythmias.
Biotin* (100 to 200 mcg)	Involved in the formation of certain fatty acids and in the production of energy from the metabolism of glucose. It is essential for the workings of many body chemical systems.	Eggs, green leafy vegetables, kidneys, liver, string beans, milk, meat. Also made by intestinal bacteria.	Rare except in infants. Mild skin disorders, depression, insomnia, muscle pain, anemia.	*See* vitamin B_1.
Folic acid (folate or folacin) (150 to 200 mcg)	Assists in the formation of certain body proteins and genetic materials for the cell nucleus and in the formation of red blood cells.	Green leafy vegetables, liver, wheat germ, legumes, bran, nuts, orange and grapefruit juice.	Impaired cell division and altered protein synthesis leading to megaloblastic anemia (abnormal red blood cells) or macrocytic	Could mask a B_{12} deficiency. Convulsions in epileptics. At very high doses, can interfere with zinc absorption.

		One fresh, uncooked vegetable or fruit prevents deficiency.	anemia (oversized red blood cells). Weight loss, gastrointestinal disturbances, irritability. Alcoholics, pregnant women, and poor people more prone to deficiency.	
Pantothenic acid* (4 to 7 mg)	A key substance in the body metabolism involved in changing carbohydrates, fats, and proteins into molecular forms needed by the body. Also required for formation of certain hormones and nerve-regulating substances.	Found in most animal and plant foods; also manufactured by intestinal bacteria.	Not known in humans except under experimental conditions.	May increase need for thiamine and lead to thiamine deficiency.
Vitamin C (ascorbic acid) (50 to 60 mg)	Helps bind cells together and strengthens walls of blood vessels. Needed for healthy gums. Helps body resist infection. Promotes healing of wounds and cuts.	Citrus fruits and juices, green leafy vegetables, tomatoes, melon, cauliflower, strawberries, potatoes, cabbage, peppers, snow peas.	Bleeding gums; loose teeth; hemorrhages under the skin; slow healing; dry, rough skin; loss of appetite. Scurvy in extreme cases.	Bladder and kidney stones, urinary tract irritation, diarrhea, and blood disorders. Overconsumption can lead to dependency that can cause deficiency symptoms when reduced to normal doses.

*RDAs not established; amounts are estimated safe and adequate dietary intakes.

Most people do not need to take extra vitamins, although exceptions might be made for certain medical conditions that increase the need for certain vitamins.

Despite the rareness of true vitamin deficiencies in this country (they tend to be found in alcoholics or others who do not consume an adequate diet), many people worry that they somehow are not getting enough vitamins and minerals from their food. Some resort to taking supplements, frequently in megadoses that are many times the recommended allowance. This can lead to potentially dangerous overdosing.

Since metabolism and body needs change with age, the RDAs for some nutrients change with age as well. For example, older people may need additional thiamine (vitamin B_1), but this does not mean that they need to take it in pill form. Simply increasing their intake of pasta, poultry, whole-grain cereals, or other thiamine-rich foods will suffice.

Many vitamins can be diminished or destroyed in food preparation—for example, by overcooking or boiling vegetables in large amounts of water, which is then drained off. Minimal cooking, such as steaming or stir-frying, conserves vitamins.

Megadosing. Too much of a good thing can be bad, and this statement is especially true of vitamins and minerals. As mentioned previously, vitamin and mineral deficiencies are relatively rare in the United States. Nutritional deficiencies are usually limited to a few groups of people: those addicted to alcohol or drugs; the homeless and other economically disadvantaged individuals; people who have underlying diseases that hinder absorption of nutrients; and those who follow a limited diet, such as strict vegans (vegans eat no animal foods, not even milk, cheese, or eggs).

Most of us do not think of vitamins as being drugs, but when they are consumed in amounts that are greater than the body can handle, they become pharmacological agents with the same potential for adverse reactions and side effects as any chemical drug. For example, taking large amounts of vitamins A or D can cause serious liver damage and may even be life-threatening. In general, unsafe dosages start at about three times the RDAs for minerals, five times the RDAs for fat-soluble vitamins, and ten times the RDAs for water-soluble vitamins. Before taking any supplements, you should consult your doctor first and make sure that the pills do not exceed the RDAs. Unless your doctor specifically prescribes a higher dosage, you probably don't need supplements. And contrary to popular belief, it does not make any difference (except in price) whether a vitamin supplement is "natural" or synthetic; both types are chemical compounds that are utilized the same way by the body.

Other overused vitamins are C and E. Megadoses of vitamin C have long been touted as a preventive for everything from the common cold to cancer, but to date, no solid scientific evidence supports these claims. Nevertheless, many people have taken to giving themselves megadoses of vitamin C, just in case. Usually, large amounts of vitamin C are harmless because the excess will be excreted, but evidence has shown that megadoses can cause adverse effects such as nausea, cramps, diarrhea, and urinary tract irritation in some people. Megadoses can also interfere with the accuracy of certain laboratory tests, the efficacy of certain drugs, and the metabolism of certain other vitamins and minerals.

Most of the claims for megadoses of vitamin E are just as far-reaching as for C, and equally unproved. For example, vitamin E has been touted as capable of promoting new hair growth, preventing ulcers, and increasing sex drive, among other things. Again, no sound evidence supports these claims. And although low-cholesterol diets may increase the body's need for vitamin E, these diets have built-in sources of extra vitamin E. It can be found in vegetable-oil margarines, for instance.

There *is* evidence that vitamin E may play a role in the prevention of heart disease. A study by the World Health Organization (WHO) found that in 62 percent of subjects who were dying from heart disease, vitamin E levels were low. Only 20 percent of the subjects were smokers or were found to have high total cholesterol or high blood pressure. Another small study involved 504 men, 110 of whom had angina. It found that the level of antioxidants, including vitamin E, was higher than average in the men who did not experience angina. This evidence is not conclusive. Results from controlled clinical trials will determine the final word. In the meantime, a supplement of 200 to 600 milligrams per day, taken under a doctor's supervision, may be beneficial. In general, supplements should be avoided by people who take anticoagulant drugs or who have a blood-clotting disorder. High doses of vitamin E are also contraindicated in people who have a genetic tendency to conserve iron—about 10 percent of the population.

Mineral supplements can be particularly dangerous for any older person whose kidneys or liver cannot metabolize the excess. And taking too much of one mineral can upset the balance of others. For instance, excess phosphorus interferes with the body's ability to absorb calcium. Excessive minerals also can interfere with the action of a number of drugs, so a person on medication should never take vitamin or mineral supplements without first consulting his or her physician. Calcium supplements, for example, can interfere with the body's ability to utilize certain antibiotics. Consult with a doctor and pharmacist if such a combination is necessary.

MINERALS

Minerals are inorganic substances that, like vitamins, are needed in very small amounts for a wide array of essential body functions. Three minerals—calcium, phosphorus, and magnesium—are referred to as *macrominerals* because the body needs these minerals in relatively large amounts. The other essential minerals are *microminerals,* or trace elements, and are needed only in very small amounts. But these amounts are all relative: The difference in dosage is between milligrams and micrograms—and as with vitamins, mineral overdoses can be dangerous. A well-balanced diet should supply all the body's needs (see Table 1.4).

TABLE 1.4
Basic Facts About Minerals

Nutrient (RDA for adults)	What it does	Sources	Signs of deficiency	Signs of overdose
		MACROMINERALS		
Calcium (800 to 1,200 mg)†	Helps build strong bones and teeth. Helps blood clot. Helps muscles and nerves function normally. Needed to activate certain enzymes that help change food into energy.	Milk and milk products, green leafy vegetables, citrus fruits, dried peas and beans, sardines (with bones), shellfish, tofu.	Rickets in children; osteoporosis or osteomalacia (soft bones) in adults.	Drowsiness, calcium deposits, impaired absorption of iron and other minerals, peptic ulcer, mental confusion, lethargy, muscle pain, calcium kidney stones.
Phosphorus (800 to 1,200 mg)	With calcium, helps build strong bones and teeth. Needed by certain enzymes that help change food into energy. Promotes proper nerve and muscle function.	Meat, poultry, fish, eggs, dried peas and beans, milk and milk products, egg yolk, and phosphates in processed foods and soft drinks.	Weakness, bone pain, decreased appetite (rare).	Upset of the calcium-phosphorous ratio, hindering uptake of calcium.
Magnesium (280 to 350 mg)	Activator for enzymes that transfer and release energy in the body. Necessary for production of genetic material. Promotes bone growth.	Raw leafy green vegetables, nuts, soy beans, whole grains, oysters, scallops.	Muscular tremors, twitching and leg cramps, weakness, irregular heartbeat. Deficiency is sometimes seen in people with severe kidney disease, prolonged diarrhea, or alcoholism, or in people who take diuretics.	Upset of the calcium-magnesium ratio, leading to impaired nervous-system function. Especially dangerous for people with impaired kidney function.

TRACE MINERALS

Iron (10 to 15 mg)	Combines with protein to make hemoglobin, the red substance in the blood that carries oxygen from lungs to cells, and myoglobin, the substance that stores oxygen in muscles.	Liver, meat products, egg yolk, shellfish, green leafy vegetables, peas, beans, dried prunes, raisins, apricots, whole-grain and enriched bread and cereal.	Iron deficiency anemia, pallor of skin, weakness and fatigue, headache, shortness of breath.	Toxic buildup in liver, pancreas, and heart (very rare). Diabetes, interference with zinc absorption, arrhythmias.
Iodine (150 mcg)	Necessary for normal function of the thyroid gland.	Iodized salt, seafood.	Thyroid enlargement (goiter). Causes cretinism in infants.	Damaged thyroid function.
Zinc (15 mg for men; 12 mg for women)	Element of enzymes that work with red blood cells to move carbon dioxide from the tissues to the lungs.	Meat, fish, egg yolk, milk.	Loss of taste and delayed wound healing. Growth retardation and delayed sexual maturation in children.	Gastrointestinal symptoms such as nausea, vomiting, bleeding, and abdominal pain. Premature labor and stillbirth in pregnant women.
Copper (2 to 30 mg)	Used by several important proteins, including enzymes, involved in respiratory and red blood cell function. Also needed for making red blood cells. Responsible in part for body's pigment. Enhances iron absorption.	Organ meats, shellfish, nuts, fruit, dried legumes, raisins, mushrooms.	Rarely seen in adults. In infants, hypochromic anemia with abnormal development of bone, nervous tissue, lungs, and pigmentation of hair.	Liver disease and gastrointestinal symptoms such as vomiting and diarrhea. Overdoses can occur as a result of eating foods cooked in unlined copper pots.

TABLE 1.4
Basic Facts About Minerals (*cont'd*)

TRACE MINERALS *(cont'd)*

Nutrient (RDA for adults)	What it does	Sources	Signs of deficiency	Signs of overdose
Fluorine* (fluoride) (1.5 to 4 mg)	Contributes to solid tooth and bone formation, especially in children. Enhances body's uptake of calcium, possibly helping prevent osteoporosis.	Fluoridated water, food cooked in fluoridated water, fish, meat, tea.	Tooth decay.	Mottling of enamel on teeth.
Chromium* (0.05 to 0.2 mg)	With insulin, it is required for metabolism of glucose.	Dried brewer's yeast, whole-grain breads, peanuts.	Diabetes-like symptoms.	Unknown.
Selenium (40 to 70 mcg)	Interacts with vitamin E; prevents breakdown of fats and body chemicals.	Seafood, egg yolk, chicken, meat, garlic, whole-grain cereals, mushrooms, onions.	Unknown.	Nausea, abdominal pain, diarrhea, hair and nail damage, fatigue, irritability. Can be fatal.
Manganese* (2.5 to 5 mg)	Needed for normal tendon and bone structure; part of some enzymes.	Bran, coffee, tea, nuts, peas, beans.	Unknown.	Nerve damage.
Sulfur (RDA unknown)	Component of several amino acids; used to make hair and nails.	Wheat germ, dried beans, beef, clams, peanuts.	Unknown.	Unknown.

Molybdenum* (0.15 to 0.5 mg)	Forms part of enzymes necessary for metabolism. Helps regulate storage of iron.	Legumes, cereals, dark green vegetables, liver, other organ meats.	Unknown.	Loss of copper; joint pain similar to gout.
MINERALS THAT ARE ELECTROLYTES (MAINTAIN PROPER BODY CHEMISTRY)				
Sodium* (1,100 to 3,300 mg)	Helps maintain water balance inside and outside cells.	Table salt, processed foods, ham, meat, fish, poultry, eggs, milk.	Loss of sodium through extreme perspiration can cause muscle cramps, headache, weakness.	High blood pressure, kidney disease, water retention (edema), congestive heart failure.
Chloride* (1,700 to 5,100 mg)	Part of hydrochloric acid found in gastric juice and important to normal digestion.	Same as sodium.	Upsets balance of acids and bases in body fluids (very rare).	Upsets acid-base balance.
Potassium* (1,875 to 5,625 mg)	With sodium, helps regulate body fluid balance. Needed for transmission of nerve impulses, for muscles to contract, and for proper metabolism.	Bananas, dried fruits, peanut butter, potatoes, orange juice, other fruits and vegetables.	Muscular weakness, irritability, irregular heartbeat (rare but may result from prolonged diarrhea or use of diuretics), kidney and lung failure.	High levels of potassium can cause severe cardiac irregularities and can lead to cardiac arrest. Nausea, diarrhea.

*RDAs not established; amounts are estimated safe and adequate daily dietary intakes.
†Many experts now recommend that women consume 1,000 to 1,500 mg.

Osteoporosis. In recent years, the public has become increasingly aware of the importance of calcium, and the food and drug industries have been quick to respond. Calcium is now being added to everything from breakfast cereals to soft drinks, and there are dozens of highly advertised calcium supplements on the market.

Calcium is the body's most abundant mineral. (All adults need about 800 to 1,500 milligrams of calcium daily.) Calcium is needed to build and maintain bones and teeth; it also helps regulate blood clotting, muscle tone, and nerve function; it is necessary for the absorption of vitamin B_{12} through the intestines as well as for the release of energy from carbohydrates, fats, and proteins. The bones serve as the body's calcium storehouse; about 98 percent is in the bones, 1 percent is in the teeth, and the remaining 1 percent circulates in the blood. Calcium constantly moves in and out of the bones, too. When blood calcium levels fall, the bones release enough of the mineral to restore the proper balance. Conversely, when blood levels exceed a certain amount, the calcium is absorbed by the bones or excreted by the kidneys.

Excessive loss of bone calcium can eventually lead to osteoporosis, a condition in which the bones become weak and porous with an increased tendency to fracture. Older women are especially prone to osteoporosis for a number of reasons. After menopause the ovaries no longer make the female sex hormone, estrogen, which appears to be essential in proper calcium metabolism. Women also have less bone mass than men, which makes them more susceptible to osteoporosis.

Adequate calcium intake throughout life is important in building and maintaining bones. Unfortunately, many women shun high-calcium foods—milk, cheese, and other milk products—to cut calories. Waiting until middle age or until after bone-thinning problems appear before taking calcium supplements is like the proverbial locking of the barn door after the horse has fled. Starting to increase calcium intake at age 50 will not by itself prevent osteoporosis or repair already damaged bones. But adequate calcium is an important component—along with estrogen replacement after menopause, exercise, and adequate intake of vitamin D—in the prevention and treatment of osteoporosis.

Aging interferes with the body's ability to absorb calcium. And when people are inactive or are immobile for a period—following injury or illness, for example—their bones do not absorb calcium as efficiently and become further weakened. Other factors that hinder the body's ability to absorb calcium or that increase its excretion include a high-protein, high-fat diet; cigarette smoking; and excessive consumption of caffeine, dietary fiber (especially bran), and foods high in phosphorus and oxalic acid (for example, spinach).

Low-fat, preferably skim, milk is the ideal source of calcium because lactose, or milk sugar, seems to enhance calcium absorption. Unfortunately, many older people cannot drink milk, often because their digestive system cannot handle the lactose. But calcium is found in tofu, green leafy vegetables (except spinach), canned sardines with bones, and other foods (see Table 1.5).

Table 1.5
Dietary Sources of Calcium

Food	Serving size	Calcium (mg)
MILK AND MILK PRODUCTS		
Milk (skim, whole,* etc.)	8 oz	300
Yogurt, whole milk*	8 oz	275
Yogurt, skim with nonfat milk solids	8 oz	452
Nonfat dry milk	1 tbsp	57
Ice cream, vanilla*	1 cup	208
Ice milk, vanilla	1 cup	283
CHEESE		
American*	1 oz	195
Cheddar*	1 oz	211
Cottage, creamed	1 cup	211
Cottage, low-fat dry	1 cup	138
Cream cheese*	1 oz	23
Parmesan, grated	1 tbsp	69
Swiss*	1 oz	259
FISH/SEAFOOD		
Mussels	3½ oz	88
Oysters	5–8 medium	94
Salmon, canned with bones	3½ oz	198
Sardines, canned with bones	3½ oz	449
Shrimp	3½ oz	63
FRUIT		
Figs, dried	5 medium	126
Orange	1 medium	65
Prunes, dried	10 large	51
NUTS/SEEDS		
Almonds or hazelnuts*	12–15	38
Sesame seeds*	1 oz	28
Sunflower seeds*	1 oz	34
VEGETABLES		
Bean curd (tofu)	3½ oz.	128
Beans, garbanzo	½ cup	80
Beans, pinto	½ cup	135

TABLE 1.5
Dietary Sources of Calcium (*cont'd*)

Food	Serving size	Calcium (mg)
	VEGETABLES (*cont'd*)	
Beans, red kidney	½ cup	110
Broccoli, cooked	⅔ cup	88
Chard, cooked†	½ cup	61
Collard greens, cooked†	½ cup	152
Fennel, raw	3½ cup	100
Kale, cooked†	½ cup	134
Lettuce, romaine	3½ cup	68
Mustard greens, cooked†	½ cup	145
Rutabaga, cooked	½ cup	59
Seaweed, agar, raw	3½ oz.	567
Seaweed, kelp, raw	3½ oz.	1,093
Squash, acorn	½ medium, baked	61

*High fat content
†Foods high in oxalic acid, which hinders absorption

Many nutritionists urge people past middle age to keep a food diary to see just how much calcium they are getting. If it is less than the recommended 1,000 to 1,500 milligrams, they should make up the difference with a calcium supplement, although deriving calcium from their food is preferable (see Table 1.6). Also, it is not beneficial to take in more calcium than is necessary. The body absorbs about 30 to 40 percent of the calcium in the diet, and it tends to do so at that level even when dietary calcium is increased with supplements. Moreover, consuming much more than is necessary can increase the risk of kidney stones in susceptible people.

Fluoride, or fluorine, one of the essential trace minerals, is also essential in maintaining strong bones and may be included in the treatment regimen for osteoporosis.

SODIUM. There is little doubt that, to most people, salt is indeed the king of condiments. Once more precious than gold, in ancient times it was so scarce that men went to war for it and explored the earth in its quest. Today, of course, salt is plentiful throughout the industrialized world, and the average American consumes 2 to 4 teaspoons of salt a day—many times what the body actually needs. Many experts think that our large intake of salt contributes to our great incidence of high blood pressure and heart disease. However, this is still unproved and controversial.

Salt is made up of two essential minerals, sodium and chlorine. Dr. Derek Denton, an Australian scientist and researcher, contends that our appetite for salt is a powerful

TABLE 1.6
Sample High-Calcium Menu

The following menu illustrates how a person can get adequate calcium, in this example about 1,400 mg, from an ordinary diet. If the milk is eliminated, a 600-mg calcium supplement or other high-calcium foods can be substituted.

Food	Calcium (mg)
BREAKFAST	
Fresh orange	65
Cereal with ½ cup skim milk	150
8 oz skim milk	300
LUNCH	
Sandwich made with lean ham and 1 oz low-fat cheese	260
Green salad	40
2 fig bars	100
Beverage	0
DINNER	
Vegetable soup	30
Roast chicken	0
Broccoli	88
Baked potato	0
Green salad	40
½ cup ice cream	100
BEFORE BED	
1 glass skim milk	300
Total calcium	**1,473**

instinct developed over 30 million years of evolution. He points out that it is no accident that salt is one of the four primary elements of taste because, without it, life cannot exist. Sodium is one of the essential electrolytes that help cells maintain their delicate fluid balance. Our need for salt is believed to be a holdover from our evolutionary origin in the sea. As multicellular organisms evolved and moved onto land, they carried with them their saltwater origin in their blood. In fact, our blood plasma today is chemically similar to seawater.

Like all essential nutrients, ingesting either too little or too much salt can be harmful. Excess sodium is normally excreted in the urine. However, if the kidneys cannot handle all the salt, the body will increase its fluid or blood volume to restore a more normal sodium balance. This may lead to high blood pressure and a buildup of body fluids. People who are genetically predisposed to *hypertension* (the medical term for high blood pressure) may develop high blood pressure when they consume too much sodium; in fact, their predisposition may be due to an increased sensitivity to the effects of sodium. Excessive sodium also can worsen kidney disease and congestive heart failure, as well as the bloating that many women experience during their premenstrual phase.

Sodium is found naturally in a variety of foods, including cheeses, eggs, meat, and fish. The average person can usually satisfy the recommended daily intake of 1,100 to 3,300 milligrams without any added salt. The American Heart Association's dietary guidelines recommend consuming no more than 3 grams of sodium per day. (One gram of sodium is equal to slightly less than one-half teaspoon of salt.)

Removing the saltshaker from the table and not adding salt during food preparation are two good ways to cut down on sodium intake. But for people who should markedly reduce sodium consumption, these steps may not be enough. Studies have found that most of the sodium we consume is actually hidden in processed foods—everything from breakfast cereals to canned goods, including many that don't taste at all salty. Sometimes salt can be reduced in convenience foods by draining or rinsing. For example, high-salt canned foods such as tuna can be drained and rinsed in water for one minute to lower sodium content.

A diet designed to cut down on sodium should emphasize fresh fish and poultry as well as fresh vegetables, fruits, and grains. Alternative seasonings are highly recommended and readily available. Remember, though, that seasoned or flavored salts, such as garlic or onion salt, are just as high in sodium as regular table salt. Soy sauce is especially high in sodium, although there are now low-salt varieties. Check the labels for the sodium content of processed foods. Many foods are labeled "lite," but this does not necessarily mean that they are truly low in salt (or calories or fat); it simply means that the product contains less than what would normally be found in it. Not all sodium is listed as such on the label: Baking soda and monosodium glutamate (MSG) are examples of high-sodium ingredients not so listed.

Remember, too, that food is not the only source of sodium: It is also found in many beverages, such as soft drinks and beer, as well as in a wide variety of medications.

Potassium. Reducing salt is only half the story. Studies suggest that a low-potassium intake may also contribute to high blood pressure. Like sodium, potassium is an essential electrolyte needed to maintain fluid balance. Potassium is also vital for proper nerve and muscle function. It is abundant in a number of fruits and vegetables—the staples of our prehistoric ancestors' diets. Because potassium was plentiful and sodium rare, our bodies evolved to conserve sodium and excrete potassium. Today the situation is reversed: Our typical diet—high in fats, meat, sugar, and sodium—is relatively low in potassium. But our bodies have not changed to accommodate the modern diet, and our kidneys are still designed to conserve sodium and excrete potassium.

"HIDDEN" SOURCES OF SODIUM

The following ingredients are contained in many processed foods. Their listing on a food label indicates an added source of sodium.

- *Baking powder (baking soda plus acid):* used to leaven quick breads, muffins, and cakes.
- *Baking soda (sodium bicarbonate or bicarbonate of soda):* used to leaven breads and cakes; sometimes added to vegetables in cooking to keep them bright green.
- *Brine:* table salt and water used to flavor corned beef, pickles, and sauerkraut, as well as to preserve vegetables and condiments.
- *Disodium phosphate:* used in some quick-cooking cereals and processed cheeses, and in meat to retain liquids.
- *Dry skim milk:* used in a number of products, including baked goods.
- *Hydrolyzed vegetable protein:* used as a filler.
- *Monosodium glutamate (MSG):* a tenderizer and flavor enhancer used in cooking and preserving foods.
- *Sodium alginate:* used in many chocolate milks and ice creams for smooth texture.
- *Sodium ascorbate:* used as a preservative.
- *Sodium benzoate:* used as a preservative in many condiments, such as relishes, sauces, and salad dressings.
- *Sodium citrate:* used as a flavoring.
- *Sodium cyclamate and sodium saccharin:* used in some low-calorie soft drinks and desserts.
- *Sodium hydroxide:* used in food processing to soften and loosen skins of ripe olives, hominy, and certain fruits and vegetables.
- *Sodium nitrate and sodium nitrite:* used to cure meats and sausages.
- *Sodium propionate:* used in pasteurized cheeses and in some breads and cakes to inhibit the growth of mold.
- *Sodium sulfite:* used to bleach certain fruits in which an artificial color is desired; also used as a preservative in some dried fruits.
- *Soy sauce and soy isolates:* used as a flavoring.
- *Whey solids:* the liquid drained from yogurt; used as filler.

Societies that consume a largely vegetarian (high-potassium), low-salt diet have very little high blood pressure and associated problems. Ongoing studies by Dr. Louis Tobian and his associates at the University of Minnesota continue to find that a low-

INTERPRETING FOOD LABELS

The Food and Drug Administration (FDA) has established the following criteria for labeling regarding sodium content.

When the Label Says:	It Means:
Lite	Processed with less than the usual amount of sodium (or calories, color, or fat)
Low sodium	140 mg or less per serving
Reduced sodium	Processed to reduce the usual level of sodium by 75 percent
Sodium-free	Less than 5 mg per serving
Unsalted	Processed without the normally added salt
Very low sodium	35 mg or less per serving

salt, high-potassium diet protects animals, including strains of mice that are genetically susceptible to hypertension, from developing high blood pressure, strokes, and kidney damage. The studies showed these conditions to be common in litter mates fed high-salt, low-potassium diets.

Potassium can be added to the diet simply by increasing one's intake of fruits and vegetables (see Table 1.7). People taking diuretics (popularly known as "water pills") should be particularly careful to increase potassium intake, since they will excrete large amounts of potassium. But a word of caution: Too much potassium can cause serious problems. Some salt substitutes contain large amounts of potassium. There have been cases of potassium toxicity among people who use these in addition to potassium supplements prescribed with their antihypertensive medication.

Iron. Although normally a person on a well-balanced diet should not be at risk for iron deficiency, this is the most common nutritional deficiency seen in the United States. Iron is essential to make hemoglobin, the part of the red blood cell that carries oxygen to all of the body's cells. Prolonged iron deficiency can lead to anemia; signs include fatigue, pallor, shortness of breath, and general malaise.

Organ meats and red meat are among our best sources of iron, although it is also found in small amounts in a variety of foods (see Table 1.8). Since many elderly people tend to subsist on a low-calorie diet, they are at risk of developing iron-deficiency anemia. Iron deficiency may also be caused by internal bleeding from stomach ulcers, the

TABLE 1.7
High-Potassium, Low-Salt Foods

Food	Serving size	Potassium (mg)	Sodium (mg)
Apricots	3 medium	281	1
Asparagus	6 spears	278	2
Avocado	½ medium	604	4
Banana	1 medium	559	1
Beans, green	1 cup	189	5
Beans, white, cooked	½ cup	416	7
Broccoli	1 stalk	267	10
Cantaloupe	¼ medium	251	12
Carrots	2 small	341	47
Dates	10 medium	648	1
Grapefruit	½ medium	135	1
Mushrooms	4 large	414	15
Orange	1 medium	311	2
Orange juice	1 cup	496	3
Peach	1 medium	202	1
Peanuts (plain)	2½ oz	740	2
Potato	1 medium	504	4
Prunes (dried)	8 large	940	11
Spinach	½ cup	291	451
Sunflower seeds	3½ oz	920	30
Tomato	1 small	244	3
Watermelon	1 slice	600	6

intestinal tract, or other organs. Frequent use of aspirin or other anti-inflammatory drugs used to treat arthritis, for example, also can cause intestinal bleeding, resulting in iron deficiency.

Although only a small amount of iron is needed daily by the body (10 to 15 milligrams), our bodies do not absorb all the iron we consume. With age, iron absorption tends to decrease even more, so it is possible to eat foods that contain iron without supplying the body with an adequate amount. Liver, red meat, and eggs are the richest and most easily absorbed sources of iron, but they are also high in cholesterol.

Only about 5 percent of the iron from plant sources is absorbed. However, consuming iron-rich foods, particularly the less-absorbed plant sources, at a meal with citrus or other foods high in vitamin C appears to increase iron absorption. Including a small amount of meat, fish, or poultry also boosts iron absorption. The iron content of

TABLE 1.8
Sources of Iron

Food	Serving size	Iron (mg)	Food	Serving size	Iron (mg)
Apricots (dried)	8 halves	2.5	Liverwurst	3 oz	4.5
Avocado (Calif.)	½ medium	1.3	Molasses (blackstrap)	1 tbsp	3.2
Bean curds (tofu)	3½ oz	1.9	Mustard greens	1 cup (cooked)	2.5
Beef, roast	3 oz	6.1	Oatmeal	1 cup (cooked)	1.7
Beet greens	1 cup (cooked)	2.8	Orange (Valencia)	1 medium	1.0
Blood sausage	2 oz	1.0	Pork chop	3½ oz	4.5
Calf's liver	3½ oz	14.2	Pumpkin seeds	3 oz	7.1
Chicken	3 oz	1.5	Raisins	½ cup	2.5
Chicken livers	3 oz	7.0	Rice (enriched)	1 cup (cooked)	1.6
Clams or oysters	3 oz	5.0	Sardines	3½ oz	5.2
Collard greens	1 cup (cooked)	1.7	Shrimp	3 oz	2.5
Corn grits	¼ cup (cooked)	1.4	Spinach	1 cup (cooked)	0.8
Egg	1 medium	1.1	Sunflower seeds	3 oz	7.1
Farina	1 cup (cooked)	2.0	Veal cutlet	3½ oz	3.0
Kidney beans	½ cup (cooked)	2.8	Walnuts	¼ cup	1.1
Lima beans	½ cup (cooked)	3.5			

foods also can be increased by cooking in uncoated iron utensils. The greatest increase in iron will come from acidic foods with a high moisture content that require a long cooking time.

Iron deficiency can be treated with iron supplements, but these should be taken only on the advice of a physician after true anemia has been documented. If the deficiency is due to internal bleeding, its source must be found and treated.

EXCESS IRON. Excessive iron may be a risk factor for heart disease, according to a recent study in Finland which showed that men who had higher-than-average iron levels had an increased incidence of heart attack (implying that too much iron may set into motion the process that causes atherosclerosis). This finding has opened a new line of research. It may explain why low-dose aspirin, which causes microbleeding that lowers the body's iron levels, is effective in preventing heart attacks and why premenopausal women, who have lower iron levels because of menstruation, are less prone to heart disease than men. Because one-third of all men are genetically predisposed to conserve iron, a diet high in meat and other iron-fortified foods, along with this tendency to conserve iron, may be important in the development of heart disease in men.

Although this finding has not yet been confirmed, it does appear to add weight to the apparent value of a diet that is relatively low in protein (and fat) and high in carbohydrate content.

WATER

About 65 percent of body tissue is actually water. Aside from oxygen, it is our most essential nutrient. It regulates body temperature, circulation, and excretion; it also holds substances in solution and aids digestion. Water comes both from the liquids we drink as well as from foods, such as fruits, vegetables, and even meat. All adults should consume six to eight glasses of liquid a day. Coffee and tea, probably our most common sources of water, should not be our exclusive sources because they have a diuretic effect and also contain caffeine as well as other potentially harmful substances. Soft drinks and juices are other common sources of water, but remember, these contain calories (or in the case of low-calorie drinks, artificial sweeteners). If you dislike plain tap water, try keeping a pitcher of water with lemon slices in the refrigerator. This makes a low-cost, refreshing drink. Seltzer, either plain or fruit-flavored, is another noncaloric alternative to regular soft drinks.

OTHER DIETARY FACTORS

FIBER

Dietary fiber, or roughage, is the part of plant food that we cannot digest because our intestinal tract lacks the needed enzymes to break it down. There are several types of fiber in our diet, the most common of which are cellulose, pectin, hemicellulose, lignin, and the gums and mucilages used either as thickening agents or to improve the texture of processed foods. A diet that provides a variety of whole-grain cereals and breads, vegetables, and fruits will contain ample amounts of different fibers (see Table 1.9).

Fiber is the fashion today. And like most other fads, it has its pluses and minuses. Moderate amounts of dietary fiber (approximately 20 to 30 grams a day) can benefit the body in several ways:

- □ It may help reduce the risk of cancers of the colon and rectum.
- □ It may help reduce the incidence of diverticulosis and other intestinal disorders.
- □ It helps prevent constipation.
- □ It may help control blood sugar levels.
- □ It may help lower cholesterol.

Table 1.9
Foods High in Fiber

Food	Portion	Fiber (g)
CEREALS		
Bran	½ cup	2.3
Bran flakes	1 cup	1.3
Bran flakes with raisins	1 cup	1.5
Oatmeal, cooked	1 cup	0.6
Wheat, cracked (bulgur), dry	2 tbsp	0.2
Wheat, shredded	2 biscuits	1.1
BREADS AND CRACKERS		
Bread		
Cracked wheat	1 slice	0.1
Pumpernickel	1 slice	0.4
Raisin	1 slice	0.2
Rye	1 slice	0.1
Whole wheat	1 slice	0.4
Crackers		
Graham, plain	4 crackers	0.3
Whole wheat	4 crackers	0.4
FRUITS		
Apples, unpared	1 small	1.0
Apples, pared	1 small	0.6
Apricots	2–3 medium	0.6
Bananas	1 small (6 in)	0.5
Blueberries	½ cup	1.2
Grapes	22 medium	0.6
Oranges	1 small (2½ in)	0.5
Papaya	½ cup pulp	1.1
Peaches	1 medium	0.6
Pears, with skin	1 medium (3 x 2½ in)	2.8
Prunes, dehydrated, uncooked	8 large	2.2
Raisins, dried, seedless	½ cup	0.7
Raspberries, black	½ cup	3.7
Raspberries, red	½ cup	2.0
Strawberries	10 large (⅔ cup)	1.3
VEGETABLES		
Artichoke, Jerusalem, raw	4 small (1½-in diam)	0.8
Asparagus	5–6 spears raw or ⅔ cup cooked	0.7
Avocados, California	½ medium	1.9
Avocados, Florida	½ medium	2.8
Beans, green or yellow	1 cup cut	1.0
Beets	2 medium (2-in diam)	0.8
Broccoli, cooked	⅔ cup cut	1.5
Brussels sprouts, cooked	6–7 (⅔ cup)	1.6
Cabbage, raw	1 cup shredded	0.8
Carrots	1 large or 2 small raw or ⅔ cup cooked	1.0
Cauliflower	½ cup cooked or 1 cup raw	0.6
Celery, raw	1 cup diced	0.6
Corn, cooked	1 medium ear	0.7
Cucumbers, unpared	½ medium	0.3
Cucumbers, pared	½ medium	0.15
Eggplant, cooked	½ cup diced	0.9
Lettuce, raw	3½ oz	0.6
Mushrooms, raw	10 small or 4 large	0.8
Okra, cooked	8–9 pods	1.0
Onions, cooked	½ cup	0.6
Peas, green, cooked	⅔ cup	2.0
Potatoes, cooked with skin	1–2½-in diam	0.5
Spinach, raw or cooked	3½ oz	0.6
Squash, summer, cooked	½ cup	0.6
Squash, winter, cooked	½ cup	1.4
Tomatoes, ripe, raw	1 small	0.5
Turnips, cooked	⅔ cup diced	0.9
Watercress, raw	3½ oz or 100 sprigs	0.7

TABLE 1.9
Foods High in Fiber (*cont'd*)

Food	Portion	Fiber (g)
LEGUMES, GRAINS, AND NUTS		
Almonds	⅔ cup	2.6
Barley, pot or Scotch, raw	½ cup	0.9
Beans, lima, cooked	½ cup	1.6
Beans, mung, sprouted, raw	1 cup	0.5
Beans, red, cooked	½ cup	1.7
Beans, white, cooked	½ cup	1.5
Black-eyed peas (cowpeas), cooked	½ cup	1.8
Brazil nuts	25 medium or ⅓ cup	3.1
Lentils, cooked	⅔ cup	1.2
Macadamia nuts	6 whole	0.4
Peanut butter	1 tbsp	0.3
Peanuts, roasted, with skins	2½ oz	2.7
Pecans	12 halves	0.3
Pistachio nuts	30 whole	0.3
Popcorn, plain	1 cup popped	0.3
Rice, brown, cooked	1 cup	0.5
Soybeans, cooked	½ cup	1.6
Soybeans, sprouts, raw	1 cup	0.8

Source: U.S. Department of Agriculture

Many people mistakenly assume that increasing fiber intake means adding bran to a variety of foods or consuming large amounts of bran cereals. But there is increasing evidence that too much bran fiber can actually be harmful: It can irritate the intestinal tract and reduce the body's absorption of calcium, zinc, and other essential minerals.

CONSERVING DIETARY FIBER

- Avoid peeling potatoes, apples, and other fruits and vegetables that have edible skins.
- Stir-fry or steam vegetables to minimize breakdown of fiber.
- Use brown rice instead of white.
- Substitute whole wheat flour whenever possible.
- Use the dark green outer leaves of lettuce, cabbage, and other vegetables: They contain more fiber and nutrients than the softer inner leaves.
- Use pectin instead of cornstarch to thicken fruit pies or stewed fruits.
- Avoid removing the strings from celery, beans, and other such vegetables.
- Avoid overcooking vegetables and fruits: Many can be served raw or cooked only until just tender.

Nutritionists agree that no more than 10 to 15 grams of bran fiber should be consumed per day. Any more than that can upset intestinal function and actually create some of the problems it is intended to prevent or solve, such as intestinal gas, constipation, or even intestinal blockage.

CAFFEINE

In moderate amounts, caffeine is generally considered harmless. Moderation, however, is the key, especially since a person's tolerance for caffeine declines with age. (A cup of coffee contains about 150 milligrams of caffeine.) Although coffee is perhaps our most common source of caffeine, it is by no means the only one. Chocolate, colas and other soft drinks, tea, some aspirin compounds, and other medications also contain caffeine. If you are trying to cut down on caffeine, check labels on medications and other items for sources of hidden caffeine (see Table 1.10).

The effects of too much caffeine range from anxiety and irritability to insomnia, migraine headaches, diarrhea, indigestion, and irregular heartbeat. The possible link between coffee and heart attacks is disputed: The long-term ongoing Framingham

TABLE 1.10
Sources of Caffeine

Source (amount)	Caffeine (mg)
COFFEE (5-OZ CUP)	
Drip	146
Percolated	110
Regular instant	53
Coffee/grain blends	35
Decaffeinated instant	2
TEA (5-OZ CUP)	
1-minute brew	9–23
3-minute brew	20–46
5-minute brew	20–50
Instant	12–28
Canned iced tea (12 oz)	22–36
COCOA AND CHOCOLATE	
Cocoa from mix (6 oz)	10
Milk chocolate (1 oz)	6
Baking chocolate (1 oz)	35
SOFT DRINKS (12-OZ CAN)	
Dr. Pepper	60
Regular colas	30–45
Diet colas	50
Mountain Dew	50
Tab	45
NONPRESCRIPTION DRUGS	
Prolamine	280
NoDoz, Caffedrin, Vivarin	200
Aqua-ban	200
Dietac, Dexatrim	200
Excedrin	130
Midol	65
Anacin	65
Dristan and other cold remedies	20–35

(Mass.) Heart Study has failed to find a connection, and other studies have been poorly designed. For example, some studies didn't isolate this possible risk from factors such as smoking, while others were based on boiled coffee, which few Americans drink.

In 1990, however, a study on coffee drinking by more than 45,500 men was reported in the *New England Journal of Medicine.* For the most part, it has quelled the controversy by concluding that even at high levels—6 cups or more a day—caffeine in coffee did not increase the risk of heart disease or stroke.

Moderation is still recommended: 5 cups or fewer a day for healthy people and little or none for people who are prone to abnormal heart rhythms. Excessive caffeine may also lead to palpitations and irregular heart rhythms in susceptible individuals—for example, those with valvular heart disease. Switching to a decaffeinated brand (water-processed rather than chemically processed) may be the best course in such cases.

NITRITES

Nitrites (and nitrates) are added to food to prevent the growth of botulism and to add color and flavor. Although there is no concrete evidence that nitrites are linked to cancer, when they combine with the muscle fat of meats they form carcinogenic nitrosamines. Since this evidence became known, the U.S. government has been instituting regulations regarding nitrite use. Federal law requires that four parts ascorbate (another preservative) be added for each part nitrite or nitrate, which prevents nitrosamines from forming. Avoiding cured meats such as bacon and frankfurters, unless the label specifically states that they are nitrite-free, cuts down on exposure to nitrites.

FOOD ADDITIVES

Anyone who regularly reads the lists of ingredients on processed foods (something everyone *should* do) frequently comes across terms like BHA, BHT, ascorbyl palmitate, potassium bisulfite, and dozens of other equally mysterious terms. Obviously they are chemical additives, but beyond that, most people have no idea what they are doing in our food.

Food purists have long decried the presence of chemicals in food. But all food, both natural and concocted, is made up of chemicals. Indeed, as human beings we are a complex arrangement of chemicals. Some chemicals are essential to sustain life, others are beneficial, and still others are highly toxic.

A wide array of chemicals is used in food processing, some to improve nutritional content and others to make food more attractive or flavorful. Perhaps the most important chemicals are the large number of preservatives that are added to keep food from spoiling. Some preservatives, such as salt, sugar, and certain acids, have been used for centuries. In recent decades, these have been joined by scores of other formulations that make it possible for us to enjoy a wide variety of foods from all over the world in every season. But many people worry that these additives may be harmful or alter the nutritional quality of food.

Since the early 1970s, the Food and Drug Administration (FDA) has been studying the safety of various preservatives, including more than two dozen that have been used for many years but never scientifically tested. This summary discusses the pros and cons of the major classes of preservatives. It also discusses the GRAS (*G*enerally *R*ecognized *A*s *S*afe) status of each, a listing limited to substances in use before 1961.

TWO BASIC TYPES

Modern preservatives fall into two categories: (1) the *antimicrobials,* which inhibit the growth of molds, yeasts, and bacteria, the microorganisms that spoil food; and (2) the *antioxidants,* chemicals that keep food from becoming rancid or developing off-flavors, odors, and discolorations.

Ascorbates and Erythorbates. These are basically antioxidants that include ascorbic acid (vitamin C), which also has some antimicrobial properties, ascorbyl palmitate, calcium ascorbate, erythorbic acid, sodium ascorbate, and sodium erythorbate. They are used in small amounts to prevent some foods, such as pears or potatoes, from turning brown. They also are used in baked goods, candies, fats and oils, cereals, pickling brine, and processed meats. Calcium ascorbate is a derivative of vitamin C and has a rather limited use in foods. The FDA recognizes all these antioxidants as safe.

Benzoic Acid and Sodium Benzoate. These antimicrobials are used to retard the growth of yeasts, bacteria, and some molds in many foods, especially those that are acidic. Benzoic acid occurs naturally in raspberries and other berries, prunes, tea, cinnamon, and cloves. It is used mostly in soft drinks and alcoholic beverages, soft candies, chewing gum, fats and oils, baked goods, condiments, nondairy creamers, gelatins, puddings, frozen dairy products, and cheese. Sodium benzoate appears in these foods as well as in baked goods, processed vegetables, margarine, instant coffee, cereals, and meat products.

BHA (butylated hydroxyanisole) and BHT (butylated hydroxytoluene). These chemically similar compounds are widely used as antioxidants to keep foods from turning rancid, especially those made with fats and oils. They have been used in foods for more than 40 years, but their safety is still under study by the FDA, which has ruled that BHA and BHT, either alone or in combination, cannot make up more than 0.02 percent of the fat and oil content of a food.

Parabens. These antimicrobial agents, chemically similar to benzoic acid, include methylparaben and propylparaben. Their safety has been reaffirmed by the FDA, and they are used to inhibit the growth of molds and yeasts in acidic foods. They also may be added to jams, jellies, pickles, syrups, grain products, cheese, soft drinks, baked goods, processed vegetables, and frozen dairy products.

Propionic Acid and Its Salts. These antimicrobial agents include calcium propionate, sodium propionate, dilauryl thiodipropionate, and thiodipropionic acid. They are most effective against fungi and are widely used in baked goods and cheese products. The FDA has confirmed all as safe, but calcium propionate and sodium propionate should be used only in very small quantities.

Propyl Gallate. This is an antioxidant that has been reaffirmed as safe. It is often combined with BHA and/or BHT and is widely used in fats, oils, meat products, nuts, grain products, snack foods, baked goods, soft candy, gum, and soft drinks.

Sorbates. These include sorbic acid and calcium, potassium, and sodium sorbate. Their safety has been affirmed, and they can be used in small quantities in a variety of processed foods.

Stannous Chloride. This is an antioxidant sometimes referred to as tin chloride. It prevents food from changing color or developing offensive odors. It has been reaffirmed as safe but can be used only in very minute quantities because it is derived from metallic tin.

Sulfiting Agents. These are antioxidants that prevent discoloration of foods, especially vegetables, potatoes, and fruits. Sulfiting agents include potassium and sodium bisulfite, potassium and sodium metabisulfite, and sulfur dioxide. There have been numerous reports of serious, even fatal, allergic reactions to these agents, especially when consumed by asthmatics. The FDA has advised food processors and restaurants that consumers should be informed if sulfiting agents are used. However, this is not always done; anyone with serious allergies or asthma should specifically ask if sulfiting agents have been added to vegetables, fruits, and other foods. If in doubt, it is a good idea to avoid foods that may have been treated with them. Most wines also contain sulfites.

Tocopherols. These chemically related substances contain vitamin E and are used as antioxidants. Many occur naturally in meat, vegetable oils, cereal grains, nuts, and leafy vegetables. They are used in baked products, cereals, dairy products, infant formulas, and other foods to prevent them from turning rancid. Tocopherols are generally considered safe by the FDA.

CHOLESTEROL

No doubt about it, Americans have become increasingly cholesterol-conscious in recent years. We are eating less red meat and butter, fewer eggs, and more fish and poultry.

Even so, misinformation and confusion abound, and many people who think they are using low-cholesterol substitutes actually end up consuming more cholesterol and saturated fats than before. For example, many people eating in a fast-food restaurant will order a fish sandwich or fried chicken instead of a hamburger, thinking that they will be cutting down on cholesterol and calories. Actually, if the hamburger is reasonably lean and broiled, it is likely to contain less fat and cholesterol than deep-fried breaded fish or chicken. Or a person may shun beef in favor of Cheddar or some other hard cheese. Unless the beef is very fatty, the cheese is likely to have, ounce for ounce, more cholesterol and fat than the meat.

Remember, too, that some fast-food restaurants cook fried potatoes in beef fat (suet), adding a hefty amount of fat and cholesterol to a naturally low-fat vegetable that normally would be cholesterol-free.

Cholesterol is a waxy alcohol that is essential in forming all animal cell membranes. It also is needed for proper nerve function, for reproduction, and for a number of other vital processes. Without it, we cannot survive. But it is not necessary to derive any cholesterol from the diet; our bodies are capable of manufacturing all that we need.

Essential fatty acids are converted to cholesterol in the liver. Each day we require about 100 milligrams of cholesterol, and under normal circumstances the body manufactures 500 to 1,000 milligrams, depending upon need. The American Heart Association advises that we limit cholesterol consumption to no more than 300 milligrams per day—about 80 milligrams more than are found in one large egg yolk (213 to 220 milligrams). If the diet provides too much cholesterol, the amount circulating in the blood rises. In time, this can lead to atherosclerosis (hardening of the arteries). The deposits of fatty plaque that clog the coronary arteries and are responsible for most heart attacks are made mostly of cholesterol.

Americans tend to have high levels of total cholesterol: Readings of 250 to 300 milligrams/deciliter or even higher are very common, and the *average* cholesterol level for adult Americans is now about 213. The American Heart Association recommends that adults have cholesterol levels between 160 and 200 milligrams/deciliter. It should be noted, however, that cholesterol rises somewhat with age, so a level of up to 240 milligrams/deciliter in a person over 40 constitutes only a moderate risk. Such a level would indicate a high risk for a younger person.

A cholesterol level below 160 milligrams/deciliter has been linked to increased risk of death, especially from bowel cancer and, interestingly, from violence (accident, homicide, suicide). These findings have shown up in several studies, including the Multiple Risk Factor Intervention Trial (MR FIT), an ongoing study of 350,000 middle-aged men. The reasons for these correlations are not known.

"Good" Cholesterol. Total cholesterol is not the whole story, however. Because cholesterol is a fatlike substance and fat and water do not mix, cholesterol must be attached to a water-soluble substance in order to travel through the blood, which is

mostly water. Three proteins, called *lipoproteins,* have this function. Two lipoproteins—low-density and very-low-density, or LDLs and VLDLs—carry cholesterol to the blood vessel linings and are instrumental in the development of atherosclerosis. LDL levels should be below 130 milligrams/deciliter. Studies show that lowering the LDL levels to about 100 milligrams/deciliter can be beneficial, even in people who already have coronary heart disease. Lowering the LDL level can slow the disease and, in some cases, reverse some of its effects.

The third, high-density lipoprotein, or HDL, carries cholesterol away from the vessel walls and is referred to as "good" cholesterol because it seems to protect against atherosclerosis. When blood cholesterol is measured, the test results should include a breakdown of HDL and LDL cholesterol and should also state the ratio of total cholesterol to HDL. A person can have a relatively low total cholesterol level and still develop atherosclerosis if the HDLs are very low. In general, if the ratio of total cholesterol to HDL is greater than 4.5:1 or if the HDL level is 35 milligrams/deciliter or lower, efforts should be made to raise HDL. Of course, total cholesterol should also be reduced, especially if it is about 220 to 240 (see Table 1.11).

Factors that appear to raise HDLs include exercise, a vegetarian diet, estrogen replacement in postmenopausal women, pectin, and high-dose niacin.

Another, less-substantiated factor in heart disease may be the level of triglycerides, or blood fats, which are transported by the lipoprotein VLDL. This does not, however, appear to be an independent risk factor. Rather, a moderately high triglyceride level (between 200 and 400 milligrams/deciliter) probably is of concern only in people who have a high LDL level or who already have coronary heart disease or diabetes. A severely high triglyceride level (above 400 milligrams/deciliter) is relatively rare, but it

TABLE 1.11
Cholesterol and Cardiovascular Risk

The following table, developed by the National Cholesterol Education Program, a government-sponsored organization, shows cholesterol levels and the corresponding risk of a heart attack.

Cholesterol (mg/dl)	Risk	Recommended action
200 or less	Normal	Recheck within five years
200–239		
No heart disease or risk factors	Borderline	Recheck annually; dietary counseling
With heart disease or two risk factors	High	Measure HDL/LDL levels
Over 240	High	Dietary therapy plus drugs if needed

should be treated immediately because of its potential effect on the pancreas. Studies continue to assess the role of triglycerides in heart and other disease.

Sources of Cholesterol. Many people are still confused about the sources of cholesterol in their diets, and much of this confusion is fueled by food advertising. *Cholesterol is found only in animal products, not in any vegetable oils or other plant products.* Thus, advertising claims that products such as a certain brand of margarine or peanut butter contain no cholesterol are misleading and irrelevant. Unless animal fats have been added, plant products obviously do not contain cholesterol. They may, however, be high in palm, coconut, or hardened oils. These are high in saturated fats and therefore capable of raising our own cholesterol levels. In fact, these fats are thought to raise blood cholesterol more than cholesterol-rich foods do.

Cholesterol is usually, but not always, found in association with fat. Egg yolks, fatty meats, whole milk, butter, liver and other organ meats, and hard cheeses all are high in cholesterol (see Table 1.12). Contrary to popular belief, fish, chicken, and other poultry also contain cholesterol and in about the same amounts as in beef and other meats. In fact, some fish and seafoods contain more cholesterol than beef. But the fish still would be a better overall meal choice because its fat tends to be unsaturated, which helps lower total cholesterol and increase protective HDL cholesterol.

Polyunsaturated fats, which are fatty acids with two or more *unsaturated bonds* (double bonds between carbon atoms, with no hydrogen atoms), are found in corn and soybean oils. They usually do not increase the cholesterol level. An identifying feature of polyunsaturated fats is their liquid form whether at room temperature or refrigerated.

Monounsaturated fats, which are found in olive and peanut oils, are liquid at room temperature and semisolid or solid when refrigerated. They usually do not increase the cholesterol level.

In contrast, saturated or hydrogenated fats, which are found in animal and milk products, raise cholesterol. When saturated fats are ingested, the liver converts them to cholesterol. These fatty acids are solid or hard at room temperature.

Ideally, less than 30 percent of our total calories should come from fats, and these should be evenly distributed among saturated, monounsaturated, and polyunsaturated fats. Virtually everyone with even moderately elevated cholesterol can benefit from a low-fat, low-cholesterol, high-carbohydrate diet.

The American Heart Association recommends the following heart-healthy diet choices:

Fruits and Nonstarchy Vegetables

- □ All are acceptable choices (except coconuts, avocados, and olives, which are listed under fats).
- □ Allow four servings of each per day. A serving equals ½ cup cooked or

Table 1.12
Cholesterol and Fat Content of Foods

Food	Cholesterol (mg)	Fats (g) Saturated	Monounsaturated	Polyunsaturated
MEAT, POULTRY, AND FISH				
1 oz lean beef	26	0.9	0.8	0.1
1 oz fatty beef	27	2.2	2.0	0.2
1 oz veal	28	0.9	0.8	0.1
1 oz chicken (dark meat)	26	0.8	1.0	0.6
1 oz chicken/turkey (white meat)	22	0.3	0.3	0.2
1 oz pork	28	0.9	0.8	0.1
1 oz beef liver	83	0.1	0	0
1 oz lean fish	28	0	0.1	0.1
1 oz fatty fish	25	0.9	1.1	1.1
1 oz water-packed tuna	11	0	0	0
1 oz lean lamb	17	0.1	0.2	0.2
FATS AND OILS				
1 tsp margarine (1.6/1.9 poly/sat)	0	1.4	3.3	2.4
1 tsp corn oil	0	0.6	1.1	2.6
1 tsp safflower oil	0	0.4	0.6	3.3
1 tsp vegetable oil	0	0.7	1.0	2.6
2 tsp avocado	0	0.8	2.1	1.3
EGGS AND DAIRY PRODUCTS				
1 egg	213	1.7	2.2	0.7
1 tsp butter	12	1.9	1.4	0.2
2 oz 5%-fat cheese	20	1.6	1.0	0.1
2 oz Cheddar cheese	56	12.0	6.0	0.5
1 cup whole milk	34	4.8	2.4	0.1
1 cup 2% milk	22	2.4	2.0	0.1
1 cup skim milk	4	0.3	0.1	0
1 cup 1% yogurt	14	2.3	1.0	0.1
1 cup ice cream	56	16.8	9.6	0.3

canned, 1 cup raw vegetables, 1 medium-size piece of fruit, or 6 ounces juice.

- □ To cut calories, use unsweetened or juice pack; avoid cream, butter, or margarine sauces; use herbs, spices, lemon juice, etc., for flavorings.

Bread, Cereals, and Starchy Foods

- □ Use any plain breads, rolls, cereals, rice, pasta, starchy vegetables, and low-fat crackers.
- □ Avoid commercial cookies, cakes, pies, other such baked goods, croissants, eggs, butter or cheese breads and rolls, granola-type cereals with coconut or coconut oil, chow mein noodles, french fried potatoes or other fried vegetables, and other baked goods high in fats.
- □ Reduce serving sizes to 75- to 100-calorie portions (for example, 1 slice bread, ⅔ to ¾ cup prepared cereals, ½ cup potato, lima beans, or green peas).

Crackers and Snack Foods

- □ Use low-fat crackers, bread sticks, melba toast, matzo, rusks, zwieback, unbuttered air-popped popcorn, etc.
- □ Avoid sweets and other high-calorie foods.
- □ Use fruits and vegetables as snacks.

Milk

- □ Use only skim or low-fat (1 percent butter fat or less) milk, either dry or fluid.
- □ Use low-fat (2 grams or less per ounce) cheese.
- □ Use dry-curd, low-fat cottage cheese.
- □ Use skim or low-fat plain yogurt.
- □ Avoid all other dairy and nondairy substitutes that contain butterfat or saturated fats.
- □ Use sherbet, frozen yogurt, or ice milk in place of ice cream.

Meat, Poultry, Seafood, and Eggs

- □ Reduce consumption of red meat in favor of veal, poultry, fish, seafood, and meat substitutes. Increase use of meatless main dishes to three or more per week.
- □ Reduce total cholesterol intake to 300 milligrams or fewer per day.
- □ Reduce total fat consumption to 30 percent or less of total calories.
- □ Avoid prime or marbled meats, sausages, spare ribs, all cured meats, duck, goose, poultry skin, any other fatty poultry, fatty organ meats (for exam-

ple, brains), pork and beans, gravy, and any commercial fried meats, poultry, or seafood.

- □ Increase use of legumes and other meat substitutes.
- □ Reduce egg consumption to no more than two egg yolks per week (egg whites can be used in any quantity).
- □ Consume 6 ounces or less of meat per day.

FATS AND OILS

- □ Increase use of polyunsaturated fats (for example, safflower, sunflower, corn, soybean, and cottonseed oils) in preference to saturated fats (especially butter, lard, or other animal fats).
- □ Avoid use of coconut, coconut oil, palm or palm kernel oils, other hardened oils, shortening, cheese dressings, chocolate, meat drippings, cashews, pistachios, and macadamia nuts.
- □ Use margarine or polyunsaturated oil in place of butter or shortening.
- □ Prepare homemade salad dressing using safflower, corn, or sunflower oil.
- □ Use fat-free desserts.

The way food is prepared can also make a major difference in whether it will raise or lower your cholesterol level. The fat content of meat and poultry can be lowered considerably simply by buying lean cuts and then trimming off as much visible fat and/or skin as possible. Many people who have given up meat in favor of cheese, nuts, or peanut butter may be surprised to learn that they are now consuming more fat, ounce for ounce, than before (see Table 1.13).

TABLE 1.13
Suggested Daily Food Portions for a Low-Fat, Low-Cholesterol Diet

Food group	Portion size
Fruits and vegetables	Four or more servings of ½ cup fruit or vegetable juice, ½ cup cooked fruit or vegetable, or one medium (3-in) fruit or vegetable
Breads, cereals, and starchy foods	Four or more servings of one slice bread; 1 cup dry cereal; ½ cup cooked cereal, pasta, rice, or noodles; one tortilla; 1 cup popcorn, or two graham crackers
Milk and cheese	Two or more servings of one 8-oz glass of low-fat or nonfat milk or buttermilk, one 8-oz carton low-fat yogurt, 1 oz low-fat cheese, or ⅓ cup low-fat cottage cheese
Fish, poultry, meat, dried beans, peas, nuts, egg yolks	Maximum of two servings daily of 2–3 oz meat, fish, or poultry. Unlimited egg whites.
Polyunsaturated fats, oils	Two tablespoons per day

TIPS FOR LOWERING CHOLESTEROL

Experts agree that diet and exercise are key factors when it comes to lowering cholesterol. Studies have found that increasing exercise and shedding excess weight will lower total cholesterol and improve the HDL/LDL ratio.

People who have very high cholesterol or signs of atherosclerotic heart disease may need to take additional steps. A number of cholesterol-lowering drugs may be pre-

BETTER FOOD LABELS—AT LAST

It took an act of Congress, years of research, and some last-minute government wrangling: New nutrition labels for all processed foods began to appear on supermarket shelves in early 1993. All processed foods—some 300,000 varieties—must carry the new nutrition information by May 1994.

The U.S. Food and Drug Administration, which developed the labeling rules, successfully resisted food-industry pressure and held to its plan to present nutrition information as percentages of "daily values." That will help people compare different foods to see how they fit into an overall diet.

The final label format (see sample chart) has several refinements over earlier drafts. Most significantly, the label lists daily values for a 2,000 calorie diet. (Earlier versions used a 2,350-calorie diet.) The label also lists nutrient limits for a 2,500-calorie diet, useful mainly for larger men but helpful to other consumers who want to extrapolate nutrition information for other caloric intakes.

The 2,500-calorie diet was a concession to the U.S. Department of Agriculture, which feared—along with such constituents as cattle ranchers—that people would shun foods seemingly too high in fat in a 2,000-calorie diet. But the USDA also made significant concessions. It agreed to use the FDA's label format for any processed foods under its jurisdiction. That's a significant gain for consumers, who might otherwise have faced two different labels in the stores—one for meat lasagna (USDA), another for cheese lasagna (FDA), for example.

The FDA's daily values for fat—no more than 65 grams in a 2,000-calorie diet—equal 30 percent of calories from fat. (It might have been preferable if the government had set a limit of 25 percent.) The FDA's regulations also standardize meanings for claims: A food can't be called "light," for example, unless it has at least 50 percent less fat than the product with which it's compared. Foods labeled "fresh" cannot have been frozen, processed, heated, or chemically preserved. Finally, the new rules limit the labels' health label hype to only a few, well-substantiated claims, such as the link between fiber and prevention of some types of cancer.

The following is a sample label for a package of macaroni and cheese:

NUTRITION FACTS

Serving Size ½ cup (114g)
Servings per Container 4
Amount per Serving

Calories 260	Calories from Fat 120
	% Daily Value*
Total Fat 13 g	20
Saturated fat 5g	25
Cholesterol 30 mg	10
Sodium 660 mg	28
Total carbohydrate 31g	11
Dietary fiber 0g	0
Sugar 5g	
Protein 5g	

Vitamin A 4% *	Vitamin C 2%
Calcium 15% *	Iron 4%

*Percent Daily Values are based on a 2,000-calorie diet. Your daily values may be higher or lower, depending on your calorie needs.

	Calories	2,000	2,500
Total fat	less than	65g	80g
Saturated fat	less than	20g	25g
Cholesterol	less than	300mg	300mg
Sodium	less than	2,400mg	2,400mg
Total carbohydrate		300g	375g
Fiber		25g	30g

Calories per gram: Fat 9* Carbohydrates 4* Protein 4

scribed, but for older people the side effects must be weighed against the potential benefits. It must be remembered that drug therapy is still only an adjunct to dietary and other measures. The drugs now available include cholestyramine (Questran), colestipol (Colestid), gemfibrozil (Lopid), lovastatin (Mevacor) and probucol (Lorelco). Other drugs—fenofibrate (Lipidil), simvastatin (Zocor), pravastatin (Pravachol) and fluvastatin (LoChol)—have recently been introduced or may be available soon. Any cholesterol-lowering drug should be used only under the close supervision of a doctor, since its potential adverse effects include impaired liver function.

Large doses of niacin, one of the B vitamins, also have been found to lower LDL and raise HDL cholesterol, but niacin should not be taken without consulting a doctor. Studies at Beth Israel Hospital in Boston found that 1,000 to 3,000 milligrams of niacin a day can lower cholesterol by up to 30 percent. But there are side effects—people may experience hot flashes and other unpleasant effects such as itching, rashes, flushing, or stomachaches. In high doses—7,000 to 8,000 milligrams per day—niacin can cause liver damage. Liver enzymes, blood sugar, and uric acid levels may need to be tested on a regular basis. Taking niacin in its sustained-release form, even at low doses of 500 milligrams a day, can cause severe damage to the liver.

By starting patients on 300 milligrams of niacin a day and working up gradually to 1,000 to 3,000 milligrams over a period of several weeks, the Boston researchers found that most patients could tolerate the drug and still gain the cholesterol-lowering benefits. Taking aspirin once a day can help relieve the flushing and itching that usually accompany the onset of therapy.

Niacin, also referred to as nicotinic acid, offers another important advantage over other cholesterol-lowering drugs—it is not as expensive. For example, cholesterol-lowering therapy with cholestyramine (Questran) can cost as much as $350 a month, compared to about $15 a month with niacin.

AGE-RELATED CHANGES IN WEIGHT

As we grow older, our metabolism slows. We also tend to lose some of our muscle mass while the percentage of body fat increases. Typically, our physical activity also decreases. Taken together, these factors mean that as we grow older we do not need to eat as much; as a rule of thumb, a person's caloric requirement falls by approximately 2 to 10 percent for each decade past 20. Thus, a middle-aged person who continues to eat as he or she did at age 20 will gain weight. But attention to diet and sound nutrition, plus maintaining a high level of physical activity, will help keep the pounds from creeping up.

Acceptable weight is what is comfortable and healthy, not what may be fashionable. Generally, a gain of 20 to 25 pounds after age 30 is not considered harmful to health, but it may be upsetting to find you can no longer fit into a certain size dress or suit. If this is so, then there is no harm in undertaking a moderate reduction in calories, coupled with increased physical activity, to provide for a gradual weight loss until you again achieve the weight comfortable for you.

Insurance companies have devised standard height and weight tables that give "ideal" weights according to sex and body type (see Table 1.14). Total weight, however, is not the only indicator of overweight; the ratio of muscle to fat is just as important. The skin-fold test can serve as a guide: If a person can pinch more than one inch in a place like the abdomen above the hip bone or the loose skin fold on the underside of the upper arm—places where fat usually accumulates—he or she is overweight.

TABLE 1.14
Desirable Weight for Height

MEN

Height (in shoes)	Small frame	Weight (when dressed) Medium frame	Large frame
5′2″	112–120	118–129	126–141
5′3″	115–123	121–133	129–144
5′5″	118–126	124–136	132–148
5′6″	121–129	127–139	135–152
5′7″	123–133	130–143	138–156
5′8″	128–137	134–147	142–161
5′9″	132–141	138–152	147–166
5′10″	136–145	142–156	151–170
5′11″	140–150	146–160	155–174
6′	148–158	154–170	159–179
6′1″	152–162	158–175	164–184
6′2″	156–167	162–180	168–189
6′3″	160–171	167–185	173–194
6′4″	164–175	172–190	182–204

WOMEN

Height (in shoes)	Small frame	Weight (when dressed) Medium frame	Large frame
4′10″	92–98	96–101	104–119
4′11″	94–101	98–110	106–122
5′	96–104	101–113	110–125
5′1″	99–107	104–116	112–128
5′2″	102–110	107–119	115–131
5′3″	105–113	110–122	118–134
5′4″	108–116	113–126	121–138
5′5″	111–119	116–130	125–142
5′6″	114–123	120–135	120–146
5′7″	118–127	124–139	133–150
5′8″	122–131	128–143	137–154
5′9″	126–135	132–147	141–158
5′10″	130–140	136–151	145–163
5′11″	134–144	140–155	149–168
6′	138–148	144–159	153–173

Maintaining acceptable weight can bring numerous health benefits. Extra weight puts extra stress on bones and joints, and may worsen arthritis or osteoporosis. Obesity has been associated with hypertension, adult-onset diabetes, certain forms of cancer, and heart disease. In addition, excess pounds can complicate other health problems and restrict a person's mobility, which in itself can lead to health problems.

The keys to successful weight loss are moderation, balance, and maintenance. All too often, however, we resort to crash or fad diets. Most of these diets have little regard for proper nutrition or good eating habits. They all have one common denominator—a reduced intake of calories—which is why all of them, when followed for any period of time, result in weight loss. But studies have found that more than 95 percent of those who lose weight on a crash diet regain it within a few months. Typically, a person will "go on a diet," lose the desired 10 or 15 pounds, and then go off the diet and resume the same old eating habits that produced the original weight problem. Recent studies have shown that this yo-yo pattern of weight loss and weight gain can cause more health problems, including increased cancer risk, than staying at the higher weight. The secret to long-term weight control is to forget about dieting and instead to modify daily eating habits to prevent taking in more calories than are burned up.

Although this may sound simple, in practice it can be quite difficult. Eating habits are firmly ingrained from an early age, and most people find them difficult to change, especially when they try to tackle everything all at once. It is far better to concentrate on one or two of the most important areas at a time and gradually adopt a more healthful eating pattern. For example, if you determine that reducing your intake of fats and cholesterol should take priority, then concentrate on these first; leave things like cutting down on sugar and salt for later, after you have succeeded with your initial goals.

Although most overweight problems can be traced to consuming more calories than are expended, with the excess being stored as body fat, there are instances in which the extra weight is related to hormonal problems or other diseases. Certain drugs, such as cortisone and other steroid hormones, also promote weight gain. And some people have a genetic tendency to gain weight: They simply metabolize food more efficiently than others and do not need as many calories.

Even people who do not have a genetic predisposition to gaining weight may inadvertently alter their metabolism, through crash dieting, to produce the same effect. When the body is deprived of calories, it will naturally slow down its metabolism to conserve energy, burning calories at a lower rate. After all, the body's centers of metabolism and appetite control do not differentiate between deliberate dieting and involuntary starvation. They know only that the body is running short of fuel, and will reset the metabolic rate at a lower level to conserve it. When dieting ends, the body does not necessarily reset the metabolic rate at its previous level. As a result, a person may gain weight more rapidly than ever.

Always check with your doctor before making any major dietary change, especially if you are more than 20 percent overweight. Successful weight loss requires a balanced, flexible eating plan that will produce a gradual weight loss and a permanent change in eating habits. Some people may find that joining a group, such as Weight Watchers or Overeaters Anonymous, makes this easier to achieve than solo dieting.

Exercise is an essential part of any weight-reduction program. In addition to burning up calories (see Table 1.15), exercise improves muscle tone and provides a trimmer look. Exercise will also help maintain the body's normal metabolic rate, in addition to helping control appetite.

DETERMINING YOUR CALORIC NEEDS

All of us, whether overweight or not, need a certain number of calories each day simply to carry on essential body processes—blood circulation, maintaining body temperature, digestion, breathing, etc. This is called the basal metabolic rate (BMR), the body's minimum daily need for calories. To calculate your approximate BMR, multiply your weight (in pounds) by 10. Men should add twice their weight to this total, and women should add their weight one time. For example, the calculation for a 180-pound man would be:

$$180 \times 10 = 1{,}800 + 360 = 2{,}160 \text{ calories per day}$$

For a 125-pound woman, the calculation would be:

$$125 \times 10 = 1{,}250 + 125 = 1{,}375 \text{ calories per day}$$

Now add to this the number of calories you burn up in your various daily activities—working, sitting, watching TV, walking the dog, etc. (see chapter 2 for tables on the calorie expenditure of various activities). As a rule of thumb, you can use the for-

TABLE 1.15
Calorie Expenditures for Physical Activities

Activity	Calories used per hour
Walking	100 × number of mph
Racewalking	500
Jogging	600
Running	800–1,000
Cycling	250 for speed of 5 mph
Tennis (doubles)	350–450
Tennis (singles)	400–500
Swimming (breast or backstroke)	300–600
Swimming (crawl)	700–900
Aerobic dancing	600–800
Ballet exercises/calisthenics	300
Handball	650–800
Cross-country skiing	700–1,000

mula in the following box, "Average Caloric Needs," to calculate how many calories you need to sustain your BMR and normal activities.

A reasonable goal for a weight-loss program is a loss of one or two pounds a week. One pound equals 3,500 calories, so consuming 500 calories fewer than are burned up each day should produce the desired weight loss. The 500 calories can come from a combination of decreased food intake and increased physical activity. For example, you might cut your food intake by 300 calories a day, a very modest reduction. This can be accomplished by simply eating smaller portions of most foods or by making substitutions (for example, a 90-calorie apple instead of a 350-calorie piece of apple pie, a 90-calorie glass of skim milk instead of a 150-calorie glass of whole milk). Then, by increasing exercise by 200 calories (for example, a 45-minute brisk walk), you will accomplish your goal of one pound a week. You can double the weight loss if you cut your food intake by 600 calories (but you should consume at least 1,000 to 1,200 calories a day) and if you double your exercise—swim for 45 minutes in addition to a 45-minute walk or an equivalent activity.

AVERAGE CALORIC NEEDS

Divide your weight by 2.2 to arrive at kilograms.

	Activity level (values are calories needed per kilogram)		
Weight status	**Sedentary**	**Moderately active**	**Very active**
Overweight	15–20	25	35
Normal	25	30	40
Underweight	30	35	45

Examples: If you are a sedentary woman weighing 160 pounds (about 73 kilograms) who should lose 25 pounds, you would calculate your daily caloric needs using the weight status for overweight individuals. If you aim to consume 18 calories per day per kilogram, your total intake should be about 1,314 calories, and your weight will come down.

If you are a moderately active and normal-weight woman weighing 132 pounds (60 kilograms), your daily caloric intake should be 30 calories per kilogram, or about 1,800 calories.

If you are very active, weigh 120 pounds (about 54.5 kilograms), but should weigh 132, you should consume about 45 calories per kilogram, or about 2,450 calories per day.

KEEPING A FOOD DIARY

Almost any weight-loss program is doomed unless it is accompanied by a conscious effort to adopt more healthful food habits. And to alter food habits, it is essential to know where you are going wrong. Most people actually have no idea how much they eat and under what circumstances. Many overweight people insist that they eat very little but still gain weight. When they keep careful food diaries, however, they are surprised to learn just how much they do consume each day. Keeping a food diary before starting on a diet is also a good way to analyze current eating habits to find out what triggers eating—social situations, boredom, stress—and at what times during the day one's temptation to eat is greatest.

SAMPLE FOOD DIARY

Alan Greene, who is 40 pounds overweight and has high blood pressure, insists he's a light eater, and for most of the day that's true. Up until 6 P.M. he had only consumed 705 calories, less than one-third of what his nutritionist determined was his total daily requirement. But from 6 P.M. until he went to bed he consumed a whopping 4,545 calories. He joined a couple of friends at a local pub for a beer and ended up munching on a cup of salted peanuts—bad for both his diet and hypertension. His wife, thinking

Alan Greene's Sample Food Diary

Name: Alan Greene **Date: 7/20/92**

Food eaten	Time/circumstance	Calories
Coffee (cream and sugar)	7:15 A.M. bkfst.	40
Orange juice		110
Doughnut		130
Coffee (cream and sugar)	10:30 A.M. break	40
Yogurt (fruit)		200
Coffee (cream and sugar)	12:30 P.M. lunch	40
Coke	4 P.M. break	145
1 beer	6 P.M. relaxing after work	150
Peanuts (1 cup)		1,200
Fried chicken (3 pieces)	7:30 P.M. dinner with family	500
French fries (1 g)		220
Lettuce salad		15
Blue cheese dressing		220
Ice cream (1 cup)		300
Coffee (cream and sugar)		40
2 beers	8:30–10 P.M. watching TV ballgame	300
Potato chips (8 oz)		1,170
Ice cream (½ cup)	10:30 P.M. late-night snack	150
3 cookies		280
Total calories		**5,250**

that chicken is healthier than Mr. Greene's favorite steak, served a frozen fast-food variety, loaded with extra fat, for dinner. The same amount of skinless roast chicken would have had one-third the calories. Similarly, a baked potato would have had less than one-half the calories of his french fries. By adding 3 tablespoons of blue cheese dressing to his salad, he turned a 15-calorie dish into one with 235 calories. For dessert, a piece of fruit or frozen ice would have had fewer calories than the ice cream. Popcorn and a low-calorie beer or seltzer would have saved more than 1,000 calories while he watched TV. A before-bed snack of a glass of skim milk and one cookie again would have saved 245 calories.

Mr. Greene's diet, typical of what millions of Americans eat every day in varying quantities, is high in fat and sugar, low in complex carbohydrates and fiber. By increasing the last two elements and distributing the food more evenly throughout the day to prevent extreme late-day hunger, Mr. Greene could stay on his recommended 1,500-calorie reducing diet. In the course of a year, he can lose his excess weight, and in the process, he also may be able to bring his high blood pressure under control. What's more, he would acquire eating habits that would help maintain his proper weight for life.

Alan Greene's Revised Menu

Food eaten	Time/circumstance	Calories
½ grapefruit	7:15 A.M. bkfst.	40
Shredded wheat		90
Skim milk (1 cup)		90
1 slice whole wheat toast		55
1 tsp low-calorie margarine		15
Coffee (skim milk/½ tsp sugar)		15
Skim milk	10:30 A.M. break	90
Bran muffin		100
Sliced turkey sandwich on rye bread	12:30 P.M. lunch	250
Apple, medium		90
Coffee (skim milk/sugar)		15
Seltzer	4 P.M. break	0
2 rye crackers		45
Roast chicken breast	7:30 P.M. dinner with family	180
Baked potato/1 tsp margarine		100
Green salad/"lite" dressing		40
Broccoli with lemon		35
Pear		60
Coffee (skim milk/sugar)		15
Popcorn (1 cup unbuttered)	8:30–10:30 P.M. watching TV ballgame	10
Seltzer		0
Skim milk	10:30 P.M. late-night snack	90
1 low-calorie cookie		15
Total calories		**1,440**

The Columbia University Institute of Human Nutrition developed a model weight-loss plan that includes food choices from all the basic groups. If preferred, total calories can be divided into five or six meals instead of three, which may keep hunger from tempting a person to overeat when mealtime finally arrives. A supply of nutritious, low-calorie snacks such as fresh vegetables or whole-grain crackers will stave off hunger and prevent overeating if they are incorporated into the day's eating plan and caloric allowance. Eating slowly allows the body to register the feeling of fullness, and serving smaller portions on luncheon plates (instead of dinner plates) reduces the temptation to overfill one's plate and can prevent feelings of deprivation.

The diet plan is designed to bring about gradual weight loss with a nutritionally balanced, varied, and flexible eating plan. But remember, any weight-loss plan, no matter how balanced and sensible, will fail if you view it as a temporary measure to achieve a short-term goal. After your goal is achieved, you may slip back into your former eating habits and gain back the weight.

VEGETARIAN DIETS

Many of us associate vegetarian diets with rebellious young people, offbeat religious sects, or boring regimens of seeds, nuts, and beans. Actually, there are many different kinds of vegetarian diets, and when approached with common sense and sound nutritional principles, they can be varied, interesting, and healthful—naturally low in cholesterol and saturated fats and high in complex carbohydrates, vitamins, and minerals.

Not all vegetarian diets are the same. People who eat milk, eggs, and other dairy products, or those who occasionally have fish, have no trouble getting enough complete proteins. Others who eat only plant foods will need to match vegetable proteins to ensure that they consume all of the needed amino acids—the building blocks that make complete proteins.

TYPES OF VEGETARIANS

- *Strict vegetarians, or vegans:* Diet provides no animal foods, not even milk, cheese, or eggs.
- *Lactovegetarians:* Diet does not include meat, fish, or eggs, but milk, cheese, and other dairy products are allowed.
- *Ovolactovegetarians:* Eggs are added to the lactovegetarian diet.
- *Part-time vegetarians:* Diet is mostly ovolactovegetarian, with occasional additions of fish or poultry.

SAMPLE WEIGHT-LOSS MENUS

The following menus show how you can space your food through the day to prevent excessive hunger, stay within calorie limits, and still consume an interesting, healthful diet.

1,200 Calories

BREAKFAST

¼ cantaloupe

1½ cup puffed wheat

1 cup skim milk

Tea/coffee

MIDMORNING SNACK

½ bagel/1 tsp margarine

¼ cup herbed low-fat cottage cheese

LUNCH

¼ cup tuna with 1 tsp. mayonnaise and lettuce on a bun

Sliced tomatoes

Apple

Tea/coffee

MIDAFTERNOON SNACK

Rye crackers/1 oz Swiss cheese

Skim milk

1,500 Calories

BREAKFAST

Orange

½ cup farina/½ cup skim milk

½ English muffin/1 tsp margarine

Tea/coffee

MIDMORNING SNACK

¼ cup herbed low-fat cottage cheese

Rye crackers

Tea/coffee

LUNCH

Tomato and rice soup

2 oz turkey breast/1 tsp mayonnaise/ lettuce/rye bread

Tea/coffee

MIDAFTERNOON SNACK

Crackers

2 tsp peanut butter

1,800 Calories

BREAKFAST

½ grapefruit

1 cup shredded wheat/½ banana/ skim milk

Boiled egg

1 slice whole wheat toast/margarine

Tea/coffee

MIDMORNING SNACK

Small corn muffin

1 cup skim milk

LUNCH

Spaghetti with tomato and meat sauce

Green salad with oil-and-vinegar dressing

Angel food cake

Tea/coffee

1,200 Calories	1,500 Calories	1,800 Calories
DINNER	DINNER	MIDAFTERNOON SNACK
Clear broth soup with pasta or rice	Fruit cup	½ cup raw vegetables with ¼ cup herbed cottage cheese
2 oz roast chicken	Chili with rice	DINNER
Broccoli	Green salad with oil-and-vinegar dressing	Clear soup
Lettuce and endive salad with lemon juice	Sherbet	Chinese stir-fry dinner (sprouts, tofu, Chinese cabbage, strips of lean beef, soy sauce, peanut oil)
Yogurt with fresh berry topping	BEFORE BED	Rice
	1 cup skim milk	Green salad with low-fat dressing
	Pear	Stewed pear
		Tea/coffee
		BEFORE BED
		¼ cup yogurt flavored with cinnamon

Aside from the potential problem of inadequate or incomplete protein, many vegetarian regimens may fall short of providing enough iron and vitamin B_{12}. Iron is added to many foods, including fortified cereals and enriched bread and pasta; it is also found in raisins and other dried fruits, nuts, dried beans and peas, blackstrap molasses, and green leafy vegetables. Cooking acidic foods in cast-iron pots also can increase dietary iron.

Vitamin B_{12} occurs naturally only in meat, other animal products, and some types of seaweed, but it is added to fortified breakfast cereals and brewer's yeast. Eventually some strict vegetarians may need B_{12} supplements, although deficiency symptoms or pernicious anemia are rare except in alcoholics or others who are malnourished. Getting adequate calcium may be a problem for strict vegetarians who shun milk and milk products, the best sources of this mineral. Those who do not eat dairy products should emphasize dried peas and beans, green leafy vegetables, citrus fruits, and nuts, all of which contain calcium. Women in particular should be sure they are getting enough calcium; those who are strict vegetarians and do not drink milk may want to discuss with their physician the possible need for a calcium supplement. With proper planning and balance, however, most vegetarians do not need vitamin and mineral supplements.

SPECIAL PROBLEMS OF THE ELDERLY

As a whole, our elderly population is probably the most poorly nourished group in the United States. People living alone, sometimes without adequate cooking or refrigeration facilities, subsist on tea, toast, canned soups, candy, and snack foods. Many have difficulty shopping, and still others have little incentive to prepare themselves nutritious and appetizing meals.

Economics may often be the primary cause of poor nutrition in the elderly. Developing thrifty shopping habits with an eye to sound nutrition can solve some of the problems in the food/money equation. (See box "Food Tips for Older People.") A pound of pasta, fresh tomatoes, and squash can be the ingredients of a healthy meal and are less expensive than many convenience foods. Often, an older person on a fixed income is forced to choose between not paying the rent or medical bills and cutting back on food. Many older people are unaware that they may be eligible for food stamps; others are too proud to apply. A phone call to the local food stamp office or Department of Aging will clarify the requirements.

Cutbacks in government-supported meal programs, such as Meals on Wheels and meals served at senior citizen centers, have been especially hard for the elderly poor. And, of course, availability and programs vary widely from area to area. What may be readily available in an urban area may be totally lacking in a rural or suburban community. Still, there are many resources, and very often people simply do not know what is available. The local Department of Aging, the Health Department, Visiting Nurse Association, senior citizen center, and the individual's own physician, minister, or rabbi are good sources of information.

Very often, older people complain that they simply do not feel like eating. Taste and smell tend to decrease with age, which is another reason some elderly people may eat less. Some try to compensate for this by adding extra salt. A better alternative is to use different spices and pungent herbs like thyme, sage, or basil. Serving foods that have always been favorites in a way that is visually pleasing can also be an incentive to eat well.

FOOD TIPS FOR OLDER PEOPLE

1. *When shopping:*
   - Plan menus for several days or a week. Don't forget to include leftovers in your planning.
   - Buy items in quantities that you are sure you will use—for example, a half carton of eggs or a pint of milk. If necessary, ask a grocer to open packages of produce so you can buy the quantity you need.
   - When buying fruit, select only one or two pieces that are ripe for immediate eating and others that are less ripe for later use.
   - If access to a supermarket is a problem, check with your local agency on aging or social service department to see if there is a bus service or other transportation program for people in your situation. Consider working out an exchange with a neighbor—for example, baby-sitting in exchange for transportation to a shopping center.
2. *If you are on a limited budget:*
   - Check whether you are eligible for food stamps, Meals on Wheels, or other food programs.
   - Check with your local community center or senior citizen program for other assistance programs that may apply to you.
   - Check newspaper ads or store circulars for specials.
   - Use coupons, but only for items you use and need.
   - Read nutrition labels.
   - Look for unbranded or store-brand items.
   - Buy fresh fruits and vegetables in season.
   - Look for less-expensive sources of protein (peanut butter, legumes, liver, chicken, canned fish, eggs).
   - Avoid "health" or "organic" foods, which are more expensive and no more healthful than regular foods.
   - If you have freezer space, use it for extras and leftovers.
3. *If you lack a refrigerator, try stocking the following items:*
   - Nonfat dried milk
   - Peanut butter
   - Enriched or whole-grain cereals and breads (small loaf)
   - Canned fish, stew, chunky soups, hash, pork and beans
   - Dried fruits and nuts
   - Dried peas and beans
4. *If chewing is a problem:*
   - Use fish, ground meat, baked beans, cottage cheese, and other "soft" protein foods.

- Cook stews, soups, and casseroles, and freeze leftovers for future use.
- Chop or puree vegetables and fruits.

5. *If your appetite is poor or you eat alone:*
   - Plan regular meals and try to exchange cooking with a friend occasionally.
   - Resist eating out of a pan; treat yourself to an attractive table and eat from real dishes.
   - A glass of wine may help perk up your appetite (but don't substitute alcohol for food).
   - A pet may provide needed companionship.
   - Try to get some exercise each day, even if it's only a walk to the corner and back.
   - Turn on some music or a favorite radio or TV program while you eat.
6. *If you are trying to lose weight:*
   - Eat smaller portions.
   - Use low-fat milk, diet margarine, and other low-calorie foods.
   - Eat more often; don't let yourself get too hungry. Five small meals consumed throughout the day will prevent you from getting so hungry that you end up overeating at night.
   - Avoid fad or crash diets.
   - Eat pasta, fruits, vegetables, and sources of vegetable protein (dried peas, beans, rice, etc.) instead of meat. If you eat meat, buy low-fat cuts and trim off all visible fat. A gram of fat contains 9 calories, compared to 4 calories in a gram of carbohydrate or protein foods. High-fiber foods, or roughage, contain fewer calories because the fiber is not digested.
7. *If you are trying to gain weight:*
   - Use whole milk and fortify your drinks with an egg, ice cream, or dried milk.
   - Eat more often: Include snacks of cheese, peanut butter, or nuts in your diet.
   - Add cheese or cream cheese to soups, casseroles, and other dishes.

HELP FOR OTHER PROBLEMS

Chewing. A blender, food processor, or grinder is helpful if chewing is a problem. The diet should emphasize soft but nutrient-rich foods like fish and chicken, yogurt, and eggs. In many cases, properly fitting dentures will eliminate chewing problems, so a dental checkup is important.

Medications. More than 85 percent of all people 65 and older take at least one prescription drug, and many take several. The more drugs consumed, the greater the chance of interactions with food or other drugs. Many medications alter the nutritional status of, or the way the body uses, different foods. For example, large numbers of older people take diuretics for high blood pressure, edema, or congestive heart failure. These drugs can lead to urinary loss of potassium, sodium, and other important minerals. The problem may be compounded by a diet that is restricted in one or more of these nutrients.

Many drugs cause a loss of appetite; others may produce nausea, constipation, diarrhea, and other side effects. One should be aware of possible adverse reactions and side effects associated with various medications, and report these to one's doctor if they occur. Sometimes the problem can be remedied by the timing of medications: Some should be taken with meals, others before or after eating. Remember, too, that alcohol is a drug and can produce adverse reactions when combined with other drugs. It also affects metabolism, and excessive alcohol consumption can cause serious nutritional deficiencies.

Constipation. Many older people complain of being constipated and frequently resort to overuse of laxatives. Sometimes the constipation is a *result* of laxative abuse. Older people who have difficulty chewing may shun high-fiber foods in favor of soft, easy-to-eat items. Lack of exercise and inadequate fluid intake can also promote constipation. Some laxatives, such as mineral oil, decrease absorption of the fat-soluble vitamins A, D, E, and K. Others interfere with absorption of minerals and other important nutrients. Increasing the intake of foods that are high in fiber or roughage, yet still easy to chew, will help. Examples include whole-grain hot cereals like oatmeal or farina; whole-grain cold cereals like bran or wheat flakes; stewed or canned fruits; cooked dried beans, lentils, or vegetables that are steamed until tender; brown rice; and salads made with lettuce, tomatoes, and other "soft" greens or vegetables.

Indigestion. The production of gastric juices may decrease with age, resulting in increased susceptibility to digestive problems. A hiatal hernia, resulting in heartburn from a backflow of gastric juices from the stomach into the esophagus, also becomes more common with age. Eating small, frequent meals, avoiding foods that seem to promote stomach upset, judicious use of antacids (some are also good sources of extra calcium), and not lying down for an hour or two after eating usually will minimize the problem.

NUTRITION QUACKERY

Older people, especially those with chronic diseases, are particularly vulnerable to food faddism and nutrition quackery. Nutrition charlatans do not hesitate to promise that their particular diet, supplement, or potion will help a person recapture lost youth, overcome infirmities, live longer, and so on. Their products tend to be expensive, even harmful, or at least worthless. It is far better to spend the money on wholesome nutritious foods than on an assortment of supplements, expensive "organic" foods, and other unproven nutritional remedies.

One of the most common of the questionable nutritional practices involves promoting megadoses of vitamins and minerals. Many people who shun taking needed medications because they fear side effects think nothing of taking pharmacological doses of vitamin A, B-complex, C, E, and other nutrients. Whenever a nutrient is taken in amounts that exceed what the body can utilize, it takes on the property of a drug and carries a risk of side effects and adverse reactions. Before taking any vitamin or mineral in excess of the RDA, a person should check with his or her doctor.

Similarly, people should avoid herbal potions that are marketed as nutritional products but that in reality have little or no nutritional value and may even be harmful. Remember, there are no licensing requirements or educational standards for "nutritionists." While many may be well-qualified and dispense legitimate advice, many others have little or no qualifications, and trade in nutritional nonsense. Many call themselves "doctor," but further investigation discloses that their degrees are from mail-order "diploma mills." Dr. Victor Herbert, a leading nutrition educator, demonstrated how easy it is to get a "nutrition degree, complete with an impressive-looking certificate." He enrolled his dog Sassafras and cat Charlie as professional members of the American Association of Nutrition and Dietary Consultants. All he had to do was fill out forms and send in $50 for each certificate. "At least 10,000 people have obtained similar certificates," he says, "and it is safe to assume that many, if not most, are now practicing nutrition 'therapists.'"

There are numerous legitimate sources of sound nutritional advice and information. Anyone who claims to be a nutrition therapist should have a degree from an institution accredited by the Council of Postsecondary Accreditation in Washington, D.C. Be particularly wary of strange-sounding degrees like Doctor of Naturopathy (N.D.), Doctor of Metaphysics (Ms.D.), or Doctor of Holistic Medicine (D.H.M.). A qualified registered dietitian (R.D.) or physician who has taken extra courses in nutrition is your best source of nutritional counseling.

2

Exercise— The Key to Lifelong Fitness

Increasingly, exercise is emerging as one of the best ways to avoid many of the infirmities associated with growing older. In fact, studies have shown that many problems thought to be chronic diseases of aging are really symptoms of muscle and joint disuse. A regular program of exercise may help retain joint movement as well as strengthen muscles, thereby countering the effects of age-related arthritis. Exercise also is vital in maintaining healthy bones and is part of the prevention of and the treatment regimen for osteoporosis. People who exercise also have an enhanced feeling of well-being and are not as vulnerable to depression. Active people have fewer problems controlling their weight, sleep better, and feel better about themselves. And, of course, the benefits of regular exercise in improving cardiovascular and lung functioning are now an accepted tenet of modern medicine. In fact, in 1992 the American Heart Association labeled physical inactivity, or lack of exercise, as a major risk factor for coronary heart disease.

DESIGNING YOUR OWN EXERCISE PROGRAM

Many over-50 people, especially those who have led relatively sedentary lives, often feel that it is too late for them to take up exercise, that the damage caused by their inactivity is too advanced to overcome. The good news is that it is never too late to start exercising. According to an eight-year study released in 1989 by researchers at the Institute for Aerobics Research in Dallas, those who stand to gain most from a low-level exercise program—a brisk walk lasting 30 to 45 minutes six or seven days a week—are sedentary individuals. Every day people of all ages and physical conditions discover that even moderate exercise can make a huge difference in the way they feel and look.

Granted, there are dozens of excuses to avoid exercise: "I don't have the time," "I don't have the right shoes (or equipment, or clothes, etc.)," "It's boring," and on and on. But none of these is really valid. As little as 20 to 30 minutes a day, four times a week—time all of us waste watching TV, talking on the telephone, or performing any number of other nonessential tasks—is all it takes to get started on an exercise regimen. As for fancy clothing and equipment, all that is really needed for most activities are a pair of comfortable shoes and a loose-fitting pair of sweatpants and a T-shirt.

COMMON PITFALLS OF STARTING AN EXERCISE PROGRAM

1. *Trying to do too much too soon.* Injuries slow progress and take a longer time to heal as the body ages. The tortoise approach—slow and steady wins the race—is much more effective than trying to do too much too fast and winding up sidelined with an avoidable orthopedic injury or some other physical problem.
2. *Wearing uncomfortable clothing.* It's not necessary to spend a lot of money on chic exercise wear. All you need is loose clothing that does not restrict movement and is made of a material that breathes.
3. *Failing to warm up and cool down.* Always do warm-up exercises to avoid injuries, but avoid overstretching. Move slowly and methodically. All movements should "flow." Cool-down exercises are also important, especially for heart patients.
4. *Taking pain relievers.* Before exercising, avoid taking any drugs or medications that can mask dangerous aches and pains and lead to injury.
5. *Risking injury.* Vigorous jogging, rope jumping, aerobic dancing, or other jumping and pounding motions can cause joint injury.
6. *Keeping it moderate.* Exercising too vigorously or not vigorously enough can cause your heart rate to climb too high or stay too low. Keep your heart rate within your conditioning target range.
7. *Exercising too often or not often enough.* Three to five workouts per week, lasting 20 to 30 minutes, is optimum.
8. *Taking hot baths after exercising.* Spending time in a sauna or hot tub immediately after exercising can exacerbate circulatory problems such as high blood pressure and varicose veins.

When embarking on an exercise program, many of us make the mistake of trying to overcome the effects of years of sedentary living overnight. We often equate exercise with jogging, aerobic dancing, or some other very intense activity when, in fact, walking at a moderately brisk pace, combined with stretching exercises to keep joints flexible and prevent muscle strain, is preferable to the jarring motions of jogging or dancing.

BEFORE YOU START

A number of factors should be considered in developing your exercise program. After appropriate medical tests, your doctor will be able to suggest exercise activities based on any medical problems you may have. In addition, an exercise physiologist or

THE PRE-EXERCISE CHECKUP

Before embarking on an exercise conditioning program, all sedentary people over the age of 50 should probably have the following medical examinations:

- An exercise tolerance (stress) test. This entails exercising on a treadmill or exercise bicycle while undergoing continuous electrocardiogram (EKG) monitoring of the heart. The test will determine safe levels of activity and also may help detect unsuspected coronary disease or heart rhythm abnormalities.
- Blood pressure measurement. People with high blood pressure have a higher-than-average risk of a heart attack and may require a special exercise prescription.
- Evaluation of blood cholesterol.

In addition, people with specific health problems may require additional examinations. Depending upon the problem, these may include:

- *Diabetes.* Measurement of blood glucose before and after exercise.
- *Arthritis.* Evaluation of joints to design exercises that increase mobility without damage to structures.
- *Emphysema, asthma, and other lung disorders.* Pulmonary function tests.
- *Obesity.* Evaluation of heart and joint function.
- *Circulatory problems.* Evaluation of heart function.

sports medicine specialist may be consulted regarding flexibility, muscle strength, percentage of body fat, and other factors that affect exercise ability. When beginning a new program of exercise, remember that different types of physical activity require different sets of muscles. Proficiency at one form of activity does not mean a person can perform other exercises at the same level of intensity.

In developing an exercise program, many people overlook one of the most important factors, namely, personal likes and dislikes. If you feel uncomfortable in water, swimming obviously is not a good exercise choice for you, even though it may be one of the most physically beneficial. People who enjoy companionship and have a good sense of rhythm may enjoy aerobic dancing, while others may find this activity more of a chore than a pleasure. Competitive individuals may do better if they select tennis, handball, or some other game; more solitary types may prefer walking or a stationary bicycle.

There are things to do to make the exercise period more interesting. Exercising with your spouse or with a good friend, for instance, can change the experience from solitary drudgery to a pleasant catching-up-with-each-other routine. Riding a stationary bicycle can be timed with the morning or evening news or an interesting television program. Some bikes will accommodate a rack for reading material, and a spellbinding book may be just the ticket for keeping your mind off your exertion. Exercise can also serve a purpose: For instance, walking to the store to get the newspaper can be substituted for having it delivered.

Your overall level of fitness also is a factor in developing your own exercise program. Even without a medical checkup, you can get a good idea of your level of fitness by timing yourself on a brisk walk. If you can walk a mile in less than 15 minutes, chances are you are reasonably fit.

TYPES OF EXERCISES

There are three basic kinds of exercise:

Flexibility Training and Stretching. Stretching and flexibility training act to halt loss of joint mobility. This type of exercise loosens muscles, enabling them to relax, and prepares them for further exercise stress. Gently bending, extending, or rotating the neck, shoulders, elbows, back, hips, knees, and ankles increases the flexibility of tissues and protects against injury.

Aerobic and Endurance Activity. Rhythmic, repeated movement, done rapidly and long enough that breathing and heart rate become faster than usual, leads to improved efficiency of heart, lungs, and muscles, as well as to an increase in their capacity to do work and withstand stress. The most basic and safest aerobic exercise is walking. Cycling, swimming, and dancing are also enjoyable aerobic activities for older people. To be effective, aerobic conditioning should take place at least three times a week for at least half an hour. (People not in shape should work up to this level.)

Strength Building. Strength building, such as weight lifting and other isometric activities, increases muscle mass and also promotes improved muscle tone. Moderation should be the key to strength building, especially for older people. Age entails the loss of a certain amount of muscle mass, which can be minimized or even reversed to a degree by strength building. These exercises also protect bones and soft tissues from injury.

An ideal exercise regimen includes these three basic types of exercise. Sports medicine experts recommend this mix, called *cross-training,* and the variety may make exercise more enjoyable. Remember, the benefit of any exercise is really the product of two factors: the intrinsic value of the activity and the ability to do it regularly. The highest gain is likely to come from activity that can begin with a minimum of fuss, bother, and travel time. It shouldn't feel like punishment (or you won't keep doing it), but it does have to feel like exertion. Listen to signals from your body. Soreness in unused muscles is common after beginning exercise, but pain is a signal to rest the body.

EXERCISE EQUIPMENT AND HEALTH CLUBS

Many people make the mistake of assuming that, in order to exercise, you must join an exercise club or buy a lot of expensive equipment. While exercise clubs and a well-equipped home gym may be nice, they certainly are not essential. Indeed, many people invest large sums of money in club memberships or exercise equipment only to have them go unused. The only essential "equipment" is your own motivation; all the rest is like icing on the cake.

Still, many people find the companionship and motivation that come from exercising with a group important in helping them stick to a regimen. For them, an exercise club or group may be an ideal solution. Many Ys have special exercise programs. Community organizations, church groups, senior citizen centers, adult education programs, and work-site fitness centers are among the many groups offering exercise classes and programs. But before joining a club or program, you should follow some guidelines to make sure your choice is appropriate for your needs. Specific questions you should ask before joining an exercise club include:

1. Does the club welcome visits by prospective members at various times of the day or only at a prearranged time? Although many clubs will not permit nonmembers to actually try out their facilities (for insurance reasons), you should be able to visit at the times of day that you are most likely to use the club. In this way, you can observe how crowded it is and whether the activities are appropriate for you.
2. Are the instructors qualified? Is someone trained in emergency medical procedures available at all times when the club is in use?
3. Does the club require medical clearance before enrolling? This is impor-

tant for over-40 members who are embarking on exercise conditioning for the first time.

4. Are you likely to fit in with the other members? A group composed mostly of young, competitive handball enthusiasts probably will not have much in common with a middle-aged person who wants to tighten sagging abdominal muscles. Also, exercising with younger people may cause an older person to overdo it. Find companions in your age group or in your physical condition to avoid that temptation.
5. Is the equipment in good repair and adequate for the number of users? No one wants to spend a large portion of his or her workout time waiting in line for equipment.
6. Do the exercisers have adequate space? Overcrowding promotes injury and discourages a good workout.
7. Does each workout include a warm-up and cool-down segment?
8. Are the locker and changing rooms adequate and clean? Ask other members if theft has been a problem.
9. Are you being pressured into signing a long-term contract before you have a chance to read it carefully? Can you clearly determine what things are included and what are extras? Can you get a refund if you move away or have to give up your membership for some unforeseen reason?
10. Does the facility offer classes in other areas that may be of interest to you, such as nutrition, weight control, or smoking cessation?

TIPS ON BUYING HOME FITNESS EQUIPMENT

Selecting appropriate home exercise equipment entails the same sort of research and questioning as picking an exercise club. There is no single piece of equipment that will exercise every part of the body, but several types come close.

The basic types of home fitness equipment are rowing machines, ski simulators, stair climbers, stationary bikes, treadmills, and strength-training units. Considerations include overall fitness benefits; appropriateness of equipment for different age groups and for people with different health concerns, such as lower-back or knee problems; required maintenance; durability of equipment; size of the unit; and price.

Before buying any piece of equipment, be sure to try it out yourself. Also, understand that good, quality equipment can be expensive. This is especially true of rowing machines and treadmills. The old adage that you get what you pay for applies in full.

Cross-country Ski Simulators. These machines have become popular additions to the home gym. They work the upper and lower body together and provide an excellent cardiovascular workout with minimal stress to the back, hip, and knee joints, and no impact trauma. The independent pulley systems require some learning and coordination to operate. Dependent systems, where the pulley action moves the "skis," are easier to operate but less realistic simulations. Many experts consider this the best package for the price.

Downhill Ski Simulators. These are newer products and thus have a less-established track record. They work both upper and lower body muscles and provide a good cardiovascular workout. According to downhill buffs, this is a realistic simulation of the movements required in alpine skiing.

Rowing Machines. These machines work the upper and lower body, primarily the back muscles and upper arms and shoulders, promoting the V-shaped torso. They rate very high aerobically, but they can stress the lower back. A realistic simulation is extremely expensive.

Stair Climbers. The focus of these very popular machines is on the legs and buttocks, although some of them have components that work on the upper body. They provide an adequate cardiovascular workout and little learning is required, but the movement may place too much stress on knees, hips, lower back, ankles, and wrists (if you lean on bent wrists). Of course, if you have stairs in your home, you can perform this exercise without buying any equipment at all. Use care, however, to maintain balance.

Stationary Bikes. This is one of the most popular pieces of home equipment and one that is generally recommended for everyone except those who need to limit movement of knee joints. There are two types of stationary bikes, upright and recumbent. Recumbent bikes allow the rider to sit in a kind of bucket seat, with legs outstretched and parallel to the floor. People often find the recumbent bikes to be more comfortable, especially the seats. The uprights, however, take up less floor space. Both types provide an adequate cardiovascular workout, and the primary muscular focus is on the hamstrings and buttocks. There are also dual-action bikes available that work both the upper and lower body. Whether the stationary bicycle is an exercycle or an ergometer (which comes with built-in gauges for instant feedback on how much energy you're using), it should have a heavy flywheel weighing at least 30 pounds, plus a comfortable seat that lets you fully extend your legs to the pedals. The knee on the forward leg should not extend over or beyond toes, as this can cause knee strain. The *wheel tension* ("speed and resistance") of the bike should be easy to adjust. There are many, many models to choose from, so try out several models and pick the one that pedals smoothly and feels best to you at the right price.

Treadmills. An efficient tool for weight control, a treadmill works all the muscles in the lower body. It provides the same benefits as walking, jogging, or running outside.

It also provides almost the same impact stress. However, the most significant problem with treadmills may be the price. Good, dependable machines are expensive, listing for a thousand dollars or more.

Strength-Training Equipment. The American College of Sports Medicine (ACSM) recommends strength training as an adjunct to all cardiovascular fitness programs. It enhances not only appearance but also the ability to perform lifting, pushing, pulling, and other everyday living tasks without injury. Also, you can start a program with a few inexpensive pieces. You can wear ankle and wrist weights, usually weighing about 2 pounds each, while walking or doing other exercise to expend more energy and build strength. This does not build up muscle bulk, but can help you improve tone, endurance, and power. The weights should not be too heavy, and they should be placed evenly on the body to avoid feeling off balance. Other more elaborate weight-training and multipurpose gyms are available for home use, but they are expensive and may not be recommended for people with chronic heart disease. Be careful when buying equipment, because a number of companies sell over the phone or through ads. Again, always try out equipment before buying it.

EXERCISE VIDEOS

There are many exercise programs on television as well as a growing number of exercise videos for home use. Proceed cautiously with these: Most are designed for in-shape, vigorous exercisers, and even these people may have trouble keeping pace with a professional exercise leader. Little attention is paid to the beginning, older person in these types of programs. Becoming overly enthusiastic while exercising to a film program—especially one that is done to fast, catchy music without a proper warm-up—can cause injury or at least serious soreness that will inhibit further exercising.

Any exercise program or equipment should be discussed with your physician. As in all types of exercise, moderation is most important, especially in the beginning.

FITNESS WALKING

At times, it may seem that jogging is the national pastime and that health club memberships and exercise equipment are essential, but all you really need for a good exercise program are a pair of comfortable walking shoes and a place to walk. Fitness walking does not carry the risk of joint and muscle injury that is inherent in jogging or running. And, when done at a brisk pace, it can provide the heart with an equally good workout. In fact, racewalking is a recognized Olympic sport. For those who can no longer take the constant pounding and jarring of jogging but need the psychological benefits of competition and the same physical benefits as running, this revved-up version of normal walking may be the answer.

Racewalking, which entails a rhythmic form of brisk walking and a pumping arm movement, provides a more vigorous workout and may not be recommended for people with certain forms of heart disease or a chronic pulmonary disorder. For those suited to racewalking, the sport provides a good workout for virtually every major muscle group—buttocks, thighs, calves, arms, chest, back, and abdominals—and in less time per session than is needed with regular walking.

For most of us, simply walking at a brisk pace is sufficient. With proper shoes, just about everyone can walk for fitness. Challenge yourself, but don't overdo it. A brisk walk of 60 minutes three or four times a week is enough to provide cardiovascular conditioning. A walk to the corner and back or getting off the bus and walking the last mile to or from work may be the way to begin.

An increasing number of people, especially those in the over-40 age group, are exchanging their running shoes for walking shoes. Shopping malls have become favored places for informal exercise groups that meet regularly and walk briskly on indoor "courses." A park, high school track, sparsely traveled road, or quiet side street are other ideal walking places.

WATER WORKOUTS

For many people, especially those with orthopedic or weight problems, exercising in water is an ideal alternative to brisk walking, jogging, and other types of land exercise. Swimming, for example, works the cardiovascular system as effectively as running

---

MALLWALKING

Mallwalking is an exercise phenomenon that has grown out of the common need for exercise in a comfortable environment, combined with the desire for companionship. Informal groups of people meet at designated places and times in a nearby shopping mall, usually in the early morning hours before shoppers descend in full force. The walks follow a "course" inside the mall. Shopping malls are open almost every day for long hours year-round, supplying a free, stable environment. This practical approach to fitness has spread so that most malls today have at least one such group. For information on your local mallwalking group, contact the administrative office of the shopping mall near you, your city's chamber of commerce, or local chapters of the American Association of Retired Persons (AARP), or look for flyers and advertisements that the groups might place in community newsletters and newspapers.

---

and provides a powerful workout for the upper body and legs, without the joint-jarring, injury-causing drawbacks of running, aerobic dance, and other land sports.

Water aerobics—dancing exercises done to music while standing in waist-deep water—is now offered by a number of exercise programs geared to older people. These exercises are particularly suitable for older women who may be experiencing early signs of osteoporosis. Water aerobics or swimming provides the benefits of activity without placing undue strain on already weakened bones (see Figures 2.1 to 2.4).

WHEN AND HOW TO BEGIN

There is no right or wrong time to exercise. For some people, a workout first thing in the morning gets them going; some prefer a midday exercise break, and still others find an evening session helps them relax and makes sleep easier. It's all a matter of personal preference. The important thing is to make exercise a part of your regular routine, just like brushing your teeth.

Wear loose-fitting clothing that breathes to allow for air circulation. Wearing a hat outdoors is a good idea in cold weather because it prevents losing too much body heat and reduces the chance of sunburn on sunny days. Rubberized, vinyl, and plastic warm-up clothes should be avoided; they don't allow for proper air circulation and evaporation of perspiration, which are necessary to regulate body temperature. Comfortable, well-fitting shoes appropriate to the exercise are also important. Joggers and runners should always carry identification, as well as change for emergency phone calls.

EXERCISE CAUTIONS

Exercise can be stimulating and fun, but caution must be observed when working out in cold or extremely warm weather. And no matter what the climate, don't eat immediately before exercising.

In Cold Weather. Dress in warm layers of clothing that can be removed as needed during exercise. Beware of strong, cold winds, which can increase the chance of frostbite, and always seek shelter if any tingling or numbness occurs in your fingers or toes. Also, be cautious when exercising at higher altitudes. Upon arrival in a mountainous area, don't be surprised if the thinner air makes breathing difficult at first. It may take several days for you to adjust, and activity should be kept at a comfortable level until then.

In the Heat. An older person, especially one with heart disease, should take special precautions when exercising in hot weather or when using a sauna or hot tub. This becomes critical for the many people who retire to Florida, Arizona, or other areas with warm climates. To avoid heat exhaustion and heatstroke, drink plenty of water or elec-

EXERCISING IN WATER

People who find it difficult to exercise on land because of arthritis or other joint problems usually can work out in water, which makes the body buoyant and also absorbs the impact an exerciser would normally encounter when the foot strikes the ground during walking or jogging. These exercises are designed to maintain joint flexibility.

Swimming, water walking, or jogging also will provide an excellent aerobic workout. If a person has trouble keeping his or her balance in the water, there are special flotation vests available that athletic trainers use to train competitive athletes without the danger of muscle injuries.

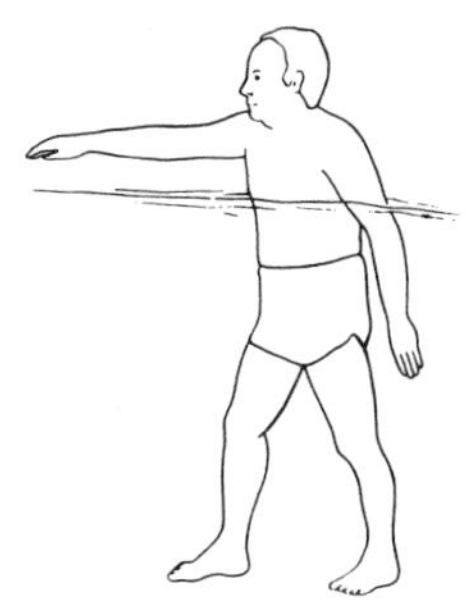

Figure 2.1
Water walking. Stand in water that is chest high (or deeper if upper body joints are affected) with one arm extended for balance and the other in the water. Rotate the arms as if you were swimming, and walk from one end of the pool to the other. This exercise is good for people with hip or knee problems.

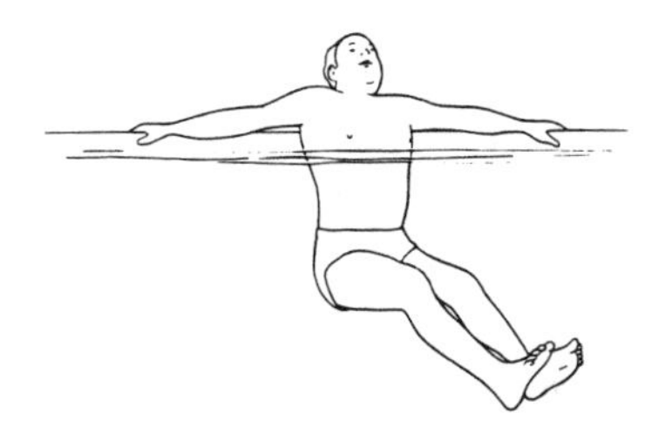

Figure 2.2
Leg and abdominal muscle stretches. Stand at the edge of the pool with arms extended and hands grasping the side of the pool. Lift lower body off pool bottom, and extend legs outward. Repeat 10 to 20 times.

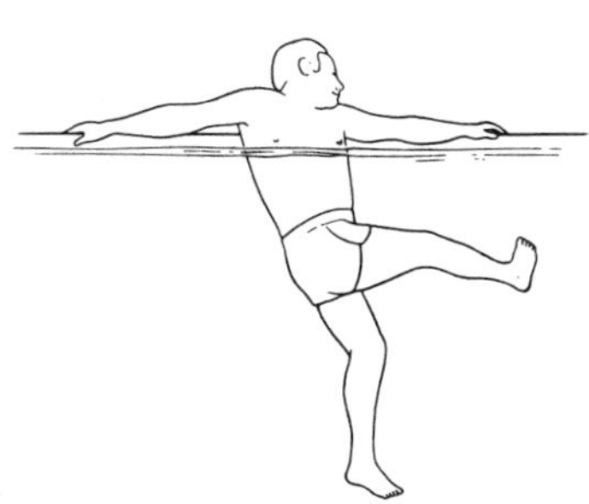

Figure 2.3
Lower body stretch. Stand with back to the side of the pool, arms extended and hands grasping the edge. Lift one leg, and try to touch side of pool. Alternating legs, repeat 10 times.

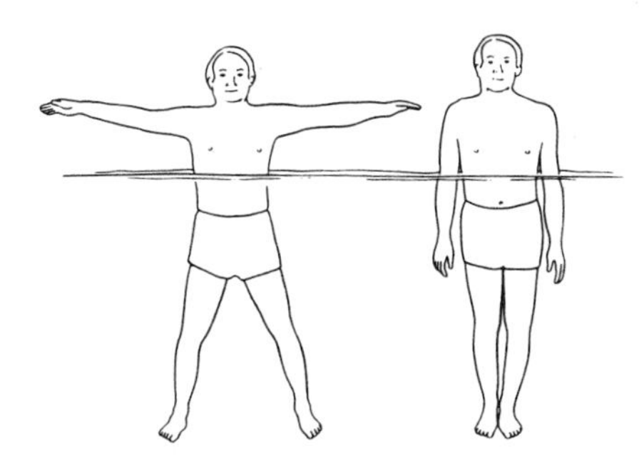

Figure 2.4
Water jumping jacks. Stand in water chest deep with arms extended at sides. Using arms for balance, with legs extended, bounce up, landing with legs together. This provides an aerobic workout similar to jumping rope, but without the impact on knees, ankles, and other weight-bearing joints.

CHOOSING THE RIGHT SHOE

The athletic shoe market—and accompanying advertising—has expanded so rapidly that buying a pair for exercise may seem a rather mind-boggling task. Ads proclaim the superiority of shoes cushioned with air, gel, or other "high-tech" materials, many of which come with a high price tag as well.

There are, however, orthopedic advantages to buying shoes designed for specific sports, although the movement—not the sport itself—should be the indicator. For instance, aerobic dance shoes may be a good choice for people who jump rope because both activities involve up-and-down motions and the shoes have extra cushioning for the forefoot and good lateral support for side-to-side movements. Running shoes can make good walking shoes. Cross-training shoes combine several design features for people who regularly engage in more than one sport or activity, but should only be used for moderate or light exercise.

Evaluate shoes on the following criteria: cushioning, stability, flexibility, construction, price, comfort, and fit. Test the cushioning by jumping lightly on a hard surface. You should feel a bounce to your step, and there should be no shock to the foot or leg. Check side-to-side flexibility by rotating the shoes back and forth while holding the toes in one hand and the heel in the other. High-top shoes, which come up around the ankle, provide extra stability for people with weak ankles. While wearing the shoes, assess flexibility, especially important in the forefoot, by lifting the heel while pressing the forefoot on the floor. The shoes should bend easily.

Time is the only true test for durability. (Check *Consumer Reports* magazine for buying advice and Ratings on running shoes and other types of athletic equipment.) It is important to realize, however, that athletic shoes must be treated as exercise equipment and should be replaced when they become less effective. Running shoes, for instance, should be changed about every 200 to 400 miles or so. In many cases, the midsole, which cushions the foot and dampens shock, wears out long before the outsole, the bottom outer layer of the sole, starts deteriorating.

The way the shoe fits your foot is the most important of all these criteria. If possible, try shoes on at the end of the day, when your feet are most swollen. Always use the sock that you would wear when exercising. There should be about ¼ to ½ inch (your thumbnail's length) between the tip of the shoe and the tip of your longest toe. The widest part of the shoe should fit comfortably around the ball of your foot. (Some manufacturers make special widths for people with wide or narrow feet.) When walking around the fitting room, your feet should not "move about" within the shoe, that is, shifting with every start and stop. Never buy a shoe with the hope that it will "stretch" out. It will be no more comfortable at home than it is in the store.

Many people's feet are different sizes, so always try on both shoes. Buy for the larger foot, and, if necessary, use an insert to fill up the other shoe.

Before you shop, find out whether you have such motion-control problems as over-pronation (the feet roll inward more than usual while running) or supination (the feet don't roll inward enough). You can diagnose your running style yourself. If you have flat feet, if your shoes wear down toward the inside ball of your foot, and if the toe box of your shoes bulges toward the inside, you're probably a pronator. You're a supinator if you have high arches and if the wear on your shoes is along the outside edge. Even wear indicates a neutral running style—and no need for shoes with special motion control.

Once you find the shoe that is right for you, your next athletic shoe shopping trip will be less involved. Even though shoe manufacturers are updating their stock continually, a knowledgeable salesperson should be able to steer you toward a like model in the same line.

trolyte-replenishing fluids before, during, and after exercise, whether you are thirsty or not. Dehydration is dangerous, and in times of heavy sweating, drinking enough cool liquids is vital. Avoid ice-cold drinks, however, as they may cause cramps.

Wearing lightweight clothing that breathes is especially important. Polypropylene is a good first-layer synthetic material that keeps the skin dry by carrying away perspiration.

Always stop exercising at the first sign of dizziness, breathing difficulty, or nausea, and use common sense when assessing the likelihood of heat-related problems. During hot weather, exercise in the cooler morning or evening hours and reduce the intensity of the exercise. And if it's 100 degrees outside, either exercise in an air-conditioned indoor space or don't exercise at all.

WHEN TO EXPECT RESULTS

Most people begin to see the benefits of regular conditioning exercise within a few weeks. True physical fitness is the ability to exercise at or near your body's maximum potential, and that may take up to three months of gradual buildup to reach. Studies have found that a year of regular conditioning exercise can bring the body back to the level that it was 10 years previously. Unfortunately, there are no shortcuts to achieving your full potential, but getting in shape is not as difficult as many people assume. And despite what you hear, it should not be painful.

Pain during exercise is a warning sign that should not be ignored. It usually means you are trying to do too much too fast or that you have injured a muscle, tendon, or other structure. Minor soreness that comes from using long-dormant muscles may be relieved by a heating pad or warm bath; a little massage at the point of soreness also may help. Sore muscles should be rested for a day or two, although gentle stretching and moderate walking usually will not provoke further pain. If the pain worsens or the soreness persists for more than a couple of days, consult your doctor.

EXERCISE GUIDELINES

Frequency, intensity, and duration are all important in a conditioning exercise program. Most conditioning programs require a minimum of three or four 20- to 30-minute sessions a week, preferably on alternating days; and some exercise physiologists recommend four or five sessions. Most physiologists caution against daily workouts because the body needs a day off now and then to allow for muscle growth and repair and to heal the minor injuries that may occur. As we grow older, the repair process may be slower. In short, heed your body's warning signs: Slow down if it tells you that you are doing too much too fast. The level of intensity depends upon physical condition, but for most people the pulse rate is the best indicator of whether or not the exercise is sufficiently vigorous to produce a conditioning effect.

GUIDELINES FOR PHYSICAL FITNESS PROGRAMS

The 1990 American College of Sports Medicine (ACSM) guidelines recommend:

- Physical activity three to five days a week.
- Aerobic activity that increases the heart rate to 60 to 85 percent of its safe maximum rate and goes on continuously for 20 to 60 minutes (longer for activity of lower intensity). Beginners should keep to 60–65 percent.
- Activity such as swimming, rowing, stair climbing, or walking/hiking that requires continuous use of large muscle groups in a rhythmic motion.
- Moderate resistance and strength training for all major muscle groups. The minimum should be one set of 8 to 12 repetitions of 8 to 10 calisthenic-type exercises at least two days a week.

HOW TO DETERMINE YOUR EXERCISE POTENTIAL

Your pulse rate, or number of heartbeats per minute, is a key indication of whether you are exercising in your conditioning zone. During exercise the pulse rate should rise. Cardiovascular conditioning takes place when the heart beats at 60 to 90 percent of its maximum safe rate. Your maximum heart rate is approximately 220 beats minus your age.

You should take your pulse before starting to exercise, again after exercising for 10 or 15 minutes, and immediately after stopping. In the beginning, your doctor may also ask you to take your pulse 15 minutes after stopping to see how long it takes your heart to return to its normal rate.

The heart rate can be measured at any place where you can feel your pulse—usually on the inside wrist or over the carotid artery in the neck. Using a stopwatch, count your pulse for 10 seconds, then multiply by 6 to get the beats per minute. An adult resting pulse rate is about 70 to 80 beats per minute, although this varies from person to person. A person in good physical condition often has a slower resting pulse because his or her heart is working more efficiently than that of a more sedentary person. During exercise, a pulse that is slower than your target range indicates you should speed up, while one that is faster means you should slow down. (Table 2.1 lists average pulse ranges. Check with your doctor to make sure your range is appropriate for you.)

At first, regular exercise may seem more of a bother than it is worth. But within a couple of weeks, most people begin to see the results—firmer muscles, an enhanced feeling of well-being, increased endurance, better appetite control, and more energy for day-to-day tasks. After a month or so, most exercisers admit they are "hooked," that they somehow don't feel right if they go more than a day or two without exercising. (See Table 2.2 for activities that build endurance and burn calories.)

Table 2.1
Target Pulse Ranges

Age	Maximum heart rate	Target range
50	170	119–145
55	165	115–140
60	160	112–136
65	155	109–132
70	150	105–128
75	145	102–123
80	140	98–119
85	135	95–115
90	130	91–110

TABLE 2.2
Activities that Build Endurance

In addition to increased heart rate, the conditioning value of a specific physical activity is assessed according to the number of calories consumed during a certain time period. The following table lists a variety of activities and the number of calories consumed per minute.

Activity	Calories used per minute
Walking	
1 mile per hour	1.5–2
2 miles per hour	3–3.5
3 miles per hour	4–5
3.5 miles per hour	5–6
5 miles per hour	7–8.5
Cycling	
6 miles per hour	4–5
10 miles per hour	5–6
11 miles per hour	7–8
12 miles per hour	8–10
13 miles per hour	10–11
Swimming (breaststroke)	
1 mile per hour	6–7
1.6 miles per hour	7–8
Swimming (sidestroke)	
1 mile per hour	8–10
Swimming (backstroke)	
1.6 miles per hour	10–11

Activity	Calories used per minute
Jogging	
5.5 miles per hour	10–11
Running	
8 miles per hour	11–12
Tennis	
doubles	5–6
singles	7–8
Vigorous dancing	5–6
Aerobic dancing	7–8
Skating (ice or roller)	6–7
Squash or handball	10–11
Rowing	11–12
Cross-country skiing	11–12
Competitive handball or squash	11–12

EXERCISES FOR HEART PATIENTS

Over the last 30 years, exercise has increasingly become an important part of treatment for heart patients. At one time, heart patients were cautioned to avoid exercise in the mistaken fear that activity might increase the chances of a heart attack. The late Dr. Paul Dudley White, physician to President Dwight D. Eisenhower, demonstrated to the world that a person could resume an active life, even after a severe heart attack. Within weeks after Eisenhower suffered his heart attack, Dr. White not only had him back in one of the world's most demanding jobs but also out on the golf course and again leading an active, vigorous life. Since then, many thousands of other heart attack patients have learned that exercise is an essential key to recovery.

Exercise also has become an important part of preventive medicine, especially for people who already have signs of coronary disease or who have a high risk of developing it. Numerous studies during the last few decades have confirmed that regular conditioning exercise lowers many of the major cardiovascular risk factors. For example, exercise can bring about a gradual reduction in moderate high blood pressure; it also can lower total cholesterol as well as increase the ratio of beneficial HDL cholesterol to harmful LDL cholesterol. Exercise is important in overall weight control, thereby reducing obesity, still another factor that raises heart attack risks.

Exercise benefits the heart in several ways. Since the heart is made up mostly of muscle (*myocardium*), any sustained physical activity will strengthen it, enabling it to pump more blood with each beat. Indeed, exercise conditioning enables the entire body to function more efficiently. For example, well-trained muscles are capable of taking more oxygen from the blood. The lungs also function more efficiently, and this combination of factors improves endurance. Most people notice that after only a few weeks of exercise conditioning, they do not tire as rapidly when exercising. Tasks that once produced breathlessness or perhaps even anginal pains—climbing a flight of stairs, for example—no longer have these effects.

AFTER A HEART ATTACK

Getting a heart attack patient out of bed is now an early treatment goal. As soon as a patient has stabilized and the immediate danger has passed (usually within a couple of days, depending upon the severity of the heart attack and other circumstances), a doctor will have him or her sitting up and taking a few steps around the room. This early activity prevents the muscle wasting and weakness that comes with prolonged bed rest; it also is an encouraging sign to the patient. Before leaving the hospital, the patient may be given a modified exercise test to determine a safe level of physical activity. Many heart attack patients now leave the hospital with an exercise prescription in hand;

EXERCISE-RELATED WARNING SIGNS

Any of the following are signs to stop exercising and see your doctor:

- excessive fatigue
- any unusual joint, muscle, or ligament problem
- chest pain
- pain in the teeth, jaws, or ear
- light-headedness, dizziness, or fainting
- nausea and/or vomiting
- headache
- shortness of breath
- sustained increase in heart rate after slowing down or resting
- irregularity of pulse

others may be enrolled in a cardiac rehabilitation program that includes exercise as well as other life-style changes, such as smoking cessation or diet and behavior modification.

Whatever the approach, postcoronary treatment almost always includes a gradual program of progressive exercise to improve heart function and increase tolerance, and to overcome the fear and depression that are so common after a heart attack. Even persons with serious heart disease can benefit from a supervised conditioning program.

In general, moderation is advised in beginning an exercise program after a heart attack, and it is sometimes a good idea to exercise in a group setting under the guidance of a person trained in handling medical emergencies. But very few people with heart disease encounter exercise-related problems. Studies have found a higher cardiovascular death rate among sedentary persons than among those who undertake a commonsense exercise regimen.

AN EXERCISE PROGRAM FOR HEART PATIENTS

Moderate aerobic exercise, coupled with stretching warm-up and cool-down routines, forms the basis of any exercise prescription for heart patients. Walking is considered the ideal exercise; stationary bicycles, water workouts, or swimming also may be recommended, especially for people who have orthopedic problems that make walking difficult.

In general, heart patients should avoid strenuous weight lifting, especially if it entails downward straining, which can result in a buildup of lung pressure. Lactic acid, which is created as a waste product by muscles during isometric or static exercise, can increase the possibility of cardiac arrhythmia.

Cool-down routines are particularly important for heart patients. Clinical studies show that the period just after exercise is when a person is most vulnerable to rhythm disturbances. Thus patients should avoid abruptly stopping exercise; instead, they should gradually allow the heart to return to its resting rate.

Each exercise session should include a 10- to 15-minute warm-up period, then the aerobic phase, followed by the cool-down. Keep a record of your exercise, and remember to check your pulse count frequently, especially in hot or humid weather, when the body is under greater stress. Drink plenty of water before, during, and after exercise. Be flexible. A physically exerting day at the office or at home can make you feel fatigued prior to exercise, so adjust your exercise accordingly. Your heart rate may increase to your target with a lower level of exercise; there is no need to match a previous session's level.

If for some reason you miss a week or so of exercise, don't attempt to pick up where you left off when you resume your sessions. Instead, again work up gradually, just as you did when you originally started exercising. Although it may take several weeks or even longer to reach your exercise potential, it takes only a few days off to begin to lose the conditioning effect.

EXERCISE AND ARTHRITIS

Almost everyone who lives long enough will develop some degree of arthritis, a term that is used to describe a whole group of disorders characterized by joint inflammation and pain. Most people with arthritis learn to live with their joint problems without serious handicap. However, some forms of the disease are more disabling than others; this is especially true of rheumatoid arthritis, a progressive, systemic disease that can produce marked joint destruction and deformities (see chapter 13).

Exercise is an important component in the treatment of most forms of arthritis because it helps maintain flexibility and joint mobility. But unlike the strenuous workouts of aerobic conditioning exercises, the regimens prescribed for arthritis should emphasize gentle, range-of-motion movements. Maintaining a full range of motion is especially important to prevent stiffening or even immobility of the joints. These exercises are designed to maintain muscle strength and proper joint alignment without placing too much stress on inflamed joints. Arthritis causes pain with movement, and the amount of pain a person feels is an important guide to safe exercising. Pain should not last longer than two hours after exercising. Any joint that is inflamed or feels "hot" to the touch should be rested, although the rest of the body should be put through its full range of movement.

The joint cartilage is lubricated and nourished by synovial fluid. Movement increases the amount of this fluid, thus increasing the lubrication to the joints and connecting tissues.

It is important to remember that if a loss of function has occurred, it will not be recovered immediately. Still, a daily program of individually prescribed exercises can help most arthritis sufferers regain at least some lost function and, in most instances, again perform the day-to-day tasks that are so important to maintaining independence. An exercise program of daily walking can also increase mobility and decrease pain in those people who suffer from osteoarthritis, the most common form of arthritis.

To begin an exercise program, the first step is to select a place for exercising that allows for full movement on all four sides of the body. Timing is also important; some arthritis patients have less pain and more mobility at the beginning of the day, while others may find the opposite is true: They are stiff in the morning, but gradually loosen up as the day goes on. Remember, pain is a signal that something is wrong; if you have a tendency to overexercise when using painkillers, it may be a good idea to time your sessions before, instead of after, taking your medication. However, before embarking on an exercise regimen, you should check with your physician or physical therapist to make sure that the exercises are right for you.

EXERCISE AND LUNG FUNCTION

Most of us give very little thought to the way we breathe, which is natural, since breathing is an automatic function. As we grow older, our lungs' vital capacity—the maximum amount of air that can be expelled in a single, forceful breath—declines steadily, but most researchers now believe that this is due more to the way we breathe than to physical factors related to aging.

There are two ways in which we can improve maximal *oxygen uptake* (the greatest amount of oxygen the heart-lung system can deliver in a given span of time): aerobic exercise conditioning and improved patterns of breathing. Most adults breathe too shallowly. When inhaling, you should expand your chest and use the diaphragm—the muscle that lies just below the rib cage. The ribs should expand outward and the abdomen should tighten.

BREATHING EXERCISES

Basic Deep Breathing

1. Relax. Let your neck and shoulders droop.
2. Rest both hands on your abdomen.
3. Breathe in through your nose and let your abdomen come out as far as it will. Keep your upper chest relaxed. Breathe out slowly through pursed lips. If you feel dizzy, wait a few breaths before trying it again.

Important: To be sure your diaphragm is moving properly, ask your doctor, nurse, or physical therapist to check your technique.

Chest Muscle Exercise

Deep breathing is easier when all the breathing muscles are used. The following exercise helps loosen tight chest muscles and increases your ability to expand the lower lungs.

1. Place your hands on the side of your lower chest.
2. Breathe in slowly through your nose. Your lower chest should move your hands out. Keep your shoulders and upper chest relaxed.
3. Breathe out slowly through pursed lips. Your hands should move in.

Practice this exercise several times a day for a few minutes at a time. Rest if you feel dizzy.

Note: Exercise is helpful in some types of lung disease but not in others. Be sure to check with your doctor before making it a part of your daily program.

A number of exercises, including yoga, improve breathing techniques. Deep breathing should not be confused with hyperventilation, the tendency to take shallow, rapid breaths of air. People who suffer from anxiety sometimes feel they are not receiving enough air and, panicking, they begin to breathe rapidly. This changes the balance of oxygen and carbon dioxide in their blood and can result in alarming symptoms, such as rapid heartbeat, light-headedness, and increasing panic. Breathing into a paper bag can ease the symptoms and restore the normal oxygen balance.

Practice breathing correctly as part of your exercise warm-up. Or you may want to schedule five to ten minutes of breathing exercises as part of a daily relaxation routine. People with specific respiratory problems, such as emphysema or asthma, also can benefit from breathing exercises to control their shortness of breath.

EXERCISES FOR A BAD BACK

At one time or another almost everyone suffers from backaches, and for a distressingly large number of people, the problem becomes chronic. However, the majority of back problems can be alleviated and/or prevented with exercises designed to strengthen the supporting muscles.

Typically, a person will suffer a back injury, perhaps a strained muscle or even a ruptured disk. This can cause inflammation and pressure on nerves, resulting in pain and muscle spasms. Increased pain leads to more muscle spasm and inflammation—in effect, a vicious circle. Depending upon the nature of the injury, rest may be prescribed during the initial period. Muscle-relaxing drugs also may be prescribed to ease the muscle spasms. Long-term preventive therapy for the problem invariably entails a program of exercise. The exercises illustrated in Figures 2.5 to 2.8 are typical of those recommended for a bad back. Before attempting them, however, you should check with your doctor. An added caution: If a back exercise provokes pain, stop it and consult your doctor or physical therapist.

HOW EXERCISE CAN OVERCOME PROBLEMS

People find many aspects of aging unpleasant, including the tendency to huff and puff after minor exertion, diminished muscle strength, general stiffening of the joints, and loss of bone mass (osteoporosis). But physical inactivity can make the body age prematurely. Muscles atrophy quickly and bones begin to lose calcium soon after a person becomes inactive. Fortunately, all of these conditions can be helped by exercise. Just learning to improve your posture can help minimize joint and back problems.

People who exercise are less prone to chronic fatigue and are able to sleep more easily. Tiredness is often the result of poor circulation, which in turn arises from a lack of physical activity. Exercise improves circulation. Another often-overlooked benefit of

EXERCISES FOR A HEALTHY BACK

These are gentle exercises, designed specifically to strengthen abdominal and back muscles.

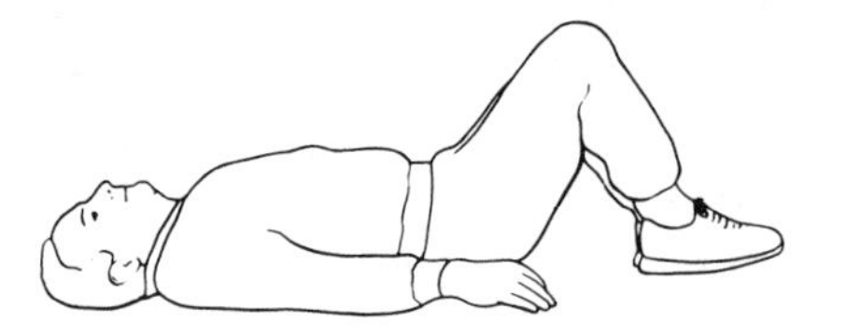
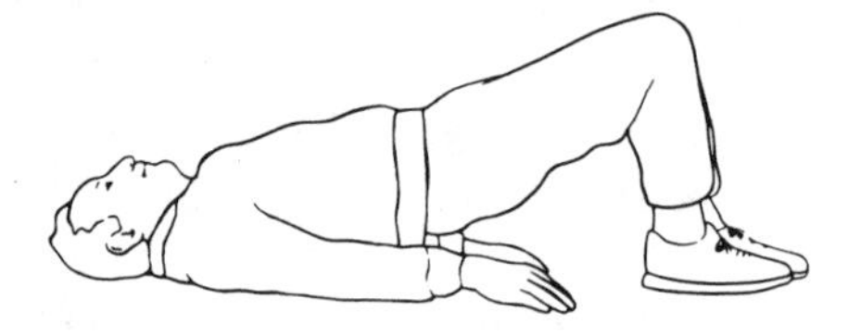

Figure 2.5
Pelvic tilt. Lie flat on the floor with arms at sides and knees slightly bent. Pull in stomach so that the small of the back is flat on the floor. Squeeze buttocks and slowly raise hips off the floor. Hold for a count of 10. Work up to 5 to 10 per session.

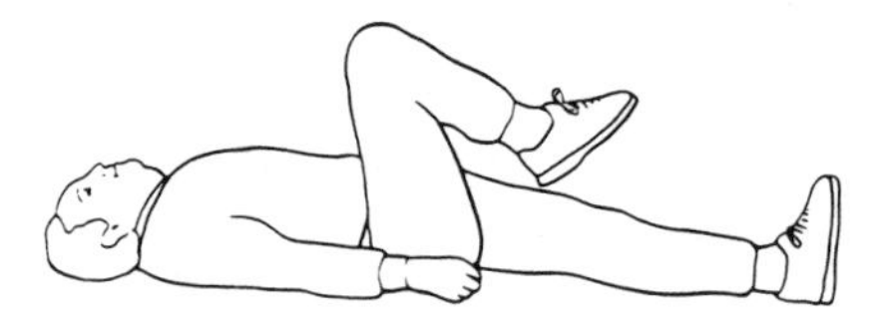
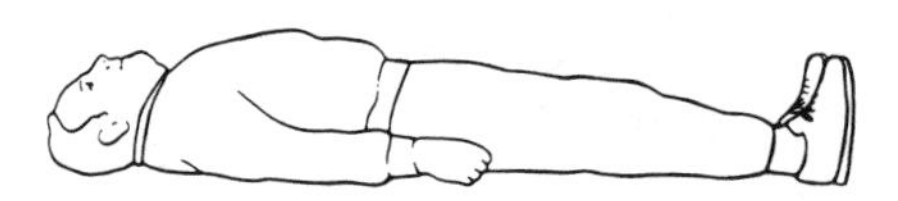

Figure 2.6
Lower back stretch. Start from basic position, lying flat on the floor with legs straight and toes pointed upward. Gently bring one knee as close to the chest as possible, then return it slowly to the starting position and relax. Repeat up to 10 times for each leg.

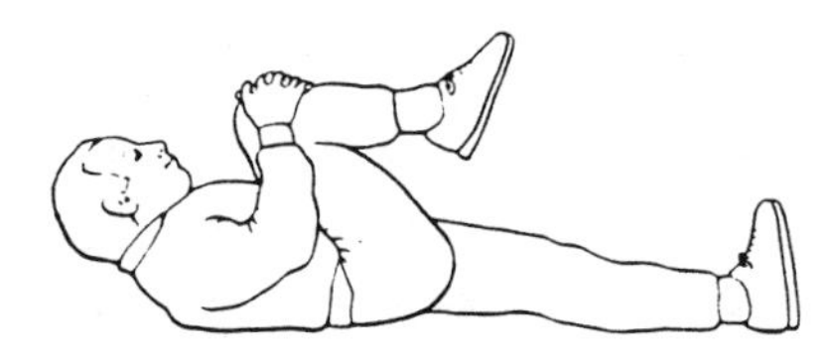
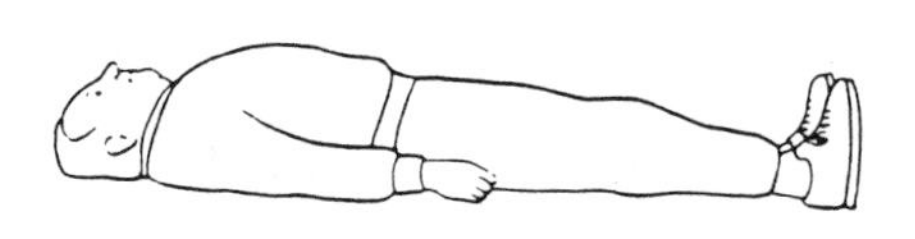

Figure 2.7
Knee to forehead. Start from basic position, lying flat on the floor with legs straight and toes pointed upward. Bend one knee as close to forehead as you can without producing pain. Return slowly to the starting position. Alternating legs, repeat 5 to 10 times.

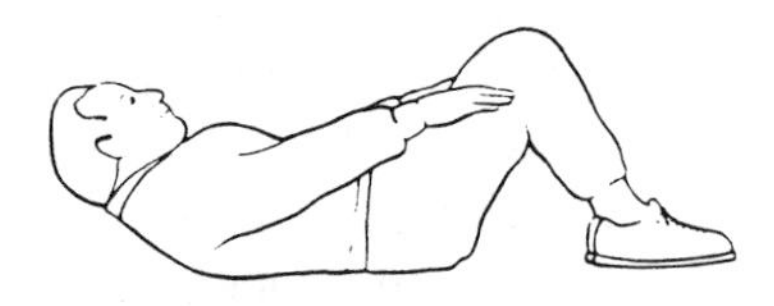
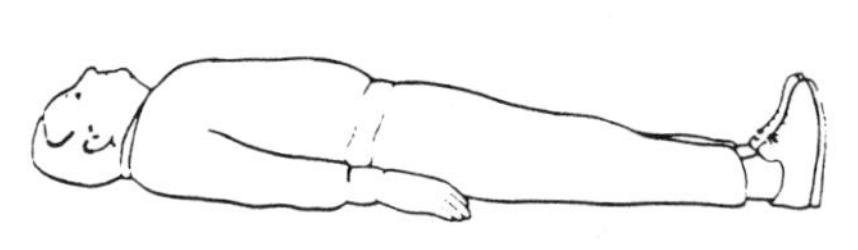

Figure 2.8
Modified sit-ups. Start from basic position. Bend knees and, with arms extended and raised off floor, raise upper part of body 6 to 8 inches off floor. Return to original position and relax. Repeat up to 10 times.

STAND TALL

Good posture not only gives a more youthful appearance, it also tells the world you are self-confident and proud of who you are. Of course, certain diseases like osteoporosis or arthritis can produce bad posture, but for most of us, slouching is more of a habit than a result of physical causes. To improve your posture, do the following routine at least three times a day.

1. Wearing low-heeled shoes (or no shoes at all), stand with your back against a wall. The feet should be pointing straight forward or slightly outward. Knees should be straight but not locked. The heels should be about 3 inches from the wall.
2. Shoulders should be relaxed but straight. Press the back of head, shoulders, and buttocks against the wall; tilt hips forward so that spine also touches the wall. The space between the wall and the small of your back should be no wider than 1 inch. Practice walking away from the wall with your head, shoulders, and hips aligned in this position.

Once you have felt correct posture, practice doing daily activities while maintaining correct alignment. It will take time and effort at first, but it will become easier and will actually give you more energy and make you less prone to backaches and other joint problems.

exercise is improved balance and agility. People who wear bifocal or trifocal lenses are especially prone to lose their sense of balance. A well-maintained sense of balance can compensate for dizziness caused by optical changes. Agility lessens the chances of falling and also allows one to move more quickly in an emergency.

The joints of older persons often go through a cycle of increasing stiffness and limitation. An episode of arthritis or bursitis, causing pain in movement, may make it impossible to swing a joint through its full range of motion. Activities are then restricted to accommodate the stiff joint. However, this inactivity causes more stiffness.

Disuse of a joint takes a toll in two ways: The lubricant that keeps the joints working (synovial fluid) dries up, and the connective tissue surrounding the joint begins to shorten and lose its resilience. But unless there is significant damage inside the joint itself, mobility can be regained with training. Also, the increased strength of the muscle helps to take some of the strain off arthritic joints.

The increasing fragility of bones (osteoporosis) in aging is a particularly common problem for certain groups of postmenopausal women and for many men as well. As bones age, they lose some of their mineral content, becoming light and more prone to breakage. Exercise—the action of muscle working against bone—helps strengthen the bones by increasing calcium absorption. (Estrogen replacement after menopause may also be needed to help maintain bones.) Thus it is particularly important for older people to maintain joint flexibility so they can engage in the types of exercise that will promote bone strength (see Figures 2.9 to 2.13).

Flexibility and range-of-motion exercises are best done daily. The fingers, arms, shoulders, knees, ankles, hips, back, and neck all should be rotated slowly and carefully to their full range of movement. Many people who have started flexibility exercises in their later years, even in their seventies and eighties, have made remarkable progress in increasing their range of movement. In beginning a program, start with relatively easy, short-term goals. For example, if it is difficult for you to bend over to put on stockings or tie your shoes, make performing these tasks with greater ease an initial goal. Then move on to more difficult goals.

Remember, too, that progress in exercising is never made in a straight upward line. There will be days when less is accomplished than on other days. Avoid being overly competitive with yourself or others. After all, your goal is increased independence and peace of mind, not winning a self-styled competition.

PREVENTING BROKEN BONES AND OTHER ACCIDENTS

All older people, whether they have arthritis or not, should take elementary precautions against accidents that occur because of "overdoing it." We have all heard stories of people who have fallen, breaking their now more-brittle hip and leg bones, while attempting household tasks that would tax even a much younger person. For example, merely replacing a light bulb has accident potential when it requires climbing a ladder. Caution requires that the ladder be securely placed or that someone help you; you must also take your time making the repair. Optimism about the possibilities in the second 50 years must be tempered with realism about potential dangers in and out of the home.

HOW TO PREVENT ACCIDENTS IN THE HOME

- *Interior stairs.* If you do not live in a single-floor residence, consider redesigning the space so that living areas that are used most often are on the first floor. If this is not possible, make sure that stairways have handrails and are not steep, and that the area is well lit.
- *Exterior steps.* Take time to look before you step. Use salt, sand, or cinders to gain traction through ice or snow. Install railings, or use outdoor carpet that is firmly affixed.

RANGE-OF-MOTION EXERCISES

These exercises are designed to maintain joint flexibility and are particularly good for people with arthritis. Try doing them in the morning after you have had a shower and a chance to limber up a bit.

Figure 2.9
Arms and elbows. Stand in a comfortable position. With elbows bent, bring hands chest-high and slowly straighten arms. Repeat 10 times to a count of 7.

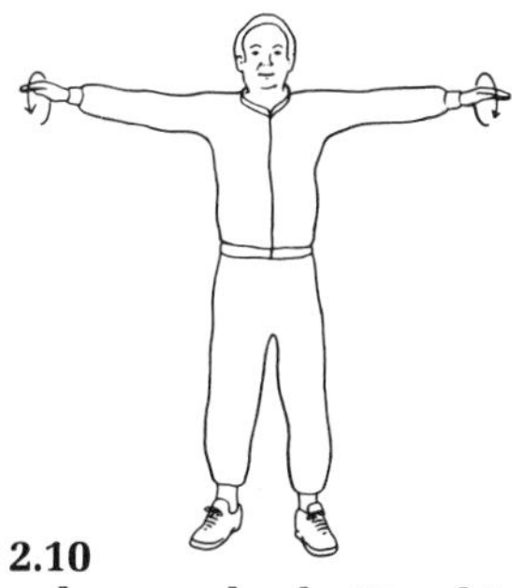

Figure 2.10
Arms and upper back. Stand in a comfortable position with arms extended straight from shoulders. Make small circles, using entire arm. Repeat 20 times.

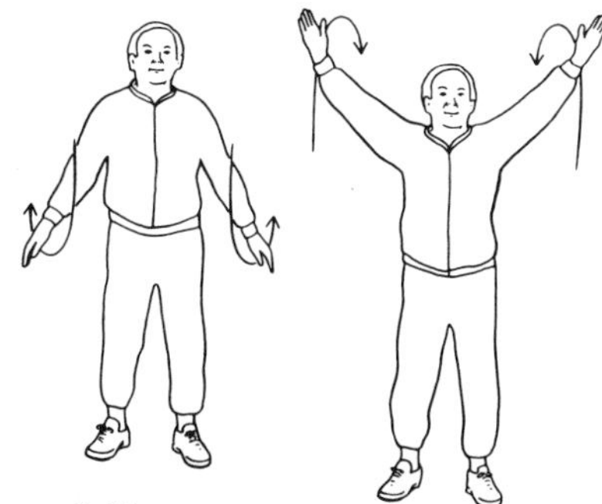

Figure 2.11
Arms and shoulders. Stand in a comfortable position and, to a count of 7, slowly make large circles with arms, raising hands as high over head as you can. Repeat 10 times.

Figure 2.12
Neck. Stand in a comfortable position, with hands relaxed on hips. To a count of 5, slowly flex neck to side, forward, backward, and flex to opposite side. Repeat 5 times.

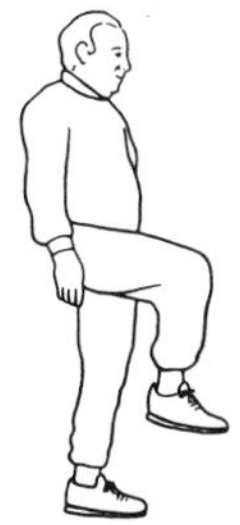

Figure 2.13
Lower back, legs, and knees. Stand in a comfortable position with arms at sides. With knee bent, slowly raise one leg and lower it to a count of 5. (If this is too difficult, stand using the back of a chair for support.) Alternating legs, repeat up to 10 times.

- *Bathroom.* Install no-slip rubber pads on the bottom of bathtubs and grab-rails next to tubs, showers, and toilets. Install scald-guard shower valves and shower stall doors instead of shower curtains that blow around and get in your way.
- *Bedroom.* Remove all obstacles in the path between the bed and the door, and have a sturdy piece of furniture—a chair or a table—near the bed for support.
- *Kitchen.* Arrange the kitchen so often-used items are within easy reach. When a step stool is necessary, make sure it is sturdy and has a slip-resistant base. Install a fire extinguisher near the stove, and learn how to use it.
- *Other rooms.* Install *working* smoke alarms near every room. Eliminate throw rugs that slip and slide, and remove cords, wires, and other clutter from floors. Keep rooms well lit. Install especially bright lights near doorways and stairwells (with switches at both ends). Place night-lights in hallways, especially near the bathroom.

3

Breaking Bad Habits

Almost from the beginning of time, humans have sought pleasure from mind- or sensation-altering substances. Virtually every culture and society has drugs that will produce a "high." Some are used for religious purposes, others simply for pleasure.

An occasional drink, cigarette, or even marijuana "joint" may not produce any long-term harm. But many people find it difficult, if not impossible, to limit their use. And once addicted to any of these substances, a person begins to suffer the physical and psychological consequences.

Surprising to some, statistics show that older people are more likely to be successful in making life-style changes, especially breaking bad health habits, than younger people. On the other hand, some older people continue their smoking or excessive drinking habits on the assumption that "the damage is done—why stop now?" In reality, it is never too late to change and never too late to reap the benefits of adopting a more healthful life-style.

SMOKING

A few years ago physicians often did not urge older smokers to quit because they assumed that a few more years of smoking was not going to significantly increase the risk of cancer or heart disease. However, new statistics show that many of the adverse effects of smoking can be reduced or, in some cases, eliminated by quitting.

By now, we all know that smoking is bad for you. The Surgeon General's latest report on the effects of smoking claims that tobacco use is directly linked to 390,000 deaths a year. It is by far the leading cause of lung cancer, emphysema, and other chronic lung diseases, and it is also a major factor in heart attacks. The statistics are well known; less well known is what is actually happening each time you take a puff.

WHAT'S IN A CIGARETTE?

There are more than 4,000 components in tobacco smoke, many of which are known toxins and carcinogens. If those substances were in our food, we would eat something else. We fight to reduce and control the amount of toxic substances in the air in our cities, yet millions of people continue to smoke, ignoring the realities of the toxins they breathe in with every puff.

Smokers contend that they enjoy smoking: It relaxes them; it increases their productivity; it wakes them up. They say they know it is bad for them, but they are willing to take their chances. Usually these claims ignore the dangers of nicotine addiction.

Nicotine. Nicotine is a powerful stimulant. It prompts the adrenal glands to secrete catecholamines such as adrenaline (epinephrine). This causes a rise in the heart rate and blood pressure, as well as constriction of the capillaries. Tobacco smoke decreases the amount of oxygen available to the heart and brain. In essence, it simulates stress and keeps the body in a state of heightened tension. When that tension wanes, the smoker reaches for another cigarette to start the process all over again.

Nicotine is detoxified in the liver. Just as chronic drinking can cause liver damage, smoking may also impair liver function. Women who smoke are at greater risk of osteoporosis (thinning of the bones) than are women who don't smoke. The statistics bear this out: Women smokers have reduced levels of estrogen, which appears to be important in proper calcium and bone metabolism.

Carbon Monoxide. Combine the effects of nicotine with the toxins in cigarette smoke, such as carbon monoxide, and the result can be lethal. Because the smoker is breathing in many other gases in addition to oxygen with each puff, the blood receives less oxygen. Moreover, carbon monoxide displaces the oxygen attached to the protein hemoglobin found in red blood cells, making oxygen less available to the heart and other tissues. The heart has to work harder just to keep the smoker going, one reason smokers run out of breath faster and more often than nonsmokers.

Chronic exposure to carbon monoxide in tobacco smoke raises the concentrations of hemoglobin bound carbon monoxide in the blood to 3 to 8 percent, far above the concentrations for the average nonsmoker (0.5 to 0.8 percent). This is within the danger zone of 5 to 10 percent that can result in impaired function of the central nervous system—that is, reduced vision and learning ability. For older people worried about failing eyesight and memory, quitting smoking has special benefits.

Because smoking makes the heart work harder and carbon monoxide in the smoke decreases the oxygen available to the heart, the smoker is more susceptible to coronary heart disease. In fact, heart and blood vessel diseases are the major causes of death for smokers, and 40 percent of deaths from heart attack are linked to cigarette smoking. People who smoke are twice as likely to have a heart attack and more likely to die from it. According to the Surgeon General's report, cigarette smoking is the major factor in 30 percent of all heart disease, and the American Cancer Society states that smoking is the biggest risk factor for sudden cardiac death and for peripheral arterial disease. Since being over 50 also increases your risk for heart attack, quitting smoking is especially important for older people.

Stroke is another health concern of older people. Cigarette smoking, by contributing to the artery-clogging arteriosclerotic process, is definitely a major factor in this often life-threatening circumstance. In addition to impeding the circulation of blood to the brain, cigarette smoking can also reduce the amount of oxygen-carrying blood to the skin. This may result in increased susceptibility to wrinkles and age lines.

Cyanide. Large doses of hydrogen cyanide, an additive found in cigarette smoke, reduces the mobility of the microscopic cilia that line the lungs and help to sweep out unwanted particles, or tars.

Tars. In addition to the poisonous gases in cigarette smoke, the smoker also inhales small particles of tar. Even filters on cigarettes cannot strain out all of the particulate matter in the smoke. Basically the smoker breathes in these small particles, which break down the tiny hairs (cilia) that clean the lungs. The breakdown of the cilia impairs the ability of the bronchial tubes to propel mucus up toward the trachea and larynx, where it can be removed by coughing. This leads to the accumulation of mucus, creating a hospitable environment for the development of infections. People who smoke have more bronchitis, influenza, sinusitis, and emphysema than nonsmokers. Smokers report more sick days, more days in bed, and higher medical costs than nonsmokers do—some $52 billion a year in lost productivity and added health-care costs in the United States alone, according to the Department of Health and Human Services.

Carcinogens. Some of the particulate substances in cigarette smoke contain known carcinogens. Although it has not been determined which substances are instrumental in the development of cancer in smokers, the eight different nitrosamines identified in cigarette smoke are known animal carcinogens and are the most likely culprits. Researchers have been unable to induce cancer in laboratory rats exposed to cigarette smoke, but the statistics on smoking and cancer are overwhelming proof of the connection. Eighty-five percent of lung cancer patients are longtime smokers (20 years or more). Smokers, especially those who are also heavy drinkers, run an increased risk of oral and esophageal cancers. Cancers of the bladder and pancreas are also much more common among smokers than nonsmokers.

The facts are there: Cigarette smoking takes years off your life and reduces the quality of the time you have left. Experts have estimated that for every cigarette smoked, 5½ minutes of expected longevity are lost. And those minutes can add up to years rather quickly.

REASONS TO QUIT SMOKING

1. Adds years to your life.
2. Helps you avoid lung cancer, emphysema, bronchitis, and heart attacks.
3. Gives the heart and circulatory system a break.
4. Gets rid of smoker's hack.
5. Makes you feel more vigorous in sports.
6. Improves stamina.
7. Stops smoke-related headaches and stomachaches.
8. Helps you regain sense of smell and taste.
9. Lets you have smoke-free rooms and closets.
10. Ends cigarette breath.
11. Saves money.
12. Eliminates stained, yellow teeth and fingers.
13. Stops burning holes in clothes or furniture.
14. Gets rid of messy ashtrays and ashes on carpets.
15. Sets a good example for others.
16. Improves self-control.
17. ______________________________
18. ______________________________
19. ______________________________
20. ______________________________

WHAT SMOKING IS DOING TO THOSE AROUND YOU

Smokers are not the only ones adversely affected by their habit. Spouses, children, grandchildren, and friends—in short, everyone coming in contact with you, and your cigarette—run the risk of compromised health. That's because there are actually two sources of cigarette smoke: mainstream and sidestream. Mainstream smoke is exhaled into the air by the smoker; sidestream smoke is emitted by the burning end of the cigarette between puffs—for example, when it is sitting in an ashtray.

Chemical studies show that sidestream smoke, because it does not go through the dual filtering system of the cigarette tip and the smoker's lungs, actually contains higher concentrations of many of the poisonous elements. These include carbon monoxide, formaldehyde, and nicotine. Eighty-five percent of the smoke in a smoke-filled room is from the sidestream source.

The effects of cigarette smoke on nonsmokers include increased risks of heart disease, pulmonary disorders, and lung cancer. People exposed to great amounts of passive cigarette smoke, especially young children, have higher incidences of bronchitis, pneumonia, and middle-ear infections. Exposure to cigarette smoke can induce an asthma attack in susceptible asthma sufferers. In addition, many people exposed to passive smoking report allergy symptoms such as watery eyes, coughing, nasal congestion, headaches, wheezing, and sneezing.

Exposure to cigarette smoke may provoke angina in those with coronary heart disease. Emphysema sufferers will have even more trouble breathing in the presence of cigarette smoke. Clearly, the benefits of quitting extend to everyone around the smoker, as well as to the smoker.

HEALTH BENEFITS OF QUITTING

And now the good news. Almost immediately after your last cigarette, your body begins to repair itself. The release of stress hormones, such as epinephrine (adrenaline), recedes to normal levels. Your circulation improves as you breathe in more oxygen, and your capillaries expand to allow easier passage of the blood to the extremities, heart, and brain. Studies have shown that, within a few months of quitting, the amount of blood getting to the brain increases significantly, thus reducing the risk of stroke and improving cerebral functions.

No longer barraged by the particulate matter in cigarette smoke, the cilia in the lungs regrow and start to function again, cleaning foreign matter from the lungs. At first your cough may get worse, but actually this is part of an increased mucus production as the cells repair themselves. Researchers estimate that in smokers with no permanent lung damage, lung function is back to normal within three months of quitting.

Of more concern to most people are risks of cancer and heart disease. After one year of not smoking, the risk of coronary heart disease drops significantly. After 10 years, the risk is comparable to that of a person who never smoked. Breathing rates also improve, and deterioration of the lungs is slowed. After 10 to 15 years, risks of cancer of the lung, larynx, and mouth approach that of nonsmokers. Life expectancy is also prolonged to near normal, although it is always somewhat lower than that of people who have never smoked.

HOW TO QUIT SMOKING

Quitting is no easy task, but in the United States almost half of all people who have ever smoked have quit, and millions more kick the habit each year. The large majority—95 percent—quit on their own, usually cold turkey; the others seek outside help from stop-smoking clinics, behavior modification therapy, hypnosis, stop-smoking aids, or a combination of these approaches. Although those who quit cold turkey report a somewhat higher success rate, it is best to use whatever technique is effective for you. Every smoker is different, so different methods will be better suited to each person. And remember, if at first you don't succeed . . . try again and again and *again.* Each time you try to quit, your chances of succeeding improve.

TIPS FOR QUITTING SMOKING

BEFORE YOU TRY TO QUIT

- □ *List your reasons for quitting.* Include your own individual motivations as well as the health and cosmetic reasons. Place this list where you will see it several times a day to remind yourself of your goals.
- □ *Think positively.* If you expect to succeed, chances are good that you will. Even if you break down and have one cigarette, it does not mean you have failed to become an ex-smoker. Just decide to stop again, and with even greater resolve.
- □ *Keep a record of your smoking habits.* For a couple of days, record each cigarette you smoke. Note the time and situation and how much you feel you wanted each cigarette. This record will help you prepare for or avoid situations in which you will most likely crave a cigarette.
- □ *Set the date for quitting and stick to it.* Pick a date that will not coincide with other periods of stress. Vacation time or other low-stress periods may be the best time to try to quit smoking. The first day of the month, the first day of spring, your birthday, and New Year's Day are all dates that signify new beginnings; use one to begin your new life without cigarettes.
- □ *Involve other people.* Some smokers are hesitant to make known their intention to quit for fear of public failure. However, most people—even nonsmokers—know that quitting is difficult. They will have some idea what you are going through and are likely to be encouraging, not judgmental. Their support and encouragement may be just what you need to keep you away from cigarettes.
- □ *Start to get in shape physically.* Aerobic exercise, such as running, swimming, aerobic dancing, or cycling, is a great way to strengthen your heart and your resolve to be an ex-smoker. While you're exercising, you can't smoke, and the more you exercise, the more you'll realize how much smoking holds you back. Building your endurance is yet another reason to quit.
- □ *Change brands of cigarettes.* While there is no "safe" cigarette, low-tar and low-nicotine brands may reduce your pleasure in smoking and therefore

make it easier to quit. Buying one pack at a time will make smoking less convenient.

□ *Talk with your doctor.* Research indicates that even a short conversation with a physician will increase your chances of success. Your doctor may have some special advice or tips that may help you.

THE FIRST FEW DAYS

□ *Throw away all of your cigarettes.* Hide all the ashtrays, matches, and other objects associated with smoking at home and at the office.

□ *Know what to expect.* Physical withdrawal symptoms from smoking may last about one to two weeks, but the worst are usually over in three days. Forty to 50 percent of smokers report no withdrawal symptoms at all.

□ *Distract your attention from cravings.* After the first few days of quitting, the process of withdrawal is mostly psychological. Intense craving is to be expected, but you can effectively distract your attention from it by taking two or three deep breaths, talking to someone, or taking a brisk walk.

□ *Join the nonsmokers.* Seek out places where smoking is prohibited, and avoid situations in which you would usually smoke (refer to your record of cigarette smoking). Plan to go to a museum, theater, or health club instead of to a cocktail party. If you must attend a function where there are many smokers, prepare yourself in advance and make a conscious effort not to smoke. Find nonsmokers or ex-smokers to talk to. Once you get through the event, plan something special to celebrate.

□ *Keep alcohol consumption to a minimum.* Cigarettes and alcohol often go hand in hand, so it may be wise to forgo drinking completely after you first quit. (Alcohol also affects your willpower adversely.) The same is true of coffee. If you always have a cigarette with your coffee, try going for a walk or drinking something else until you can divorce the two in your mind.

□ *Watch what you eat.* Many people who want to quit worry that they will gain weight. Indeed, many people do gain a few pounds, both because of improved metabolism and a perked-up appetite. But even those few can be avoided. Your appetite will improve after quitting, so have carrot and celery sticks handy. Try not to increase the size of your meals; if you must, fill up on nonfattening items such as salad with low-fat dressing. However, protein is important for the body's mending process, so be sure you're eating enough of it. Exercise will not only burn off calories but also help release the tension caused by nicotine withdrawal as well. (Note that although quitting smoking causes tension, it is actually less than the tension caused by smoking itself.) If you do gain weight, remember that experts have estimated that you would have to gain over 75 pounds to offset the benefits of quitting smoking.

NICOTINE GUM AND SKIN PATCHES

Nicotine is a highly addictive substance, which is one reason why quitting smoking is so difficult. Withdrawal symptoms such as restlessness, anxiety, irritability, frustration, and increased appetite often cause even the most resolute quitters to fall back into the habit. For some people, nicotine gum or special patches that transfer nicotine through the skin can provide physical relief during the period of early smoking cessation. The theory behind their use is that if a smoker can first deal with the psychological aspects of quitting, he or she will then be able to cope effectively with nicotine withdrawal.

Nicotine chewing gum, first introduced in 1984 under the brand name Nicorette, releases nicotine that is absorbed directly into the bloodstream through the lining of the mouth. It does not offer the nicotine "rush" a smoker experiences when inhaling, but it does enter the bloodstream in levels similar to those associated with smoking. The gum is available only by prescription, so it may require you to pay for a doctor's office visit as well. Some health insurance policies cover both treatment and the cost of the gum. (A box containing 96 pieces should cost about $20 to $30, and most people use a total of four to eight boxes.) The gum may have side effects, including hiccups, sore throat and jaw aches, nausea, heartburn, and, ironically, addiction. An estimated 1 to 2 percent of users transfer their addiction from cigarettes to the gum. For this reason, it should not be used for more than six months.

The most recently introduced stop-smoking aid is the transdermal nicotine patch, available by prescription only. Approved by the Food and Drug Administration (FDA) in 1991 and marketed under names such as Habitrol, Nicoderm, and ProStep, these approximately 2-inch-square or circular adhesive patches are affixed to the skin and slowly release a steady supply of nicotine that eventually reaches the bloodstream. The different brands differ somewhat in dose and delivery. ProStep delivers the nicotine equivalent of about 15 cigarettes in 24 hours, and the others contain diminishing doses over a 10- to 12-week course. Each patch lasts for 12 to 24 hours. A 6- to 12-week supply costs $200 to $300. The most notable side effects are minor skin irritation and insomnia and other sleep disturbances (which may be less common with the 12-hour patch). *Note:* Anyone beginning nicotine-patch therapy must stop smoking immediately to prevent nicotine overdose and the potentially fatal adverse effects associated with it, such as a heart attack.

In the short term, both nicotine gum and skin patches are considered useful. Studies have shown that smokers who use them as directed are about twice as likely to quit as those who use placebos. However, their long-term efficacy depends primarily on the motivation of the smoker.

SOURCES OF HELP

There are many organizations devoted to helping people quit smoking (see appendix A). Nonprofit groups such as the American Cancer Society, American Heart Association, and Seventh-Day Adventist Church give out free information or hold stop-smoking clinics. SmokEnders, Smoke Stoppers, and other commercial programs also have a high success rate, and the money you spend to join such a program may act as an extra incentive. Many employers also offer smoking-cessation clinics. Check with your company's medical benefits coordinator. Even if your company does not offer such programs, the situation may change if there is sufficient employee interest. Employers have a special interest in inducing people to stop smoking. Studies have shown that each smoker costs his or her employer at least $1,000 a year more in increased insurance and health costs than is paid for an individual nonsmoker.

Self-hypnosis is another method that works well for large numbers of people. The technique seems to work best for smokers who are readily hypnotizable and who have a spouse or partner concerned with their well-being.

ALCOHOL DEPENDENCY

Alcohol dependency among older people has only recently begun to receive the attention the problem warrants. It is estimated that 10 to 15 percent of all Americans over age 60 use alcohol to excess. While this percentage is comparable to statistics for other age groups, older drinkers are more likely to be adversely affected by excessive drinking and less likely to be detected and treated for their problem.

Older people often have more time and fewer responsibilities, which can sometimes lead to boredom and less self-restriction when it comes to drinking alcohol. They may be lonely because their children have left home or they've lost their spouse or best friend. These factors contribute to the ease with which some people slip into alcoholism, perhaps best defined by Alcoholics Anonymous, the oldest and most popular support organization for those who use alcohol inappropriately. A pamphlet for older people, titled *Time to Start Living,* states: "Whether or not you are an alcoholic is not determined by where you drink, when you started drinking, how long you've been drinking, . . . what, or even how much. The true test is the answer to this question: What has alcohol done to you? If it has affected your relationships; if it has influenced the way you schedule your days; if it has affected your health, . . . if you are in any way preoccupied with alcohol—then the likelihood is that you have a problem."

WHAT HAPPENS WHEN YOU DRINK

Because alcohol is so readily available, we often forget that it is in fact a drug. And, as with most drugs, alcohol can be both beneficial or toxic, depending on its use and its user.

In small doses, alcohol relaxes the body, stimulates the appetite, and produces a feeling of well-being. (Even so, there may be some adverse effects for people who have high blood pressure. Pregnant women especially should avoid alcohol at all times during pregnancy.) In large doses, it is a powerful poison that accounts for 10 percent of all

WHAT ARE THE SIGNS OF ALCOHOLISM?

Numerous screening tests have been devised to identify alcoholics. One of the most well-known is the Michigan Alcoholism Screening Test (MAST), which asks the following questions:

Points		Yes	No
	0. Do you enjoy a drink now and then?	____	____
(2)	1. Do you feel you are a normal drinker? (By normal we mean you drink less than or as much as most other people.)	____	____
(2)	2. Have you ever awakened the morning after some drinking the night before and found that you could not remember a part of the evening?	____	____
(1)	3. Does your wife, husband, a parent, or other near relative ever worry or complain about your drinking?	____	____
(2)	4. Can you stop drinking without a struggle after one or two drinks?	____	____
(1)	5. Do you ever feel guilty about your drinking?	____	____
(2)	6. Do friends or relatives think you are a normal drinker?	____	____
(0)	7. Do you ever try to limit your drinking to certain times of the day or to certain places?	____	____
(2)	8. Have you ever attended a meeting of Alcoholics Anonymous?	____	____
(1)	9. Have you ever gotten into physical fights when drinking?	____	____
(2)	10. Has your drinking ever created problems between you and your wife, husband, a parent, or other relative?	____	____

Points		Yes	No
(2)	11. Has your wife or husband (or other family members) ever gone to anyone for help about your drinking?	____	____
(2)	12. Have you ever lost friends because of your drinking?	____	____
(2)	13. Have you ever gotten into trouble at work or school because of drinking?	____	____
(2)	14. Have you ever lost a job because of drinking?	____	____
(2)	15. Have you ever neglected your obligations, your family, or your work for two or more days in a row because you were drinking?	____	____
(1)	16. Do you drink before noon fairly often?	____	____
(2)	17. Have you ever been told you have liver trouble? Cirrhosis?	____	____
(2)	*18. After heavy drinking have you ever had Delirium Tremens (D.T.s) or severe shaking, or heard voices or seen things that really weren't there?	____	____
(5)	19. Have you ever gone to anyone for help about your drinking?	____	____
(5)	20. Have you ever been in a hospital because of drinking?	____	____
(2)	21. Have you ever been a patient in a psychiatric hospital or on a psychiatric ward of a general hospital where drinking was part of the problem that resulted in hospitalization?	____	____
(2)	22. Have you ever been seen at a psychiatric or mental health clinic or gone to any doctor, social worker, or clergyman for help with any emotional problem, where drinking was part of the problem?	____	____

Points		Yes	No
(2)	**23. Have you ever been arrested for drunk driving, driving while intoxicated, or driving under the influence of alcoholic beverages? (If YES, How many times? ____)	____	____
(2)	**24. Have you ever been arrested, or taken into custody, even for a few hours, because of other drunk behavior? (If YES, How many times? ____)	____	____

*5 points for Delirium Tremens   **2 points for *each* arrest

SCORING SYSTEM: In general, 5 points or more would place the subject in an "alcoholic" category. Four points would suggest alcoholism, 3 points or less would indicate the subject was not alcoholic.

Programs using the above scoring system find it very sensitive at the 5-point level and it tends to find more people alcoholics than anticipated. However, it is a screening test and should be sensitive at its lower levels.

Source: *American Journal of Psychiatry* 127 (1971): 1653–58. (Reprinted in *Treatment of Alcoholism and Addictions*, copyright © 1989, American Psychiatric Press.)

deaths, either directly (from physical damage to the body caused by the alcohol itself) or indirectly (from accidents caused by alcohol users).

Alcohol contains calories (see Table 3.1) but no other useful nutrients. In fact, it can even deplete the body's source of vitamins and minerals or make them difficult to absorb.

When alcohol is ingested, 95 percent is absorbed from the stomach and small intestine, or duodenum, directly into the bloodstream. Within minutes, the alcohol has permeated every part of the body that contains water: lungs, kidneys, heart, and brain. The presence of small amounts of alcohol in the brain initially acts as a stimulant. The drinker at this point feels more sociable and active. However, as more alcohol is absorbed, it begins to act as a sedative or depressant with a calming or tranquilizing effect. If enough alcohol is ingested, it will start to act as a hypnotic, thereby inducing sleep.

Reaction time, physical coordination, eyesight, and depth perception are all compromised by the presence of alcohol in the blood. Driving, or any other activity involving complete and rapid decision making or calling for physical action, should be avoided completely while drinking and for a period of time afterward.

TABLE 3.1
Caloric Content of Alcoholic Beverages

Drink	Amount	Calories
WINES		
Champagne	4 oz	85
Dessert (18.8% alcohol)	4 oz	155
Port	4 oz	180
Red, white, or sherry	4 oz	100
Dry vermouth	4 oz	120
Sweet vermouth	4 oz	190
BEER AND OTHER MALT LIQUORS		
Beer	12 oz	150–160
Lite beer	12 oz	100
Ale	12 oz	150
DISTILLED LIQUORS		
Gin, rum, whiskey, or vodka		
80-proof	1 oz	70
86-proof	1 oz	75
90-proof	1 oz	80
94-proof	1 oz	83
100-proof	1 oz	90
Fermented cider	6 oz	70
Cognac or brandy	1 oz	70

The relationship of body weight to the cumulative effects of alcohol in the system is significant. Alcohol circulates with the body's fluids, and the amount of body fluids is directly related to the body weight. In short, the person of lower body weight is affected more severely by the alcohol in the drink than is the heavier individual.

Alcohol affects body functions by slowing down metabolism, breathing, and circulation. In fact, alcohol has the potential to paralyze breathing altogether, leading to death. This is a relatively rare occurrence, since the body at some point starts to rid itself of the toxin by vomiting, or the drinker passes out before consuming a fatal amount of alcohol. However, many older people may be more sensitive to the toxic effects of alcohol and may therefore reach the fatal dose at a lower level.

Alcohol in the bloodstream is broken down by enzymes in the liver, producing carbon dioxide and water that are then excreted. The liver can only process the alcohol at a certain rate—about an ounce of pure ethanol (less than an ounce of hard liquor) in an hour. The only antidote for drinking too much is to wait until the liver can convert the alcohol into a nontoxic substance. Black coffee, cold showers, and other popular remedies are not effective.

When the body attempts to repair itself from the onslaught of too much alcohol, a hangover occurs. Blood vessels in the brain that became dilated (opened up) by the presence of alcohol now return to their normal state, producing a headache. Gastric juices altered by the harsh alcohol produce stomach upset. The kidneys, stimulated by the alcohol, excrete too much water, resulting in dehydration. There is some evidence that older people become more susceptible to these unpleasant side effects, even at lower dosages.

The cure for a hangover? Sleep, aspirin, bland food, plenty of liquids, and time.

THE EFFECTS OF LONG-TERM ALCOHOL DEPENDENCE ON THE BODY

For most people without health problems, a hangover is the only physical consequence of an occasional drinking binge. However, long-term heavy drinking will take a toll on the body. Vision, sexual function, circulation, and nutrition are all impaired

TIPS ON SOCIAL DRINKING

- *Never drink on an empty stomach.* Always eat snacks (preferably cheese and crackers rather than salty potato chips, which increase thirst) when drinking alcoholic beverages. Hosts should always offer food when serving alcoholic beverages.
- *Dilute liquor with ice and water.* Drink slowly, in a relaxed and comfortable setting. Do not drink if you are depressed, nervous, or tired.
- *Alternate nonalcoholic drinks with alcoholic ones.* When you're serving drinks, always have plenty of soda and fruit juice on hand for those who choose not to drink.
- *Never drink and drive.* If you go to a party with a friend, decide beforehand who will drive home. That person should not drink. Even walking home when intoxicated increases the danger of being a victim of a crime or car accident. Call a cab, stay overnight, or have a nondrinking friend drive you home. If you are the host, never allow guests who are clearly under the influence of alcohol to drive. Insist they stay overnight or have someone else take them home.
- *Do not mix alcohol and drugs.* This applies to over-the-counter, prescription, and illicit drugs. Alcohol depresses the central nervous system. If you are taking a drug with the same side effect, the combination may have serious depressive effects.

by excessive alcohol use. In fact, alcohol dependence is cited by many experts as the number-one cause of vitamin and nutritional deficiencies (especially vitamin B_{12} and folic acid) in older people.

Because of its role in metabolizing alcohol, the liver is a prime candidate for the detrimental effects of alcohol dependence. The liver will choose to process alcohol as fuel rather than as the usual fatty acids. The resultant buildup of unprocessed fatty acids in the liver causes the organ to enlarge, a reversible condition referred to as fatty liver. This condition, which can be induced even by steady social drinking (four or five drinks daily for several weeks), does not usually cause any symptoms. The liver will return to normal size when excessive drinking is curtailed.

Heavy drinking may also lead to inflammation of liver cells, or alcoholic hepatitis. Fever, pain, and jaundice are common symptoms of this condition. If alcohol consumption is curtailed, alcoholic hepatitis may be reversible. However, if drinking continues, the next stage of liver deterioration—cirrhosis—is irreversible and often fatal.

In cirrhosis of the liver, fibrous scar tissue obstructs the flow of blood through the organ. As a result, the liver cannot perform its various functions: It cannot convert glycogen into usable glucose for energy, so blood sugar drops and hypoglycemia ensues. The liver can no longer effectively detoxify the blood or eliminate dead red blood cells, which leads to a buildup of waste products in the blood. The cirrhotic liver cannot manufacture bile to digest fat, prothrombin to clot blood and prevent bruising, globulin to fight infection, or albumin to maintain cell function. Liver malfunction can also lead to malabsorption of several important vitamins, including A, D, E, and K.

The heart is another organ that is adversely affected by alcohol abuse. Heart patients should be especially careful in monitoring their alcohol consumption because even a one-time binge may cause irregular heartbeat in some people. Heavy drinkers have an increased incidence of high blood pressure, heart attack, and other cardiac conditions. Since these problems already are more common among people over age 50, older people should be especially wary of the exacerbating consequences of excessive alcohol use.

Cardiomyopathy, a disease of the heart muscle, is more common among longtime drinkers. Strokes are also more common among drinkers who use even moderate amounts of alcohol than among nondrinkers. One study found that people who regularly consumed the equivalent of one or two glasses of wine, one beer, or one mixed drink had a higher incidence of stroke than abstainers. In addition, alcohol affects the central nervous system, slowing down brain activity and impairing reaction time, mental awareness, judgment, and coordination.

Studies show that as we grow older, the brain becomes more susceptible to these effects of alcohol. In turn, impaired brain activity can cause problems indirectly. The increased risk of a fall when drinking, combined with the increased injury due to a fall, makes drinking too much alcohol hazardous for older people. Choking on food—another kind of accident that can be fatal—is also much more common among people when they drink heavily during a meal. Denture wearers are especially at risk. Alcohol also has a detrimental effect on other parts of the nervous system and can cause visual problems, tremors, and other signs of nerve damage. Impotence, for example, is very common among alcoholic men.

The older person's digestive tract is also more susceptible to the detrimental effects of alcohol. As one gets older, the intestine's ability to move food through the digestive tract is reduced. Large amounts of alcohol cause intestinal membranes to swell, further inhibiting digestion. Alcohol also increases secretion of digestive juices that erode the stomach lining, exacerbating or causing ulcers.

Heavy drinking may also lead to malabsorption of certain vitamins, specifically vitamin B_{12} and folic acid. Deficiencies of these nutrients may cause fatigue and increased susceptibility to infection.

Although people over 65 constitute only 11 percent of the population in the United States, they consume 25 percent of all medications prescribed in this country. Therefore, among older people who drink, the chances of an adverse drug interaction with alcohol are greatly increased. Always let your doctor know what other drugs, both prescription and over-the-counter, you are taking in addition to the alcohol you drink. The doctor also must know what your drinking habits are whenever a new medication is advised.

DRUGS THAT SHOULD NOT BE TAKEN WITH ALCOHOL

- Allergy medications, antihistamines (both prescription and over-the-counter forms found in cold remedies), and some cold or cough preparations.
- Antidepressants: such as amitriptyline (Elavil) and imipramine (Tofranil).
- Tranquilizers: triazolam (Halcion), diazepam (Valium), alprazolam (Xanax).
- Barbiturates: phenobarbital.
- Motion-sickness pills: dimenhydrinate (Dramamine).
- Painkillers: codeine, propoxyphene (Darvon), meperidine (Demerol), morphine, oxycodone and aspirin (Percodan), and others. (*Note:* Mixing alcohol and high-dose aspirin, including nonsteroidal anti-inflammatory drugs, such as ibuprofen—Advil—can increase bleeding problems.)
- Sleeping medications: flurazepam (Dalmane), triazolam (Halcion), pentobarbital (Nembutal), secobarbital (Seconal).
- Some high blood pressure medications: methyldopa (Aldomet).

HELPING THE OLDER PROBLEM DRINKER

There are two general types of older problem drinkers: (1) chronic, longtime, excessive users and (2) situational users. Chronic, lifetime drinkers who have not received effective help for their problem make up approximately two-thirds of older alcoholics. Although many chronic users succumb to the physical damage of longtime excessive drinking before they reach age 65, a number survive to old age.

Situational heavy drinkers are older people who have turned to alcohol in response to the increased stresses associated with growing older: retirement, a fixed income, health problems, and the deaths of friends or family members.

In fact, social pressures and age-related problems play a key role for both types of alcoholics. The longtime alcoholic is likely to have alienated family and nondrinking friends. His or her drinking friends may have already died from the consequences of alcohol dependence. The situational alcoholic may also lack a close family unit because of the loss of friends and family members. In his or her case, however, the loss spurs the drinking, rather than vice versa.

Both types of older alcoholics are likely to be unemployed or retired. Again, for the longtime alcoholic, unemployment is probably a consequence of alcohol dependence. For the late-onset alcoholic, retirement or the loss of a job may have precipitated the drinking problem.

No matter which came first—the drinking or the social problems—group socialization and counseling are essential for effective treatment of older alcoholics. Involvement in volunteer activities in the community, recreational activities, and social groups will increase the older person's sense of self-worth and confidence. Counseling aimed at sharpening social skills necessary to make friends and to open up to old friends or family members is also especially helpful for the older problem drinker. The better a person's self-image, the less likely he or she is to reach for solace from a bottle.

In longtime alcoholics, however, there is a greater need for medical treatment and longer detoxification programs. Longtime drinkers are more susceptible to alcohol-related illnesses, and older alcoholics may need more time to rid their bodies of the toxins.

Counseling specifically for alcohol addiction is usually most effective when older alcoholics and recovering alcoholics are involved in group discussions. Problems with alcohol are just one issue among many that concern older drinkers, and every opportunity should be given to discuss these issues with peers.

Studies show that all of these programs are most effective in a nonthreatening environment, such as a senior citizen center. The center will often offer a variety of activities, including community meals and other social programs. Transportation is less likely to be a problem, and escort services are often available to older people concerned about traveling alone.

Since older people are more likely to live alone and to be retired or unemployed, they are not as visible to the community at large. Drinking problems may go unde-

HOW TO SPOT A DRINKING PROBLEM

Not everyone who drinks regularly is an alcoholic. The National Institute on Aging has compiled the following list of symptoms that indicate a drinking problem:

- drinking to calm nerves, forget worries, or reduce depression
- loss of interest in food
- gulping drinks, or drinking too fast
- lying about one's drinking habits
- drinking alone with increasing frequency
- injuring oneself or someone else while intoxicated
- getting drunk often (more than three or four times in the past year)
- needing to drink more alcohol to feel the same effects
- frequently acting irritable, resentful, or unreasonable during nondrinking periods
- experiencing medical, social, or financial problems due to drinking

tected. Family members, neighbors, and friends should keep a lookout for older people, especially those who have suffered a series of losses or disabilities.

Older alcoholics are very likely to deny the existence of a problem. They may be ashamed of their drinking or afraid that treatment programs would be ineffective, unnecessary, or too late for them. Families of older problem drinkers may also deny the problem or attribute it to the normal effects of aging. However, studies show that older alcoholics have a high rate of success in overcoming drinking problems if they receive the appropriate services. Many of the symptoms they previously attributed to aging are relieved by abstinence from drinking.

The bottom line is that help is available to the older person who is dependent on alcohol, and seeking help may be a step toward improving the quality of life for that person and his or her family members (see Appendix A).

DRUG ADDICTION

We tend to associate drug use with younger people, but this can be a mistake. Although the use of cocaine, marijuana, and other so-called recreational drugs may be more popular among the young, there are middle-aged and older users. More common, however, is the excessive use of prescription or other legal drugs.

COMMONLY ABUSED LEGAL DRUGS

- Painkillers
    - codeine preparations
    - meperidine (Demerol)
    - morphine
    - oxycodone and aspirin (Percodan)
    - propoxyphene (Darvon)
    - Other painkillers containing hydrocodone, hydromorphone, propoxyphene, oxycodone, and other narcotic ingredients.
- Tranquilizers
    - alprazolam (Xanax)
    - chlordiazepoxide (Librium)
    - chlorpromazine (Thorazine)
    - diazepam (Valium)
    - lorazepam (Ativan)
    - thioridazine (Mellaril)
- Sedatives and sleeping pills
    - flurazepam (Dalmane)
    - pentobarbital (Nembutal)
    - phenobarbital
    - secobarbital (Seconal)
    - triazolam (Halcion)
- Some muscle relaxants
    - carisoprodol (Soma)
    - methocarbamol (Robaxin)

Note: Alcohol should not be taken with anticonvulsants such as phenytoin (Dilantin), anticoagulants such as aspirin or warfarin (Coumadin), and certain antidiabetes drugs such as insulin or glyburide (Micronase) because it alters the drugs' actions. *Always ask your doctor if it is safe to drink alcohol while taking a medication.*

Historically, morphine addiction has been particularly notorious. A patient typically would be given morphine to control pain but would end up becoming addicted. Today a wide assortment of drugs, especially prescription painkillers, tranquilizers such as Valium, and diet pills, are used by people of all ages, and such use frequently leads to overuse and addiction. Starting with Betty Ford, the former First Lady, disclosure by public figures of their problems with both alcohol and painkillers has helped bring excessive use of legal drugs out into the open.

The problem of drug dependence should be approached in much the same manner as alcoholism. Stopping the drugs will often produce uncomfortable withdrawal symptoms, and a doctor's help is needed during the acute phase. Care must be taken at this time so that the person will not substitute one addiction for another.

4

Coping with Stress

We have a tendency to think that stress is an "invention" of our fast-paced twentieth-century world. The fact is that stress is an inevitable part of living, no matter what the culture or the age. We also talk a good deal about stress, but many people do not have a clear idea of what it really means. In simple terms, stress is any condition or situation that requires a person to make physical and/or psychological adjustments.

Although we usually think of stress as involving a negative event or situation—facing a big examination, losing a job, coming face-to-face with danger—joyous occasions also carry a degree of stress. Winning a long-sought promotion, going on a vacation, or buying a new home all produce stress. So, despite its negative connotation, a certain amount of stress adds spice to life and is even desirable in helping us reach our goals.

Just as there are different kinds of stressful events or stressors, so there are different levels or degrees. Some stress is mild and brief—missing a bus, misplacing keys or glasses, almost hitting a car or animal while driving are common examples. Moderate stress lasts longer and is more difficult to deal with: Examples might include getting ready for a wedding or even a holiday, overwork, the temporary absence of a spouse or child. Severe stress is more prolonged and difficult to endure—chronic illness or death of a spouse, threatened or actual loss of a job, or impending retirement.

It is the severe, chronic stress—the kind we often feel we cannot escape—coupled with poor techniques for dealing with it, that is the most likely to cause health problems. There is still much we do not understand about how the mind and body work together, but research indicates that stress may depress the body's immune system and make us more vulnerable to illness.

It is well known that people are more likely to become ill during high-stress periods. Increasingly, physicians are emphasizing effective stress management as an important part of health promotion and preventive medicine.

STRESS AND THE BODY

Our response to stress is firmly ingrained in our evolution. Whenever we are faced with danger or experience stress, the body reacts with a fight-or-flight response. The late Dr. Hans Selye, a world authority on stress and its effects, observed that the body has a three-phase response to stress: alarm, resistance, and exhaustion.

In the first phase, at almost the instant the body senses the stress, the pituitary gland sounds an internal alarm and stimulates the adrenal glands to secrete increased amounts of a stress hormone—adrenaline (epinephrine)—and corticosteroid hormones that ready the body to take immediate action. Heart rate and blood pressure increase, the pupils dilate, muscles become tense, and we feel a heightened alertness. The body is thus prepared to fight or flee. When appropriate action is taken and the source of stress is relieved, hormone levels drop to normal. If the source of stress is not removed, however, the body stays on the alert—or the resistance stage. Eventually this leads to a state of exhaustion, and unless relieved, a person is likely to develop a stress-related disorder: a stress headache or simply the inability to concentrate and function.

In our modern society, we are not likely to encounter the kinds of stress in which a full-blown fight or flight is appropriate. But the body will still react in much the same manner when it receives stress signals from the brain. Thus, when the boss asks us to redo a report or we are running late for an important appointment, the body reacts in much the same manner as it would if placed in a truly dangerous situation.

Over a longer period of time, repeated inappropriate responses to stress, with the accompanying bodily changes in blood pressure, an increased flow of gastric acid, and other hormone-related changes, can take their toll. Many experts believe that excessive stress—or perhaps more accurately, inappropriate responses to stress—can play a role in developing heart disease, asthma, ulcers, diabetes, and other diseases. In addition, many people seek to relieve stress by turning to cigarettes, alcohol use, or overeating, any one of which further compromises health.

SOURCES OF STRESS

As people age, sources of stress change. Common stressful events for those in midlife or older include illness of a spouse or oneself; death of a spouse, parent, family member, or friend; or a grown child leaving home. Chronic pain, such as that sometimes associated with rheumatoid arthritis, produces stress. Changing to a different line of work or even getting a promotion also causes stress. Stress can also result from *not* working. Retirement is a major stressor, for example (see Table 4.1).

DEVELOPING COPING STRATEGIES

Beyond differences in personality structure, much of what affects how we cope with stress stems from our early life experiences. Those who were overprotected as children may find it more difficult to cope with the normal stresses of adult life than those who were exposed to stress in small doses that allowed the development of coping mechanisms.

At certain times, though, it *is* beneficial not to face a stressful situation—at least not immediately. For example, a person who denies that he or she has a serious illness shortly after learning the diagnosis may actually be "buying time" in order to gather coping strengths.

In general, the feeling of being in control of a particular situation reduces the physiological effects of stress. Predictable but stressful events also give the individual time to think about how he or she will manage. Simply learning how to organize time to avoid feeling pressured can go a long way toward relieving stress.

Psychologists use the term *adaptive behavior* to describe effective stress management. This entails developing alternatives to the usual fight-or-flight response and starts with mobilizing inner personal resources to overcome stress. Each of us possesses different types of adaptive behavior. Dr. David Hamberg, formerly of the Stanford University Medical Center, classified adaptive behaviors as follows:

- *Information seeking.* This enables a person to keep his or her options open and to approach the stressful situation with a basis for sound problem solving and decision making.
- *Organizing feelings and information.* By sorting out conflicting feelings and information, a person can avoid disorganization and emotions that may preclude sound decision making. Making a list of pros and cons helps focus priorities and make wise decisions.
- *Maintaining flexibility.* Freedom of action must be retained in order to make sound decisions. This may entail making alternative plans and shifting priorities as the need arises. Flexibility in timing is also important. Today's crisis may not be a crisis tomorrow if a decision can be delayed until more information is obtained.
- *Ability to compromise.* Rigidity can make coping with stress very difficult, if not impossible. Being able to realistically assess a situation and arrive at a solution that maintains self-esteem is the key to any successful coping technique.

TABLE 4.1
The Stresses of Life

This table from Richard Rahe, a leading stress researcher, shows estimates of the relative amounts of stress associated with different events. These estimates are derived from questionnaires in which people were asked which events they had experienced recently and then asked to gauge the degree of adjustment each event required. The ratings, given in "life change units" (LCUs), range from 25, for a change in political beliefs or a minor illness, to 105, for the death of a child or spouse.

Health	LCU
An injury or illness that	
kept you in bed a week or more or sent you to the hospital	42
was less serious than described above	25
Major dental work	40
Major change in eating habits	29
Major change in sleeping habits	31
Major change in usual type and/or amount of recreation	30
Work	
Change to a new type of work	38
Change in work hours and conditions	33
Change in responsibilities at work	
more responsibilities	31
fewer responsibilities	29
promotion	31
demotion	57
transfer	38
Troubles at work	
with your boss	39
with coworkers	35
with persons under your supervision	30
other work troubles	31
Major business adjustment	38
Retirement	49
Loss of job	
laid off work	57
fired from work	64
Taking a correspondence course	29
Home and family	
Major change in living conditions	39
Change in residence	
move within the same town or city	28
move to a different town, city, or state	38
Change in family get-togethers	26
Major change in health or behavior of family member	52

Home and family	LCU
Marriage	50
Pregnancy	60
Miscarriage or abortion	53
Gain of a new family member	
birth of a child	49
adoption of a child	45
a relative moving in with you	57
Spouse beginning or ending work outside the home	37
Child leaving home	
to attend college	28
to marry	30
for other reasons	29
Change in arguments with spouse	34
In-law problems	29
Change in the marital status of your parents	
divorce	38
remarriage	33
Separation from spouse	
due to work	49
due to marital problems	56
Marital reconciliation	42
Divorce	62
Birth of grandchild	31
Death of spouse	105
Death of other family member	
child	105
brother or sister	64
parent	66
Personal and social	
Change in personal habits	31
Beginning or ending school or college	32
Change of school or college	28
Change in political beliefs	25
Change in religious beliefs	29

Personal and social	LCU
Change in social activities	28
Vacation	29
New, close, personal relationship	32
Engagement to marry	39
"Girlfriend" or "boyfriend" problems	30
Sexual difficulties	49
"Falling out" of a close personal relationship	35
An accident	44
Minor violation of the law	32
Being held in jail	57
Death of a close friend	46
Major decision regarding the immediate future	45
Major personal achievement	33
Financial	
Major change in finances	
increased income	27
decreased income	60
investment and/or credit difficulties	43
Loss or damage of personal property	40
Moderate purchase	26
Major purchase	39
Foreclosure on a mortgage or loan	57

TIPS FOR MANAGING STRESS

- Plan your day to include work breaks that physically or mentally take you away from the office. Try not to bring office work home.
- When you have an overwhelming number of things to accomplish, set priorities and postpone less important tasks. Learn to delegate matters that cannot be put off. Deal with concerns on a day-at-a-time basis.
- Make a realistic list of what you need to accomplish in a given day, with the most important things at the top. Tackle them one at a time, and don't start a second task until you have finished the first.
- Look at your modus operandi. Are you a perfectionist? If so, try to decide which tasks truly require meticulous attention to detail and which can be done casually. For example, if you have a high-powered job and a relative in the hospital, don't put a lot of energy into keeping your household spotless.
- Control the timing of stressful events. For example, if you have recently become widowed, defer moving to a different residence until you have had some time to make an emotional adjustment. Similarly, try not to make major decisions when you are overtired or anxious.

OTHER METHODS TO REDUCE STRESS

All of us possess the basic coping skills needed to deal with stress. We humans have survived largely because we are able to adapt to our environment and different situations. If you can learn how to handle stress while retaining self-esteem and a measure of control, you will have mastered dealing with stress. Of course, this is often easier said than done. But just remember, everyone has the potential to cope effectively. The following steps can help you achieve emotional equilibrium and a sense of well-being:

- □ Learn to recognize your own symptoms of stress. These may include irritability, sleeplessness, social and/or sexual withdrawal, loss of interest in activities, lack of appetite.
- □ Talk about stressful events to a friend or spouse before you reach a breaking point. If you feel the need, let go and cry. Like talking, crying externalizes pent-up feelings and may reduce the risk of stress-related illness. If you need extra help, seek counseling from a mental health professional.
- □ Recognize that some things cannot be changed, and put your energy toward those that can.
- □ Cultivate an optimistic attitude. Don't talk yourself into believing that you can't cope.
- □ Reduce your exposure to pet peeves. For example, go to the bank at an off-hour to avoid maddening lines. Mask outside noise by listening to relaxing music.
- □ Learn to express anger in a constructive way. Keeping anger pent up adds to feelings of stress; blowing up in a rage is almost as bad. Simply being able to say "that makes me very angry" and working out ways of avoiding anger-provoking situations are positive steps in dealing with anger.
- □ Focus on others rather than on your own problems. If time permits, do a few hours of volunteer work each week.
- □ Exercise every day, even if you have time only for a brisk, 20-minute walk.
- □ Pay attention to such signs of stress as a tension headache, and stop what you are doing for a rest break. If possible, take a warm bath or treat yourself to a massage during periods of stress. If this is not possible, practice deep abdominal breathing whenever you feel muscular tension setting in.
- □ Don't neglect your diet. Start off with a breakfast containing proteins and carbohydrates for sustained energy. And don't let the demands of your day get in the way of a relaxed lunch.

RELAXATION TECHNIQUES

Medical researchers have found that practicing daily systematic relaxation techniques reduces stress and in some cases produces symptom relief during illness or disease. These methods have been shown to help control blood sugar in some people with diabetes, blood pressure in some of those with hypertension, and pain in some patients with rheumatoid arthritis. How relaxation works is not clearly understood, but one

THE BENSON RELAXATION RESPONSE

Some general advice on regular practice of the relaxation response:

- Try to find 10 to 20 minutes in your daily routine; before breakfast is a good time.
- Sit comfortably.
- For the period you will practice, try to arrange your life so you won't have distractions. Put the phone on the answering machine, and have someone else watch the kids.
- Time yourself by glancing periodically at a clock or watch, but don't set an alarm. Commit yourself to a specific length of practice, and try to stick to it.

There are several approaches to eliciting the relaxation response. Here is one standard set of instructions used at the Mind/Body Medical Institute:

Step 1: Pick a focus word or short phrase that's firmly rooted in your personal belief system. For example, a nonreligious individual might choose a neutral word like *one* or *peace* or *love.* A Christian person desiring to use a prayer could pick the opening words of Psalm 23, *The Lord is my shepherd;* a Jewish person could choose *Shalom.*

Step 2: Sit quietly in a comfortable position.

Step 3: Close your eyes.

Step 4: Relax your muscles.

Step 5: Breathe slowly and naturally, repeating your focus word or phrase silently as you exhale.

Step 6: Throughout, assume a passive attitude. Don't worry about how well you're doing. When other thoughts come to mind, simply say to yourself "Oh, well" and gently return to the repetition.

Step 7: Continue for 10 to 20 minutes. You may open your eyes to check the time, but do not use an alarm. When you finish, sit quietly for a minute or so, at first with your eyes closed and later with your eyes open. Then do not stand for one or two minutes.

Step 8: Practice the technique once or twice a day.

hypothesis is that it somehow may make receptors in body tissue less sensitive to the high hormonal levels produced as part of the stress response.

Some people have a natural ability to concentrate deeply and put themselves into a relaxed state. Most others need some sort of training, either by reading a book on the subject or attending a class. In general, you can practice the techniques on page 115 in a quiet spot, wearing comfortable clothing, and not on a full stomach. Although these relaxation steps are typically practiced 20 minutes a day, the effects last far beyond this period.

OTHER STRESS-RELIEVING TECHNIQUES

Biofeedback. Using a widely available special machine that involves the application of electrodes to the skin to record muscle contractions and skin temperature, you can learn to control normally involuntary processes—such as heart rate and blood pressure—that increase under stress. The machine "feeds back" the efforts, and eventually you can recognize and control facets of the stress response by yourself. Once viewed with skepticism, the control of "involuntary" responses is now seen to be effective in the treatment of migraine headaches, asthma, and other disorders in certain individuals. This technique must be taught by a skilled professional.

Self-hypnosis. Hypnosis involves entering an altered state of consciousness in which all concentration is focused on a single objective or image, with all other stimuli blocked out. Many people think that hypnosis is something that a hypnotist imposes on his or her subject, or they confuse it with a sleeplike state. Others think they cannot be hypnotized. On the contrary, those who can lose themselves totally in an engrossing book or movie, or become so absorbed in a task that they are oblivious to their surroundings, are actually practicing a form of self-hypnosis. Once a person learns self-hypnosis, from a skilled professional, he or she can use it to relieve tension and feelings of stress or anxiety.

5

Looking Your Best

We have been conditioned to equate beauty with youth, and as we grow older, many of us become increasingly dismayed at the changes we see in the mirror. No matter what our age, it is natural to want to look our best. A man or woman of 50 or 60 cannot recapture the wrinkle-free skin and youthful appearance of a 20-year-old, but this does not mean that all is lost. Every age has its pluses and minuses, and while it may sound trite, there is considerable truth to the old saying that true beauty comes from within. Taking good care of yourself is the healthiest way to look your best.

The actress Helen Hayes proudly proclaims that she has never had a face-lift or any other cosmetic operation, and her serene beauty is an indication that true glamour cannot always be achieved through surgery. What we do about keeping our looks is largely a matter of personal preference. But simply maintaining good health and a sense of well-being—exercising to keep muscles firm and the body trim, controlling our weight, avoiding cigarette smoking and excessive alcohol use—contribute to personal attractiveness. For those who want to do more, a variety of surgical procedures are available. In this chapter some of the more popular of these procedures will be discussed, along with the risks that accompany any kind of surgery.

HOW THE SKIN AGES

Many factors contribute to the wrinkling, spotting, and sagging of aging skin. Some skin types have a genetic tendency to wrinkle more than others: White skin, for example, tends to wrinkle at an earlier age than the skin of Asians and blacks. But with age, wrinkles are inevitable for anyone. Smoking (which decreases blood flow to the skin) and exposure to the sun (which causes premature wrinkling and drying, as well as skin cancer) augment whatever genetic predispositions one might have to wrinkling. Although skin-saving measures ideally should start early in life, the benefits of quitting smoking and avoiding prolonged sun exposure will be apparent at any age.

Age-related changes may be more easily accepted by first looking at the skin's structure and understanding why changes happen. Below the epidermis or outer skin layer lies the dermis, which contains water, elastic fibers, and the protein collagen, as well as blood vessels, nerve fibers, sweat and sebaceous glands, and muscle tissue. Below the dermis is the fatty subcutaneous layer.

As skin ages, it loses moisture, sweat glands, and elasticity, which results in dryness and a loss of resilience. The natural loss of subcutaneous fat that comes with aging may exaggerate bony areas of the face. Loss of pigment-producing melanocytes drains color from the skin. (Conversely, accumulation of the pigment lipofuscin may produce "age," or "liver," spots on heavily exposed areas such as the face and hands.) The skin becomes altogether thinner, making blood vessels and uneven areas of color more prominent. Over decades, the pull of gravity on thinner, less elastic skin causes the face, eyelids, breasts, abdomen, and other structures to begin to sag. Extreme weight fluctuations over the years can also contribute to looser skin and increased facial wrinkling.

As a person ages, the rate at which cells from the base of the epidermis are pushed to the surface to form new skin decreases. The surface skin in an older man or woman, therefore, really is older, and for that reason may lack a youthful glow.

Beyond these small-scale events, the repeated pulling and pushing of facial skin into characteristic expressions—smiles as well as frowns—result in crow's-feet around the eyes, furrows between the brows, and creases running from the sides of the nose to the corners of the mouth.

Not all skin ages at the same rate or to the same extent. A man's oilier skin ages less rapidly than a woman's. Also, shaving stimulates a faster turnover of the epidermal layer, making the skin look fresher. Different complexions age at varying rates, depending on their sensitivity to the sun. Albinos, who lack the pigment melanin, are most sensitive; those with fair skin are next, followed by medium and then olive complexions. Black people have thicker skin layers and greater amounts of melanin, which afford the skin more protection from the sun's ultraviolet rays. Any skin protected by clothing, of course, ages more slowly than areas exposed to the sun.

HELPING YOUR SKIN

Regular exercise improves blood flow to the skin, nourishing its collagen fibers. Adequate amounts of fluid and vitamins A and C prevent skin-related deficiencies. Eliminating smoking is vitally important for the health of the whole body as well as that of the skin. Smoking decreases blood flow to the skin, causing premature wrinkling.

Avoiding the sun will not reverse damage to the collagen fibers or make surface blood vessels less visible, but wearing a sun-blocking agent during any prolonged exposure prevents further wrinkling and protects against skin cancer.

A balanced diet that provides vitamins A and C, both important in maintaining the skin, is important. The topical application of a vitamin-A derivative called retinoic acid (Retin A) has been somewhat successful in reversing and preventing wrinkles, especially those that are sun-induced. However, the results take about four to six months and are less than dramatic. Also, some people are unable to use Retin A because it causes their skin to become dry, red, and irritated. Although Retin A has become the second most common choice for people seeking wrinkle treatment, would-be users should note that excessive vitamin A is highly toxic, and self-treatment with megadoses of the vitamin or its derivatives should be avoided.

Scores of cosmetic products on the market claim to restore the skin by "feeding" it. But skin grows from below, nourished by a network of tiny blood vessels. The outer, visible layers are actually dead tissue, and nothing applied to them can provide nutrients for the underlying living layers. Drying of the skin does hasten wrinkling, so moisturizing creams, lotions, and oils that help the skin retain its natural oils and lubricants may help. But contrary to the claims of cosmetic manufacturers, none of these products can erase wrinkles. Even the highly promoted and very expensive collagen creams will not restore the skin's natural collagen, simply because the cosmetic's molecules are too large to be absorbed through the skin.

The same is true of advertising claims made for creams that contain hormones; some hormones are absorbed through the skin, but their topical application will not restore the skin. In short, the purpose of moisturizing creams or lotions is to provide an oily film that prevents the evaporation of water from the skin. An inexpensive moisturizing cream will do this just as effectively as an expensive, elaborately packaged, and heavily advertised product. Indeed, the basic ingredients may even be the same; the difference is in the scent and presentation.

SURGICAL PROCEDURES

DERMABRASION, CHEMICAL PEELING, AND COLLAGEN INJECTIONS

A number of procedures can make facial wrinkles less prominent. For example, dermabrasion, chemical peeling, and collagen injections are used to remove fine wrinkles and superficial changes in texture and pigmentation. They are considerably less expensive than a face-lift, but will not remedy sagging skin.

Dermabrasion makes use of a skin-planing tool that literally "sands" the skin to remove fine wrinkles around the brow, eyes, and mouth. It also may smooth out old scars, including acne marks. Dermabrasion is also effective in removing actinic keratoses, the flat, pink, scaly spots that result from overexposure to the sun and that can become malignant. The process takes about half an hour and is done under local anesthesia. After dermabrasion, the newly surfaced skin will be raw and pink, but it will gradually return to normal in about two weeks.

Sometimes the procedure does not always produce the desired results. The skin may grow back unnaturally shiny, too pink in tone, or lacking in pigmentation. Some cosmetic surgeons feel that dermabrasion is not effective on large areas of the face but should be restricted to smaller areas.

Chemical peeling, also known as chemosurgery, uses a mild acid to "burn off" the surface layer of skin. It is used to remove the leathery wrinkles that result from excess sun exposure. A smoother and sometimes paler layer grows in to take its place. The type of acid used depends on the depth of the wrinkles to be removed; trichloracetic acid (TCA) is used for superficial wrinkles and phenol for deeper ones.

Chemical peeling is a more aggressive and uncomfortable procedure than dermabrasion; it takes weeks and sometimes months for the skin to return to normal. The burned layer forms a scab that comes off in about 10 days, exposing a dark or red new layer that gradually lightens. The patient should avoid prolonged sun exposure for the next six months. If this is not possible, a sun-blocking agent should be applied before going out into the sun.

The process works best on fair-skinned individuals, with results that can last up to five years. Asians, blacks, and dark-skinned persons risk areas of irregular pigmentation when the new skin grows in.

Collagen injected into the dermis replaces the soft tissue lost as the skin ages or suffers trauma from injury, surgery, or disease. Frown lines, pronounced laugh lines at the corners of the lips and eyes, and creases running from the sides of the nose to the mouth respond to this treatment. But the injections will not erase fine lines around the mouth or eyes, nor can they hide hard scars or lines that have well-defined edges.

The treatment consists of at least two injections given at two-week intervals. One month after preliminary testing for allergic reactions, the physician injects a mixture of collagen and lidocaine, a local anesthetic, into the depression of the wrinkle or scar (see Figure 5.1). The patient may have some soreness and swelling afterward. The effects last from six months to two years, after which the shots may need to be repeated. Collagen injections are not for everyone; in rare cases, their use has been linked to adverse effects such as polymyositis and dermatomyositis, two diseases that affect the body's connective tissue.

Much of the collagen used today is taken from cattle skin and then purified. Allergic reactions are rare. Some patients may have slight swelling after drinking alcohol, after sunbathing for long periods, or during hay fever attacks. Cold sores (herpes simplex) may appear over the treated area.

People with autoimmune diseases, such as lupus, are not advised to have collagen treatments. These procedures should also be avoided by anyone with past hypersensitivity reactions or allergy to lidocaine. A tendency to develop skin infections also may be a deterring factor.

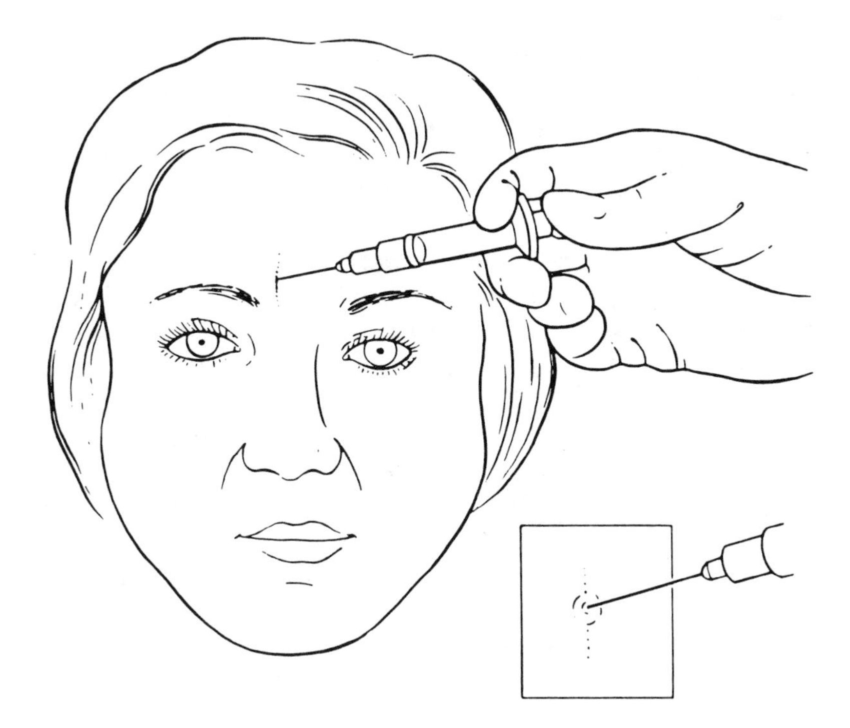

Figure 5.1 Collagen Injection
Collagen is injected to fill out a forehead wrinkle.

OTHER TREATMENTS FOR WRINKLES

Far less common than collagen injections are injections of small amounts of fat that are removed from the patient's own body. Another injectable is a compound called Fibrel, which is created by mixing a gelatin powder with an extract from the patient's own blood. Results have been inconsistent and variable: Some physicians have reported a loss in the fullness of the skin only two or three months after the fat injections. The results of the use of Fibrel are still inconclusive.

The newest procedures involve the body's own production of collagen. In a technique called *threading,* a protein-based thread is placed directly under the wrinkle, stimulating collagen production in that area. The thread dissolves in about six months. Preliminary results are promising, with the treatment lasting as long as two to five years. Another development is the use of collagen extracted from small pieces of human skin (taken from usually covered areas of the body) rather than cattle skin. The treated area may react more favorably to the human-derived product.

AGE SPOTS

Most age-related skin changes do not require cosmetic surgery. "Age" or "liver" spots, for example, will fade with the use of bleaching creams; however, the treated areas may turn blotchy when exposed to sunlight. Seborrheic keratoses—the raised black or brown wartlike growths appearing on the trunk, arms, neck, or face—are never malignant, but they may be removed for cosmetic reasons or if they rub against clothing. These growths are usually scraped, frozen, or burned off under local anesthesia in a dermatologist's office.

Moles should not be confused with age spots. A mole, known medically as a *nevus pigmentosus,* is a pigmented skin lesion that is often slightly elevated. It may range in color from light pink to dark brown or nearly black, although there are some rare white moles. Some moles are wartlike in appearance, others are smooth. Most moles are harmless, but some give rise to melanoma, a highly lethal form of cancer. There has been a marked increase in melanoma in recent years, especially among people who spend a good deal of time in the sun. It is a good idea to have any moles inspected by a physician at some point in adulthood, then check them regularly yourself for any changes. Warning signs to watch for include any change in size, shape, or color; itching; bleeding or "weeping" discharge; and blurring or invasion of borders into surrounding skin.

COSMETIC SURGERY

At one time cosmetic surgery was primarily for actors and others whose livelihood depended upon their appearance. Today this has changed; people of all ages and of both sexes are having cosmetic surgery.

Of course, not all plastic surgery is done for aesthetic reasons. Some people have a genetic tendency to develop sagging eyelids, which can eventually interfere with vision or irritate the cornea. A deviated septum in the nose can interfere with breathing.

Like any operation, cosmetic procedures do incur risks, and those contemplating plastic surgery should first determine whether their expectations are realistic. A face-lift will *not* save an unhappy marriage or help close a business deal, for example.

More than 75 percent of cosmetic surgery today is done on an outpatient basis, often in a doctor's office or freestanding ambulatory surgical clinic. If the procedure is to be done in an outpatient setting, the facility should be equipped to handle any medical or surgical emergency. You should choose a physician who is either board-certified in plastic and reconstructive surgery or in the appropriate medical specialty (for example, ophthalmology for eye surgery). He or she must also have the qualifications to do a cosmetic operation. Physicians who make unrealistic claims for an operation—for example, they promise that you will look 20 years younger—should be avoided. Names of member physicians who are board-certified, and information on specific procedures, can be obtained from:

> American Society of Plastic and Reconstructive Surgeons
> 444 East Algonquin Road
> Arlington Heights, IL 60005
> Tel.: (708) 228-9900

COST

Cosmetic plastic surgery is expensive. Costs can range from $1,000 to $8,000 or more, many procedures are not covered by insurance, and full payment may be required beforehand. The cost will depend on the type of procedure, the physician, the geographical area where the procedure is performed, and whether it is done on an inpatient or outpatient basis.

THE BODY: LIPOSUCTION

Although liposuction has been performed only since the early 1980s, it is already the most common cosmetic surgery performed in the United States. As its name implies, liposuction entails sucking fat through a thin tube inserted between skin and muscle. The procedure is for people of relatively normal weight who have a defined area—such as the abdomen, hips, buttocks, thighs, or under the chin—containing excess fat deposits. It is not for the obese person who simply needs to lose weight, and it usually is not recommended for anyone over age 45 or 50. If liposuction is performed on an older adult, the decreased skin elasticity may result in a sagging, mottled appearance when the underlying fat is removed. Anyone over 50 who is considering this procedure should have the surgeon thoroughly explain this and other drawbacks.

The procedure, which lasts from about 45 minutes to two hours, may be performed on either an inpatient or outpatient basis and under either local or general anesthesia. It is important to choose a surgeon who has undergone special training for and has extensive experience in liposuction. Keeping a supply of your own blood on hand is recommended; heavy blood loss can occur when large fat deposits are removed. The half-inch incisions made at the site of the excess fat usually disappear soon after surgery, but the recovery period can be extremely painful and may take several months. This is a serious surgical procedure. Do not undergo liposuction unless you are a good candidate and deem it absolutely necessary for your physical and mental well-being.

THE FACE: FACE-LIFTS

Face-lifts are more expensive and riskier than less drastic cosmetic procedures. Anyone considering this surgery should remember that the greater the loss in skin elasticity before the procedure, the less pronounced the effects of the operation will be.

Anyone with heart disease or other conditions that increase the risk of surgery should discuss the potential hazards with a doctor beforehand. Ideally, before a face-lift or any other cosmetic surgery, the plastic surgeon should request preoperative clearance from the patient's primary-care physician. People with uncontrolled hypertension, glaucoma, coronary artery disease, or certain other disorders may have to delay surgery until these conditions stabilize. A complete physical examination, including an electrocardiogram (ECG or EKG), chest X ray, and laboratory tests, is recommended. Depending on the patient and the surgeon, a face-lift may be done in the hospital or on an outpatient basis, using either general anesthesia or local anesthesia preceded by a sedative.

In the conventional operation, the surgeon makes an incision running from ear to ear and under the hairline, pulls down the skin flap, and cuts away excess fatty tissue underneath (see Figure 5.2). Loose neck and facial skin is then pulled back tightly, the excess trimmed away, and the skin flap sutured back into place.

After the operation, the face will be swathed in bandages for the initial recovery

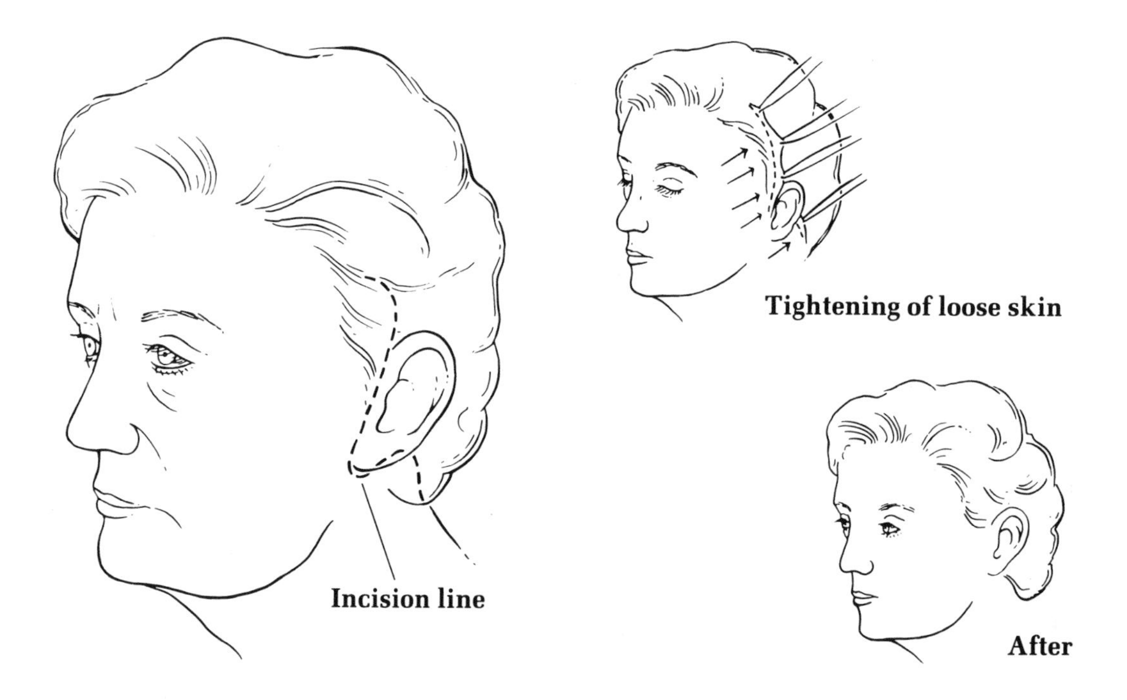

Figure 5.2 Face-lift
The drawing at the left shows the incision line and the type of facial wrinkles and sagging chin line that can be corrected with a face-lift. The drawing at the upper right shows how the skin is pulled tight and the excess removed. The lower right drawing shows the finished results—a firmer jawline and smoother facial contour.

period. It may take two or three weeks for the puffiness to disappear and the scars to heal. A woman should wait one week before applying any makeup and three weeks before using hair coloring.

Face-lifts are relatively safe operations, but some people do experience complications, such as injury to facial nerves, hair loss around the incisions, misplacement of the earlobe, skin tears or damage, infection, and *hematomas* (blood-filled swellings caused by injury to blood vessels). In rare instances, the patient may suffer eye damage caused by bleeding behind the eyes, or the death or deterioration of the skin flap that was lifted. The resulting scar tissue from these complications usually improves without treatment. However, some people—especially African-Americans, Asians, and dark-skinned whites—develop keloid scars. These are smooth, shiny, raised areas that are hard to treat.

Certain factors increase the risk of complications during or after the operation. Owing to higher pressure within the blood vessels, patients with hypertension may have increased bleeding during surgery. Those who take large amounts of aspirin run a similar risk, since aspirin acts as an anticoagulant. Because smoking impairs blood circulation and robs the tissues of oxygen, the skin of a smoker may scale or heal poorly following surgery.

Other conditions that make face-lifts and other cosmetic operations inadvisable are burns that have left scarring, previous radiation therapy that can damage blood vessels, psoriasis and other skin diseases, and any disorders that affect blood circulation. People with skin that has healed poorly in the past should approach surgery with caution, if at all.

THE EYES: BLEPHAROPLASTY

Like skin on other parts of the body, the eyelids lose elasticity with age. Changes around the eyes may be even more pronounced because the skin here is somewhat thinner than on other parts of the face. Repeated actions such as blinking and squinting contribute to sagging lids. Smoking and overexposure to the sun age skin here as they do elsewhere on the body. Aging, inherited tendencies, or certain diseases may cause puffiness, or "bags," under the eyes. The bags develop when ligaments around the eyes weaken, allowing fat to bulge outward.

Eyelid surgery, or blepharoplasty, is the fourth most common cosmetic operation (behind liposuction, breast enlargement, and collagen injections). The procedure is performed under local anesthesia, takes about an hour to complete, and is often done on an outpatient basis (although a 24-hour postoperative hospital stay is preferable to monitor for signs of bleeding). The loose tissue is cut away through incisions made in the fold of the upper lid and immediately below the lower lash line (see Figure 5.3). Dark glasses may be worn to hide any swelling or discoloration during the approximately two weeks it takes for the eyes to return to normal.

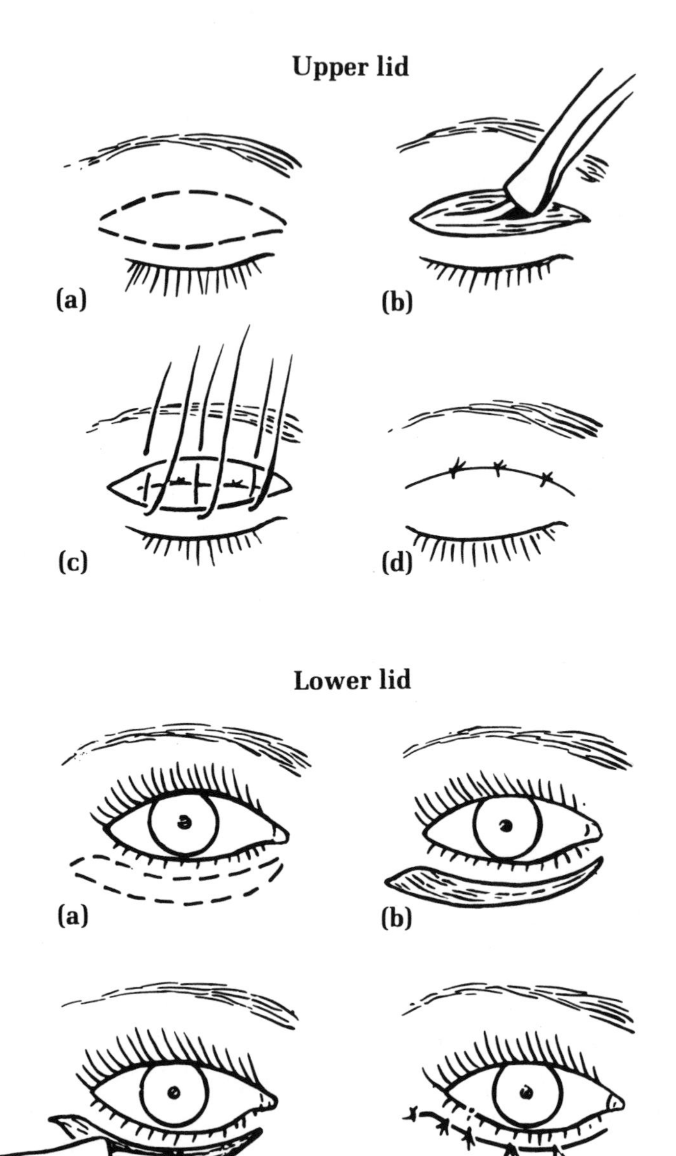

Figure 5.3 Eyelid Surgery
This shows the traditional procedure for removing fat pads and excessive skin from both upper and lower eyelids. Incisions are made in the fold of the upper lid and just below the lower lashes. The excess material is cut out, and the incisions are closed. Another method involves inserting an electric needle into the fat pockets and vaporizing the fat.

Complications, if any, are rare and usually temporary. One of the most serious is a sudden rise in blood pressure after surgery, which can lead to a hematoma. If the blood-filled swelling presses against the skin, cutting off the blood supply, the skin can slough off. Other complications include increased tearing and double vision due to swelling of the membranes lining the eyeball and eyelid (the *conjunctiva*) or to disturbances in the underlying muscle. Patients may find that they cannot close their eyes completely for several days after the operation. If this problem persists, the patient will have to use eyedrops to help distribute tears over the eyeball, a function normally performed by the lid. The most troublesome complication of blepharoplasty is *ectropion,* where the eyelid is turned out and away from the eye when too much skin has been removed. Skin grafts must then be used to rebuild the lid.

A procedure known as fat-melting blepharoplasty was developed by Dr. Michael E. Sachs, director of research and associate professor of facial plastic and reconstructive surgery at the New York Eye and Ear Infirmary of New York Medical College. Dr. Sachs's procedure, which removes eye bags without surgery, utilizes an electric needle that, in effect, vaporizes the fat. The entire procedure takes about 30 minutes using a local anesthetic: A tiny incision is made to identify the fat pockets; the needle is then inserted into the fat. Since fat is about 90 percent water, it can be vaporized with the needle's electric current. The heating actually strengthens the supporting ligaments, so there is less likelihood that sagging will recur. This operation also carries less risk of bleeding or other complications than does traditional eyelid surgery. Complete healing takes about a week.

THE NOSE: RHINOPLASTY

A rhinoplasty, or "nose job," is the fifth most popular of all cosmetic operations. At one time most people who underwent rhinoplasties all ended up with pretty much the same upturned nose. Today, however, plastic surgeons are more skilled in reshaping a nose to fit an individual face.

In a typical operation, the surgeon makes an incision through the nostril, separates the skin from cartilage and bone lying underneath, and reshapes the bone for the desired result (see Figure 5.4). The nostrils are then packed with absorbent material, and the nose is splinted to hold the new shape. For the first 24 hours after surgery, the patient will be on a liquid diet and must rest in bed, whether at home or in the hospital. The splint is removed after five to seven days. It may take two or three weeks for the discoloration around the nose and eyes to disappear, but the patient can usually resume light, normal activity within a week or two.

Complications associated with rhinoplasty are rare. The most serious is bleeding, which can show up as late as two weeks after surgery. This is usually treated by inserting a medicated packing into the nostril. Severe hemorrhage, although very uncommon, may require hospitalization. Other side effects are usually minor—a diminished sense of smell for several weeks, nasal congestion, or skin irritations from the bandages.

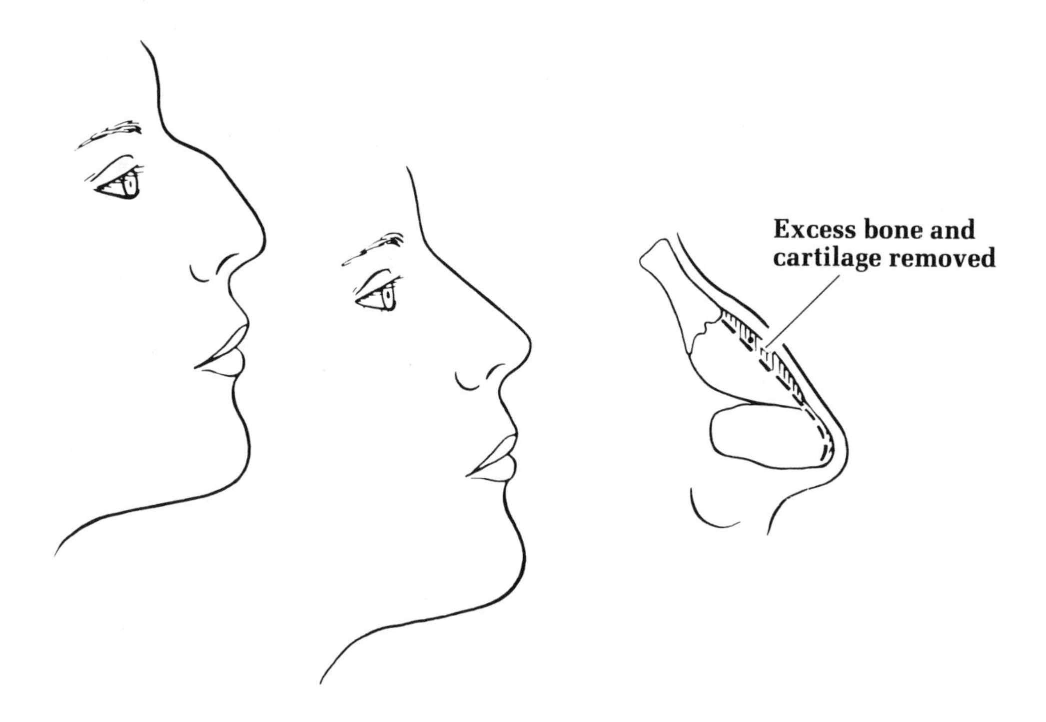

Figure 5.4 Rhinoplasty
The drawings at left and center show before and after a nose contour procedure. At right the nose is reshaped from inside the nostril.

THE CHIN

Chin remodeling is often done at the same time as a rhinoplasty or face-lift. A prominent chin can be made smaller simply by removing some of the bone. Receding chins can be remedied by inserting a hard silicone implant (not the silicone gel implants that have been so controversial), or alternatively, bone transplanted from elsewhere in the body. In one of the more common procedures (see Figure 5.5), the surgeon makes an incision inside the lower lip or under the chin, slips in the prosthesis, and bandages the area to limit movement during the initial healing period. The main risk is that the implant will protrude from the chin. If this occurs, or in the unlikely case the implant shifts, it can be replaced.

Sometimes the problem is related to misalignment of the teeth. In such instances the chin surgery may be preceded by orthodontic work to correct the dental problem.

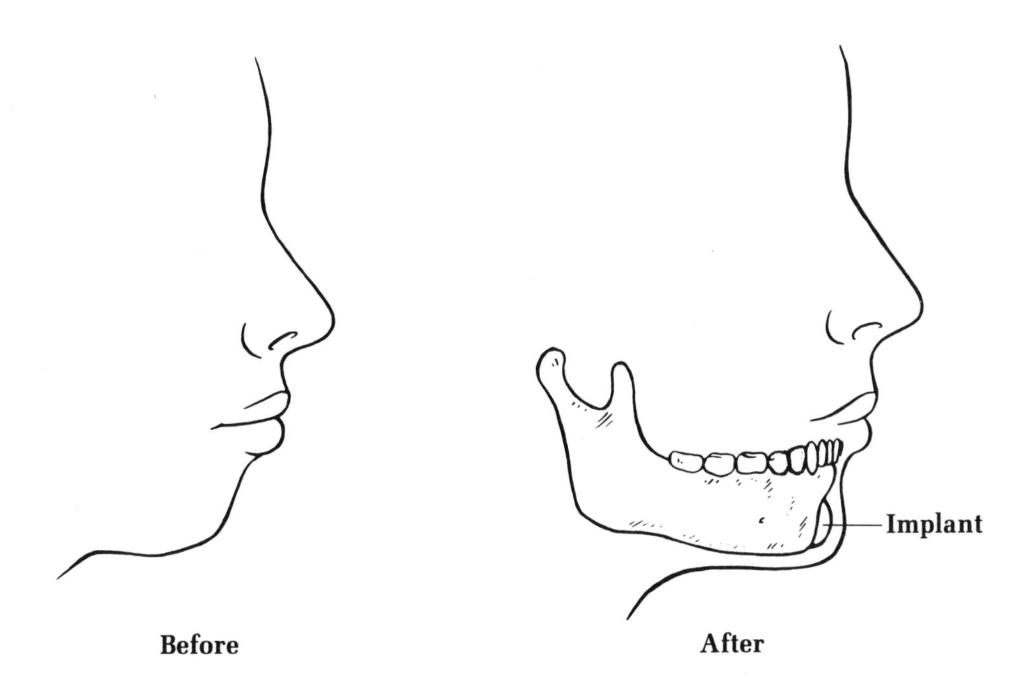

Figure 5.5 Chin Implant
At left is a receding chin that can be corrected with the insertion of an implant, shown at right.

BEYOND THE FACE

Today's cosmetic surgery is by no means limited to the face. There also are a number of body-contouring operations aimed at altering bustlines, sagging abdomens, fatty thighs, and other perceived "imperfections." It should be noted that for many older people, these operations may be riskier and less successful than facial plastic surgery. Body skin in general is thicker than facial skin and may heal unevenly, leaving prominent scar tissue. And most cosmetic operations on the body require general anesthesia, which carries a greater risk than local anesthetics.

BREAST AUGMENTATION AND REDUCTION

In recent years breast surgery has become increasingly common. The majority of operations are performed in conjunction with a mastectomy for breast cancer, a disease estimated to affect one in nine women. These operations entail reconstructing the missing breast and, if needed, altering the remaining breast to match the reconstructed one (see chapter 12).

Other breast operations may be performed to change the contour of the natural breast. Breast enlargement, or augmentation, was the second most common cosmetic procedure in 1990, according to the American Society of Plastic and Reconstructive Surgeons. An implant is inserted under the glandular tissue to "fill out" the breast. The surgeon makes the incision in the fold under the breast, creates a pocket to hold the implant snugly, then slips in the prosthesis (see Figure 5.6). Some implants have an adhesive backing that adheres to tendons in the chest for extra protection against unwanted movement. Because the implant is under natural tissue, there is usually no decrease in sensation in the breast.

In the past, the most commonly used material for breast implants has been silicone gel. However, as a result of newly instituted regulations by the Food and Drug Administration (FDA) and its April 1992 ruling, these implants are available only to women who agree to enter a controlled clinical trial and who have an "urgent need," including those undergoing reconstruction after mastectomy or injury. The agency's action was a result of concern about the side effects of silicone implants; a tendency to produce false mammography results, hardening of the surrounding breast tissue, infection, pain, and silicone leakage. A polyurethane foam–coated implant, in particular, has been taken off the market because of reports that it could break down into 2-toluene diamine (TDA), which has been shown to cause cancer in laboratory animals. Women who already have silicone gel implants should consult with their physicians and seek new information as the FDA makes it available. Still, the risks of having the implant removed are probably more serious than the risks of these side effects. Until further FDA action, breast augmentation will be done with saline (saltwater) implants, which were not affected by the ruling. (It should be noted, however, that these implants are also at risk for leakage.)

Breast reduction can produce firmer breasts with a greater lift in the older woman who has large, sagging breasts. Cutting into the skin fold under the breasts, the surgeon removes excess fat and skin then sutures the skin flap back into place (see Figure 5.7). In both augmentation and reduction operations, scar tissue is largely hidden by the fold.

Augmentation and reduction surgeries are done under general anesthesia and usually require three to five days in the hospital, although some augmentation is done on an outpatient basis. It takes about three weeks for tissues to heal well enough for the patient to resume normal activity. During this recovery period, she should not lift even moderately heavy objects or move her arms excessively.

Complications include postoperative infection, skin abscesses, failure of the wound to close properly, and fluid buildup under the skin flaps. Less common risks include excessive bleeding or impairment of blood circulation.

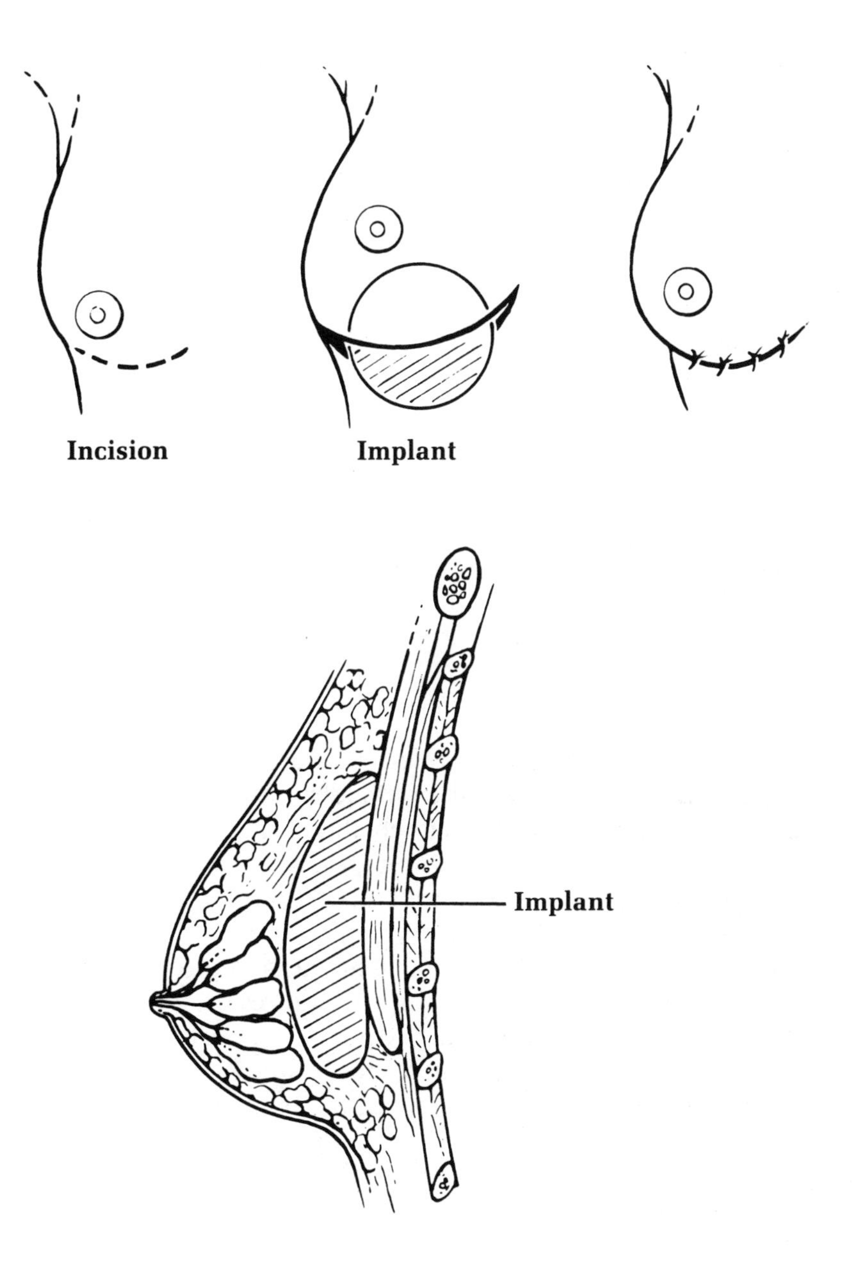

Figure 5.6 **Breast-enlargement Surgery**
An implant is inserted under normal tissue to augment the breast.

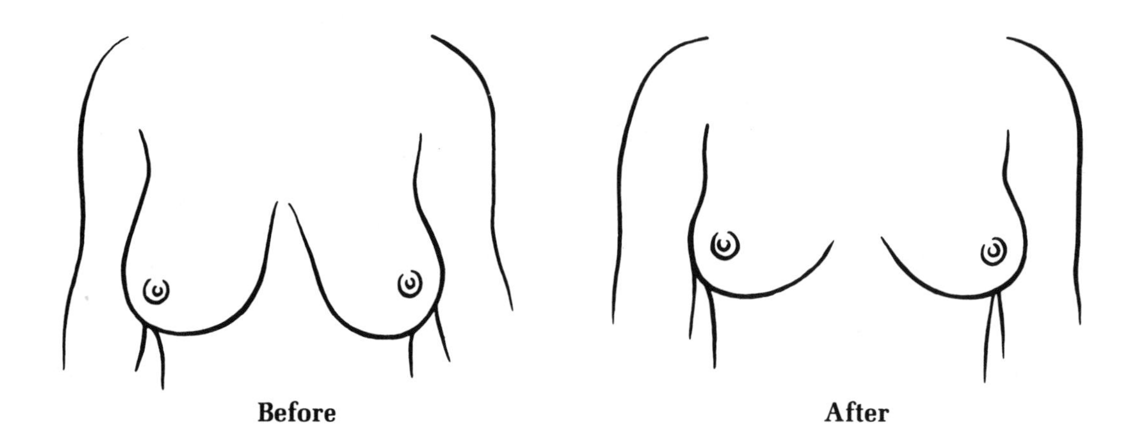

Figure 5.7 Breast-reduction Surgery
Excess tissue is removed through incisions in the fold under the breasts, giving them a firmer, higher contour.

THE ABDOMEN

Abdominal plastic surgery, often referred to as a "tummy tuck," is intended to correct the sagging that occurs most often in older women who have had several children. Weight loss and exercises to strengthen abdominal muscles may be just as effective as the surgery, and much safer. Although the term "tummy tuck" may sound benign or even frivolous, this is a serious operation with a relatively high risk of complications.

In a typical operation the surgeon makes an incision through a fold, usually above the pubic area, removes excess fat and skin, and sutures back the skin flap. The procedure is done under general anesthesia and requires two weeks in the hospital, followed by another two to three weeks of convalescence in which a limited amount of activity is possible. During the initial recovery period, the patient will usually feel discomfort when sitting or walking. Support hose and an abdominal girdle must be worn for several months to support the tissue and prevent phlebitis. Possible complications include infection, bleeding, and circulatory problems. The enforced bed rest also carries a risk of thrombophlebitis.

HAIR

As we age, differences in hair distribution become apparent between the sexes. Women may grow more body and facial hair while men may become bald.

As women go through menopause, estrogen production by the ovaries declines, while male hormone production persists. As a consequence, women develop increased body and facial hair. Shaving, tweezing, bleaching, and depilatory creams will temporarily remove or lighten hair. Because they can irritate sensitive skin, bleaching or depilatory preparations should be tested on a small sample of skin before each application. Another method is hair waxing, a relatively long-lasting process that strips both surface hair and part of the shaft below the skin.

The only permanent way to remove hair is by electrolysis. This expensive, painful process destroys the hair root through the use of a weak electric current. Because this method is not without risk of infection, it should be done only by a licensed operator.

TREATMENTS FOR BALDNESS

Although some men make it into their later years with a full head of hair, the majority will experience at least some balding by the time they reach 60. Aging, heredity, and a not completely understood interaction between the androgen hormones and

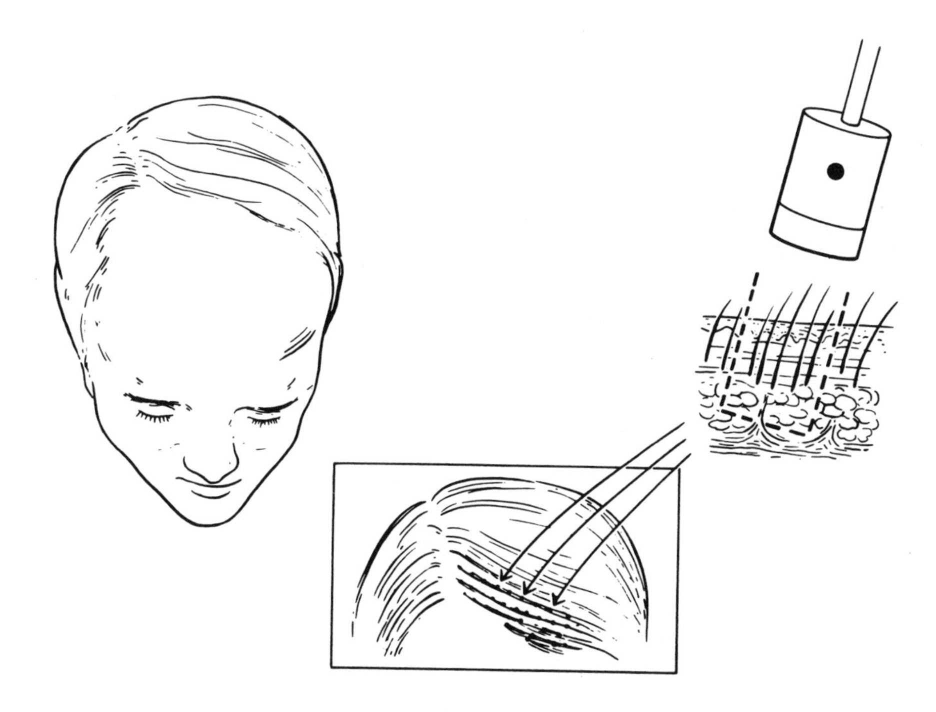

Figure 5.8 Hair Transplants
At upper right is an enlargement of the plug used to move a small portion of the skin and follicles from one part of the scalp to the balding area, such as the forehead shown at center.

hair follicles are responsible. Artificial hairpieces or hair weaving can hide a balding head, but the only permanent way to restore hair is to transplant it. In this form of cosmetic surgery, small plugs of flesh containing hair and hair follicles are transplanted, using local anesthesia, from a hairy portion to a bald section of the scalp (see Figure 5.8). From 10 to 60 plugs are done per session, with the entire procedure taking two to three months.

Although the transplanted hairs usually fall out, new ones begin to grow in the transplanted follicles after about three months. Hair transplantation can be uncomfortable at best, but complications or rejection of the plugs is rare when done by a skilled physician.

The treatment for baldness that has received the most attention is the topical application of the drug minoxidil, used to treat high blood pressure when given orally. When applied to the scalp, this prescription medication causes the fuzz on a bald head to thicken and darken. In about a third of the men, new hair growth appears. However, treatment with minoxidil shows little benefit for men over age 50, and it does not *cure* baldness in anyone. Once the applications are stopped, the fuzz returns to its former appearance and any new hair falls out.

THE EYE OF THE BEHOLDER

As we mentioned at the beginning of this chapter, physical attractiveness is largely a matter of personal style and outlook. Some people proudly proclaim that they've earned their wrinkles and have never had a face-lift. Others, on the other hand, talk openly about the psychological boost they got from cosmetic surgery. A good lesson in how to apply makeup may be just as effective as a face-lift or eye job—and a lot less costly and risky. Even the most wrinkled face is beautiful to an adoring grandchild, loving spouse, or people who admire qualities that are more than only skin-deep.

Part II

Emotional Well-Being and Relationships

6

Mid-life Crisis: Men

A man's realization that he is growing older usually hits hardest just as he enters his forties, and it can lead to major shifts in attitudes and emotional upheaval—in short, to the so-called mid-life crisis.

During middle age many men go through what is often described as a second adolescence, or "middlescence." Like adolescence, this mid-life transitional period is characterized as a time of risk taking and appraisal (or reappraisal) of life's situation and direction.

Although often touted as a negative time of restlessness and irrational change, the mid-life transition can be a positive opportunity from which one can achieve a greater sense of satisfaction and self-awareness. It is also a time when a man's personality may take a major developmental step forward. For example, many men find they become more self-confident and less intolerant of shortcomings in others. Ultimately, the type of mid-life experience a man has is totally dependent on his ability to determine his goals and to adapt to change. Basically, it can be whatever you expect it to be.

THREATS FROM WITHOUT AND WITHIN

As a man approaches middle age, changes become more frequent and perhaps more frightening. These changes may be physical, such as the graying or thinning of hair or the need to wear eyeglasses; or they may be external and socially demonstrated, as in increased competition with younger people. If a man has measured his masculinity by the traditional yardsticks of sexual performance, acquisition of money, and success on the job, he may be more susceptible to a negative mid-life experience and likely to perceive these changes as a threat.

A balding man may worry about his physical attractiveness and his sexual capacity—even though baldness has nothing to do with either of these things. As a result, he may pursue younger women in the hope of rebuilding his ego through sexual conquest. Infidelity during the mid-life transition often is based on this attempt to prove attractiveness and strength.

The man who feels increased competition on the job from younger associates moving up may start to doubt his own capacity to be useful. New ideas may become threatening to him, and the office may become a source of anxiety. To soothe this tension and enable him to face the competition, he may turn to alcohol or drugs.

Actually, prolonged use of alcohol and drugs diminishes a man's capacity to be successful and useful on the job, and his fears become a self-fulfilling prophecy. His decreased performance may lead to demotion or unemployment. However, these two painful and negative scenarios can be avoided by a positive attitude toward the changes encountered in mid-life. Concentrating on the positive aspects of growing older can lead to acceptance and even enjoyment of the changes a man experiences.

For example, there is no evidence that intelligence diminishes as one grows older. In fact, years of experience increase one's capacity to bring together stored knowledge and provide valuable advice to less experienced colleagues. Instead of fearing new ideas, a man in middle age can use what he has learned through the years to judge the viability of his juniors' suggestions. He is actually at the peak of his usefulness within the company. In his role as adviser, he can take pleasure in his unique ability to guide younger employees toward innovative ideas that can work.

One's flexibility is the key in dealing with the mid-life transition effectively. Those who are rigidly set in their ways become defeated by an ever-changing world that won't stand still for them. Unless a man actively adapts to his new roles and new abilities, he will become antiquated and less useful. Again, an unfounded fear can become a self-fulfilling prophecy.

THE ROAD NOT TAKEN

The mid-life transition is also a time of reassessment of life's achievements and directions. A man may begin to dwell on "what might have been" and vow to change his life-style in his remaining time. He may seek a totally new and different lover or profession, or even start a family in order to explore the possibilities he opted against earlier in life.

However, starting a new family or career later in life may present some problems. Young children demand a great deal of time, energy, and patience, and a man in his fifties may not have adequate supplies of any of these. Stepchildren may also present a whole new set of problems, stemming either from the new family situation or from the children's own personalities. Gaining acceptance from a reluctant stepchild is difficult at any time, but later in life it can be more trying.

This is not to say that there are no valid reasons for divorce in middle age or that a man (or woman) should accept the status quo of a bad marriage. But very often people are too willing to give up a troubled relationship before attempting to make the changes that might make their present situation more rewarding.

Flexibility and adaptability are also necessary in order to start a new job. Of course, these qualities are needed in order to be successful anytime we switch jobs, but it may be more difficult for the older person to put them into practice without some extra effort. Although it is certainly unhealthy to remain in an unsatisfying or unpleasant job just for the sake of avoiding change, it may be easier for a man to restructure his job within his present company or to take a comparable position in another similar company rather than start over again.

At a time of personal reevaluation, a man has the unique opportunity to confront the contradictions in himself and therefore come to know himself more clearly. Daniel J. Levinson in his book *The Seasons of a Man's Life* summarizes these attitudinal contradictions as young versus old, destruction versus creation, masculine versus feminine, and attachment versus separateness. Throughout life these opposite qualities and capacities within each human are encountered, but during the explorative mid-life transition, Levinson says, a man is afforded a special chance to come closer to integrating and resolving them within himself. As a result, a man may emerge from the mid-life crisis as a more sensitive, loving partner and a wiser, more cooperative colleague—more willing to reveal and explore both sides of his nature.

EMPTY NEST SYNDROME

Although depression after the children leave home is more often associated with women than men, empty nest syndrome does affect fathers. Suddenly without the diversion of children and their activities, the husband and wife must deal directly with each other. This mutual rediscovery may be negative, but it is most often experienced as the positive reawakening of a time-tested and valued friendship.

SINGLE IN MIDDLE AGE

Owing to divorce or death of a spouse, many men may find themselves again living the single life in middle age. Maintaining friendships with married people may be difficult, particularly after one's divorce. A single friend among a group of couples may make hosts feel uncomfortable, as if they must provide a date for him. During and after a divorce, friends of the couple may not want to appear to be "taking sides" by inviting the husband and not the wife, or vice versa. Therefore, the newly single man may have to make a special effort to stay in touch, even though he may feel that others should be reaching out to him.

The single man must embark on a new search for identity, make new friends, and sometimes restructure old friendships to meet his needs as a single individual. Friendship skills that may have had little use during married life must be rediscovered. Dating, romance, companionship, and sex all become issues again. Seeking out people in similar situations (for instance, in church or synagogue groups for single people, or in organizations such as Parents Without Partners) may provide a supportive network of friends.

PHYSICAL CHANGES

Middle age is a time when many men become preoccupied with their health, fearing that every twinge or symptom means an impending heart attack, cancer, or some other dreaded disease. Others take an opposite tack, ignoring serious warning signs and pretending that nothing can possibly strike them down.

Obviously, the best approach lies in between—careful attention to commonsense preventive measures and a life-style that promotes good health without making it a major preoccupation. Keeping your weight under control; eating a prudent, low-fat diet; learning how to cope with stress; staying physically active but knowing your limits—these are but a few of the positive health measures that we all can and should adopt.

In the past, men were urged to have a complete physical every year. This is no longer considered necessary, but all men should undergo certain tests periodically.

MEDICAL TESTS FOR MEN

All men over 40 should have the following medical tests periodically, as recommended by the U.S. Preventive Services Task Force, an independent panel formed by the U.S. Department of Health and Human Services. The list is not all-inclusive; other tests may be required under special circumstances or as dictated by symptoms. Also, ages and intervals are not absolute.

Physical Examinations

- *Blood pressure.* Check blood pressure every year or two. Controlling hypertension prevents complications such as heart and kidney failure.
- *Weight.* Obesity is a risk factor for many problems, including hypertension and diabetes.
- *Height.* Needed to correlate with weight.

- *Skin exam.* Every one to three years, to look for skin cancer, including melanoma.
- *Neck exam.* Needed for two reasons:

  1. Men over 60 should be examined every one to three years, for noises (bruits) sometimes heard over carotid arteries on the side of the neck. Noises many signify arteriosclerotic narrowing of the vessel, impeding blood supply to brain.
  2. Middle-aged and older people should be examined every one to three years (more frequently if history of radiation to neck or face in childhood), to detect thyroid nodules that may require further testing for thyroid cancer.

- *Heart exam.* Every one to three years, to detect murmurs that may require use of antibiotics before certain surgical procedures to prevent endocarditis (infection of a heart valve).
- *Abdominal exam.* Every one to three years, for men over 20, to detect evidence of liver or spleen enlargement. Also every one to three years for men over 60, to check for aortic aneurysm.
- *Lymph node exam.* Every one to three years, to check neck, underarms, and groin for signs of early lymphoma and other disorders.
- *Groin exam.* Men should be examined every one to three years, to detect inguinal hernia.
- *Testicular exam.* Every one to three years, to detect testicular tumors in men 20 to 35. Men should learn how to examine themselves.
- *Prostate exam.* Annually in men over 55, to detect nodules that may require further testing for prostate cancer.

Laboratory Tests

- *Complete blood count and peripheral blood smear.* Every one to three years, to test for anemia, white-blood-cell disorders such as leukemia, and platelet count.
- *Urinalysis.* Every one to three years, to examine urine and urinary sediment for the presence of glucose, protein, blood cells, bacteria, and crystals.
- *Chemical profile.* Every one to three years, automated analysis of 8 to 22 blood chemistries, including (in rough order of importance):

  Glucose. An abnormally high value may indicate diabetes.

  Total cholesterol. Coronary disease risk factor.

  HDL cholesterol. The "good" kind.

LDL cholesterol. The "bad" kind.

Triglycerides. A blood fat. Used in the calculation of LDL cholesterol.

Blood urea nitrogen/creatinine. May indicate impaired kidney function.

Liver function tests (AST, ALT, LDH, GGTP, ALP, bilirubin). To detect impaired liver function.

Uric acid. May indicate gout.

Thyroxine. May indicate thyroid problem.

Calcium. May indicate parathyroid problem.

Diagnostic Procedures

- *Tonometry.* To detect glaucoma, a leading cause of blindness. Testing should be done every three years after the age of 45 (earlier and more frequently for diabetics). Visual acuity should also be tested every three years after the age of 45.
- *Electrocardiogram.* To detect coronary heart disease in people with risk factors; frequency depends on clinical indications. Virtually useless in healthy people without risk factors, but a baseline should be done in the mid-thirties.
- *Stool test for occult blood.* To detect hidden blood in stool, which may indicate polyp or cancer. Every year after 40.
- *Flexible sigmoidoscopy.* To detect colorectal cancer by viewing the lower 12 to 24 inches of the bowel. Exam should be done after age of 50 every three to five years after two negative exams one year apart.

PROSTATIC DISORDERS

During their fifties, most men for the first time become aware of their prostate gland. This is the time when this small gland is most likely to start causing problems.

Surrounding the male urethra (the 8- to 10-inch-long tube through which urine and ejaculate pass on their way out of the body), the prostate gland starts to grow during puberty in response to the release of the male hormone testosterone. In a healthy adult, the gland is about the size of a walnut.

The function of the prostate gland is limited but important. As the ejaculate passes from the seminal vesicle to the urethra in preparation for orgasm, the prostate gland secretes the enzyme-containing portion (about one-third) of the seminal fluid that activates the sperm. Although the prostatic fluid is not necessary for sexual performance, the lack of it causes infertility.

In most men, the prostate gland goes through another growth spurt around age 50. Indeed, the gland shows some signs of enlargement in most men by age 45; by age 65, virtually all men are affected to some degree (see Figure 6.1). The growth in most cases is benign and, depending on the location of the enlargement, causes few if only minor symptoms and requires no special treatment.

Researchers are not certain what causes the prostate gland to enlarge as a man grows older. A hormonal imbalance may be the cause, or it may just be a normal part of the aging process. The prostate may double in size without causing severe symptoms in some men, while in others even a small enlargement in the wrong place may cause symptoms distressing enough to warrant surgery. If urinary flow is obstructed by the enlarged prostate, surgery becomes necessary.

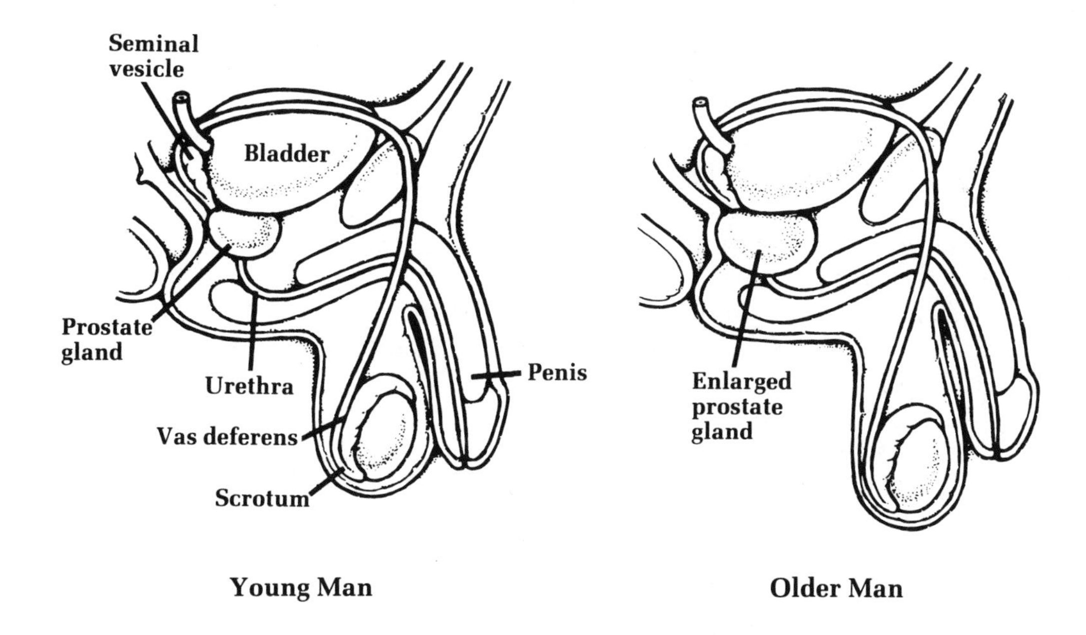

Figure 6.1 Enlarged Prostate
The drawing at left shows a normal-size prostate gland in a young man; at right, the enlargement that typically occurs after age 50.

Symptoms. The prostate gland's location is at the root of the problem. When enlarged, the gland can press on the urethra, leading to difficulty with urination. The blockage of the urethra may cause a small amount of urine to become trapped in the bladder, leading to bladder or kidney infections. Sleep may be disturbed by the frequent need to urinate (*nocturia*).

Difficulty in starting the urinary stream or in emptying the bladder completely and painful urination can be caused by an enlarged prostate gland or infection. They may also be precipitated by certain drugs, especially antihistamines and decongestants. Cold remedies, and allergy medications, should be used with caution by older men.

Treatment. Currently, the usual treatment for prostatic enlargement is surgical removal of a portion of the gland (prostatectomy). The most common procedure for treating a benign prostatic growth is known as transurethral resection of the prostate, or TURP. About 400,000 of these surgeries are performed each year in the United States. A fiber-optic instrument called a resectoscope is inserted through the urethra into the urinary bladder. The surgeon uses the electrified loop at the end of the instrument to shave away the excess prostate tissue, thus removing the obstruction to urinary flow. A catheter that facilitates the flow of urine from the bladder is left in place for three to five days. Within five to seven days the patient can return home. With recent advances in anesthetic techniques, this operation is relatively safe even for men in their nineties.

However, there is always some risk involved with general anesthesia, and it is important to note that unless the symptoms are seriously affecting the quality of the man's life, surgery may not be the answer. If increased bladder and kidney infections and frequent urination are the only symptoms, then treatment of those symptoms with antibiotics or sulfa drugs may be sufficient.

In a Veterans Administration (VA) study of men age 55 to 64 who underwent prostatectomy, many had serious difficulties such as impotence and continued urinary problems following surgery, and half of the men obtained no relief at all from the procedure. Cases are also known in which the operation has had to be repeated.

In patients with complete urinary obstruction, however, no alternative to surgery exists as yet. Usually a partial prostatectomy will return normal urinary function without adversely affecting sexual potency and orgasm. In many cases (about 50 percent), however, the semen is passed to the bladder rather than through the penis, rendering the man infertile. The impotence that may follow a partial prostatectomy is often temporary; it may be due to postoperative swelling or to psychological factors.

Drug therapy for an enlarged prostate is another frequently used treatment. The drug finasteride (Proscar) blocks the conversion of testosterone into dihydrotestosterone, which regulates the gland's growth. In half of the 1,600 patients treated in clinical trials, the prostate shrank by 20 percent, and the drug had few side effects. Another drug, terazosin (Hytrin), is an alpha-adrenergic blocker currently used in the treatment of hypertension that also relaxes the smooth muscle in the prostate. In studies its effect has helped improve urinary flow and unpleasant symptoms. Side effects are minimal—light-headedness and dizziness. Hytrin is awaiting approval by the Food and Drug Administration (FDA) for this use. Finasteride (Proscar) has been approved by the FDA. The downside to this therapy is that these drugs must be taken daily for life to stave off symptoms permanently. Also, surgery will most likely continue to be necessary for men who have severe symptoms, such as repeated urinary tract infections. Such men constitute about 20 to 30 percent of the affected group.

Cancer. Another possible indication for surgery is a suspicious nodule on the prostate that is discovered during a rectal examination, regardless of the presence of other symptoms of prostatic enlargement. The nodule should be biopsied for cancerous cells. In addition to a rectal exam, screening by ultrasound offers good results in the detection of prostatic lesions 2 millimeters in size. The severity of the cancer is dependent on the type and malignancy of the cells.

Experiments with laser surgery offer new hope for more precision and effectiveness. By using the laser (a concentrated beam of light)—in effect, to vaporize a portion of the prostate without surgically removing it—relief can be provided with no danger of postsurgery bleeding problems. Although the procedure is too new for adequate follow-up statistics, laser surgery may improve results of prostatectomy.

In the past, almost all men who have undergone the standard procedure for radical prostatectomy have become impotent as a result. The reason is that the nerves that trigger erection and ejaculation are located along the back of the prostate gland. Although the gland itself is not necessary for sexual functioning, these nerves, which are often damaged or severed during the operation, are crucial. Another 5 to 15 percent of such cancer patients also have experienced postoperative urinary incontinence.

However, a technique developed at Johns Hopkins University offers a cure without such a high risk of impotence. The modified surgery avoids the essential nerves, leaving them intact. Preliminary results showed that 70 percent of men undergoing this procedure retain potency—a vast improvement over the standard operation.

Radiation or hormonal therapy is an alternative treatment for prostatic cancer. Fifty to 60 percent of men undergoing radiation treatments remain sexually functional. A final treatment option is chemotherapy, which can have considerable side effects, including damage to the heart muscle.

Early detection and treatment of prostate cancer is important, especially now that a treatment with fewer side effects has been developed. Almost three-quarters of prostatic cancers go undetected until they are in an advanced stage in which curing them is more difficult. The most tested and effective method of detection is the annual rectal examination that is recommended for all men over the age of 45. Normally, the prostate gland is smooth and soft. A hard, irregular gland with a nodular surface may indicate prostatic cancer; in such cases, a biopsy of the gland should be performed. Rectal ultrasonography has become a useful tool for localizing an area suspicious for prostate cancer.

A blood test that detects an antigen to prostate cancer appears to be more precise for early screening than either rectal examination or ultrasound. Patients find it preferable as well. Prostate-specific antigen (PSA) may be elevated in men who have an enlarged prostate and in many men with prostate cancer. Until recently it had been used only to check the progression of the cancer and response to treatment. In a study group of 1,653 men, 37 were found to have prostate cancer, and a high PSA level was the only suspicious result that led to early detection for 5 of them. The blood test is not infallible; it may fail to detect some cancer or cast false suspicion in some healthy cases. The test is also not reliable when a patient is taking finasteride (Proscar). The combination of these diagnostic tools provides a better chance for proper and early detection.

THE SPECIAL PROBLEM OF IMPOTENCE

Impotence affects about 10 million American males. Until recently many physicians thought that 90 percent of these cases were due to psychological causes. However, sleep studies of spontaneous erections in most men now lead researchers to believe that 50 to 60 percent of impotence has a physical cause.

Most men have experienced short periods when they cannot achieve an erection, and they are perhaps related to work or family problems. But true impotence is the persistent inability to have an erection. A man whose impotence stems from emotional factors will still have erections during periods of REM sleep, the portion of sleep characterized by dreaming and rapid eye movement (REM). Lack of erections during REM sleep strongly suggests a physical basis. Resolution of the problem may be as simple as changing a blood pressure medication that causes impotence as a side effect.

FINDING THE CAUSE

Comprehensive testing at a sleep laboratory is desirable in order to establish whether impotence falls into the psychological or physical category. But for those who cannot afford this or who live far from such a facility, there are several simple ways a couple can check for nightly erections at home. One is for the woman simply to stay awake and observe her sleeping partner. A second is to paste a strip of stamps around the flaccid penis at bedtime. If the strip is torn in the morning, erection has probably occurred. This test should be repeated several times for maximum reliability.

If erections occur, the couple should seek counseling from a sex therapist affiliated with a local university or teaching hospital, or from a qualified psychotherapist with experience in sex counseling. If there are no erections, see your physician or urologist.

Once a physical cause is suspected, the physician will try to pinpoint it by doing a complete history and physical exam, including blood tests for hormone levels, measurements of blood flow to the penis, and nerve conduction studies as necessary.

PRESCRIPTION DRUGS THAT MAY CAUSE IMPOTENCE OR OTHER SEXUAL DYSFUNCTION

Here is a list of some of the more common medications that may cause sexual dysfunction. Not everyone on a particular medication will have the same side effects. Report impotence or any other problem to your doctor, but do not stop taking any drug on your own.

Antihypertensives

Alpha-Adrenergic Blockers
doxazosin (Cardura)
prazosin (Minipres)
terazosin (Hytrin)

Angiotensin-Converting Enzyme (ACE) Inhibitors
lisinopril (Zestril)

Beta-Adrenergic Blockers
metoprolol (Lopressor)
propranolol (Inderal)

Combined Alpha- and Beta-Adrenergic Blockers
labetalol (Normodyne, Trandate)

Centrally Acting
clonidine (Catapres)
methyldopa (Aldomet)
reserpine (Serpasil, Raudixin, Ser-Ap-Es)

Diuretics
spironolactone (Aldactone)
thiazide drugs (Diuril, HydroDIURIL, and others)

Sympathetic Nerve Blockers
guanethidine (Ismelin)

Antiulcer Medications

cimetidine (Tagamet)

Cholesterol-Lowering Medications

clofibrate (Atromid-S)

Psychiatric Medications

Antidepressants
amitriptyline (Elavil)
amoxapine (Ascendin)
desipramine (Norpramin)
doxepin (Sinequan)
isocarboxazid (Marplan)
maprotriline (Ludiomil)
nortriptyline (Aventyl, Pamelor)
phenelzine (Nardil)
protriptyline (Vivactil)
tranylcypromine (Parnate)
trazodone (Desyrel)

Antimania Medications
lithium carbonate (Eskalith, Lithobid)

Antipsychotic Medications
chlorpromazine (Thorazine)
chlorprothixene (Taractan)
fluoxetine (Prozac)
fluphenazine (Prolixin)
haloperidol (Haldol)
mesoridazine (Serentil)
perphenazine (Trilafon)
thioridazine (Mellaril)
thiothixene (Navane)
trifluoperazine (Stelazine)

Stimulants
amphetamine sulfate (Benzedrine)
dextroamphetamine sulfate (Dexedrine)

Tranquilizers
chlordiazepoxide (Librium)
diazepam (Valium)

POSSIBLE CAUSES OF IMPOTENCE

- *Circulatory disorders.* Blocked blood vessels or other conditions that decrease blood flow to the penis.
- *Congenital or other structural defects of the penis.* In Peyronie's disease, scar tissue builds up near the corpora cavernosa, causing contorted erections that make intercourse difficult or impossible.
- *Diabetes.* As many as half of all diabetic men are impotent. The disease's scar tissue builds up near the corpora cavernosa, causing contorted erections that make intercourse difficult or impossible.
- *Hormonal causes.* Disorders of the hypothalamus, pituitary, or thyroid gland, resulting in decreased sex hormones or increased prolactin, a hormone that is normally found in low levels in men but can stimulate the production of breast milk if the level increases.
- *Illnesses.* Impotence can occur simply because one does not feel well due to influenza or any other illness that causes fever, body aches, and other aggravating symptoms.
- *Neurological disorders.* Injuries or diseases affecting the spinal cord, such as multiple sclerosis and syphilis.
- *Substance abuse.* Cocaine and even moderate use of alcohol may cause temporary impotence. Alcoholism causes damage to the liver, which metabolizes sex hormones. Narcotics can cause nerve damage.
- *Surgery.* Repair of aneurysms in the abdominal aorta and extensive surgery on the bladder, colon, or prostate gland can sever nerves involved in erection. However, new techniques using laser beams in prostate surgery reduce the risk of impotence.
- *Toxic chemicals.* Ingredients used in pesticide production and other toxic substances can cause impotence.

FORMS OF TREATMENT

Treatment of impotence may be as simple as changing the type, dose, or time that a medication is given to avoid such a side effect. Endocrine-related impotence may be treated with hormone supplements. Drug or alcohol detoxification may help substance-dependent men, provided liver or nerve damage is not widespread. Surgery to unblock blood vessels and increase blood flow to the penis has become quite successful in recent years, with the best results occurring in men with well-defined blockages in medium or large arteries. Although surgery is successful in about a third of all cases, about half of these are temporary; in those cases, impotence returns within a year. Also, some of these men—up to a third—experience *priapism* (persistent painful erections).

For those with nerve damage due to diabetes, spinal cord injury, or other irreversible cause, penile prostheses offer a way for men to resume sexual intercourse. These are inserted into the corpora cavernosa under local anesthesia to simulate natural erections. The simplest of four types available consists of a pair of semirigid silicone rods that keep the penis constantly erect. Close-fitting underwear can be worn to push the penis against the lower abdomen or thigh, thus avoiding an embarrassing bulge.

Another type of prosthesis consists of a flexible metal wire sheathed in plastic or rubber. As with the first type, the penis will be constantly erect but will bend up or down to be concealed. Other malleable-type devices have internal cables that allow the penis to go flaccid when necessary. Another type involves a hinge that, when locked into place converts the penis from flaccid to rigid.

Finally, the most complicated prosthesis uses a miniature hydraulic pump and small inflatable tubes to simulate erections. The surgeon inserts the tubes into the corpora cavernosa, places a small water-filled reservoir behind muscles in the lower abdomen, and implants a pump into the scrotum. By alternately squeezing the scrotum or activating a release valve, the tubes fill up with water, causing an erection, or empty back into the reservoir, leaving the penis flaccid. More recently introduced inflatable prostheses are self-contained and are stimulated by manipulation of a valve in the tip of the penis. Your doctor will discuss the specific advantages and drawbacks of each type of penile prosthesis with you.

Cost of the implants, hospitalization, and surgeon's fees can be as high as $10,000 to $12,000. If organic impotence is documented, the costs may be covered under your medical insurance plan. Be sure you and your partner have explored all types of treatment before choosing this expensive surgery (see Appendix A for sources of help).

7

Mid-life Crisis: Women

Just as different cultures help define an age-related crisis or transition, so do different times. Financial need, the women's movement (which influenced more women to join the work force), the tendency to postpone childbearing until a later age, and advances in medicine and awareness of preventive measures all are changing our definition of what is popularly called the "mid-life crisis." Still, for today's woman, the forties and fifties represent decades that may produce significant stress. The departure of children and the onset of menopause remain major turning points that must be recognized and dealt with in a woman's life.

Mid-life crisis may be defined as the reaction both to increasing physical signs of aging and to major life events, such as a reduction in income due to retirement, a divorce, or the death of a longtime partner. For the woman whose identity and major preoccupation have been tied to the mothering role, the so-called empty nest may bring on both loneliness and a sense of loss of purpose in life. Furthermore, the loss of the reproductive function at menopause may trigger both psychological and physical stresses.

But there is a plus side. Mid-life brings the freedom to pursue interests that were subordinated to the parental role and the cost of raising a family. While it may be painful to see children leave home to establish their own lives, most women at this time also experience a deep sense of accomplishment and pride at having launched their children successfully into adulthood. This sense of accomplishment should be a valuable source of self-esteem that can be transferred to other pursuits. The departure of children may also provide an opportunity to renew a relationship with one's spouse or to end an unhappy marriage that was endured only "for the sake of the children."

Rather than being viewed as the beginning of the end, this period in a woman's life can and should be perceived as a new beginning—it is all a matter of attitude. With age, people tend to see the positive side of negative events as well as the negative side of positive ones. But this viewpoint is one that does not necessarily come naturally; it must be actively cultivated.

Being open to new experiences, rather than giving in to rigid behavior and attitudes, can help retain intellectual vitality and can expand one's horizons in exciting ways. More than ever, commonsense health practices should be a part of daily routines; in large measure, health maintenance during these middle years will determine whether or not a person enjoys a healthy, vital old age or joins the ranks of the frail elderly. And there are other benefits. Maintaining appropriate weight through good nutrition and regular exercise can forestall certain health problems and maximize physical attractiveness. Practicing sound preventive medicine, which includes periodic medical checkups and tests, should also be a priority.

MEDICAL TESTS FOR WOMEN

All women over 40 should have the following medical tests on a periodic basis, as recommended by the U.S. Preventive Services Task Force, an independent panel formed by the U.S. Department of Health and Human Services. The list is not all-inclusive; other tests may be required under special circumstances or as dictated by symptoms. Also, ages and intervals are not absolute.

Physical examinations

- *Blood pressure.* Check blood pressure every year or two. Controlling hypertension prevents complications such as heart and kidney failure.
- *Weight.* Obesity is a risk factor for many problems, including hypertension and diabetes.
- *Height.* Needed to correlate with weight. May be useful in assessing progression of osteoporosis in postmenopausal women.
- *Skin exam.* Every one to three years, to look for skin cancer, including melanoma.
- *Neck exam.* Needed for two reasons:

1. Women over 60 should be examined every one to three years, for noises (bruits) sometimes heard over carotid arteries on the side of the neck.

Noises many signify arteriosclerotic narrowing of the vessel, impeding blood supply to brain.

2. Middle-aged and older people should be examined every one to three years (more frequently if history of radiation to neck or face in childhood), to detect thyroid nodules that may require further testing for thyroid cancer.

- *Breast exam.* Annually, to detect lumps. Important especially in women 40 to 65, when incidence of breast cancer is highest. However, majority of breast tumors are found by self-exam, not by professional exam. All women should learn how to examine themselves.
- *Heart exam.* Every one to three years, to detect murmurs that may require use of antibiotics before certain surgical procedures to prevent endocarditis (infection of heart valve).
- *Abdominal exam.* Every one to three years, for women over 20, to detect evidence of liver or spleen enlargement.
- *Lymph node exam.* Every one to three years, to check neck, underarms, and groin for signs of early lymphoma and other disorders.

Laboratory Tests

- *Complete blood count and peripheral blood smear.* Every one to three years, to test for anemia, white-blood-cell disorders such as leukemia, and platelet count.
- *Urinalysis.* Every one to three years, to examine urine and urinary sediment for the presence of glucose, protein, blood cells, bacteria, and crystals.
- *Chemical profile.* Every one to three years, automated analysis of 8 to 22 blood chemistries, including (in rough order of importance):

Glucose. An abnormally high value may indicate diabetes.

Total cholesterol. Coronary disease risk factor.

HDL cholesterol. The "good" kind.

LDL cholesterol. The "bad" kind.

Triglycerides. A blood fat. Used in the calculation of LDL cholesterol.

Blood urea nitrogen/creatinine. May indicate impaired kidney function.

Liver function tests (AST, ALT, LDH, GGTP, ALP, bilirubin). To detect impaired liver function.

Uric acid. May indicate gout.

Thyroxine. May indicate thyroid problem.

Calcium. May indicate parathyroid problem.

Diagnostic Procedures

- *Tonometry.* To detect glaucoma, a leading cause of blindness. Testing should be done every three years after the age of 45 (earlier and more frequently for diabetics). Visual acuity should also be tested every three years after the age of 45.
- *Mammography.* Saves lives. Follow American Cancer Society guidelines for mammography: women ages 35 to 39, one baseline for future comparison; ages 40 to 49, every 1 to 2 years; age 50 and over, annually.
- *Electrocardiogram.* To detect coronary heart disease in people with risk factors; frequency depends on clinical indications. Virtually useless in healthy people without risk factors, but a baseline should be done in the mid-thirties.
- *Stool test for occult blood.* To detect hidden blood in stool, which may indicate polyp or cancer. Every year after 40.
- *Flexible sigmoidoscopy.* To detect colorectal cancer by viewing the lower 12 to 24 inches of the bowel. Exam should be done after age of 50 every three to five years after two negative exams one year apart.
- *Pap smear.* To detect cervical cancer. Should be done annually in all sexually active women.

MENOPAUSE

Traditionally, menopause has been looked upon not only as the end of a woman's reproductive years but also as an end to her sexual attractiveness—and the beginning of old age. But today American women enter menopause at a later age—the average is about 52 years—and live longer than their counterparts at the turn of the century, when the average age of menopause was about 46 and life expectancy was 51 years. Now the average life expectancy for women has been increased to 78 years, so most can expect to live 25 or 30 years, or even longer, following menopause. For a growing number of women, these years—roughly one-third of their life—are even more productive and rewarding than those that came before. Today women in their fifties and sixties are entering public life, forging new careers, going back to school to earn degrees ranging from high school diplomas to Ph.D.s—all after menopause. No longer is menopause the beginning of the end, but instead, for increasing numbers of women, often a new beginning.

THE PHYSICAL SIDE OF MENOPAUSE

Actually, reproductive capacity begins to decline long before a woman has her last menstrual period. Production of estrogen, the hormone controlling ovulation, may start to drop by the late twenties or early thirties. At the same time, the number of egg-containing follicles in the ovaries continues its decline from the nearly half a million present at birth. By the time a woman reaches her fifties, the ovaries cannot produce enough estrogen to stimulate egg maturation and ovulation. Progesterone, the hormone that promotes the shedding of the uterine lining and thus produces the menstrual flow, depends upon ovulation. Thus, when ovulation stops, menstrual periods will taper off and gradually cease. This does not happen overnight; menopause is a process that may take two to five years to complete.

The age of menopause is largely determined by genetic makeup; daughters of women who entered menopause in their forties are likely to follow suit, while those whose mothers menstruated until their mid-fifties are likely to experience a late menopause. However, removal of the ovaries, which is frequently performed as part of a hysterectomy, will result in an abrupt menopause if the woman is still menstruating. In these cases, menopausal symptoms are more severe than those occurring under natural conditions. Heavy smoking, tubal ligation, or removal of the uterus but not the ovaries may also bring on a somewhat earlier menopause.

MENOPAUSAL SYMPTOMS

The vast majority of menopausal American women—at least 75 percent—experience some symptoms that are related to decreased ovarian estrogen production. Some are barely noticeable, but other symptoms may be severe enough to cause one to seek medical attention.

Hot Flashes. Surveys of menopausal women have found that hot flashes, sweats, and chills are among the most common and troubling symptoms. These sensations of intense heat travel up the body from the waist to the neck. The decline in estrogen blood levels is believed to affect the temperature control center in the brain, resulting in a slight elevation of body temperature and dilation or opening of the skin's blood vessels. This causes the sensation of heat and reddening of the skin (the flash). Increased blood flow to the skin causes perspiring, sometimes drenching, which cools the skin by evaporating the moisture, thus lowering the body temperature (the chill). Hot flashes range from mild to severe; they can occur infrequently or, in severe cases, 40 to 50 times a day. They also are usually more intense at night and may even wake a woman from a deep sleep. Although hot flashes can be unnerving, they are harmless and often disappear by themselves within two to three years. Taking replacement estrogen medication suppresses the abnormal activity of the brain's temperature center and eliminates hot flashes. Alcohol, caffeine, hot beverages, and spicy foods provoke hot flashes. Stress and emotional upsets are additional triggers.

Vaginal Dryness. The sharp reduction in estrogen also leads to atrophy or thinning of the vaginal lining, causing it to lose its natural lubrication and distensibility.

Although regular sexual stimulation helps postpone the atrophy, many women will begin to experience pain during intercourse within five to ten years after the onset of menopause. In addition to discomfort, these vaginal changes can also lead to increased irritation and inflammation. Urinary tract infection can occur as well. Good personal hygiene and the use of estrogen in the form of vaginal cream are effective countermeasures. Vaginal atrophy is reversible when estrogen replacement therapy is given.

Urinary Irritations. A similar tissue-thinning process takes place near the opening of the urethra, making the urinary tract more vulnerable to irritation and infection. Estrogen replacement and drinking plenty of liquids help reduce the risk of urinary infection. After menopause, many women also experience increased problems of stress incontinence, the involuntary loss of urine when sneezing, reaching, or exercising. The Kegel exercises that strengthen muscles controlling the flow of urine often can help.

Bone Thinning. Perhaps the most serious consequence of estrogen deficiency is osteoporosis, the thinning of bone. More than 25 percent of women develop osteoporosis within 10 to 15 years after menopause. Currently, about 15 million women have

KEGEL EXERCISES

In the 1950s, Dr. Arnold Kegel, a surgeon at UCLA, devised a series of exercises to strengthen the pubococcygeal (PC) muscles, between the vagina and the anus. This area, known as the pelvic floor, slackens during pregnancy and childbirth. Many women are unaware of their weakened PC muscles until menopause, which brings a thinning of tissue in this area. The Kegel exercises attempt to reverse this condition.

1. As a first step, learn to identify the PC muscles. You can do this by attempting to stop the flow of urine in midstream, or alternatively, by inserting a finger into your vagina and tightening the muscles until you feel your finger being squeezed.
2. Tighten these muscles in a front to back motion, starting first with the muscles that control urination and ending by tightening the anus. Hold for a count of 5 and repeat 15 to 20 times at each session.

These exercises can be performed anywhere at any time. For maximum effect, they should be repeated 50 to 100 times a day.

it to some degree, and each year between 2 and 5 million people seek help for osteoporosis-related problems. As the bones become increasingly thin, even a very minor fall or injury can result in a fracture; sometimes a bone can break even in the absence of trauma. Deaths—some 30,000 each year—typically occur in cases where an older woman breaks a hip, undergoes surgery, and then succumbs to such common complications as pulmonary embolism or pneumonia.

In recent years we have become increasingly aware of osteoporosis as a major health problem (see Figure 7.1). Much of this attention has focused on the role of dietary calcium in the maintenance of bone strength. While adequate dietary calcium throughout life can decrease the number of cases of serious osteoporosis, it will not entirely solve the problem of postmenopausal osteoporosis in women who are at high risk because of other factors. The body requires estrogen for the calcium to be retained in the skeleton. Weight-bearing exercise and vitamin D also are important.

Women who are at high risk of developing osteoporosis should be particularly diligent about preventive measures. Adequate calcium (about 1,000 to 1,500 milligrams

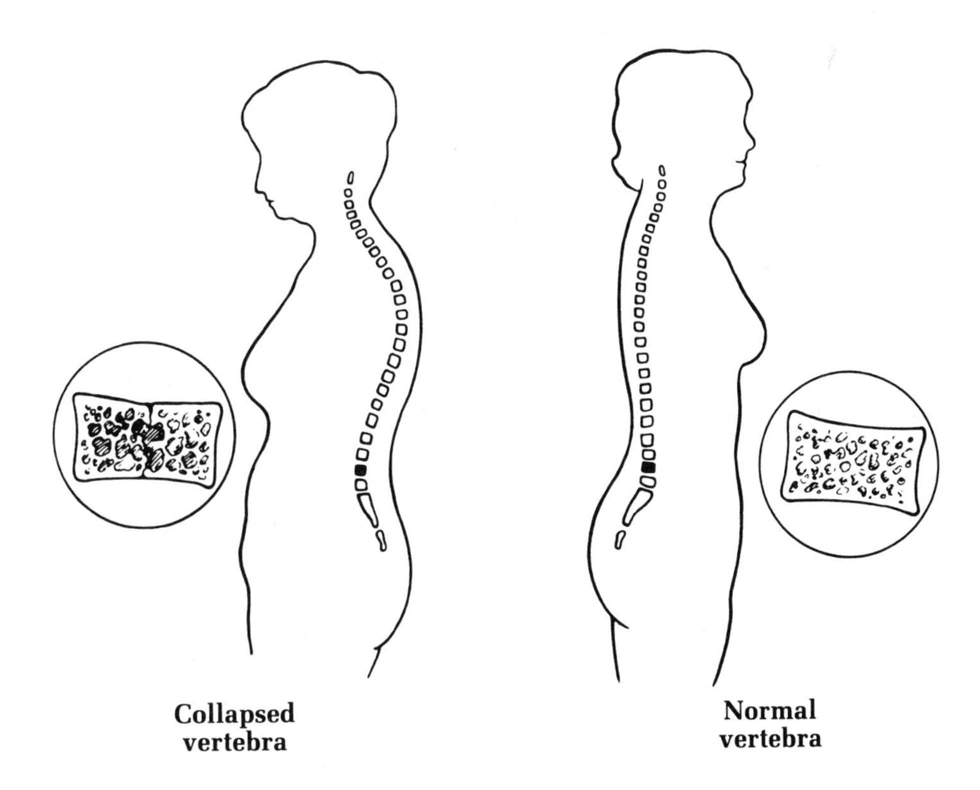

Figure 7.1 Height Loss Due to Osteoporosis
A height loss of 3 to 8 inches is not unusual in advanced osteoporosis.

a day), vitamin D, and exercise all are important in maintaining bone strength. But without estrogen, none of these measures will be effective in preventing and halting the progression of osteoporosis. For maximum benefit, estrogen replacement should be started soon after menopause, although it has been shown to prevent further bone thinning even when started by women in their seventies and eighties. Another treatment for osteoporosis uses an oral compound called etidronate (Didronel), which slows bone reabsorption. However, this treatment is not only less proven but is also an expensive alternative.

Heart Disease. After menopause, women also become more vulnerable to heart disease. In fact, heart disease is the number-one killer of women over 50. Estrogen has a beneficial effect on the heart, presumably by raising HDL cholesterol, which is pro-

FACTORS THAT INCREASE THE RISK OF OSTEOPOROSIS

- *Gender.* Women are more likely than men to develop osteoporosis.
- *Ethnic background.* Caucasians of northern European descent, especially women with light eyes and fair skin, have the highest incidence, as do Japanese and certain other Asians.
- *Physical build.* Women with a small bone structure have less bone mass to start with and are at a higher risk than larger-boned women and men. A slender build also increases risk; fatty tissue converts adrenal hormones into estrogen, so very thin women have lower levels of estrogen.
- *Early menopause.* Women who have an early, abrupt menopause because of a hysterectomy or ovarian failure develop osteoporosis at an earlier age, with more pronounced bone loss than women who undergo a later, natural menopause.
- *Sedentary life-style.* Physical activity and stress on the bones is essential for proper bone metabolism.
- *Cigarette smoking.* Smoking lowers estrogen levels and also hinders calcium metabolism.
- *Heredity.* Women with a family history of osteoporosis are more likely to develop the disease.
- *Calcium deficiency.* Many women, especially those who shun milk, cheese, and other dairy products, may have a chronic calcium deficiency without knowing it. The problem may be compounded among women who have had several children and breast-fed their babies without taking adequate dietary calcium.

tective against the buildup of fatty deposits in the coronary arteries. Estrogen does increase the tendency for blood to clot, so women who already have clotting problems, high blood pressure, or atherosclerosis may be advised not to take it or to compensate by adding low-dose aspirin to suppress the blood platelets and prevent excessive clotting. A doctor should be consulted before self-treatment with aspirin, however, because it can promote bleeding problems.

Weight Gain. Many women notice that they begin to gain weight at about the time of menopause and that the extra pounds seem to be centered around the waist and abdomen—the dreaded middle-aged spread. Metabolism slows down as we grow older, so we do not need as many calories. Increased exercise and a lowered intake of food can help prevent weight gain. But this is not the whole story. Changing hormone levels help redistribute fat: Breasts and buttocks may lose fatty tissue while the abdomen gains fat. This is believed to be a result of lowered estrogen and high levels of androgens, which cause women to acquire the fat padding in the midsection that is common in men. Poor tone of the abdominal muscles also can cause sagging; toning exercises such as leg lifts and partial sit-ups will help prevent this and keep the midsection flat.

Loss of Libido. Sexuality becomes a major concern for many women going through menopause. They worry that, with the loss of their reproductive function, they will no longer be attractive to their sexual partners. Some women experience diminished sexual desire with menopause, but this is by no means universal. Many women, no longer fearing an unwanted pregnancy, find that they are even more sexually responsive. Sexuality is a fragile combination of physical and psychological factors, and something that requires considerable nurturing to keep fresh and alive. If a couple experiences sexual problems and is unable to discuss them, the help of a qualified therapist is the next step.

A word of warning regarding contraception during menopause: Many women assume that once they stop menstruating, they no longer have to worry about birth control. This may be true in many instances, but there are enough unplanned pregnancies among women going through menopause to dispel this notion. Experts recommend that birth control be practiced until periods have stopped completely for a full year and a doctor has verified that the woman is no longer ovulating, even sporadically.

Finding an appropriate means of birth control is often a problem for older women. In general, the pill is not recommended for women over the age of 40, although the progesterone-only pill, or mini-pill, is a safe and acceptable alternative for older women. Because ovulation is erratic, the rhythm or natural family-planning methods are even more unreliable than they are in younger women. Barrier methods—the diaphragm and spermicide for women, condoms for men—are reliable if used properly and consistently, carry no side effects, and in the case of condoms help prevent transmission of the AIDS virus. If a woman experiences pain or irritation during intercourse and the man is wearing a condom, it should be lubricated. Problems arising from sensitivity to latex can be remedied by using the more hypoallergenic condoms made from lamb intestines, but these are a less effective barrier to the AIDS virus.

Heretofore, intrauterine devices (IUDs) have been a favored contraceptive for older women; however, all but two IUDs have been taken off the market in the United States because of lawsuits over complications brought against manufacturers of the devices. One IUD that remains is medicated with small amounts of progesterone, and it must be replaced each year. The other contains copper and may remain in the body for up to seven years. IUDs are still widely available in Canada. Many doctors still think IUDs are suitable for older, monogamous women. They are not recommended for a woman with multiple sex partners or a history of pelvic infections.

And, of course, sterilization is an increasingly popular method of birth control for couples whose families are complete. Many women in their early forties think that there is little point in undergoing sterilization at that age, but considering that they may have 10 or more years of contraception ahead of them, it is still a viable alternative to other methods.

Mood Swings. Not all problems associated with menopause are physical; depression, insomnia, irritability, and other largely psychological disturbances also are common during this time. While many of these problems may be related to all of the other life changes taking place during the late forties and early fifties, they also have organic causes related to shifting hormone levels.

Psychological changes accompanying menopause can be very disturbing, especially since many doctors and spouses tend to dismiss them as trivial or imaginary. Any woman who has regularly experienced symptoms associated with premenstrual syndrome (PMS) knows that they are not "all in her head" and that the mood swings, crying spells, irritability, and other psychological symptoms are related to cyclical hormonal changes. During menopause, hormonal levels also are shifting and can produce many of the same symptoms, only on a more constant basis. The symptoms also may be exacerbated by a woman's attitude toward aging and other circumstances, such as the stress of having children leave home or the prospect of losing a mate. Psychological therapy can help—it can take the form of individual counseling, group therapy, or simply sharing experiences with other women with similar problems. Coming to terms with the physical changes of menopause and developing a positive attitude about the future can go a long way toward easing the psychological stresses and symptoms.

PROS AND CONS OF HORMONE REPLACEMENT THERAPY (HRT)

Doctors still are not in full agreement, but more are recommending lifelong estrogen replacement for most postmenopausal women. Proponents of estrogen replacement note that today's increased life expectancy means that women are living longer in a menopausal and therefore estrogen-deficient state, and that hormone replacement is

SYMPTOMS ASSOCIATED WITH MENOPAUSE

Not all women experience all of the following symptoms, but these are among the more common signs and symptoms related to menopause:

- tapering off and then cessation of menstruation
- hot flashes
- sweats, including night sweats
- depression, mood swings
- insomnia
- feelings of anxiety
- irritability
- palpitations
- generalized itching
- vaginal dryness, itching, increased susceptibility to infection
- thinning of scalp and pubic hair
- increased facial hair
- increased thinning of bones
- weight gain, bloating
- increased brittleness of nails, with grooving and slower growth
- joint pain
- headaches
- rise in LDL cholesterol

vital in preventing osteoporosis and heart disease while relieving the distressing symptoms of menopause. Compelling results from an ongoing study by Harvard University have influenced many physicians. The Nurses' Health Study followed 48,470 post-menopausal women, finding that those who take estrogen and have no history of heart disease have half as many heart attacks and a 50 percent lower cardiovascular-related death rate when compared to women who do not take estrogen.

On the other side are physicians who fear that long-term hormone therapy may increase the risk of cancer or other problems. They point to studies published in the 1970s that report a marked increase in endometrial cancer among women on long-term estrogen therapy. Following these reports, there was a marked swing away from long-term estrogen replacement, which is thought to be a factor in the current increase in osteoporosis among older women. Even the Nurses' Health Study found that women taking estrogen have approximately a 35 percent higher risk of developing breast cancer.

Today the pendulum is swinging back in favor of estrogen replacement. Most doctors point to statistics that prove heart disease to be a much larger threat to over-50 women than breast or endometrial cancer. The choice, however, is a personal and difficult one. Results from much-needed further research, such as a 3-year study and a 14-year clinical trial planned by the National Institutes of Health, should give women a more definitive basis for this decision.

There have been a number of modifications in hormone replacement therapy since the 1950s and 1960s. The dosage of estrogen is now lower than in the early days of hormone therapy, and one current regimen also incorporates progesterone, another female sex hormone. Typically, a woman will take 0.625 milligram of estrogen (e.g., Premarin) for 20 days, then take 5 to 10 milligrams of progesterone (e.g., Provera) for 10 days, and nothing for the next 5 days. This combination of hormones mimics the body's normal levels of estrogen and progesterone. Taking progesterone decreases the therapy's ability to protect against heart disease, but it also lowers the risk of endometrial cancer by preventing a buildup of the uterine lining. Women who have had the uterus removed do not have to take progesterone.

After stopping the progesterone, a woman will have about three days of light bleeding, similar to what happens during menstruation. The bleeding is usually lighter than a regular period, and after a couple of years of hormone therapy, it tapers off and eventually stops. Recent studies indicate that this regimen may actually lower the risk of cancer. What's more, the introduction of the estrogen skin patch eliminates some of the side effects associated with oral estrogen by providing a more constant level in the blood and by bypassing the liver. The patch, marketed under the name Estraderm, contains 0.05 milligram of estrogen. It must be changed twice a week, and if progesterone is part of the regimen, it is taken orally on the same schedule as the oral estrogen.

Depending on the reason for taking hormones, estrogen is administered in the

HORMONE REPLACEMENT THERAPY STATISTICS

- Reduces the risk of heart attack or cardiac death by half. Heart attack is the number-one killer of American women, and cardiovascular disease claims the lives of more than 480,000 women each year.
- Increases chance of breast cancer by 35 percent. The estimated number of deaths in 1992 attributed to breast cancer is 46,000, lower than the number of deaths from heart disease.
- Increases risk of endometrial cancer. The estimated number of deaths in 1992 attributed to endometrial cancer is 5,600.

form of a pill, transdermal (skin) patch, or vaginal cream (which relieves vaginal dryness but does not help protect against osteoporosis or heart disease). Some indications, such as risk for osteoporosis and vaginal atrophy, require lifelong estrogen treatment; others, such as most cases of hot flashes, may be short-term and given at a higher dosage than long-term replacement therapy. Estrogen may also be given as a long-lasting injection, but this is not recommended because there is no way to eliminate it quickly from the body in case of serious side effects. In addition, injections of estrogen are associated with a higher risk of endometrial cancer than other forms of estrogen therapy.

Possible contraindications for estrogen therapy include cancer of the uterus, estrogen-dependent breast cancer, and a family history of either. A past medical history of phlebitis (a blood clot in a vein, usually in the leg) may also be a contraindication, although replacement estrogen doses and the risk of clotting are significantly lower than for oral contraceptives. Women with gallbladder disease, once a risk factor, may now safely use the transdermal estrogen patch, which, unlike the oral form, bypasses the liver.

Routine estrogen replacement therapy usually does not start until a woman has had 12 consecutive months without a period, although larger doses of estrogen may be prescribed earlier to relieve symptoms such as hot flashes. Before starting estrogen replacement therapy, all women should have a complete physical examination, including a breast examination and mammogram, pelvic exam, and Pap smear. In addition, blood tests for cholesterol and glucose as well as thyroid and liver function are necessary. A biopsy to check for abnormal cells in the endometrium is also recommended. At this time, however, there is no widely available, reliable, and inexpensive way to screen for risk of osteoporosis. Use of a densometer to check bone density is still controversial but may help. Presence of risk factors and/or loss of height also can be used to determine the need for estrogen replacement.

POSSIBLE SIDE EFFECTS OF HRT

Side effects from estrogen replacement are usually temporary and include breast tenderness, fluid retention, nausea, and slight weight gain. More serious side effects include persistent severe headaches, swelling, redness, and warmth or tenderness in the extremities, any of which might mean formation of a blood clot. If any of these side effects occur, they should be reported to a doctor immediately and may be an indication to stop hormones.

Many women will experience vaginal bleeding when progesterone is a part of their regimen. This occurs after the progesterone is stopped at the end of the cycle, but the bleeding is light, lasting for only two or three days. Any heavy bleeding or blood clots, bleeding lasting more than three to five days, or bleeding at any other time in the cycle is abnormal and should be checked as soon as possible by a doctor.

Women on hormone replacement therapy should see their doctors every six

TABLE 7.1
Hormone Replacement Therapy Medications

Estrogen doses vary according to the reason for treatment. In general, atrophic vaginal changes usually require the lowest dose; osteoporosis or protection against osteoporosis and heart disease, an intermediate dose; and hot flashes, the highest dose. The initial dosage may be adjusted up or down as determined during the individual course of treatment. Your physician may prescribe the hormone on a continuous or cyclical basis.

Brand name	Generic name	Route	Dose (per day)
		ESTROGENS	
Estinyl	ethinyl estradiol	oral	0.02 to 0.05 mg
Estrace	estradiol	oral vaginal cream	1 to 2 mg 2 to 4 g (as marked on applicator)
Estraderm	estradiol	skin patch	0.05 mg per patch, twice per week
Estrovis	quinestrol	oral	100 mcg
Ogen	estropipate	oral vaginal cream	0.75 mg to 6 mg 2 to 4 g (as marked on applicator)
Premarin	conjugated estrogens	oral vaginal cream	0.3 to 0.125 mg ½ to 1 applicatorful
		PROGESTERONES	
Amen	medroxyprogesterone acetate	oral	5 to 10 mg for 10 days each cycle
Cycrin	medroxyprogesterone acetate	oral	5 to 10 mg for 10 days each cycle
Provera	medroxyprogesterone acetate	oral	5 to 10 mg for 10 days each cycle

months for follow-up breast and pelvic exams, a Pap smear, and other pertinent tests—for example, blood sugar and blood pressure measurements for those with diabetes or hypertension. Some physicians recommend that women who take only estrogen have annual endometrial biopsies.

IF HORMONE THERAPY IS NOT FOR YOU

Some women cannot take estrogen replacement for medical reasons. Others may feel that their symptoms are not troublesome enough to warrant hormone therapy. Here are some of the alternative means of coping with menopausal symptoms:

DIET. To keep supplementary estrogen production at a maximum, be sure to take in sufficient protein and calories. A minimum of 1,200 calories a day is necessary for adequate nutrition, although lower-calorie diets may be permissible for a week at a time for people who are overweight. Vegetarians should know how to combine foods to obtain complete protein. Remember, however, that too much protein interferes with calcium absorption, increasing the risk of osteoporosis (see chapter 1).

Temperature Regulation. To help moderate hot flashes, drink cool beverages, have a cool shower, or turn on the air conditioner if a room is warm. Wear layers of clothes that can be removed in the event of a hot flash.

Sleep Inducers. In case of insomnia, either due to hot flashes or as a separate symptom, try a glass of warm milk or a warm bath before bedtime. Learn relaxation techniques or make up your own, but worrying about falling asleep is the worst way to fight insomnia. Exercising earlier in the evening (but not immediately before going to bed) also helps induce sleep. Self-hypnosis is another effective way to overcome insomnia.

Coping Techniques. Biofeedback training, meditation, relaxation exercises, and self-hypnosis all have been shown effective in helping some women control hot flashes, mood swings, and other symptoms. Self-help discussion groups in which women with similar problems discuss their difficulties and solutions are also helpful.

Women need to recognize that menopause does entail change, but it is a natural milestone that can be passed with a minimum of difficulty with the right attitude, plus medical and personal support. A woman often hesitates to discuss her fears of growing older with her spouse and children; simply being able to talk about what is happening, both physically and psychologically, can make a big difference.

CHANGING LIFE-STYLES AND RELATIONSHIPS

Preventive medicine and advances in treatment of many diseases mean that today's couples live longer after retirement than those of 50 years ago. For the woman who has worked while rearing her children, the effect of not being needed by either children or colleagues on the job may be psychologically disruptive. She may have trouble just getting out of bed in the morning, having no deadline, time clock, or child's needs to attend to. It is important to combat this feeling by taking the time to serve her own needs after so many years of helping others.

For a woman who has not had a job outside the home since her children were born, the departure of children may be particularly unsettling. In effect, she suddenly finds herself "out of work," with no recent experience that qualifies her to compete in the job market. Of course, holding a job is not the only alternative, but it is important for the nonworking woman to develop new interests if she is to lead a satisfying life.

For those who do not want or need a paying job, taking on volunteer work or finding a consuming interest will not only provide mental stimulation but also enlarge the circle of friends and ease emotional dependence on a spouse. Local hospitals, community agencies, churches, and synagogues may have a wide variety of volunteer opportunities. For anyone who has ever felt the desire to remedy any of society's ills, working with the homeless or pregnant teenagers might be satisfying. Or there are scores of political organizations that constantly need volunteers for everything from stuffing envelopes to handing out campaign literature and manning polls during elections. Schools and day-care centers are still other possibilities that offer a woman an opportunity to use her mothering skills to help youngsters of all ages.

In caring for a family, many women have not had the time or energy to focus on their own development. Now is the time to do so. Some women might consider parlaying writing ability, handicraft, or cooking skills into a business. Teaming up with others to form a catering service can be fun and profitable, as well as time-consuming and demanding. Other women might satisfy creative leanings by joining a local theater group, learning to play a musical instrument, or learning how to make pottery, quilts, or other handicrafts. The possibilities are endless; the task is to focus on an activity that will be a pleasurable and rewarding one rather than merely time-filling.

THE CHANGING MARITAL RELATIONSHIP

Once children leave home, both an empty house and the need that many women feel to redefine their identity may put a strain on the marriage. Physical signs of aging plus the loss of reproductive function may be devastating to a woman whose feeling of femininity is closely tied to her appearance and the ability to bear children. At the same time, her husband may be struggling with his own feelings about aging. Unrealized career hopes and the awareness that he has limited time left to make his mark may leave him feeling that he is in a rut, producing a restlessness that may spill over into other areas of his life, such as the marriage.

The high divorce rate among couples who are suddenly faced with an empty nest and the need to reestablish their own relationship attests to the difficulties involved. Still, if a couple can resist focusing on problems alone, this can be a time of joyous rediscovery and strengthening of a marriage. Finding shared interests is an important key to revitalizing a marriage. Reading aloud to each other, listening to music, and sharing a mutual hobby provide an opportunity for rediscovery and growth.

Communication is vitally important in keeping a marriage healthy. A good sense of humor, an open attitude toward developing new interests, seeing new sides of a mate, and a lot of patience are important in getting through this often-difficult transition period. Of course, in some instances, despite the desire and efforts of partners to stay together, the marriage may break up. Or the early death of a spouse may leave a woman alone. According to the March 1990 "Current Population Report" produced by the U.S. Bureau of the Census, only 42 percent of married women 65 and older had a living spouse, compared to 77 percent of married men in the same age group.

The greater number of women, plus the tendency of men to marry younger partners, makes remarriage far less likely for older women compared to older men—all the more reason for a woman to develop independent interests and a network of supportive friends. Very few of us enjoy the extended family situation of past generations and other societies, which eased the strain of adjusting to the newly single or widowed state, but all of us have access to friends or other people in similar circumstances. To tap these resources, it may be necessary to make the first move—something many people find difficult—in reestablishing a social life. Some suggested starting points are:

- *Keep active.* The more time you have to brood, the worse your outlook will be. Even if you initially engage in an activity just to keep busy, chances are it will soon become enjoyable in and of itself.
- *Become a joiner.* Find a group that fits in with your interests. Church or synagogue groups, health clubs, gardening clubs, or a local Y or library are only a few of those available.
- *Take in a roommate.* If you live alone and have extra space, why not share it? Large urban areas often have roommate referral services that do preliminary screening. In smaller communities, check public bulletin boards and classified ads or ask friends or coworkers. A local college also may need housing for students or staff. Be sure to interview any prospects carefully. Honesty, financial responsibility, consideration for others, and similar attitudes toward household chores are as important as compatibility.
- *Speak up.* We grow up being warned against talking to strangers; still, conversations started in a museum, laundry room, bookstore, library, etc., can lead to friendships. Of course, discretion and common sense are important, but it is also important to realize that most people are not out to cause you misery or harm.
- *Tap local resources.* Think twice before moving to another community. Although this may be an ideal time to relocate, a totally new environment may be very lonely and unsettling.
- *Look your best.* Wearing makeup and flattering clothing can lift your spirits, even though you may have to push yourself to do so at first.
- *Get back in circulation.* If you are ready to date, consider some of the newer methods of meeting men, as well as the tried-and-true friendship or work contacts. Urban communities may have video-dating services that enable you to see and be seen before actually meeting a date. Special-interest or metropolitan magazines often run personal ads placed by people seriously interested in establishing relationships. (Publications that charge more for placing an ad—rates may be as high as $80 or $100—may attract more reputable, professional men compared to those that charge less.)
- *Go back to school.* Young people have long known that class is an ideal place to meet others with similar interests. Almost every community offers some sort of adult education at the local high school, college, community center, etc.

GOING BACK TO WORK

Returning to work or taking a job for the first time can be a matter of necessity, choice, or a combination of both. In ever-growing numbers, women of all ages are reentering the work force. According to the January 1992 "Employment and Earnings," produced by the U.S. Department of Labor's Bureau of Labor Statistics, 72 percent of women age 45 to 54, and 45 percent of those between 55 and 64, are employed outside the home or are looking for work.

Now is the time to explore career options. Even if pressing financial needs dictate that a woman return to work, she should make every effort to investigate available opportunities fully to find truly satisfying employment. Too many of us spend our lives working at jobs that really do not excite or interest us, but we simply do not know how to change our situation. The following suggestions may be helpful:

- Make an inventory of your interests. Do you like to work with figures or with people, with children, or the elderly? Do you like to be left on your own or do you like to work under close supervision in a structured environment?
- Make an inventory of your skills. Do you speak a second language? Can you type? Use a computer? Perhaps you sew well or are knowledgeable about books. Or you may be skilled in a sport or can tell the difference between an antique and a reproduction. Remember, almost any skill can be marketed.
- Are you willing to relocate? To travel for a certain percentage of time?
- Make an inventory of what you need for a given job. To qualify, you may need to take a refresher course, obtain a license, or take special training.
- What are your minimum salary requirements? Perhaps you can afford to do volunteer work or take a part-time job to get the necessary background. Or you may be willing to accept temporary employment that might eventually turn into full-time work.

Once you have analyzed your skills and interests, check the *Dictionary of Occupational Titles* and the *Occupational Outlook Handbook,* both of which are available in most library reference departments, for actual job descriptions and growth opportunities in various fields. If possible, try to spend a day observing someone who works in your area of interest to see what the job actually entails.

JOB SEARCH TACTICS

If you have good clerical skills but haven't decided on a particular field of interest, consider registering with a temporary employment agency. Working for different com-

WRITING YOUR RÉSUMÉ

- *Make it look professional.* A résumé should be typed on plain paper, single-spaced, and run no more than two pages.
- *Find an appropriate format.* Check sample résumés and pick a format that is appropriate for you. List all previous jobs, dates, and a brief description of duties.
- *Emphasize experience and skills.* If work experience is limited, mention high school or college courses in which you excelled, significant extracurricular activities, scholarships, and academic honors.
- *Emphasize accomplishments.* If you performed beyond the specific job description or accomplished special tasks—for example, increasing production, exceeding fund-raising goals—list these.
- *Analyze your relevant life skills.* If you are seeking a job in health care and cared for a seriously ill relative, you may have performed various nursing functions and have become familiar with social service agency resources.
- *Be concise.* Employers are not impressed by inflated descriptions.
- *Include a cover letter addressed to a specific person.* Briefly state how you would be a valuable employee and say that you will call the following week to discuss job opportunities.
- *Follow up.* Don't wait for a prospective employer to call you; instead, call him or her to arrange for an interview.

panies will give you an idea of which ones have desirable environments, and it may also lead to a permanent job.

For those seeking work in a specific area, it is important to read the classified ads regularly and perhaps register with an employment agency. Attend any "career days" your community sponsors, and talk to relatives, friends, or others in your community who might have contacts in your field of interest. Read trade publications, available at any good library, for possible leads. Employment agencies may be helpful, but use caution in selecting one that is right for you.

Many jobs never appear in the classified ads. A company may promote from within; the person who chooses the candidate may have a stack of unsolicited résumés; or the employer simply may not have seen a particular need that could be filled by an applicant with the right combination of talents. To find a job in this "hidden" market, check with the reference section of a good library for a wealth of directories that list businesses, hospitals, miscellaneous associations, and other categories. Select promising possibilities, and note the names of those heading the relevant departments. Always write to an area head rather than to the personnel department, which may not hear of an opening that the employer can easily fill. If there are 30 interesting companies, send your résumé to all of them. Only a small percentage may be interested in you, and "blanketing the market" is the best way to find those few.

SORTING OUT PRIORITIES

In this chapter, we have covered a wide range of situations that are ripe for creating mid-life crises. But it would be a mistake to assume that the middle years always bring major life problems. Many women move through mid-life with enviable equanimity; they seem to have their priorities in order and are able to sort out what really matters.

For all of us, these middle years are a period of setting priorities. What seemed terribly important at 20 or 30 may be trivial today, and vice versa. The midpoint is a good time to look both back and ahead—to readjust goals and make realistic assessments.

8

Changing Relationships

At the turn of the century, it was assumed that an elderly parent, grandparent, aunt, or uncle would always have a home—and a place in life—with members of the younger generation. This is no longer the case. Today's society is much more mobile than any in the past. Grandparents may live on one coast, their children on the other, and grandchildren somewhere in between. The increased financial independence of older people means that more can live on their own and do not need to depend upon children or other relatives. This can be a blessing for both the elderly and their family, though financial independence does not necessarily resolve the emotional need for close human contact.

Families today not only are more scattered than in the past but also are smaller. At the turn of the century, it was not unusual for a person to have seven or more siblings; today one or two is more likely the norm. (Or, in the sociologist's terms, each family has approximately 1.8 children.) A host of other demographic changes is at work, which means it is not just that the total size of the family is smaller but that the nature of the relationships is different now, too. People today live much longer. It is not uncommon for four generations of a family to be alive at the same time; even five is not so unusual.

The more common practice of divorce and remarriage is also changing our traditional approach to family relationships. Today's children may have two sets of living grandparents and an equal number of, or even more, stepgrandparents. Sometimes grandparents lose contact with grandchildren when custody is granted to a daughter-in-law or son-in-law.

IMPORTANCE OF NETWORKS

Throughout life all of us establish various networks that we can draw upon for friendship, emotional support, and other needs. In general, women fare somewhat better than men in establishing and maintaining networks of both friends and relatives. This is particularly important in cases of divorce or death, because it is usually the woman who winds up alone. Married couples generally have wider circles of friends than widowed or divorced people, except in the case of elderly widows.

Friendships are particularly important during times of transition, such as retirement. Retirees, however, sometimes find it difficult to make friends to replace the former coworkers and friends from the workplace. Since the older person may not have a built-in social network like the workplace, it is particularly important for him or her to have other friendships. Making an effort to join in new activities, to attend events at the community center, and to renew old friendships that may have faded during the working years are all useful strategies.

Siblings can become important sources of support and friendship in the later years. Many people report that they grow closer to their siblings as they get older, seeing or speaking to them more frequently, sharing memories, and offering moral support during times of stress or transition. Any rivalry or competition that may have existed has usually dissipated by the later years, and the siblings can enjoy their shared histories and keep track of events in each other's present lives. Although adult children are the primary source of support when an elderly person needs help, siblings are considered reliable sources of assistance and will usually offer to do what they can.

As the family grows older, the nature of relationships is bound to change gradually; in fact, it is often the function of the family to promote changes in those relationships. The middle-generation adults in the family configuration may face several transitions in relationships all at the same time—for example, coping with the departure of the last child at a time when one of their own parents is dying. Coming to grips with the major comings and goings within a family's structure is never easy; still, planning for inevitable changes and being prepared for their consequences can make them less stressful.

DEPARTURE OF CHILDREN

When children first leave home, they create a huge gap in the lives of their parents: The house may seem empty, too big, and devoid of activity. For women who have not worked outside the home or who worked only part-time, this period is equivalent to the stage of losing a job or seeing their husband retire. The woman whose main role came from her function as a mother may feel a loss of identity and have more difficulty coping with this period than other women who have maintained a career or other interests over the years.

After an initial period of adjustment, however, this time of life can become a satisfying and fulfilling one. In surveys, many people at this stage of life report that they are happy to be free of household and financial responsibilities and that they enjoy the increased freedom to do things by themselves and for themselves. The parents' relationship with their children is now a more mutual, voluntary one based on enjoyment rather than obligation and involves a more evenhanded, give-and-take quality.

Obviously the departure of children prompts a major change in a couple's own relationship. Unfortunately, divorce at this stage of life is all too common. A couple may be faced with the fact that they had little in common aside from their role as parents; when this ends, so does the marriage. For those couples who stayed together "for the children" or whose marriage has fundamental problems not dealt with while the children were at home, it would be illogical to expect some magical transformation to the same kind of relationship they had as newlyweds. Marriage counseling can be a helpful option for some couples who may need objective professional help to deal with long-term problems as well as to cope with the ways in which each person may have changed over the years. For some, divorce may be the best solution; for others, rebuilding the marriage is possible.

Of course, not all couples find this a difficult time. Many look forward to moving on and anticipate this stage of life as a time to renew their relationship, to get to know each other again. Many couples say that their marriage improves during this period, since they can concentrate on each other, free of the pressures and presence of children. There is also less personal uncertainty at this stage. As a rule, the couple will be more financially secure, with no major changes expected in the near future. Most people by now are established in their chosen careers, and retirement is likely to be a decade or so in the future.

This is a time to develop new interests and activities that can be shared by both spouses, providing not only a focus for this period of life but also a good preparation for retirement. Remember, however, that too much togetherness can be just as detrimental to a relationship as too little. Individual activities and private times are important.

Women generally direct their attention to outside interests during this time, concentrating on nondomestic achievements. At the same time, men become somewhat less achievement-oriented and are more likely to seek to satisfy domestic and inner needs.

Whatever the personal direction, this is a period during which people concentrate on achieving personal satisfaction, whether that comes from finally finishing a degree, getting a job, or cutting down on working hours. It is a time when people need to expand their network of friends, and a natural way to do so is to get involved in new activities. The way people deal with changes during this period of life has important consequences for the future.

AGING PARENTS

One of the effects of the changing longevity pattern is that more and more people are surviving into what is considered "old" old age. Therefore, middle-aged people may be called on to support their aging parents with financial aid or varying degrees of care.

The majority of people enter old age with better health and a more stable financial situation than in the past. Elderly people, while they may want to live near their children and to see them often, express a desire to maintain their own residence and independence whenever possible. However, eventually inflation, illness, or physical handicaps may create conditions that erode the independence of the elderly and make it necessary for their adult children to help in some way. Generally an elderly man who becomes ill or deteriorates physically will have a wife to care for him, since women live longer and men tend to marry younger women. Women are not so fortunate; all too often an elderly woman who is left on her own may find she needs some sort of assistance, and this usually comes from adult children.

Studies have shown that most adult children will voluntarily help their parents and that most say that they have a good relationship with their parents. However, the parents' need for help often comes at a time when the middle-aged children are dealing with many other demands on their resources: helping their young married children, still supporting younger children at home, planning for their own retirement, anticipating a reduced retirement income, or coping with the changes produced by aging or health problems themselves. The resulting situation is sometimes referred to as the "middle-generation squeeze," when middle-aged adults have to try to balance the demands of younger children, aging parents, and their own personal and financial needs.

Traditionally the daughter has been the caregiver in families. This may have worked well in the past, but in today's world, where the daughter is more likely to work outside the home, caring for an elderly parent can be a source of major stress, something neither the adult child nor the parent wants.

There are no pat solutions, but many problems can be avoided by realistic planning and early preventive action. Obviously health is a major determinant: It is the frail elderly who are most likely to wind up dependent upon others. It cannot be overemphasized that sound preventive health measures—good nutrition, appropriate exercise, varied interests that will help retain psychological well-being, and supportive formal and informal networks—are major keys to avoiding joining the ranks of the frail elderly. There are numerous examples of independent people in their nineties or even older who still care for themselves and lead vital, interesting lives. NBC's "Today" show has long featured a segment of daily birthday greetings to people who have passed the 100-year mark, and it is interesting to note how many proudly proclaim they still keep house, garden, and perform myriad other activities.

Even if an elderly person moves in with an adult child, it is important for all concerned that the parent retain a feeling of independence. Of course, this may not be possible in the face of serious, disabling illness, but this is the exception rather than the rule; most older people do not end up severely disabled. Ideally, there should be adequate space to ensure privacy for all. Converting a basement playroom into a small apartment, or declaring Grandma's or Grandpa's room off-limits to other family members except upon invitation, should be considered if at all possible.

All too often, parent and child feel that their natural roles have been reversed and that the child has, in effect, assumed the parenting role. Understandably, this can be emotionally and physically trying, unless approached with considerable give-and-take on all sides. An elderly parent who fears becoming a burden and wants to retain as much independence as possible may challenge the adult child's control of the situation, resulting in power conflicts within the family. Economic dependency may make an older person feel that he or she is losing control in all areas of life, and the resulting anxiety may cause the person to behave aggressively, manipulatively, or in other inappropriate ways. In addition, the elderly person may have different expectations of what kind of help is needed than the adult child does, leading to feelings of frustration and dissatisfaction on both sides.

There is a tendency to infantilize elderly parents, making them dependent and childlike. This provokes hostility on the part of the older parent and resentment from the rest of the family. In recent years we have heard a good deal about elder abuse, but the emphasis has been on physical mishandling. Abuse does not have to be physical; psychological mistreatment can be even more devastating than the physical.

BEFORE HAVING A PARENT MOVE IN

The following questions should be asked before you set up a multigenerational household.

- Will the adult child's marriage suffer adverse effects?
- Will there be constant conflicts and clashes?
- Is there enough space to ensure privacy for everyone?
- Is someone available to provide care if needed?
- Will the elderly person feel comfortable in new surroundings and with new people?
- Are finances adequate?
- Have all other alternatives been weighed, and is this really the best solution?
- Are there community services or other resources that can be tapped?
- Will the parent have a useful role in the household?

THE NEED TO COMMUNICATE

As more people survive into old age it is important for everyone to make an effort to understand the aging process. One of the reasons that middle-aged adults may resent caring for their parents is that they fear that they will be in the same position in a number of years. If people know what to expect, and what the potentials and limitations are, they will be able to plan better for the future and will be able to meet the needs of the elderly more effectively. Many of the problems that come up are the result of a mismatch of expectations. The child may be providing a lot of assistance—in money or time—but it may not be the kind of help that the parent feels he or she needs. Open communication between parents and children about what is needed and what is feasible can prevent situations that will lead to conflict.

Often, the way the decision to have a parent move into the home is made influences the way the situation progresses. Permanent decisions should not be made hastily at a moment of crisis; otherwise they can turn out to be serious mistakes, leading to unpleasant experiences for all concerned. For example, if an elderly mother falls and breaks a hip or suffers other serious illness, there may be a great temptation to sell the house and have her move in with one of the children. By the time everyone realizes that a mistake has been made and that everyone would have been happier with some other arrangement, such as a part-time homemaker or live-in helper, it may be too late to go back. Any arrangement should be made with the expectation that it will be examined and reviewed as a step toward more permanent solutions. Today many frail elderly are still able to remain at home with assistance from home-care services.

Everyone likes to feel in control of his or her life, and this does not change with age. Most elderly people prefer to remain in their own home with assistance from their children when needed. Sometimes adult children—out of a sense of guilt, genuine concern, or a vague feeling that they should do "what is right"—intervene too drastically in the elderly parents' life, in effect making them more dependent than they really need to be. If the parents are making an effort to stay active and are enjoying their life-style, then children should not force them to make a change simply to relieve their own guilt or anxiety. The older person's needs and wishes must be taken into consideration. If adult children are worried about their elderly mother living in an urban area, perhaps they can offer to have a visiting service check in on her periodically, rather than try to persuade her to leave her independent life to live, dependently, with them.

In many cases, what is needed is psychological and moral support. The knowledge that help is there if it is wanted and needed can relieve an older person's anxiety. And if it becomes necessary for the parent to move into the home, support services are available that can help reduce stress on everyone (see Appendix A). Day-care centers, visiting nurses, geriatric aides, and respite programs can be of invaluable assistance, depending on the needs of the elderly parent. Senior citizen centers that can offer the elderly person some means of social contact outside the family are also helpful to both parties. Surveys show that older people who have relationships with peers are more sat-

ROLE OF THE HOME-CARE WORKER

Although the duties of home-care workers (variously known as homemakers or home health aides) vary with training, amount of time spent in the home, and the particular state agency's certification requirements, the basic job description usually includes:

- Grocery shopping and meal preparation
- Personal care, including giving bed baths or assisting with tub baths; shampooing, brushing, and combing hair, and shaving (for men) with an electric razor; brushing teeth; cleaning and cutting fingernails and toenails (except for diabetics)
- Changing bed linens and making the bed, even for an individual who is bed-bound
- Helping a person transfer from bed to chair, walker, or wheelchair
- Assisting a person with medications, such as opening a pill bottle. This does not include actually giving the medication, unless the worker is properly trained and licensed.

Source: Adapted from *In-home Personal Care and Homemaker Chore Service Standards*, published by the Missouri Department of Social Services, Division of Aging, Jefferson City, Missouri.

isfied than those whose lives are completely tied up with their own family. And the social activities that the elderly parent participates in will give adult children the time and opportunity to pursue their own interests.

It is important to discuss the issue of what to do about aging parents openly, with all interested parties present. If an elderly parent can no longer live alone, what is the best solution? Perhaps a nursing home, a senior citizen community, living with one child, or alternating between the children's homes is the solution. Yet none of these options can be chosen unless everyone who will be affected is invited into the decision-making process and all of the issues—financial, psychological, practical—are discussed honestly. Once the situation is realistically appraised, it should be possible to work out a solution that will be acceptable to everyone involved.

Frequently an older person may not want to assume the responsibility of seeking help and may prefer to let things slide. In such instances a child may suggest that the parent consult a physician or other adviser, but if at all possible, the older person should be encouraged to seek help when needed and look after his or her own needs. Support from peer groups and networks, both formal and informal, is very important in establishing independence and retaining control. Sometimes this may mean taking an initiative or breaking out of old habits. For example, if you have always driven yourself to the shopping center but can no longer drive, try to make arrangements for yourself—even if it means taking a taxi or public transportation—instead of waiting for a family member to drive you. When you give up trying to solve your own problems, you may have no choice but to do what you are told instead of acting on your own. Making such concessions may not be easy, but they are better than the alternative of losing your independence.

It's also important to decide and discuss with family members your wishes for treatment in case of accident or severe or terminal illness. Advance directives such as a living will can provide written documentation of those wishes, and can help in ensuring that the health-care system recognizes your desires in this matter (see Chapter 20).

The importance of planning cannot be overemphasized. Before the need ever arises, parents and children should discuss personal preferences about the later years.

GRANDPARENTHOOD

Grandparents, who have always enjoyed a unique position in society, are finding that their role today is much different from what they may have expected. The increased tendency for couples to divorce and remarry has blurred the generational lines. More men in their fifties and sixties are remarrying, are establishing new families, and find that they have children and grandchildren of the same ages.

Today's 50-year-old is likely to be physically younger than in the past, so our traditional image of the grandparent as a wise elder is changing. Indeed, some people who are trying to hang on to their youth may react with mixed feelings to their entry into the grandparent role. Even though they may have been anticipating grandchildren for some time, the reality may make them feel that they are really "too young to be grandparents." While delighting in the child, they may feel that they are being pushed into a role that they are not ready to accept.

Although many grandparents see their grandchildren as a source of renewal of interest in life—or as a symbol of its pleasing continuity, giving them a connection with the present as well as the future—few seem to regard grandparenthood as somehow a renewal of parenting. Indeed, as a rule, grandparents see the grandchildren as a source of pleasure without the constraints and demands of responsibility. The older grandparents who have already retired have the time to do things with the grandchildren that they may not have had the time or money to do with their own children. Even younger grandparents usually have more money than they did when raising their own children, and they often enjoy being able to indulge their grandchildren with luxuries that they may not have been able to give their own daughters or sons. Becoming a grandparent also gives people the opportunity to succeed in a new role. Any regrets or failures they felt about parenting need not carry over into this new stage.

DEFINING THE RELATIONSHIP

Unlike the parenting role, grandparenthood is vaguely defined. The shape that the relationship between grandparent and grandchild will take may depend on the grandparents' current life-style, their view of their role within the whole family system, and their adult children's living situation. It might touch on whether, for instance, the adult children need financial assistance or some other kind of support. Often the grandparents' relationship with the adult children is the key. The attitude of the adult children toward their parents can determine the amount of contact or the nature of contact that grandparents have with their grandchildren. A parent-child relationship characterized by persistent conflicts, for example, may produce clashes over issues that concern the grandchildren, and this may have an effect on how frequently grandparents see their grandchildren.

Despite the deep affection that most grandparents express for their grandchildren, they do not necessarily want to see them more frequently, or (perhaps more pertinent) to be pressed into a frequent baby-sitting role. For most older people, maintaining ties with peers and remaining active in various undertakings are essential to achieving a satisfying life. The grandchildren may be an important part of that life, but they should not become the only focus. Grandparents who have to help care for grandchildren because of a divorce or financial problems inevitably must sacrifice some of their independence and personal life in this "surrogate parenting" role. Although most grandparents will offer help when it is needed—just as adult children offer help to parents when the occasion arises—doing so may be a considerable sacrifice for them. Some grandparents who live close to their children have found it helpful to put certain limitations on "nonemergency" help—such as offering to baby-sit once a week, but not more often—in order to preserve their own life-styles. This should not be considered an unloving attitude on their part but rather a way of maintaining the autonomy of both family units.

A long-distance relationship does not seem to affect the closeness of ties between most grandchildren and their grandparents. Although grandparents who live in the same town may see their grandchildren more often, those who live a greater distance away usually maintain contact by phone calls and letters and tend to have extended visits when they do come to town.

Problems may arise when there is a disruption of the adult children's family. Typically, the husband's parents are the ones who lose touch with the children if there is a divorce. The wife's parents may have a closer bond because they are the ones who will more likely be turned to for help. With the steady increase in divorce and remarriage, many grandparents find themselves with stepgrandchildren. Their reaction to the divorce, their feelings about the first spouse or about the new spouse, and their relationship with the adult child can all affect the quality of their relationship with the new grandchildren.

THE FAMILY CONNECTION

The older generation in a family, particularly the older woman, is often responsible for keeping family ties intact, maintaining acquaintances, arranging for the family to get together, keeping track of birthdays, and other tasks. The grandparents serve to preserve the integrity of the whole family system. With the arrival of grandchildren, there may be more frequent contact between the parents and adult children than before, as well as renewed contact with other members of the family. The grandparents assume the task of keeping everyone up-to-date and therefore sustain familial ties.

Grandparents may also serve a more immediate need as family "stabilizers" or arbitrators. Not uncommonly, a youngster may turn to a grandparent to serve as a confidant or to settle a conflict between parents and children. Grandparents should take care not to undermine a parent's authority by siding with the grandchild, but often just listening to the child and then suggesting that the youngster present his or her case to the parents will clear the air.

Although the role of grandparents may be changing, there is little doubt that it remains a satisfying one most of us hope we will eventually come to share. Still, we should avoid idealizing the role and having unreasonable expectations. While we may not always agree with the way a grandchild is being reared, it is important to recognize that this is the responsibility of the parents, not the grandparents. Advice may be offered when sought, but it is important to resist the temptation to interfere in the parental role.

DIVORCE OR DEATH OF A SPOUSE

Certainly the most significant change that may come in middle or old age is the loss of a spouse through death or divorce. Suddenly we are confronted with the restructuring of life at a time when we are already occupied with trying to cope with the normal stresses of aging. The personal loss of the spouse through death or divorce, difficult enough in itself, may also trigger dramatic changes in other areas of one's life: the family support network, finances, friendships, and sometimes even one's place of residence.

EFFECT ON RELATIONSHIPS

It is well known that divorce or the death of a spouse has different effects on men and women. Women tend to have a stronger network of peer and family relationships than men. Adult children may rally around their mother, if only because she is usually the one who needs some sort of financial or practical assistance in the early stages. Thus, a woman's ties with certain family members may be strengthened after divorce or her husband's death.

Sometimes, however, widows or divorcees are afraid of becoming a burden on adult children and may hesitate to ask for help. When adult children feel that the mother needs financial or other help but find it difficult to provide that help, guilt or resentment may build up. And those adult children who once may have expected financial aid from their parents often find that the newly widowed or divorced woman is no longer able to help out.

For men, the loss of a spouse through death or divorce invariably weakens his social network—a sharp contrast to the strengthened network experienced by women. His relationship with the children and with his in-laws may be affected, and since it is typically the woman who has made the effort to maintain family contacts, he may even see members of his own family less frequently. We might expect these adverse reactions following divorce, but they seem to hold true for widowers as well. Studies show that widowers tend to become socially isolated from relatives, whereas widows typically receive support and assistance from family members. It is also common for the parents of the husband to lose contact with grandchildren if there is a divorce. Many states now have specific statutes that give grandparents visitation rights; if matters deteriorate to this point, grandparents should be aware that they do have a right to see their grandchildren.

Friendships, especially with other married couples, may be altered for both men and women who divorce. This is because married couples often find it difficult to sustain a relationship with both parties after the divorce, and they are not always willing to include the divorced individuals, with their new status as singles, in their social activities. A similar situation often exists for a widow or widower, who suddenly finds that she or he is no longer invited to "couples" events.

ECONOMICS

Women frequently experience a dramatic drop in income after divorce or death of a spouse—an unfortunate circumstance that is not as common among men. Sometimes loss of economic support can further exacerbate social isolation and loss of self-esteem. Divorced women are often less well-off financially than widows, and the fact that the majority of working women 50 and over are in poorly paying positions makes their financial futures uncertain. Fortunately, a growing number of resources are responding to this situation by helping older, divorced or widowed women achieve financial independence.

ESTABLISHING NEW FRIENDS AND NETWORKS

Many widowed or divorced women are reluctant to move out of their own little niches to establish new networks and relationships. Some men also may hesitate to start anew, but most have the advantage of an established life and identity outside the home and family. An older woman who has been married for the last 20 or 30 years may already be particularly hesitant about dating, especially under the "new" rules and mores, yet there may be little opportunity to meet potential partners in her present network of friends and family members.

Even if a woman has no intention of seeking a new mate or partner, it is a good idea for her to investigate new activities and interests that will introduce her to a new set of acquaintances. The old group of friends may find it difficult to adjust to her new identity as a single person, but a new group will know only that identity, which may ease somewhat her transition into this new status. Men often can fall back on work colleagues; if not, they will often face adjustments and problems similar to those of women.

When considering a serious relationship or remarriage, one of the most important things to keep in mind is that the new person should not be seen as a replacement for the old spouse but rather accepted as a unique person in his or her own right. Trying to "re-create" the former marriage is one of the surest ways to fail in the new one. Finding entirely new interests or moving to a new home are possible ways to avoid this trap. The expectations from the first marriage must not be carried over into the second. It is equally important not to be unduly influenced by other people's opinions, pro or con, about dating or marriage—whether they come from adult children or friends. Only the newly single individual knows whether he or she wants to enter into a relationship and whether the relationship is right.

EXTENDED NETWORKS

Although close family ties are important, they are not enough for an interesting and satisfying life-style. Friendships with people of one's own generation, with those who share similar interests and who are available to participate in social activities, are essential to a full life. Older people who have ongoing friendships and who are able to establish new ones are more satisfied with their lives than those whose contact with people is limited to family members. These friendships are particularly important during times of transition, such as retirement. Retirees, however, sometimes find it difficult to find friends to replace coworkers and other friends from the workplace. Since the older person may not have any other built-in social network, it becomes particularly important for him or her to develop other such networks now. Museums, libraries, senior citizen centers, volunteer corps, adult education classes, foster grandparent organizations, churches, or synagogues are only a few of the places where people can find others with like interests. Making an effort to join in new activities, to attend events at a community center, and to renew old friendships that may have faded during the working years are all useful "networking" strategies.

9

Lifelong Learning— The Key to Mental Fitness

The mind's capacity for learning knows no age restrictions. No matter what our age, our minds crave new challenges, interesting stimuli, and variety to keep us curious, alert, and capable people—to ourselves as well as to others. The marvelous thing about being human, Ashley Montagu writes, is that we are designed *throughout* our life to continue to explore, discover, and change.

THE ABILITY TO LEARN

Studies have shown that learning is not only a potent mental stimulant but also helps promote a healthy body. The more mentally active a person is, in fact, the less likely he or she is to deteriorate physically. Researchers are trying to find out why this is true; the most popular theory is that the brain is more closely linked to the body's immune system than previously thought, and may play a role in other organ systems. Unfortunately, formal education has been traditionally viewed as a chunk of experience appropriate to the first three decades of life and not as a lifelong process. As a rule, education is thought to end when real "adult" life—work—begins. Although the setting and functions of education may vary at different times in life, stimulation, growth, and learning are as necessary—and accessible—to the mind of a 75-year-old as they are to a 15-year-old.

As we get older we seem to need more time to react and solve problems; however, this will affect us to a lesser degree when we actively pursue new interests and continue to learn and exercise our minds. Aging in itself does not affect learning ability, but learning does seem to have a positive effect on the quality of the aging process. Continuous learning opportunities and serial jobs, allowing every person the chance to explore multiple interests and learn new skills, would do much to avoid the gradual decline associated with boredom and inactivity in older persons.

Studies have shown, contrary to much of accepted opinion, that intellectual performance in a healthy person continues undiminished until at least his or her seventies. Dr. Alex Comfort (whose medical specialty is gerontology) notes that if the mind has not atrophied through disuse, there is no reason to suspect that learning ability will decline until well into the ninth decade. The overwhelming majority of older people suffer no loss of mental function. When there is a decline, it is not the result of aging but almost always has a physical cause, such as stroke. Ill health is much more likely than age to cause mental deficiencies.

In a long-term study involving members of a Seattle health maintenance organization (HMO), virtually no decline was shown in cognitive test performance up to age 60. Moreover, fewer than half of those tested at age 80 showed any measurable decline. Since most intelligence tests are designed for the young, their efficacy in testing older people may be limited. It is possible that aging brings benefits to intellectual performance in some areas, such as experience-based decision making, interpersonal competence, and the ability to evaluate alternatives and set priorities.

The only tests in which older people may show a somewhat slower reaction are those that involve a time element. Because reaction time may increase with age, it may take an older person a little longer to solve a problem, but there is no decline in the ability to do the work.

Societal prejudices that assume older people are less competent, interesting, or capable than younger ones are completely unfounded. Often this attitude is self-perpetuating; if it is adopted at an early age, many people actually believe themselves capable of less as they age and will close off many of their options. They will initiate what Ashley Montagu calls *psychosclerosis,* or hardening of the mind. Just as a limb can atrophy through disuse, so can the mind lose its ability to function for lack of exercise. The best way to ensure an alert, functioning mind at age 70 is to continue, throughout the years, to learn and entertain new ideas.

MEMORY

To associate poor memory with aging is specious. There are many young people with poor memories and older people with very reliable ones. A 30-year-old man who forgets his raincoat in the office will simply pick it up the next day without wasting any time thinking about his forgetfulness. If a 60-year-old man forgot the coat, however, he and his associates would more readily attribute the lapse to age. Research has shown that although some functions that affect memory may slow down by a fraction because of age, memory is not affected for the most part. Older people may have need for more frequent use of certain memory strategies—such as writing notes to prompt their memory—but there is no reason to believe that their recall capability cannot be as efficient as that of a young person. In fact, prospective memory—remembering to do something at the right time—actually seems to improve with age. Other memory functions, such as short-term memory and world knowledge (specific information not tied to a time or event), remain stable over time.

Certain physical conditions can masquerade as memory loss: An undetected hearing or vision deficit, for instance, may cause a person to forget names or faces because he did not hear or see them correctly. Drug or alcohol use, nutritional disorders, and depression are some of the reversible causes of mild dementia in people of all ages. Once the problem is corrected, such memory problems should disappear. If memory loss seems chronic, consult a physician to rule out metabolic disorders, chronic infections, or diseases such as Alzheimer's (see Chapter 16). Chances are that you are simply more sensitive to the normal fluctuations in recalling information. Remember that you have a much larger store of memories to sift through than you did at age 20, so it shouldn't be surprising if it takes somewhat longer to come up with the right answer.

The accuracy of memory is linked to several factors: interest, motivation, education, health, and the circumstances of the event. Because educated people normally use their memory skills extensively, they seem to have better memories. Motivation is an especially important factor: If information has no particular relevance or use, it probably will not be remembered. A sports enthusiast, for example, will easily remember the week's baseball scores, while someone with no interest in the game—even if he or she has listened to the same broadcast—will not.

MAKING THE EFFORT

Memory depends, to a large degree, on whether or not a person tries to remember and employs effective strategies to do so. Robin West, in her book *Memory Fitness Over 40,* points out that the few effects age does have on memory can easily be overcome with consistent use of memory strategies. According to West, more cues may be needed for recall because the ability to concentrate and ignore distractions becomes more difficult with age, making it harder to remember things. West advises people to evaluate their memory to see what strategies they use most effectively and then to refine and expand upon them. People with good visual memories could use mental pictures as a memory aid. For example, many parking lots use a visual aid to help patrons remember what section they parked in. You might note, for instance, that your car is to the left of the C (cat) sign. For those more verbally oriented, West suggests word and letter associations.

An organized routine and structured environment can be invaluable aids to memory. It is easier to remember an object when it is in a place that corresponds to its use.

If, for instance, it becomes routine for you to check your desk (where your appointment calendar is kept) before lunch, you will be less likely to forget afternoon appointments or errands. Always placing reading glasses on the table next to the bookshelf will help to eliminate frustrating searches. One technique that seems to come naturally to many people is to leave what is important in the most visible place; for instance, a report that has to be taken to a meeting should be left on top of the desk instead of in the file.

Researchers have found that older people have more difficulty not finding something already in its proper place than do younger people. According to research done by people at Boston Veterans Administration Hospital, this is really a perceptual and not a memory problem; all that may be required is to slow down and look in the same place more carefully again.

Like all things worth doing, memory improvement takes effort. Once the proven techniques are learned, you should practice them as you would any other skill, with the assurance that memory can be improved at any age and that the minor memory deficiencies resulting from age can be circumvented.

GOING BACK TO SCHOOL

Older people in record numbers are now realizing the rewards of, and their potential for, learning. The proportion of older Americans participating in educational programs is greater than ever and expected to increase. In addition, although the number of people reaching retirement age in good health has increased, the number of so-called college-age students seeking degrees is decreasing. With this shift in demographics, educational institutions and alternative educational programs are already adjusting some of their programs to respond to the needs and interests of the older learner.

The ability to learn is not what separates the older learner from the younger one; it is rather the distinct difference in interests between the two. Older learners are usually motivated by personal interest in a specific subject. As their numbers grow, older students will find they exert more influence on the types of courses and programs most suited to their interests—whether they are learning woodworking or a new job skill, the study of art, philosophy, the stock market, or a foreign language. Many institutions have already realized the potential of these new students and have designed programs for them. Although these programs take varied forms, they all share a common and very important element—input from participants. In some, the courses are taught by participants; in others, they may be taught by regular college faculty who are chosen by participants.

SOCIAL ASPECTS

An added advantage of enrolling in a program under the auspices of an educational institution is the availability of extracurricular benefits—cafeterias, libraries, film and theater programs, and sports centers. For some, these resources are incentive enough to participate. For others, just being on campus offers opportunities to converse with and meet others. For the retired, taking a class or going back to school might replace the social contacts and feeling of usefulness provided by the workplace. Being actively involved in a learning situation will help older people vanquish the false assumptions some younger people may have about the learning abilities and capabilities of the older generation.

EDUCATIONAL OPPORTUNITIES FOR DIFFERENT NEEDS

One of the biggest problems an older person faces in signing up for classes is simply picking a manageable number from the wide range of what is available. As a first step, it may be advisable to sort out your objectives.

Learn New Job Skills. The right class can help you keep abreast of technological changes in your field or investigate a new endeavor, such as getting a real estate license or advising on investments. Retirement may liberate you from working for financial considerations; your definition of what work can be may broaden to include volunteer or community service. Many jobs, such as working with young children or with hospital patients, or learning to read Braille books, require new skills that may, in turn, stimulate further interest in more intensive or specialized learning.

Explore a Lifelong Interest. As an adult learner, you are not necessarily constrained by what will be "useful" in terms of getting a job or what will look good on a résumé. You have the freedom to devote time and energy to whatever is of genuine interest—or to indulge a fleeting fancy. Colleges and universities now offer evening and weekend classes, certificate programs, noncredit courses, and auditing options from which the adult student can choose the most appealing format.

Keep Up with Current Affairs. Senior citizen centers, Ys, and community organizations often offer discussion groups on books, theater, world affairs, new technology, and other topics of current interest.

Take Self-help Classes. These include courses on aspects of financial management, preventive health, nutrition, coping with stress, exercise, and more.

Try Combined-interest Programs. These allow you to match your skills with other interests. If you like to travel, for example, you may want to study photography or languages during a special-interest tour. Nutrition and gardening mate well with cooking; all can be enhanced by a class taken in any one of the subjects.

DEGREE-ORIENTED LEARNING

It would be a mistake to assume that all adult education programs are necessarily divorced from degree or career-oriented programs. Because the retirement years offer an opportunity to do what finances, work, or family responsibilities may have precluded in the past, someone interested in earning a high school or college degree or pursuing an advanced degree has many options from which to choose. Many programs make working on a degree feasible and convenient in the preretirement years.

Many colleges now offer discounts on tuition to senior citizens, both to those enrolled in a regular program and to those interested only in specific courses. The Age Discrimination Act of 1975, which made discrimination based on age illegal for all programs receiving federal funds, applies to college admissions and financial assistance. The state attorney general's office can help people who suspect discrimination to devise their best course of action.

"Life experience" credit, now available at most schools, is especially attractive to the mature student working toward a degree because it recognizes the importance of experience and allows the student to turn it into course credit. Each school evaluates skills and requirements that were fulfilled in the workplace or at home and assigns an appropriate credit for them. While it sounds easy, there is a catch: You must have documentation of the experience, which might be difficult to obtain for something done 25 or more years ago. Nevertheless, careful analysis of life experience—and your own perseverance—should yield at least moderate credits prior to registration.

The College Level Examination Program (CLEP), a national program sponsored by the College Examination Board, gives credit by examination. The prospective student submits the CLEP scores to the college admissions office, which will decide whether or not to accept the credit.

University Without Walls is an individually tailored program worked out by the student and the school as an alternative to the traditional degree program. For information, contact your local college.

As schools begin to recognize the needs of the older student, and as the older population begins to lobby for programs to meet those needs, more opportunities will become available. To date, community colleges have been particularly receptive to the needs of the older student, but some private schools have also been in the forefront of education for older students.

Many adults hesitate to return to campus because they fear they will not be able to compete with younger students or that they have forgotten necessary study skills. But experience has shown no basis for these fears. Older students have no trouble with the subject matter and are often more responsible, reliable, and organized than their younger colleagues.

THE LEARNER'S ADVISORY SERVICE

Many public libraries offer a learner's advisory service that provides information on available college programs, requirements, admissions policies, and tuition grants, as well as alternative educational resources. Where it exists, this service can be one of the most comprehensive sources of information on learning resources available and is invaluable not only to the adult returning to school, but to anyone seeking information on a special interest or an alternative learning program. If your local public library does not offer this service, information can be obtained from the Adult Services Division, American Library Association, 50 East Huron Street, Chicago, IL 60611. The telephone number is (312) 944-6780.

MATCHING THE OLDER STUDENT WITH THE OPPORTUNITY

Those who find the plethora of alternatives in educational opportunities overwhelming may want to avail themselves of the services of a number of testing organizations.

Those who prefer a "high-tech" approach may want to try SIGI Plus, a computer-assisted guidance system developed for the Educational Testing Service in Princeton, New Jersey. The user enters information about his or her skills and objectives, and the computer generates a list of possible occupational or educational opportunities, including information on skills needed and advice on how to acquire those skills. The program is offered free through about 1,200 to 1,400 colleges and universities. To find an affiliated school, call the Educational Testing Service at (609) 921-9000.

Although many adults in their middle and older years may feel that they already know what interests them, many are often surprised not only at what emerges from an evaluation of aptitudes and interests but also at possibilities that never before occurred to them. Some people are unaware of skills that they possess, or do not know which skills will transfer easily from one field to another. Many factors should be taken into consideration when choosing a new activity or finding the best way to fulfill an interest. For instance, what is your learning style? Do you learn best in a lecture environment? In a hands-on situation? In a peer discussion group? Are you a visual or verbal learner? What skills are strongest—interpersonal, artistic, or investigative? A person's experience, background, personal likes and dislikes, degree of commitment and motivation—along with a number of other things—all enter into the equation. When all these things are taken into consideration, they may lead to some unexpected and appealing opportunities.

LIFE REVIEW/PERSONAL HISTORY

Reviewing one's life can give coherence and meaning to the past, help a person face the present, and plan for the future. Colleges, community centers, and senior centers recognize the importance and popularity of these projects and now offer courses and workshops in journal writing, oral history, or autobiography. Sharing life events with others may give someone the necessary momentum for what is normally a solitary endeavor. Writing or recording a personal history ensures that cherished memories are passed on to children and grandchildren, providing a sense of continuity. The recorder will also benefit (if past events have been recorded honestly) by being able to view past relationships more clearly, with the hope that the examination will improve or strengthen present ones. At a time of transition, life review can give us clues to our behavior. It can also be an excellent preretirement tool and, in the later years, can provide a sense of fulfillment and closure.

You might want to create a family tree and write a personal time line of major events. Sorting through old family records, talking to others, revisiting places from the past, and reading diaries and letters that have been saved through the years all provide a basis for this personal history.

SPECIAL PROGRAMS

In recognizing the special requirements of the older student—the desire for student-directed classes, a clear definition of interests, and an emphasis on a specific area of interest—many schools offer special programs specifically designed for the mature student.

Based on a participatory education model, The Institute for Retired Professionals (IRP) at the New School for Social Research in New York City, founded in 1962, is the precursor for other programs. Study groups, seminars, and workshops are student-led. Members of the IRP, who come from diverse professional backgrounds, study a variety of subjects from foreign languages to computers, music, economics, and tai chi. Members benefit from more than simply the learning opportunities; the IRP is also a vital center for social contacts: New friendships are formed, coffee breaks and lunch provide opportunities for conversation, and extracurricular activities are regular features of the program.

Started in 1977, the Institute for Learning in Retirement (ILR) is part of Harvard University's Center for Lifelong Learning and was modeled after the New School's IRP. Student-led groups on a variety of topics are chosen by the members of the institute. The only requirements for admission are that the individual be retired or semiretired, pay the very low fee each term, and have a desire to learn. Members of the ILR, like those at the IRP, report that the social side of the experience—the new network of friends, opportunities, and activities—is as valuable as the educational aspect. Similar programs are offered at American University, Brooklyn College, Duke University, UCLA, and undoubtedly many more schools. Check your own local community colleges.

ELDERHOSTEL

Founded in 1975 as a summer residential college program, Elderhostel offers non-credit courses in the liberal arts and sciences to people over 60. The program has expanded to include year-round and foreign study opportunities and is now found on more than 1,800 campuses around the globe. Participants consider the built-in and interactive aspects of the residential format as important pluses.

Significant requirements for these learning vacations are: age 60 or older, a spouse that age, or being 50 or older with an over-60 companion. The programs range from weeklong stays in the United States (averaging about $300, including meals and lodging) to foreign programs such as a four-week Australian excursion (about $7,000, including airfare).

The courses, taught by college-level professors and other experts, are an integral part of Elderhostel. In weeklong domestic programs, they are usually grouped as three courses per week, each meeting one and a half hours per day, but they do not include homework or tests. Curriculums depend in part on which instructors are available, so they may or may not be related to the program site. For instance, a three-week trip through Great Britain might have classes exploring Elizabethan London and Roman archaeology. One weeklong program at the University of North Carolina at Chapel Hill offered three courses on different facets of opera.

Accommodations may be in dormitories, tents, or comfortable condominiums—the luck of the draw prevails. Food is also a mixed bag. The food in Italy might be excellent, but it might be rather bland in some of the domestic programs where college food service is the norm.

All in all, though, people report good experiences with Elderhostel, and the fact that about 250,000 people enroll in the programs each year speaks for itself. Participants tend to find the companionship and mental stimulation rewarding and the various locales interesting. Free time is usually plentiful enough to spend exploring the different areas. For more information or for a catalog, write to Elderhostel, 75 Federal Street, Boston, MA 02110-1941.

INTERHOSTEL

Interhostel is a program for older adults that offers travel-study opportunities, generally of two-week duration. Lecture and field trips are arranged with educational institutions in the host country. For information, write Interhostel, University of New Hampshire, 6 Garrison Avenue, Durham, NH 03824-3529, or call (800) 733-9753 or (603) 862-1147.

TV AS AN EDUCATIONAL MEDIUM

With television reaching 99 percent of the U.S. population, it is not surprising that it is often used as a vehicle for education. The PBS Adult Learning Service, a national college credit service, is a cooperative program involving 285 public television stations and more than 1,000 colleges and universities. After enrolling in the electronic college campus through their local college, students watch the appropriate shows and study at home, then go to the college campus for exams and occasional visits with professors. A variety of subject areas are included in the course offerings. The local community college is the best source of information.

LEARNING EXCHANGES

For those who want specific knowledge on a variety of subjects, from learning a foreign language to auto repair, or who would like to get together with others to share views on a topic of interest, learning exchanges are valuable resources. They match those with a particular interest either with an individual who is knowledgeable in that field or with those sharing the same interests. The telephone directory, community center, library, or community newspaper can help locate a learning exchange in your area.

LEARNING ON YOUR OWN

There is nothing written in stone that says learning can be accomplished only in group situations. While not for everyone, self-teaching offers the motivated person the luxury of learning as quickly—or as leisurely—as desired. Without the constraints of a curriculum, one has the freedom to explore tangential interests in depth. But for self-teaching to be effective, an individual must learn to locate and use available resources; learning to use the library profitably can be a course in itself. While self-education eliminates the social contact and exchange of ideas that make learning in a class or group situation so appealing, for the disciplined student with the right temperament and interests it can be a rewarding undertaking and provide a sense of accomplishment.

The secret of successful lifelong learning is not being afraid of new experiences. Of course it can be intimidating to walk into a library and find out that computers have replaced the old card catalog that most of us grew up with. But you are not alone—and mastering the new skills yields a wonderful sense of accomplishment and self-worth. Learning may be difficult, but it can keep you young in heart and mind, and that's well worth the effort.

10

Planning for Retirement

Today more people than ever before are retiring from the workplace. Today's retirees, for the most part, have greater financial security than past generations, thanks to improved pensions and Social Security benefits. But one of the most important aspects of successful retirement is the one that is the most neglected—namely, careful preretirement planning.

We often hear horror stories about people who have been forced into retirement and ended up in a semivegetative state from boredom or who died shortly thereafter, also presumably from boredom. While this may indeed happen occasionally, surveys of retirees show that most of them are content to be retired and that many are happier than when they were working. Still, those who cope the best and report the most satisfaction are the ones who have kept busy with fulfilling activities, and who have maintained a good relationship with a spouse or a network of friends. Ideally, according to writer Richard Bolles, retirement should be part learning, part working, and part playing, although the "work" does not have to be what it was before. Those people who think that the word *retire* is a signal to stop doing, moving, or trying are those who quickly become dissatisfied with retirement, and are also those who are most likely to develop health or mobility problems soon afterward.

RETIREMENT STRATEGIES

People can do a number of things to make retirement more enjoyable and less stressful, including the following steps.

- *Start planning early.* Many people make the mistake of thinking that retirement planning entails only financial matters. Although finances are, of course, an important part of retirement planning, they are only one component among many. Retirement can provide that longed-for opportunity to pursue in depth a genuine interest, but effort and planning are still necessary to get the most out of the experience. Life-style planning is as important as financial planning in this respect.
- *Keep healthy.* Health maintenance should not be overlooked as an important part of retirement planning. Problems neglected or untreated when we are young often become serious or disabling with age. Commonsense practices such as not smoking, keeping weight under control, and regular exercise all are important preventive measures.
- *Consult your partner.* Of course, retirement planning must involve both husband and wife. If one spouse looks forward to moving to the country and tending a garden and the other has always assumed foreign travel would be the focus of the retirement years, both will be in for an unpleasant surprise when the time for retirement arrives. A couple should come up with individual plans, compare and discuss them, and make compromises and alterations until they arrive at a formula that satisfies the requirements of both as much as possible.
- *Be flexible.* A retirement plan should always be flexible enough to accommodate any unexpected changes in the economic picture, health, or personal preferences—the arrival of grandchildren, for example. There should also be a backup plan in case the original one turns out to be less than ideal. If, after a couple of months in the country, both spouses are going stir-crazy and longing to return to the city, then they should be able to do so without great stress or hardship. If possible, "safety systems" should be in place. The couple might, for instance, sublet their city apartment or suburban home for six months while they experiment with living in the country.
- *Make an inventory.* Many people plan to continue their lives after retirement more or less as they are, living near family and friends. Making an inventory of the best and worst aspects of the present situation is a good way to identify future retirement preferences. People who know that retirement is 10 to 15 years away should begin developing new interests and activities. Short-term projects, such as fixing up the house, will soon run out, leaving the retiree with a lot of unscheduled time.

STARTING A NEW CAREER

For the person whose life has been enjoyably work-oriented, retirement to a life of leisure may be a deadly prospect. Such a person may be happier finding some type of employment or even a new career after retirement. The work may be a part-time position, self-employment, or volunteer service. The opportunities and possibilities are virtually limitless. A few examples: Several Florida senior citizen health clinics are staffed by retired physicians who work on a volunteer basis. Many school districts welcome retired teachers as tutors, substitutes, or volunteers to work with special education programs or extracurricular activities. Retired executives, professors, or people with special knowledge or skills are often sought out as highly paid consultants.

Some organizations help place retired people with specific skills in the right positions. For example, SCORE—Service Corps of Retired Executives—matches people who can volunteer their knowledge to small businesses in need of their skills. RSVP—Retired Senior Volunteer Program—is a special program run by ACTION that seeks volunteers for community service programs (see Appendix A, "Resources for Retirement," under Chapter 10).

Retirement can also provide an opportunity to work for a public service group or cause. Hospitals, charities, the Foster Grandparent Program (also run by ACTION), and political organizations are just a few of the possibilities.

Even for people who have a good idea of what they want to do, a preretirement course or workshop can be helpful. There are so many variables involved, from finances to what to do with leisure time, that it would be difficult to cover all the bases on one's own. Many companies are now offering some kind of in-house planning service. Retirement counseling may also be available at the local community college, community centers such as Ys, or senior centers.

The National Council on Aging (NCOA) offers a multimedia package on retirement planning that may be purchased by any interested group—a person's company, for instance, or colleges or community centers. The council will train a staff member to present the program or will provide someone to conduct the session. The program is broken down into six parts: life-style planning, financial planning (including getting records together, fighting inflation, and savings and investment), healthful living, interpersonal relations, living arrangements, and leisure and work options. Workbooks are provided for spouses in order to encourage people to participate as couples. The program material is appropriate for a wide range of ages, interests, and occupations. Council officials recommend that people begin planning for retirement by their forties or early fifties.

The American Association of Retired Persons (AARP) also offers retirement counseling programs. The AARP will train a company representative to provide worksite retirement counseling or will send trained volunteers into a community at the request of individuals who do not have access to company-sponsored programs. These counseling sessions may be held at any available community site, such as the local library, church, or synagogue.

FINANCIAL PLANNING

Some experts estimate the cost of maintaining the desired retirement life-style at somewhere between 60 and 80 percent of your gross preretirement income, adjusted for inflation. When people begin to assess their financial preparation for retirement, they should add up all their potential sources of retirement income, including their pensions, IRAs, Social Security, life insurance, and health insurance.

A session with a tax accountant or financial planner can help you assess your future needs and begin making the necessary financial arrangements well in advance of retirement. Many colleges, companies, community centers, banks, brokerage houses, and other organizations offer retirement counseling programs, money management workshops, or computerized financial planning.

Many people who have a substantial amount of money turn to financial planners or money managers. Before taking this route, however, it is important to do some checking and choose cautiously. Financial planning is a vaguely defined and poorly regulated field. Checking the planner's credentials and background, speaking to other clients, going on the recommendation of a reliable tax lawyer or banker, and speaking to several consultants before making a choice are important tactics for choosing a trustworthy financial planner. Unfortunately, there are unscrupulous or incompetent planners who simply walk away after depleting a client's life savings.

CHECKING OUT A FINANCIAL PLANNER

Before engaging a financial planner, ask for and check references. A call to the Better Business Bureau may also be worthwhile. Financial planners also should demonstrate credentials and qualifications. Here are some of the more common planners:

- *International Association for Financial Planning.* Membership simply signifies an agreement to abide by a code of ethics.
- *Registry of Financial Planning Practitioners.* Maintained by the International Association for Financial Planning. Listing signifies that the planner must have three years of financial planning experience, meet educational standards, and pass a written examination.
- *Certified Financial Planner.* Signifies that the person has passed a series of examinations.
- *Chartered Financial Consultant.* Signifies person has passed a series of tests.

HASTY MOVES

All too many people associate retirement with selling the house and moving to a sunny clime. This may be fine for some people, but a large number find that life in a Florida or Arizona retirement community is not what they had expected, and in a few months they are back home. When asked why they returned, they will often say, "We missed our friends," or "There wasn't anything to do," or "We want to be near our grandchildren." Many find they do not enjoy the segregated feeling of living in a retirement community of mostly older people, while others may say it is exactly what they were looking for.

Before making any permanent move, a couple should thoroughly investigate their options. A depressingly large number of older people end up living in a place that is unsuitable to their interests. Others are duped out of their life savings by investing in real estate schemes or financially shaky retirement homes or communities. The lure of prepaid lifelong care is understandably attractive, but before signing any papers or investing a penny, check out the operation thoroughly with your lawyer, the Better Business Bureau, consumer protection agency, and other appropriate groups.

If you are unsure where you want to live, try sampling several places before buying and selling. House exchanges, or renting out your present home and leasing one in an area you are considering, are both low-risk possibilities. It takes more than a couple of weeks to really sample what living in another place may be like; it is better to give yourself several months or even a year's trial before making a major move.

A COMMUNITY OPTION

"Continuing care" communities are included in the range of options that have developed to meet the housing and health needs of the older population. These communities usually attract people in what is considered the second stage of retirement—the 75-year-old-and-up group. They offer living arrangements that include a studio or larger apartment, community and health centers, a nursing home on the premises, and a wide variety of elective services. Usually one meal a day is taken in the communal dining room, although residents may arrange for more meals if they wish. These communities operate in a number of ways, but they usually charge a one-time entrance fee that may or may not be partially refundable, plus a monthly maintenance fee.

Entrance fees range anywhere from $25,000 to $150,000. At some continuing-care communities, the entrance and monthly fees cover all costs; other communities operate on a "fee-for-service" arrangement, while still others charge extra only for certain items, such as nursing-home care. For the most part, these communities are designed for people who have already experienced health problems, who may not be as independent as they once were, or who simply want to give up some of their responsibilities, such as the care of a large home.

Before making a commitment, one should spend a few days in the community. Also ask for the community's financial history, including details about monthly fees and whether they have been raised frequently and what sort of reserve fund there is. State officials at the Department of Aging (see Appendix B) may be able to provide information on local communities.

Part III

A Preventive Approach to the Diseases of Aging

11

Heart Disease and Circulatory Disorders

Despite considerable medical gains made against heart disease during the last few decades, cardiovascular disease remains our leading cause of death, claiming almost one million lives a year. Of these, heart attacks account for about 498,000 deaths annually, followed by strokes with 147,000, hypertensive disease with 32,000, and miscellaneous other cardiovascular diseases accounting for the remaining 267,000-plus deaths. Of course, mortality figures are not the only factor: A huge number of Americans—more than 69 million, according to the American Heart Association—live their day-to-day lives with some form of heart or blood vessel disease.

Although the risk of a heart attack and other cardiovascular diseases increases with age, about a fifth of the deaths occur among people under the age of 65. At one time we assumed that heart disease was a factor of aging, but this is no longer true. Increasingly experts are convinced that a large percentage of heart attacks, strokes, and other forms of heart disease can be prevented by changing our life-style to avoid or minimize the factors that raise the risk of cardiovascular disease. Scores of studies conducted by researchers here and around the world have repeatedly identified these avoidable risk factors as:

- *Cigarette smoking.* Smokers have more than twice the risk of a heart attack as nonsmokers, and smoking is the leading risk factor for sudden cardiac death. More than 237,000 cardiac deaths a year are linked directly to smoking, according to the U.S. Surgeon General's office. A smoker who has a heart attack is more likely to die of it, with death often occurring within an hour of onset. Stopping smoking, however, lowers the risk to normal within a few years.

- □ *High blood pressure.* People with high blood pressure, or hypertension, are more likely to have a heart attack, stroke, congestive heart failure, and kidney failure than people whose blood pressure is normal. The risk is even greater among hypertensives who smoke or have high blood cholesterol or other cardiovascular risk factors. The risk can be reduced by lowering blood pressure and maintaining it, usually with a combination of medication, diet, and exercise.
- □ *High blood cholesterol.* Too much blood cholesterol leads to atherosclerosis, the buildup of fatty deposits along the artery walls. When the coronary arteries are affected, blood flow to the heart muscle is reduced and, if a coronary artery becomes completely blocked by the fatty plaque or a clot, a heart attack occurs.

These are the major avoidable risk factors linked to heart disease. A number of others that may not be so clearly associated with heart disease, but still important to control, have been identified. These include:

- □ *Diabetes.* Type II or adult-onset diabetes, the most common form of the disorder, occurs in middle age, especially among overweight people. It may be present for many years without causing symptoms, while still causing damage to the heart, blood vessels, kidneys, and other vital organs. Controlling diabetes through diet, exercise, and insulin or another diabetes medication, if needed, can reduce both the risk of a heart attack and complications of the diabetes itself.
- □ *Obesity.* A number of studies have found that markedly overweight people, defined as those who are 20 percent or more above ideal weight, have a higher incidence of heart attacks as well as a higher death rate from cancer and a number of other diseases. Added weight increases the risk of high blood pressure; it also increases the heart's workload.
- □ *Sedentary life-style.* Although it has not been proved that lack of exercise increases the risk of a heart attack, studies have found that people who exercise regularly have a lower incidence of cardiovascular disease. Exercise is important in weight control; it also strengthens the heart muscle and improves the efficiency of the cardiovascular system.
- □ *Type A personality and stress.* It has not been conclusively proved that personality and stress are cardiovascular risk factors, but many experts think that personality type and our individual responses to stress may affect our vulnerability to heart disease. Type A people tend to be overly competitive, aggressive, time-driven, and compulsive. They overreact to even very

minor stresses by pumping out the stress hormones that prepare the body for a fight-or-flight response. Sometimes referred to as "hot responders," these people may have several episodes a day in which their blood pressure rises, heart rate increases, and the body goes through the involuntary changes intended to protect it from danger. Some researchers hypothesize that these surges of stress hormones can in some way damage blood vessels and may be a factor that initiates atherosclerosis. Even individuals who do not fit the Type A profile run an increased risk of heart disease from severe or prolonged stress. Reducing stress and developing effective coping techniques can help minimize Type A behavior and its associated stress as risk factors.

In addition to avoidable risk factors, other circumstances increase cardiovascular vulnerability over which we have no control. These include:

- *Heredity.* A family history of early heart attacks, high blood pressure, or strokes greatly increases the risk. Anyone whose parents or other close relatives have suffered a heart attack or stroke before age 50 or 55 should make a special effort to minimize other risk factors.
- *Age.* Although we commonly associate heart attacks with striking down men in their prime, the fact is that the risk rises sharply with age. More than half of all heart attacks occur in people over age 65, and of those who die, 80 percent are 65 or older.
- *Gender.* Men are much more likely to have a heart attack than women. Even after menopause, when women's risk of a heart attack begins to rise, the cardiovascular death rate of women is still lower than that of men. Heart attack is, however, the number-one killer of American women, and more than one-half of all women over age 55 have high blood pressure. Estrogen replacement therapy has been proven to protect postmenopausal women from heart disease, providing a way for some women to decrease their risk.
- *Race.* African-Americans have almost a one-third greater chance of developing hypertension than whites, which is believed to explain why African-Americans have a much higher death rate from heart attacks and strokes.

As might be expected, the more risk factors a person has, the greater the chance of suffering a heart attack, stroke, or some other form of heart disease. Although one cannot change one's family history, age, gender, or race, a person who falls into one or more of these high-risk groups is not necessarily fated to develop cardiovascular disease. But the presence of any unavoidable risk factor should serve as an extra warning to modify or avoid those factors over which we do have control.

HOW THE HEART WORKS

To better understand how you can protect yourself from heart disease, it is important to know the basics of how this vital organ works. The heart is a simple yet marvelously engineered organ, about the size of two clenched fists and weighing 11 to 16 ounces in the average adult. It is situated between the lungs in the upper chest cavity.

The heart is made up mostly of muscle tissue known as myocardium. It is a hollow organ, divided into four chambers. The upper two are the right and left atria—chambers where blood collects—and the lower two are the right and left ventricles, the pumping chambers. The right atrium receives the blood that has circulated through the body, blood low in oxygen and nutrients, high in carbon dioxide, and with waste products that normally are expelled through the lungs. This "used" blood passes into the right ventricle and is pumped to the lungs, where the carbon dioxide and wastes are removed and fresh oxygen is added. This freshly oxygenated blood passes from the lungs into the left atrium, then through the mitral valve into the left ventricle. This chamber is the heart's "workhorse" because it must pump the blood through the aortic valve and into the aorta—the body's great artery—to begin its journey through the body's circulatory system.

In a normal, active adult, the heart beats about 100,000 times a day, in effect pumping the equivalent of more than 4,000 gallons of blood through more than 60,000 miles of blood vessels, an operation most of us totally ignore until something goes wrong. But despite the heart's prodigious workload, it is designed to last a lifetime. Autopsies performed on men and women in their eighties and nineties who died of something other than heart disease have found that their hearts often show little sign of wear and tear. This is despite the fact that the heart must beat regularly 60 to 80 times a minute (and more during exercise), without stopping, year in and year out. So, popular notions to the contrary, it does not appear that heart disease is an inevitable part of aging. Instead, it is a consequence of life-style or other unidentified factors that many experts feel can be changed or controlled to prevent a large percentage of heart attacks, especially those occurring at relatively early ages.

The heart muscle itself is nourished by a network of coronary arteries that encircle the heart like a crown, hence the name "coronary." These vessels appear to be particularly susceptible to atherosclerosis, a narrowing or "hardening" caused by deposits of fatty plaque, or atheroma. These deposits are made up of cholesterol, fats, and fibrous tissue. The cause of atherosclerosis is unknown, but it appears to start early in life and is a progressive disease. It is particularly common among Americans and has been linked to our high-fat, high-cholesterol diet. Cigarette smoking, perhaps because of an autoimmune response to something in tobacco or smoke, is believed to be a possible initiating factor. Nicotine, a vasoconstrictor, narrows the coronary arteries and allows clots to form. Carbon monoxide in the blood from smoking reduces the effective supply of oxygen to the heart muscle. Stress, an autoimmune process (a defect in the body's immune system that causes it to damage itself), and hormonal imbalances are among the other possible factors that have been linked to atherosclerosis. High blood pressure and diabetes accelerate the process.

About 5 percent of the body's total blood flow passes through the coronary arteries. As these vessels become progressively narrowed by atherosclerosis, the heart muscle may become "starved" for oxygen and other nutrients. This can result in episodes of angina—the chest pains that are characteristic of coronary disease. Since the heart muscle is extremely efficient in extracting oxygen from the blood, the coronary vessels can be markedly narrowed—as much as 70 to 90 percent blocked—before any symptoms occur. Thus, a person can have severe coronary disease without knowing it. In a distressingly large number of cases, the first sign of heart disease is heart attack or sudden death.

The rhythmic beating of the heart is controlled by a bundle of cells that generate electrical impulses to coordinate the heart's contractions. This natural pacemaker sometimes goes awry, resulting in serious disturbances of the heart's rhythm. Drugs and artificial pacemakers may be lifesaving in such circumstances.

In order for the blood to travel through hundreds of miles of vessels throughout the body and deliver oxygen to every cell, a certain pressure must be maintained within the vessels. With each heartbeat, about three ounces of blood is pumped from the left ventricle into the aorta. You can feel this sudden surge of blood at any of a number of pulse points throughout the body. The force of the heartbeat is a determining factor in maintaining blood pressure. When blood pressure is measured, two readings are taken: for example, 120 over 80. The higher number is the *systolic* pressure, which is the peak pressure when the blood is forced from the heart during a contraction of the left ventricle; the lower number is the *diastolic* pressure, which is the force exerted on the artery walls when the heart is resting between beats. This diastolic pressure is controlled by the resistance to blood flow from the arterioles, or smallest arteries, into the capillaries, microscopic vessels that feed the individual cells. If the arterioles are constricted, or narrowed, diastolic pressure will rise, and this in turn forces systolic pressure up in order to ensure continued blood flow.

To ensure that blood moves in the right direction, we have a marvelously engineered system of valves in the heart and blood vessels. Sometimes the valves in the heart become damaged, either by congenital defects or diseases, such as rheumatic fever, or by other infections. Drugs, surgery, and replacement with artificial valves now make it possible for many people with severe valvular disease to lead normal lives. More commonly, it is the tiny valves in the veins, especially those in the lower legs, that can become weakened or damaged. This can cause varicose veins and the pooling of blood in the lower extremities. Heredity, obesity, and a sedentary life-style are possible causative factors. Other circulatory problems can be brought on by a narrowing of arteries in the legs—a process similar to what happens to clogged coronary arteries.

COMMON FORMS OF HEART DISEASE

CORONARY DISEASE AND ANGINA

As the coronary arteries become progressively narrowed by atherosclerosis, many people experience angina pectoris, the medical term for chest pains behind the breastbone. Typically, a person does not have any problems while resting or carrying out moderate activities. But extra demands upon the heart—running to catch a bus, climbing a flight of stairs, an emotional upset, going out on a cold and windy day, or eating a heavy meal—will produce chest pains and shortness of breath. An attack of angina, which usually lasts for only a few minutes, is relieved by rest or drugs, such as nitroglycerin.

The pains are due to inadequate oxygen being delivered to the heart muscle, a condition called myocardial ischemia. Some people experience myocardial ischemia without pain, a condition referred to as silent ischemia; others may have pain without significant narrowing of the arteries. Typically, people with this variant form of angina may experience pain when resting, and a study of their coronary arteries may find only minor narrowing. In these instances, the angina is thought to be caused by a spasm of the coronary artery, frequently at the site of atherosclerotic plaque.

It is sometimes difficult to distinguish pain caused by myocardial ischemia from that of other conditions, such as heartburn, a hiatus hernia, chest muscle pain, and so forth. In general, the pain of angina starts in the center of the chest and is a persistent squeezing or pressing sensation that may spread to the shoulders or arms. It usually affects the left side, although both sides may be involved, as well as the back, neck, or jaw. Most people with angina can identify a triggering factor—exertion, a burst of anger—and the episodes usually pass with rest or after taking a nitroglycerin tablet.

Anyone who suspects he or she is experiencing chest pains or shortness of breath related to the heart should see a doctor promptly. Most people with angina learn to adjust their routines to live with the condition. Stopping smoking, starting a program of gradual exercise conditioning, losing weight, lowering cholesterol and other cardiovascular risk factors, taking medication to prevent or minimize attacks, avoiding precipitating factors—all are commonsense measures that can minimize the problem. In some instances, however, the attacks come with increasing frequency and severity, often without provocation. This is called unstable angina and is often a prelude to a heart attack. More intensive treatment, such as drug therapy (see Table 11.1) or a coronary bypass operation, may be needed to prevent a heart attack.

HIGH BLOOD PRESSURE

Nearly 63 million Americans have high blood pressure, making it our most common cardiovascular disease. Often referred to as the silent killer, hypertension—the medical term for high blood pressure—is the leading cause of strokes and is also a major

TABLE 11.1
Drugs to Treat Angina

BETA BLOCKERS

Action: Reduce heart rate and heart muscle contractility by blocking the response of the beta nerve receptors. These receptors send signals to the heart to work harder.

Generic name	Brand name	Possible side effects
acebutolol	Sectral	Slow pulse, weakness, low blood pressure, asthma attacks, fatigue, insomnia (for propranolol), impotence, nausea, nightmares or vivid dreams, lethargy as well as cold hands and feet because of reduced circulation
atenolol	Tenormin	
betaxolol	Kerlone	
carteolol	Cartrol	
metoprolol	Lopressor	
nadolol	Corgard	
penbutolol	Levatol	
pindolol	Visken	
propranolol	Inderal	
timolol	Blocadren	

CALCIUM CHANNEL BLOCKERS

Action: Block the passage of calcium into the muscle cells that control the size of blood vessels, thus preventing the arteries from constricting.

Generic name	Brand name	Possible side effects
diltiazem	Cardizem	Headache, nausea, swelling, irregular heartbeat, rash, fatigue
nicardipine	Cardene	Flushing, headache, palpitations, dizziness, nausea, low blood pressure, ankle swelling, rash
nifedipine	Procardia	Dizziness, light-headedness, headache, weakness, flushing, transient low blood pressure, palpitations, ankle swelling, nausea
verapamil	Calan Isoptin Verelan	Dizziness, headache, low blood pressure, slow pulse, ankle swelling, constipation

NITRATES

Action: Cause veins and arteries to dilate, thus improving coronary blood flow and increasing the supply of oxygenated blood.

Generic name	Brand name	Possible side effects
isosorbide dinitrate	Dilatrate-SR Iso-Bid Isordil Sorbitrate Sorbitrate SA	Headache, flushing, dizziness upon standing, nausea, vomiting
nitroglycerin	Deponit NTG Minitran Nitro-Bid Nitrogard Nitroglyn Nitrol Nitrolingual Nitrong Nitrostat Transderm-Nitro Tridil	Same effects as above, plus rapid pulse

Table 11.1
Drugs to Treat Angina (*cont'd*)

OTHER DRUGS

Action: Increase blood flow to the heart by dilating certain coronary arteries.

Generic name	Brand name	Possible side effects
dipyridamole	Persantine	Headache, dizziness, weakness, nausea, flushing, rash

Source: Consumer Reports Books, *The Complete Drug Reference,* 1992 edition © The U.S. Pharmacopeial Convention, Inc. Permission granted.

risk factor for heart attacks, congestive heart failure, and kidney failure. It is described as silent because it usually does not produce symptoms until its most advanced stages. By that time, the heart, blood vessels, and other organs may have suffered permanent damage.

In general, high blood pressure in adults is defined as consistent systolic readings greater than or equal to 140 millimeters of mercury (mm Hg) and a diastolic pressure greater than or equal to 90 mm Hg. The combination of the two readings can be important. A diastolic reading of more than 110 mm Hg calls for immediate treatment regardless of the systolic measurement. In older people, the systolic reading may be high while the diastolic reading is normal. This is called isolated systolic hypertension.

Not uncommonly, a person may have a high reading when blood pressure is measured in a doctor's office, yet normal readings at home or elsewhere. This is why several readings taken at different times and in different positions usually are needed to establish a diagnosis of hypertension, especially if it is in the mild-to-moderate range.

Many people mistakenly think that as they get older, blood pressure will normally rise in order to get blood to the vital organs. This is not true—the higher the blood pressure, the greater the chances of having a heart attack, stroke, or kidney failure, regardless of age. Hypertension usually develops between the ages of 30 and 45, and without treatment, it becomes progressively higher.

Causes. In more than 90 percent of people diagnosed, no cause can be found for high blood pressure; this is referred to as primary, or essential, hypertension. In a small number of cases, a cause for the hypertension *can* be identified; for example, some types of kidney disease, adrenal tumors, hormonal abnormalities, use of birth control pills, and certain medications may raise blood pressure. In some of these cases, identifying and correcting the underlying cause will cure the hypertension. But this is unusual; the large majority of hypertension has no identifiable cause, and treatment must persist for life. Recent studies have found that some patients can eventually stop the drugs after years of treatment, but experts think these are exceptional cases rather than the rule. Many eventually must resume therapy.

Many people think that chronic tension or stress causes hypertension. Although stress can produce a temporary rise in blood pressure, it has not been proved that it actually causes the sustained elevations seen in hypertension. Still, some experts think that stress or, perhaps more accurately, poor techniques in coping with stress may be a contributing factor.

Heredity appears to play a definite role in determining who will develop hypertension. Children in families where one or both of the parents have hypertension are more likely to have blood pressures that are at the high end of the scale. They also have an increased risk of developing hypertension as adults. Obesity also appears to be a factor: Overweight people have a higher incidence of hypertension than their normal-weight peers. In this country, African-Americans have almost a one-third greater chance of having hypertension than whites. The reasons for this are unknown, although heredity, poverty, stress, and high-salt diets have been suggested as possible explanations.

The role of sodium as a possible cause of high blood pressure is a matter of continuing debate among doctors and researchers. There is no clear evidence that consuming large amounts of sodium—the major ingredient in table salt—will cause hypertension among people who are not predisposed to the disease. But among those with a genetic predisposition, it appears that sodium consumption is a major contributing factor. And restricting sodium often will lower blood pressure. In fact, before the development of modern antihypertensive drugs, severe salt restriction, such as the famous rice diet developed at Duke University Medical Center, was about the only treatment for high blood pressure.

Treatment. Once a diagnosis of hypertension has been made, it is important to bring the high blood pressure into the normal range. Often this can be accomplished with weight loss, lowered salt intake, increased exercise, and developing improved techniques for dealing with stress, especially if the hypertension is in the mild-to-moderate range (140–160/90–95). But if this conservative approach fails to bring blood pressure back to normal within three to six months, most doctors will prescribe antihypertensive drugs.

These medications have truly revolutionized the treatment of high blood pressure. Just a few decades ago, malignant hypertension was a fairly common disorder; today it very rarely occurs. There are now a large number of various drugs that can be prescribed to lower blood pressure (see Table 11.2)—so many, in fact, that most cases can be brought under adequate control without undue side effects. If side effects do occur, it is important to talk to your doctor; frequently, the dosage can be adjusted or medication changed to eliminate or minimize side effects and still control the high blood pressure.

Although modern drugs can bring high blood pressure under control, they are not a cure for the disease. Almost always, one must take the medication for the rest of one's life. Many people make the mistake of taking the drugs for a few weeks or months, then stop taking them as soon as checkups show normal readings. This can be a potentially life-threatening mistake: Some drugs cannot be stopped abruptly without a rebound

TABLE 11.2
Drugs to Treat High Blood Pressure

ACE INHIBITORS

Action: Improve blood flow by preventing production of a hormone, angiotensin II, that causes constriction of blood vessels.

Generic name	Brand name	Possible side effects
captopril	Capoten	Dizziness or weakness, loss of appetite, rash, itching, a hacking and unpredictable cough, swelling
enalapril	Vasotec	
lisinopril	Prinivil	
	Zestril	

ALPHA BLOCKERS

Action: Lower high blood pressure by blocking responses from the alpha nerve receptors. These receptors send messages to the heart to work harder.

Generic name	Brand name	Possible side effects
doxazosin	Cardura	Upon standing abruptly, fainting or dizziness because of drop in blood pressure (risk increased when drinking alcohol, standing for long periods, exercising, or being exposed to hot weather), nausea, headache, palpitations
prazosin	Minipress	
terazosin	Hytrin	

BETA BLOCKERS

Action: Reduce heart rate and heart muscle contractility by blocking the response of the beta nerve receptors. These receptors send signals to the heart to work harder.

Generic name	Brand name	Possible side effects
acebutolol	Sectral	Slow pulse, weakness, low blood pressure, asthma attacks, fatigue, insomnia (for Inderal), impotence, nausea, nightmares or vivid dreams, lethargy as well as cold hands and feet because of reduced circulation
atenolol	Tenormin	
betaxolol	Kerlone	
carteolol	Cartrol	
metoprolol	Lopressor	
nadolol	Corgard	
penbutolol	Levatol	
pindolol	Visken	
propranolol	Inderal	
timolol	Blocadren	

ALPHA AND BETA BLOCKERS

Generic name	Brand name	Possible side effects
labetolol	Normodyne	Nausea and indigestion, cold hands and feet, temporary impotence, nightmares, dizziness (especially during initial treatment or as dosage is increased)
	Trandate	

CALCIUM CHANNEL BLOCKERS

Action: Block the passage of calcium into the muscle cells that control the size of blood vessels, thus preventing the arteries from constricting.

Generic name	Brand name	Possible side effects
diltiazem	Cardizem	Headache, nausea, swelling, irregular heartbeat, rash, fatigue

TABLE 11.2
Drugs to Treat High Blood Pressure (*cont'd*)

CALCIUM CHANNEL BLOCKERS (cont'd)

Generic name	Brand name	Possible side effects
nicardipine	Cardene	Flushing, headache, palpitations, dizziness, nausea, low blood pressure, ankle swelling, rash
nifedipine	Procardia	Dizziness, light-headedness, headache, weakness, flushing, transient low blood pressure, palpitations, ankle swelling, nausea
verapamil	Calan Isoptin Verelan	Dizziness, headache, low blood pressure, slow pulse, ankle swelling, constipation

CENTRALLY ACTING DRUGS

Action: Decrease nerve impulses from brain centers that control constriction of blood vessels.

Generic name	Brand name	Possible side effects
clonidine guanabenz guanfacine	Catapres Wytensin Tenex	Drowsiness or sedation, constipation, dry mouth, headache, dizziness or weakness, rash, depression, ankle swelling, cold hands, impotence
methyldopa	Aldomet	Dizziness or light-headedness, drowsiness, headache, dry mouth or stuffy nose, swelling of ankles or feet, tiredness or weakness, fever, depression, liver inflammation

DIURETICS

Action: Increase the amount of sodium and water excreted by the kidneys, thereby reducing the volume of blood. Diuretics are classified according to their site of action in the kidney.

	Generic name	Brand name	Possible side effects
Loop Diuretics	bumetanide furosemide	Bumex Lasix	Lethargy, cramps, rash, impotence (some effects may be avoided by combining with a potassium supplement or potassium-sparing drug)
Potassium-Sparing Diuretics	amiloride	Midamor	Muscle weakness and numbness (if too much potassium is retained), upset stomach, lethargy, rash
	spironolactone	Aldactone	Muscle weakness and numbness (if too much potassium is retained), nausea and vomiting, diarrhea, lethargy, irregular menstruation, breast enlargement in men, impotence, rash
	triamterene	Dyrenium	Same as for amiloride (Midamor)
Thiazide Diuretics	chlorthalidone hydrochlorothiazide	Hygroton Esidrix Hydrodiuril Oretic	Same as for loop diuretics
	metolazone	Diulo Mykrox Zaroxolyn	

TABLE 11.2
Drugs to Treat High Blood Pressure (*cont'd*)

OTHER DRUGS

Action: Cause blood vessels to dilate.

Generic name	Brand name	Possible side effects
hydralazine	Apresoline	Nausea and vomiting, headache, dizziness, irregular heartbeat, loss of appetite, rash, flushing, joint pains, drug-induced lupus
minoxidil	Loniten	Increased hair growth (especially on face and back), fluid retention, shortness of breath, tiredness, dizziness or light-headedness, nausea, headache, rash
reserpine	Serpasil	Drowsiness, diarrhea, nausea, dry mouth, dizziness, headache, depression, muscular aches, temporary impotence, weight gain, rash

Source: Consumer Reports Books, *The Complete Drug Reference*, 1992 edition © The U.S. Pharmacopeial Convention, Inc. Permission granted.

effect in which the blood pressure soars higher than ever. More specifically, abrupt cessation of beta-blocking drugs may precipitate a heart attack.

Although hypertension can be a fatal disease, when properly treated the vast majority of patients live perfectly normal lives. In fact, no one would even suspect they have a serious cardiovascular disorder. The outlook today for people with high blood pressure is excellent, so long as they continue their treatment. Anyone with high blood pressure should see his or her doctor regularly, usually every six to 12 months once blood pressure has returned to normal. Such regular checkups will help make sure that the disease remains under control. Many doctors also advise patients to measure blood pressure periodically at home. This may be done with the regular cuff and stethoscope that your doctor uses (see box below) or with one of the newer electronic monitors with a digital readout.

HOW TO TAKE YOUR OWN BLOOD PRESSURE

Monitoring your blood pressure at home is helpful to both you and your physician. Often patients find that readings taken in a doctor's office will be higher than those taken at home. Home monitoring will ensure that your blood pressure is under control and allow the doctor to monitor your medication accordingly.

Use the following procedure to take your blood pressure with a non-automated sphygmomanometer and stethoscope:

- Be sure you are in a quiet place. You have to be able to hear your blood flow.
- Take your reading in the same position each time. Blood pressure readings will vary depending on whether you are sitting or lying down.
- Rest your forearm flat on a table. Your upper arm (where the cuff will be placed) should be at the same level as your heart. This will help to avoid deviations in readings.
- Roll up the sleeve to expose the upper arm. If the sleeve is rolled tight, slip that arm free of the sleeve.
- Place the stethoscope on the brachial artery in the crook of your elbow. You can locate this artery by feeling for your pulse with your fingertips.
- Slip the deflated cuff onto your upper arm. Use the ring and Velcro wrap to make the cuff snug. (Keep the stethoscope over the artery as you fit the cuff.)
- Place the pressure gauge (manometer) where you can see it easily.
- Put the ear tips of the stethoscope in your ears. (You may have to reposition the stethoscope on your arm to get a better sound.) Inflate the cuff about 30 points (millimeters of mercury) above your expected systolic pressure. This value is determined by trial and error, or you can use the last reading taken at your doctor's office.
- Once the cuff pressure is greater than your systolic pressure, the cuff will act as a tourniquet, cutting off the blood supply. You should not hear any sound in the stethoscope. Keep your eye on the gauge and gradually release the pressure in the cuff using the release on the bulb. (Ideally, you should release the pressure slowly, about 2 to 3 points per heartbeat.)
- As soon as the arterial pressure drops below the cuff pressure, you will hear a pulse. At the first sound of your pulse, note the reading on the pressure gauge: This reading is your systolic pressure.
- Continue to release air from the cuff. The sound of your pulse will increase as more blood is allowed through the artery. Then, as the cuff pressure approaches your diastolic pressure, the sound will begin to fade. Listen carefully until the pulse disappears. The gauge level at the last sound you hear is your diastolic reading.
- Record both the systolic and diastolic readings, as well as the date and time of the measurement.
- If you want to check this reading, you can do so by taking it again. Wait a minute before you repeat the measurement. This time adjust your initial cuff pressure to exactly 30 points above your previous systolic pressure.
- If you can, record your weight and pulse as well as any unrelated events such as arguments, physical exertion, or medications you have taken that might affect your readings. This will help you and the doctor interpret any changes in pressure.

HEART ATTACKS

More than 1.5 million Americans each year suffer a heart attack, and nearly 500,000 of them die. Understandably, a heart attack is a very serious and frightening event, but it need not mean the end of a productive life. Today more than 6.1 million Americans have a history of heart attack or angina (chest pain) or both; most have returned to their jobs or former activities, even though some restrictions may be necessary. Improved treatments mean that even more people are surviving heart attacks—and with less lasting damage than in the past. For instance, the death rate from heart attack decreased from 226 persons per 100,000 in the United States in 1950 to 129 per 100,000 in 1986. Besides improved medical care, factors such as smoking cessation and reduction of fat in the diet may be partially responsible for this favorable trend.

The medical term for heart attack is myocardial infarction, which means death of heart muscle. A heart attack occurs when a coronary artery becomes blocked, cutting off the supply of blood to the nearby muscle (see Figure 11.1). Any prolonged or exten-

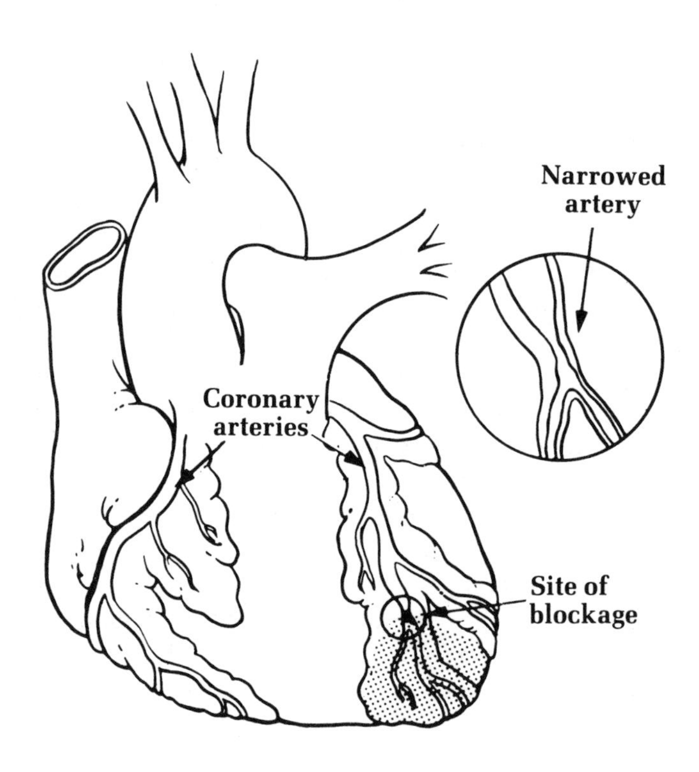

Figure 11.1 What Happens During a Heart Attack
During a heart attack, a coronary artery becomes completely blocked, resulting in death of the surrounding heart muscle, as indicated by the shaded area in the lower portion of the heart.

sive obstruction of a coronary artery can lead to irreversible injury to the heart itself, and, depending upon the location and extent of the damage, this can result in death or disability.

Early treatment of a heart attack with relatively new intravenous drugs—thrombolytics—that dissolve the obstructing clot now makes it possible to avoid much or even all of the damage that usually occurs from an infarction. The three most common of these drugs are t-PA, streptokinase, and APSAC, but usually they are used only in emergencies or in a hospital setting. Thrombolytics are seldom effective unless they are administered within the first few hours (usually one to three hours) of the attack. These agents have certainly revolutionized treatment of heart attacks—for people who receive them in time.

All too often a heart attack victim delays seeking medical help, frequently with fatal results. Most heart attack deaths occur in the first two hours, yet studies have found that many people wait four to six hours before going to an emergency room.

After a Heart Attack. It is normal to be depressed and afraid after experiencing an attack. Many people fear that this means the end of their job, a normal sex life, and all of the things that make life worthwhile. This is why rehabilitation after a heart attack is so important. A heart attack causes some permanent heart damage, but the extent of the damage varies widely from person to person. In some, it may be barely noticeable; in others it can be severe enough to impose certain limitations. But the vast majority of people who survive a heart attack are able to resume an active, normal life. Unfortunately, far too many heart attack patients opt for disability rather than rehabilitation. Most heart attack patients are able to return to their regular jobs, but some whose jobs are particularly strenuous or stressful may need reassignment. Increasingly, cardiac rehabilitation programs include occupational rehabilitation as well.

Activity is the key to any successful rehabilitation effort. This usually entails exercise conditioning, both to improve cardiovascular function and to retrain weakened muscles. Typically, today's heart attack patient will be sitting up in a day or two. He or she will be walking around the hospital room or corridor as soon as the danger of serious rhythm disturbances and other complications is past—usually in four or five days—and ready to go home by the end of the second week or even earlier. Because the prospect of leaving the safety of the hospital is very difficult for a number of heart attack patients, many hospitals now give a modified exercise test before discharging such patients. This shows the patient that he or she can safely engage in a certain amount of physical activity; it also enables a doctor to draw up a specific exercise prescription. Typically, the patient will be instructed to walk—slowly at first, then gradually building up both distance and speed. In the beginning, the person may feel weak and shaky; this is due more to the weakness that follows any stay in bed rather than to the heart attack itself. But after a few weeks most people find they again feel physically fit, and those who were sedentary before may be surprised to find they actually are in even better shape than before the attack.

WARNING SIGNS OF A HEART ATTACK

Know the warning signals of a heart attack:

- Uncomfortable pressure, fullness, squeezing, or pain in the center of the chest that lasts more than a few minutes.
- Pain spreading to the shoulders, neck, or arms.
- Chest discomfort with light-headedness, fainting, sweating, nausea, or shortness of breath.
- Not all these warning signs occur in every heart attack. If some start to occur, however, don't wait. Get help immediately. Delay can be deadly!

Know what to do in an emergency:

- Find out which area hospitals have 24-hour emergency cardiac care.
- Know (in advance) which hospital or medical facility is nearest your home and office, and tell your family and friends to call this facility in an emergency.
- Keep a list of emergency rescue service numbers next to the telephone and in your pocket, wallet, or purse.
- If you have chest discomfort that lasts 10 minutes or more, call the emergency rescue service.
- If you can reach a hospital faster by going yourself and not waiting for an ambulance, have someone drive you there.

Be a heart saver:

- If you're with someone who is experiencing the signs of a heart attack, and the warning signs last more than a few minutes, act immediately. Expect some denial of the problem; it's normal for someone with chest discomfort to deny the possibility of something as serious as a heart attack. But don't take no for an answer. Insist on taking prompt action.
- Call the emergency service or get to the nearest hospital emergency room that offers 24-hour emergency cardiac care.
- Give CPR (mouth-to-mouth breathing and chest compression) if it's necessary and you're properly trained in the procedure.

Source: American Heart Association, *1992 Heart and Stroke Facts*. Reproduced with permission.

Sexuality is a topic that all too many patients and physicians alike avoid discussing, but it is a question that is uppermost in the minds of heart attack victims and their partners. A study by researchers at Massachusetts General Hospital found that heart attack patients who resumed sexual relations had a lower incidence of subsequent heart attacks and death than those who did not, even though their physical conditions were comparable.

Contrary to popular belief, sexual intercourse requires only a modest amount of extra cardiovascular effort. Most doctors agree that a heart attack patient who can climb a flight of stairs or walk a block has enough physical stamina for normal sexual relations. Most sexual problems following a heart attack are due to fear (on the part of both the patient and his or her partner), not to cardiac-related disability. Some of the drugs used to treat heart disease also may interfere with sexual function; if this is a problem, it should be discussed with a doctor who may be able to adjust the drug dosage or prescribe an alternative medication that will not have this side effect.

Obviously, life is not exactly the same after a heart attack; chances are, healthy changes are in order. Stopping smoking, losing weight, increasing physical activity, and avoiding unnecessary stress are all commonsense life-style changes from which most of us could benefit. But it often takes something as drastic as a heart attack to prod us into action.

SURGERY TO TREAT CORONARY DISEASE

About 370,000 Americans undergo coronary bypass graft surgery each year. About 260,000 have an invasive procedure called percutaneous transluminal coronary angioplasty (PTCA) in addition to or instead of a bypass, and the number is rising. This treatment, also referred to as angioplasty or balloon angioplasty, involves using a catheter and inflatable balloonlike tip to flatten the fatty deposits in coronary arteries; it thus dilates them and improves blood flow. More costly procedures, such as heart transplants, are being done with increasing frequency. And experimental treatments, such as development of an artificial heart, continue to capture our imagination and attention. However, these operations have added billions of dollars to the nation's annual medical bill.

A number of physicians have questioned the long-term value of many of these expensive operations. About 25 percent of patients who have had angioplasty experience a gradual renarrowing of the dilated artery, and bypass surgery patients are subject to blockage of the grafted vessel at an increased rate. There is still disagreement among experts as to whether patients with certain types of coronary disease should be treated with drugs and exercise rather than surgery. Some studies have found little or no difference in survival rates between those who have a bypass and those who are treated medically with drugs, exercise, life-style changes, and other methods. Some doctors even think that coronary bypass operations will become obsolete in a few years. At present, however, many people with severe coronary disease are undergoing bypass surgery, and second and even third operations are not uncommon for people who had their first bypass five to 10 years ago.

In a bypass operation, segments of healthy blood vessels—usually the internal mammary artery, which normally supplies blood to the chest wall, or a saphenous vein from the leg—are grafted onto the heart's surface to bypass clogged areas of coronary arteries (see Figure 11.2). Studies have shown that the internal mammary artery is more likely to stay open than a transplanted vein; only 60 percent of grafts using a vein remain open after 10 years, compared to 90 percent of mammary artery grafts. The operation is more difficult and longer than the traditional bypass, however, and is performed at fewer medical centers. Even so, nearly all people who have had multiple bypass surgery have at least one internal mammary artery graft, and this type of graft is often performed along with a saphenous vein graft. Generally, the more bypass routes, the better chance of a successful long-term outcome.

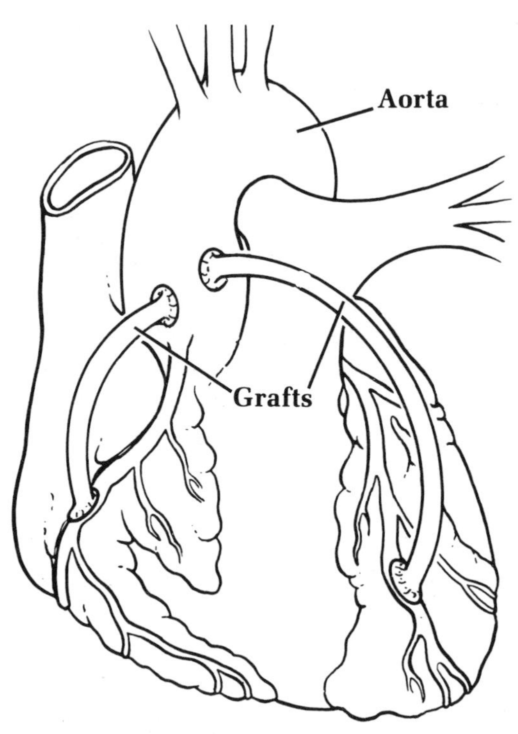

Figure 11.2 Coronary Bypass Operation
To bypass severely blocked areas, portions of a vein (usually the saphenous vein from the leg) or the internal mammary artery (located near the heart) are grafted to coronary arteries. There can be multiple grafts. For instance, a quadruple bypass refers to an operation that includes four grafts.

During the operation, which usually takes two to four hours, the heart is stopped and circulation is maintained by a heart-lung machine. Afterward most patients spend two or three days in an intensive-care recovery room, and an additional week to 10 days in the hospital. The objective is to restore normal blood flow to the heart muscle, thereby eliminating or minimizing anginal attacks and, hopefully, preventing heart attacks.

The operation is not without risks: A small percentage of patients, 1 to 3 percent nationwide, die during surgery or before leaving the hospital. In addition, a small percentage suffer a heart attack, stroke, or other serious complication during or immediately after the operation. The surgery is not a cure for coronary disease; in fact, the grafted vessels seem to become clogged by the same atherosclerotic process that damaged the original coronary arteries, only faster. Despite these very real drawbacks, large numbers of heart patients will unquestionably benefit from coronary bypass surgery, especially in terms of overcoming the symptoms and disability of severe coronary disease. If an operation is called for, however, it should be done in a hospital in which at least 100 to 150 such operations are performed annually.

Angioplasty is less costly and safer than coronary bypass surgery, but it too has its limitations and drawbacks. During angioplasty a balloon is passed through a clogged artery and expanded at the site of the narrowing (see Figure 11.3). Not all clogged coronary arteries can be treated with angioplasty. The results also tend to be temporary; many patients who undergo angioplasty eventually require a second procedure or bypass surgery. Because angioplasty is so much less traumatic than bypass surgery, it should be the procedure of choice for patients with one or two blocked arteries. That's true even when the primary goal is not just to relieve symptoms but also to reduce a high risk of heart attack. Bypass remains a later option if angioplasty doesn't help.

Experiments to use lasers and other advanced technology to unclog coronary arteries and other blood vessels are beginning to show promise. Lasers, which use concentrated beams of light instead of a surgical scalpel, are being used in a number of surgical procedures, including delicate eye surgery and gynecological operations. Many heart researchers think it is only a matter of time before lasers will be used to clean out atherosclerotic plaque from coronary arteries.

STROKES AND MINI-STROKES (TIAs)

The incidence of stroke has dropped dramatically in the last 20 years, largely because of increased detection and treatment of high blood pressure. Even so, it remains a major cause of death and disability; about 500,000 Americans suffer a stroke each year, of whom approximately 147,000 will die. Of the nearly 3 million living stroke victims, many have significant disabilities.

During a stroke the blood supply to part of the brain is cut off, resulting in death of brain tissue in the affected area. Most strokes are caused by a cerebral thrombosis, in

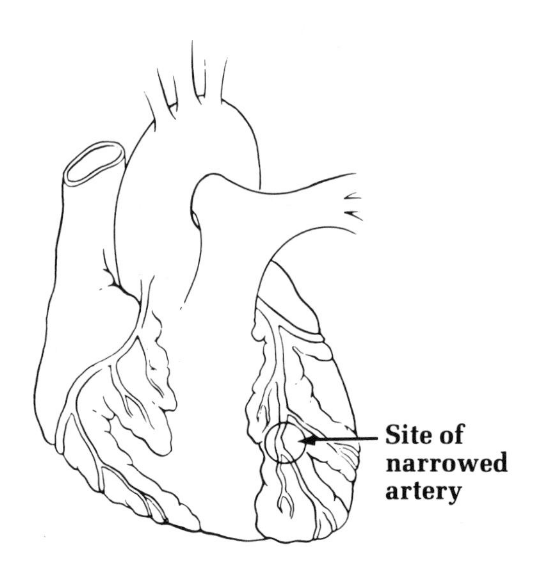

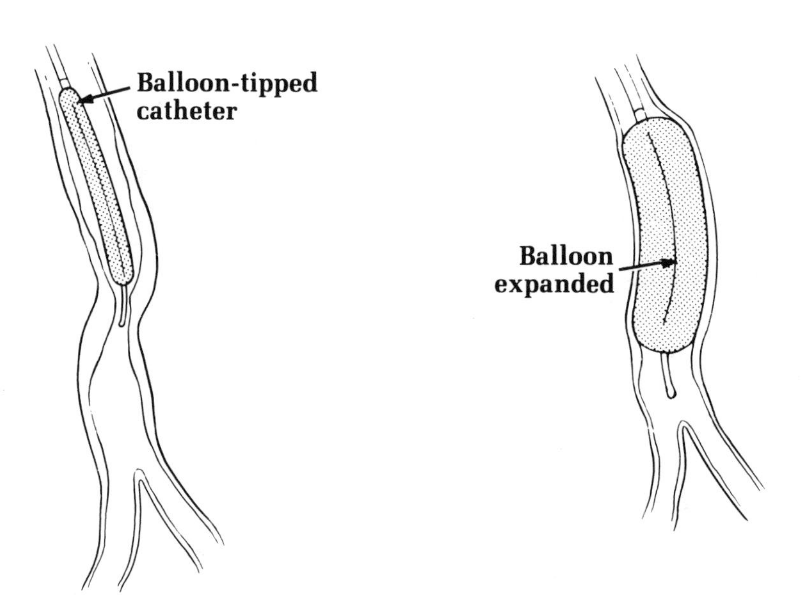

Figure 11.3 Balloon Angioplasty
In balloon angioplasty, a catheter with a balloon tip is passed through the coronary arteries to the site of blockage. The balloon is then inflated, flattening out the fatty deposits along the artery wall to allow more blood to flow through the vessel.

which a clot blocks one of the arteries serving the brain. Strokes also may be caused by bleeding or hemorrhage, usually when a weakened blood vessel bursts. This type of stroke also may be caused by a head injury or an aneurysm, a weakened section of blood vessel that balloons out from the artery wall.

In addition to high blood pressure, the risk of a stroke may be increased by:

- □ a high red blood cell count
- □ heart disease
- □ diabetes
- □ being male
- □ being over 55
- □ smoking cigarettes

About 10 percent of strokes are preceded by mini-strokes, or transient ischemic attacks (TIAs). These are temporary symptoms caused by reduced blood flow to the brain, and they are important warning signs that should never be ignored. Prompt treatment at this point often can prevent a full-blown stroke.

Treatment of strokes and mini-strokes depends on their severity and the source of blockage. Often the blockage occurs in the carotid artery in the neck, causing a ministroke. Surgery to remove the atherosclerotic plaque or to bypass the clogged area may be sufficient to prevent a stroke. As with coronary bypass surgery, the patient will find a second opinion valuable because the operation has its own risks.

If the blood vessel is blocked by a clot, drugs may be given to dissolve it and to prevent the formation of new clots. Some of these anticlotting drugs must be admin-

WARNING SIGNS OF A STROKE

- Sudden weakness or numbness of the face, arm, or leg on one side of the body.
- Sudden dimness or loss of vision, particularly in one eye.
- Loss of speech, or trouble talking or understanding speech.
- Sudden severe headaches with no apparent cause.
- Unexplained dizziness, unsteadiness, or sudden falls, especially with any of the previous symptoms.

If you notice one or more of these signs, don't wait. See a doctor right away!

Source: American Heart Association, *1992 Heart and Stroke Facts*. Reproduced with permission.

istered in a hospital setting and carefully monitored to make sure that the blood does not become too thin and result in hemorrhaging. On a long-term basis, a low dose of ordinary aspirin, usually one-half to one aspirin per day, seems to prevent the formation of potentially lethal clots. People who have had heart valve replacement also are at a high risk of stroke because clots tend to form in and around the artificial valves. This can be prevented by taking an anticlotting medication on a regular basis. Those patients who are allergic to aspirin should consult their physician regarding the use of alternative medication.

Rehabilitation is a vital part of stroke treatment. Contrary to popular belief, most people who have a stroke can be successfully rehabilitated, although this depends upon the extent of brain damage. The attitude and cooperation of the patient and family members are also very important, as is the timing and quality of the rehabilitation program. Ideally, rehabilitation should start as soon as the immediate crisis has passed. The part of the brain damaged by stroke determines the physical consequences (see Figure 11.4). Often little can be done to overcome some of the paralysis, memory loss, and other problems, but increasingly we are learning more about retraining the brain to enable a stroke victim to learn new skills and relearn old ones.

ASPIRIN AND HEART DISEASE

The role of aspirin in the treatment and prevention of heart disease has been subject to debate ever since researchers discovered its value as an antiplatelet drug. Antiplatelets work to keep platelets—tiny components of blood—from sticking together and forming blood clots. Blood clots can lead to heart attack and stroke, and may also cause discomfort or pain. Daily aspirin therapy lowers these risks.

Although the usual dose for this kind of therapy is one aspirin (325 milligrams) a day, recent research has shown that as little as 80 milligrams a day may be enough to protect some people. For those at greatest risk of a heart attack, four tablets a day (1,300 mg) may be prescribed.

Even though aspirin is a commonly used over-the-counter drug, you must consult your doctor before starting *any* drug therapy. Some people are not suited to taking aspirin on a regular basis. For example, those with ulcers or bleeding disorders should not be treated with aspirin. Even when its use is appropriate, aspirin therapy should be combined with life-style changes, such as diet and exercise modifications, in an all-encompassing preventive program.

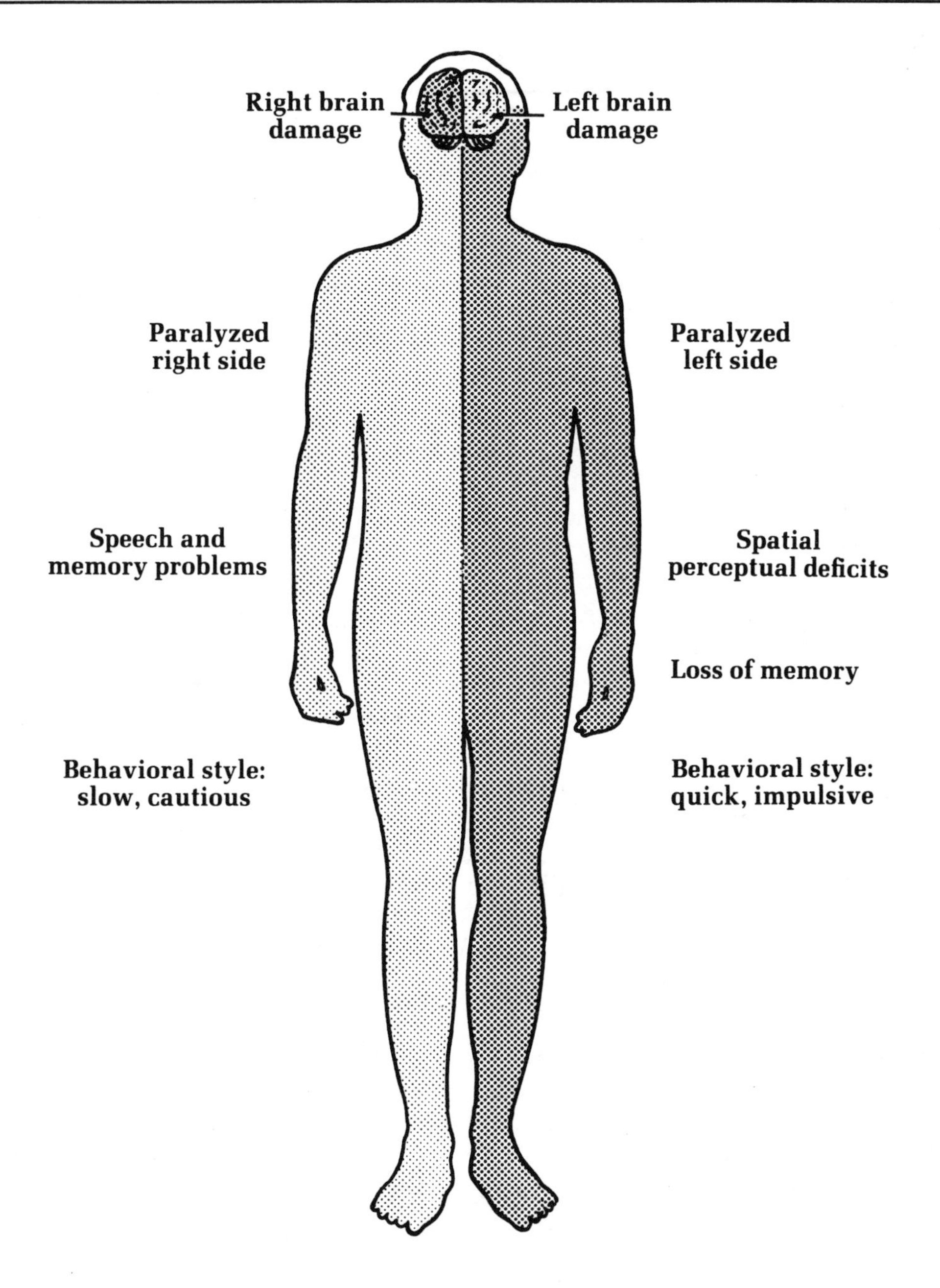

Figure 11.4 Possible Effects of a Stroke
A stroke can damage the right side of the brain, which controls the left side of the body, as well as the left side, which controls the right side of the body.

HEART VALVE DISEASE

A system of four valves—one for each chamber of the heart—ensures that blood moves in the right direction as it passes through the heart. For example, the tricuspid valve allows blood to pass from the right atrium into the right ventricle. The blood is then forced from the right ventricle into the lungs via the pulmonary valve; oxygenated blood goes from the lungs into the left atrium, where it passes through the mitral valve and into the left ventricle, the heart's main pumping chamber. Finally, blood being pumped from the left ventricle goes through the aortic valve and into the aorta, where it begins its trip through the body's circulatory system.

Sometimes, in a quiet moment after exercising, you can hear your heart making a thumping sound. It is audible when you are lying still after exercising. This is the sound of the heart valves closing. The valves work in close synchronization with each other: When the heart beats (or contracts), the pulmonary and aortic valves open to allow blood to pass into the lungs and aorta respectively; between beats, the tricuspid and mitral valves open to let the blood from the atria into the pumping chambers.

Heart valve disorders usually fall into one of two categories: (1) valvular stenosis, in which the valve becomes thickened and narrowed, preventing it from opening properly and impeding the outward flow of blood, or (2) valvular regurgitation, also referred to as insufficiency or incompetence, in which the valve is weakened and does not close properly, thus permitting a backflow of blood.

The most common type of valve disorder, affecting about 5 to 10 percent of the U.S. population, is mitral valve prolapse, also known as the click-murmur syndrome. The valve's flaplike leaflets fail to close properly because of a deformity that is believed to be hereditary. In serious cases, mitral regurgitation may occur, but usually the disorder is mild and produces no symptoms. Generally diagnosed during adolescence and early adulthood, mitral valve prolapse causes characteristic clicks and murmurs that can be heard through a stethoscope. Many more women than men have mitral valve prolapse.

Congenital defects, heart attacks, and aging all can lead to valvular disease. Heart valves also may be damaged by infections: These include rheumatic fever, caused by a streptococcal bacterium, and bacterial endocarditis, a serious heart infection that occurs when an infection in another part of the body goes untreated. It is most common among people who already have malfunctioning valves, people who have artificial valves, and intravenous drug users who use contaminated needles.

In older people, the most common cause of heart valve disease is called myxomatous degeneration. In this process, the valve (usually the mitral valve) and the mechanisms that control its opening and closing become defective as a result of lost tissue elasticity and starchy buildup. Another type of tissue breakdown, called calcific degeneration, involves buildup of calcium deposits that damage the valve. It usually affects the aortic valve or the mitral valve, producing aortic stenosis or mitral regurgitation. The causes of these two conditions are unknown, and they may produce no symptoms.

When valves become defective, the heart has to work harder to pump blood through the body. Eventually this can lead to congestive heart failure or disturbances in heart rhythm. Sometimes a defective heart valve is discovered during a routine examination, when a doctor detects a murmur or other unusual sound while listening to the heart through a stethoscope. More frequently, the problem will be discovered after it has produced symptoms. Shortness of breath and fatigue are common signs of valvular disease. A bluish tinge to the fingers or lips and fainting are also possible signs of heart valve disease.

Diagnosis of a valvular problem can be confirmed by echocardiography, an examination that uses sound waves to map the structures of the heart. Other methods are cardiac catheterization and angiography. Most valve problems can be treated with drugs, although drugs do not cure the initial valve disorder. Digitalis or other medications may be prescribed to slow the heartbeat and increase its output. Diuretics and a salt-restricted diet may be prescribed to prevent a buildup of fluid. Since diseased heart valves are a common site for blood clots to form, low doses of aspirin or other anti-clotting drugs are often needed as a preventive measure. Beta blockers or other antiarrhythmic drugs may be needed to prevent irregular heartbeats. Prophylactic antibiotics also are important in long-term treatment of heart valve disease. Defective valves are particularly susceptible to bacterial endocarditis; to prevent this, antibiotics should always be taken before any surgical or dental procedure in which bacteria might enter the bloodstream.

If a heart valve becomes so damaged that it seriously hampers the flow of blood or is causing congestive heart failure, it may be replaced with an artificial valve. A number of efficient and durable replacement valves have been developed; some of these are made from animal parts and others are made of plastic and/or metal. Valve replacement should be performed by a surgeon who does a large number of these operations each year. The hospital team should also have regular experience. Following heart valve replacement, antibiotics and blood-thinning drugs may be permanently prescribed to prevent infection and clot formation.

An alternative to surgery known as balloon valvuloplasty is being used increasingly for stenotic valves. In the same process as angioplasty, a balloon-tipped catheter is inserted and the balloon is inflated, widening the narrowed portion of the valve. The procedure is more successful when performed on the mitral valve rather than the aortic valve. The long-term success of this treatment is uncertain, but it is a safer and less expensive option, especially for those who are unable to go through surgery.

A person with severe valvular disease may need to avoid very strenuous activity or include rest periods throughout the day. With proper treatment, however, most can live reasonably normal lives.

HEART RHYTHM DISORDERS

The average adult heart will beat regularly 60 to 70 times per minute. The rhythm slows during sleep and speeds up during exercise. Normally we are unaware of our heart's rhythm; the sympathetic nervous system automatically regulates the heart's beating. All of us now and then experience a skipped heartbeat or even a series of fast beats, or palpitations. These occasional disturbances in heart rhythm usually are benign, but there are a number of diseases in which cardiac arrhythmias, or irregular heartbeats, are potentially serious.

When the heart beats too fast, its action is referred to as tachycardia; if it beats too slowly, the action is known as bradycardia. Cigarette smoking, excessive caffeine consumption, anxiety, and certain drugs all can affect the heart's rhythm. An overactive thyroid can cause tachycardia, while too little thyroid hormone results in bradycardia. Some types of heart disease, such as coronary or heart valve disorders, also cause heart arrhythmias.

Most arrhythmias are temporary and harmless, but some can be life-threatening. For example, ventricular fibrillation is a common cause of sudden death. When fibrillation occurs, the heart beats in a shallow, quivering, disorganized fashion, and it fails to pump any blood. The quivering is caused by a severe disturbance in the heart's electrical impulses. If ventricular fibrillation is not stopped almost immediately—at least within two or three minutes—and the heart's normal rhythm restored, the person will die. If you are a fan of TV medical dramas, you have probably seen emergency room doctors using electrical defibrillators, paddlelike devices that administer an electrical shock to the heart to interrupt the disturbed electrical pattern and restore a normal beat. A similarly disturbed pattern occurs during ventricular fibrillation. When ventricular fibrillation happens outside a hospital setting or where emergency help is not quickly available, it can cause sudden death.

Another common, potentially serious arrhythmia is atrial fibrillation. In this disorder, the atrium beats 500 to 600 times a minute, causing the ventricles to beat irregularly but at a slower rate—170 to 200 beats per minute. This is due to the filtering action of the atrioventricular node. In fact, the ventricular rate is sometimes normal during these episodes, and the volume of blood pumped usually remains adequate. Atrial fibrillation often occurs after heart disease or another disorder has caused the atrium to enlarge, but it may also occur when no heart disease is evident. Other factors include sleep deprivation, use of drugs such as amphetamines or cocaine, excessive consumption of caffeine or alcohol, heart valve disease, lung disease, pericarditis, and hyperthyroidism. Once established, atrial fibrillation lasts for life, but it can be controlled by drugs (see Table 11.3). Aspirin may be prescribed on a daily basis to prevent the most serious possible result of prolonged episodes of atrial fibrillation: clots that could lead to stroke.

Some cardiac arrhythmias arise in the heart's pacemaker cells, specialized cells that conduct electrical impulses. The heart may beat either too fast or too slowly; if the

Table 11.3

Drugs to Treat Heart Rhythm Disorders (Arrhythmias)

BETA BLOCKERS

Action: Reduce heart rate and heart muscle contractility by blocking the response of the beta nerve receptors. These receptors send signals to the heart to work harder.

Generic name	Brand name	Possible side effects
acebutolol atenolol betaxolol carteolol metoprolol nadolol penbutolol pindolol propranolol timolol	Sectral Tenormin Kerlone Cartrol Lopressor Corgard Levatol Visken Inderal Blocadren	Slow pulse, weakness, low blood pressure, asthma attacks, fatigue, insomnia (for Inderal), impotence, nausea, nightmares or vivid dreams, lethargy as well as cold hands and feet because of reduced circulation

CALCIUM CHANNEL BLOCKERS

Action: Inhibit the flow of calcium in and out of the heart tissue, affecting their electrical impulses.

Generic name	Brand name	Possible side effects
diltiazem	Cardizem	Headache, nausea, swelling, irregular heartbeat, rash, fatigue
verapamil	Calan Isoptin Verelan	Dizziness, headache, low blood pressure, slow pulse, ankle swelling, constipation

DIGITALIS PREPARATIONS

Action: Restore normal heartbeat by controlling the release rate and speed of electrical impulses within the heart.

Generic name	Brand name	Possible side effects
digoxin digitoxin	Lanoxin Crystodigin	Tiredness, nausea, loss of appetite, disturbances in vision, weakness, headache, slow pulse

OTHER ANTIARRHYTHMICS

Action: Highly potent drugs that restore normal heartbeat through a variety of mechanisms.

Generic name	Brand name	Possible side effects
amiodarone	Cordarone	Lung or liver inflammation, muscle degeneration and weakness, loss of balance, slow heart rate, sunburn susceptibility, thyroid underactivity or overactivity, rash, weight loss, nausea, constipation, dizziness, fainting, palpitations, changes in vision
disopyramide	Norpace	Weakening of heart contractions, dry mouth, constipation, difficulty urinating (for men), low blood sugar, worsening of glaucoma
flecainide propafenone	Tambocor Rhythmol	Weakening cardiac pumping, slow heart rate, increased blood sugar, fever, rash, liver inflammation, confusion, loss of concentration, dizziness, metallic taste in mouth, changes in vision
mexiletine	Mexitil	Fever, rash, lower blood platelet count, liver inflammation, nausea, confusion, loss of concentration, dizziness, tremors, changes in vision

TABLE 11.3
Drugs to Treat Heart Rhythm Disorders (Arrhythmias) (*cont'd*)

Generic name	Brand name	Possible side effects
procainamide	Procan Pronestyl	Fever, rash, liver inflammation, weight loss, nausea, confusion, loss of concentration, drug-induced lupus
quinidine gluconate quinidine sulfate	Duraquin Quinaglute Quinalan Quinidex	Diarrhea, drop in blood platelets, fever, rash, dizziness, ringing in the ears
tocainide	Tonocard	Weight loss, nausea, tremors, fever, rash, depressed white blood cell count, liver inflammation, confusion, loss of concentration, dizziness, disturbances in vision, lung inflammation

Source: Consumer Reports Books, *The Complete Drug Reference*, 1992 edition © The U.S. Pharmacopeial Convention, Inc. Permission granted.

problem is severe and cannot be controlled by drugs, an artificial pacemaker may be needed. This device provides electrical impulses that ensure a steady heartbeat. Some pacemakers work on demand; that is, they send out impulses only when the heart rate falls below a certain predetermined level. They do not send impulses when the heart is beating normally. Other pacemakers work constantly, sending out impulses at a fixed rate regardless of whether the heart is beating too fast or too slowly.

Another option that has become available more recently is the automatic implantable cardioverter defibrillator (AICD). It is designed primarily to prevent ventricular defibrillation—a disorder that can be fatal within minutes—by slowing down or halting the excessively rapid ventricular beats. It does this by interrupting the abnormal rhythm with brief shocks to the heart muscle. This device has been implanted primarily in people who are at high risk for sudden death. Mortality rates have dropped to 1 to 4 percent with the device, compared to 10 to 15 percent for people who receive only drug treatment.

People who are prone to cardiac arrhythmias should avoid caffeine, tobacco, and drugs that cause the heartbeat to speed up. Although most cardiac arrhythmias are relatively harmless, some can develop into serious problems. Therefore, all should be investigated by a doctor.

CONGESTIVE HEART FAILURE

Congestive heart failure occurs when the heart is unable to pump enough blood through the body, even during rest or periods of very modest activity, to enable the body to carry out normal functions. This results in a buildup of blood volume that causes an accumulation of fluids, or congestion.

An early, frequent sign of congestive heart failure is difficulty breathing when lying down. Typically, the person will awaken with a feeling of breathlessness. This is caused by an accumulation of fluid in the lungs and is eased by sitting up. Many people with congestive failure end up sleeping upright in a chair or propped up in bed with several pillows. Swelling in the legs is another early, common sign of congestive failure, as is a rapid pulse, which is produced by increased pumping action as the heart attempts to meet the body's demand for oxygen carried by the blood.

Congestive heart failure may be the result of damage to the heart muscle during a heart attack or from chronic high blood pressure. Cardiomyopathy, a disease of the muscle, and diseases of the heart valves are other causes of congestive heart failure. Early diagnosis and treatment of valvular disease or high blood pressure are important in preventing congestive heart failure. Chronic infection with fever, severe anemia, and extreme vitamin B deficiency are additional causes of congestive heart failure.

The earlier diagnosis and treatment of congestive heart failure is made, the better the outlook. Often, identifying and correcting the underlying cause will improve the heart's pumping ability. For example, treating high blood pressure or valvular disease will make congestive heart failure easier to manage.

Several drugs are used to treat congestive heart failure. Digitalis, which slows the heart rate and increases the strength of its contractions, thereby enabling it to pump more blood, is a standard drug in treating the disorder. Diuretics are often prescribed to reduce the accumulation of fluid in the legs, lungs, liver, and other tissues. Relatively new drugs used in the treatment of heart failure are vasodilators, which ease the heart's workload by dilating, or opening up, the blood vessels. One type of vasodilator, angiotensin-converting enzyme (ACE) inhibitors, which include captopril (Capoten) and enalapril (Vasotec), may sometimes be prescribed when diuretics and digitalis are not effective. They also work well in combination.

Weight loss, salt restriction, and frequent rest periods throughout the day are among the life-style changes that may be necessary to overcome problems caused by congestive heart failure. Moderate exercise aimed at improving cardiovascular function may help the body make more efficient use of available oxygen and ease the feelings of breathlessness. However, any exercise program should be carried out under a doctor's direction.

CIRCULATORY DISORDERS

Most of us immediately think of the heart when we talk about cardiovascular disorders, overlooking the blood vessels and other facets of circulatory function. In many instances circulatory disorders are independent of heart disease. The more common ones are described below.

Varicose Veins. Varicose veins are very common, especially among older women who have had several children. In these veins, weakened valves that help keep the blood flowing toward the heart cause the disorder. Blood that circulates to the legs and feet must travel upward, against the force of gravity, to get back to the heart and lungs. Blood pressure aids in promoting this upward flow, as does the constriction of leg muscles as a person moves about. These forces are aided by a series of one-way valves, flaplike leaflets that lie flat against the wall of a vein when blood is moving toward the heart. The valves billow outward if the blood starts to flow backward, helping ensure that the blood flows in one direction.

If some of the valves become weakened, a backflow of blood may result. Blood will seep backward until it is stopped by a properly functioning valve. The blood will accumulate in this spot, causing the vein's walls to expand outward. Over time, this will result in the twisted and swollen vessels characteristic of varicose veins.

Some people have an inherited tendency to develop varicose veins. Pregnancy, obesity, and standing in one position for long periods are among the other factors promoting varicose veins. Women may be more susceptible than men because their muscles may not be as well developed. The varicose veins that often develop during pregnancy are caused by the increased abdominal weight and extra blood flow, as well as the downward pressure of the fetus. These usually disappear after the baby is born, but a woman who has had repeated pregnancies accompanied by varicose veins may be more susceptible to developing varicosities later in life.

A swelling and darkening of vessels in the leg are the first symptoms of varicose veins. There is often a feeling of tightness or heaviness in the lower legs, tenderness, muscle cramps and weakness, and sometimes ankle swelling. In severe cases, bruising, infection, and swelling may form at the site of the varicosities.

Exercise is very important in both the prevention and treatment of varicose veins. People whose jobs demand that they stand for long periods—barbers, traffic officers, and surgeons, among others—should make it a point to move their legs frequently. Standing with one leg elevated on a short stool may help; taking a break now and then to sit with the legs raised to promote blood flow is also recommended. Avoid sitting with the legs crossed—this hinders blood flow in the legs.

Walking and cycling are particularly good activities for people with varicose veins. Wearing elastic support hose also may be recommended; to get the maximum benefit, however, the hose should be the prescription type, which offers better support than regular, off-the-rack support hose. Of course, anyone with varicose veins should avoid wearing tight shoes, garters, or other garments that restrict blood flow. And they should lose weight if they are heavy. Veins that are supported by firm muscle instead of fat are less likely to swell.

For people who are not helped by such conservative methods, medical treatment may be needed. One common approach entails injecting the vein with a solution that causes it to harden, thus sealing off the vessel and forcing the rerouting of blood to other healthy vessels. This may provide temporary relief but it usually is not a permanent cure. In severe cases, surgical removal of the damaged vessels may be necessary. This also forces a rerouting of blood and improves circulation in the legs.

Phlebitis and Thrombophlebitis. Phlebitis refers to inflammation of a vein, which often results in formation of a clot, or thrombus, at the site of inflammation—a condition called thrombophlebitis. There are two kinds of thrombophlebitis: (1) superficial thrombophlebitis, which is located in a superficial vein, and (2) deep thrombophlebitis, which occurs in a vessel located deeper within the leg. Superficial thrombophlebitis is uncomfortable but rarely life-threatening; in contrast, a part of a deep thrombophlebitis may break off and travel through the circulatory system to the lungs, with often fatal results. Deep thrombophlebitis is most common among people who have chronic heart or lung disease, or who are confined to bed following surgery, stroke, or a broken bone. Signs of deep thrombophlebitis include heaviness and pain in the leg, especially when it is down; swelling; and a bluish cast to the skin, which also may feel warm to the touch.

Diagnosis is usually made with a process called contrast venography, which consists of injecting a dye and following its course using X rays. This test, while considered the most accurate measure, can be uncomfortable. An alternative test known as impedance plethysmography measures blood flow in the legs with a blood pressure cuff and electrodes. It is especially useful in detecting clots above the knee. Another test, ultrasonography, uses sound waves to compose a picture that can show clots. It is noninvasive but relatively expensive. In a test called platelet scintigraphy, radioactive isotopes are injected to locate clots and to plot their path over a few days.

Superficial thrombophlebitis often occurs in people with varicose veins. It usually can be treated with periods of resting while keeping the leg elevated, and with anti-inflammatory drugs to ease the inflammation and pain. Warm compresses and elastic stockings also may help. It is important to stay active and to avoid long periods in bed or remaining in one position. In severe cases, however, bed rest with the leg elevated may be required. If these measures do not work, the patient may need surgery to remove the clot and the inflamed lining of the vessel.

Deep thrombophlebitis always requires prompt medical treatment. Anticoagulant drugs to prevent further clotting are usually needed. People taking these medications need to have their blood tested frequently to make sure that it is not being thinned too much. They also should avoid aspirin or any other drug that inhibits clotting or may cause bleeding. Bed rest with the leg elevated also may be required; wearing elastic stockings (regular or prescription-type), even in bed, will help promote circulation.

Since phlebitis has a tendency to recur, it is important that a person be aware of the warning signs and seek prompt medical attention should they reappear.

Arteriosclerosis Obliterans. Arteriosclerosis, or progressive hardening and narrowing of the arteries, can occur in many parts of the body. When it affects the lower legs, the condition is called arteriosclerosis obliterans. It typically strikes men over age 50 who smoke and have high blood cholesterol. High blood pressure and diabetes also increase the risk.

As the major arteries that carry blood to the legs and feet become progressively narrowed by fatty deposits, smaller collateral vessels attempt to take over a greater circulatory function. But these vessels usually are inadequate to meet the demands. At first the person may be troubled by leg cramps, aches, or muscle fatigue in the legs while exercising. This is called intermittent claudication, or "leg angina." The site of the pain and other symptoms is determined by the area of narrowing. For example, if the femoral artery (which runs down the thigh) is blocked, pain is likely to occur in the calves.

In most cases, the person has to stop and rest the legs after walking a block or two or climbing a flight of stairs in order to relieve the pain. As the narrowing worsens, pain is likely to occur almost constantly, even when resting. Eventually, the skin—deprived of oxygen and other nutrients—weakens and begins to break down, resulting in ulcers. In severe cases, gangrene may develop, requiring amputation in 3 to 5 percent of those with claudication. Fortunately this can usually be avoided with early treatment. Stopping smoking, lowering cholesterol and high blood pressure, and keeping blood sugar in the normal range if diabetes is present are all important first steps in controlling obstructive arterial disorders. There are other causes of intermittent claudication, such as a degenerative spinal disc. It is important to see a doctor to determine the cause of the problem so proper treatment can be initiated.

Exercise, even though it may be painful, is a vital part of treatment. Patients with arteriosclerosis obliterans and intermittent claudication usually are instructed to walk or use a stationary bicycle for 15 to 30 minutes, several times a day. Patients should rest when pain occurs, but continue exercising when it eases. A program of graduated walking and exercise improves collateral circulation and, for many patients, can ease the symptoms.

If the problem persists or worsens, vascular surgery may be attempted to improve circulation. This may entail using grafts—either taken from healthy vessels elsewhere or from synthetic material—to bypass the blocked area, as well as endarterectomy, in which the diseased vessel will be opened and the fatty deposits that are clogging it removed. Angioplasty, the procedure in which a balloon-tipped catheter is used to flatten the fatty deposits and widen the artery, has increasingly replaced endarterectomies. Researchers also are studying the use of lasers to "clean out" these blocked vessels, noting that the leg is better suited to this type of surgery than the heart is.

Aneurysms. An aneurysm is a weakened segment of an artery or other blood vessel that fills with blood and balloons outward. Congenital weakness in the blood vessel walls, high blood pressure, infection, arteriosclerosis, and injuries are among the more common causes of aneurysms.

Very often, a person can have an aneurysm without knowing it. These symptomless aneurysms may show up on an X ray or be felt during a physical examination. Some, however, will produce symptoms, depending upon their severity and location. Sometimes an aneurysm will press on an internal organ, causing pain or other problems. A person may feel a pulsating sensation; for example, an aneurysm of the large abdominal aortic artery may be felt as a pulsation in the abdomen.

Rupture of the vessel is the major danger of an aneurysm. Depending upon the location and amount of bleeding, a ruptured aneurysm can produce shock, loss of consciousness, and death. A ruptured aneurysm in the brain can cause a stroke. Sometimes an aneurysm leaks blood without actually rupturing; it may cause pain without the shock and rapid onset of other symptoms seen with a rupture, but it is still potentially life-threatening. Aneurysms also increase the danger of blood clotting, which can result in a heart attack or stroke. Sometimes an aneurysm will bleed into the wall of an artery and block some of its branches. This happens most often in the aorta.

Sometimes an aneurysm can be surgically repaired or removed; in other instances, treatment may consist of lowering blood pressure and keeping it at a low level to prevent extra strain on the weakened vessel.

12

Cancer

Despite considerable gains in the last two decades, cancer remains our second leading cause of death, second only to heart disease. Many people still harbor the mistaken notion that a diagnosis of cancer means unrelenting pain and an automatic death sentence. The fact is, using present treatments and technology, half or more of all cancers can be cured. Three million of the 5 million living Americans who have had cancer were treated five or more years ago, and most of these are considered fully cured of the disease.

As for the question of cancer pain, it is true that some cancers are painful. Many other kinds, however, produce little or no pain. For many patients, what pain does exist can be controlled with aspirin or prescription drugs or self-help techniques. In fact, the pain of chronic arthritis is often considered worse than the pain of many cancers.

Fortunately, the social stigma and many of the groundless fears that were associated with cancer in the past seem to be disappearing, but misconceptions remain. For example, many former cancer patients still find employers reluctant to take the chance of hiring or promoting them, although studies have found that recovered cancer patients do not display as much job absenteeism as people with heart disease or diabetes. Cancer rehabilitation remains a largely neglected aspect of treatment, even though most cancer patients can resume normal, productive lives if given the opportunity.

Cancer prevention is another area largely neglected by the general public. Experts contend that the majority of cancer cases—some say as many as 85 percent of the more common cancers—could be prevented simply by avoiding known carcinogens, such as tobacco. Despite the available information on the relation of cancer or survival after cancer to such factors as smoking, diet, and early detection, attention to cancer prevention does not seem to be a personal priority with the American public. But as more information is made available and as evidence to support some claims about risks and benefits grows stronger, health-care professionals and other concerned individuals hope to see a movement away from health-endangering practices and toward health promotion. The fact is, an informed, participatory public is the best equipped to prevent cancer from happening in the first place.

It may seem difficult to correlate the fact that cancer causes so many deaths with the statistics that show that survival rates for most cancers have been steadily improving over the past decades. In the 1940s, only one in four patients was cured of the disease, cure being defined as being alive and free of the disease five years after diagnosis. Today two out of five achieve this goal. The increase in the number of deaths despite the improved survival percentage rate is due largely to an increase in the number of new lung cancer cases each year, particularly among women who smoke cigarettes.

Survival—being symptom-free for five years following treatment for cancer—has improved for a variety of reasons, among them improved forms of therapy and methods of getting treatments directly to malignant tissue, more sophisticated screening techniques leading to earlier detection, and heightened public awareness, which can also lead to earlier detection.

WHAT IS CANCER?

Cancer is a family of diseases that includes more than a hundred types. Basically, cancer is uncontrolled cell growth. Normal cells have a specific function in the maintenance of the body and a regulated growth process that controls the ratio of old or dying cells to new cells. Cells can be divided into three types as far as their growth potential is concerned: *static* cells, such as muscle and nerve tissue, which do not divide or grow after they have reached a specific size; *committed* cells, which stop growing when the organ or tissue achieves its normal size, though they may be reactivated if damage occurs to the tissue or organ; and *stem* cells, which are continually dying and being replaced, but which appear to have an internal control system that maintains a balance between new and old cells.

Cancer cells, on the other hand, do not serve any assigned function in the body and do not obey any such regulatory process. They grow, therefore, without restraint, and they do not die or "shed" as do normal cells. Cancer cells live longer than normal cells and divide also more often during their lifespan, thus fueling the growth of tumors that may start to encroach on neighboring tissue.

Another distinguishing characteristic of cancer cells is their ability to migrate from their original site to other parts of the body through the blood or lymph systems, forming metastases (new cancer growths). Initially, this spread may be confined to one region of the body, but depending on the type of cancer and the time in which it is left untreated, the disease may eventually spread throughout the body.

Cancer is not contracted in the same way as a cold or stomach virus. Some cancers tend to run in families, and people in those families are assumed to have a genetic predisposition to a specific cancer. Typically, cancer develops slowly over a period of many years, but it can also occur very suddenly. There may be a substantial gap between exposure to a cancer-causing agent and the first symptoms, or diagnosis, of cancer: the time-bomb effect. It is possible that many cancers develop by means of a two-stage process: first, exposure to initiators, substances that may pave the way for cancer; and second, exposure to promoters, carcinogens, or other cancer-causing agents.

The risk of cancer substantially increases with age. Studies have shown that your risk of developing cancer at age 65 to 69 is greater than it was 10 years earlier. Approximately 85 percent of all new cancer cases diagnosed in 1990 occurred in people over 50.

Some experts estimate that environmental factors—including overexposure to the sun, smoking, alcohol, diet, or exposure to other carcinogenic substances—account for the majority of cancers in this country, and that a majority of those cases could be avoided.

CAUSAL FACTORS

SMOKING

If the claim that reducing one's cancer risk substantially is within the power of the general population sounds extravagant, a look at the statistics for lung cancer may provide supporting evidence. Of the 168,000 annual cases of lung cancer—a cancer with one of the lowest five-year survival rates, at 13 percent—the American Cancer Society estimates that 100,000 could be prevented if no one smoked. Lung cancer is now the number-one cancer killer in both sexes. The disease has recently surpassed breast cancer in women because of the increase in smoking among women. Tobacco is commonly blamed as the primary cause of lung cancer, but it is also implicated in cancers of the mouth, throat, larynx, esophagus, pancreas, and bladder. And cigarette smoking enhances one's risk from other environmental hazards. Asbestos exposure, for example, places a person at risk for lung cancer, but in conjunction with smoking, that risk is substantially increased.

Other agents that increase susceptibility to lung cancer include:

- radioisotopes
- mustard gas
- asbestos dust
- polycyclic aromatic hydrocarbons

- □ halogen ethers
- □ nickel and chromium dust
- □ inorganic arsenic
- □ iron ore
- □ wood dust
- □ leather-tanning agents
- □ vinyl chloride
- □ printing ink and textile dye (possibly)

Not only the simple incidence of lung cancer but the death rate from lung cancer is higher among smokers; those who smoke two or more packs of cigarettes a day face a 15 to 25 percent higher mortality rate than do nonsmokers. Risk increases with the number of years the person has smoked, the number of cigarettes smoked per day, and the tar and nicotine content of the cigarettes. Therefore, the single most effective strategy for preventing lung cancer is unquestionably to stop smoking.

Although cigarette smoking is the primary factor in lung cancer, cigar and pipe smoking substantially increase the risk of other cancers, especially those of the mouth, lip, tongue, pharynx, larynx, and esophagus. Smokeless tobacco—moist "dip" tobacco and loose-leaf chewing tobacco—significantly increase the risk of mouth and throat cancers.

SUN EXPOSURE

Overexposure to the sun is considered to be a factor in almost all cases of non-melanoma skin cancers. The American Cancer Society estimates that about 90 percent of the approximately 600,000 cases of skin cancer diagnosed each year could have been prevented by protection from the sun's rays. These cancers, basal cell carcinoma and squamous cell carcinoma, are almost always cured once correctly diagnosed. Sun exposure has also been shown to be a factor in malignant melanoma, a relatively rare cancer that has been increasing dramatically in the United States in recent decades. The mortality rate from melanoma, which strikes those over 45 the most frequently, is about 20 percent.

Many people over 50 take vacations to tropical locales or retire to warm climates such as Florida, Arizona, and southern California, and they should especially be aware of the effects of sun exposure. Baking in the sun poolside is not an option anymore, unless you want to significantly increase your odds of developing skin cancer.

RADIATION

Exposure to ionizing radiation can come from diagnostic radiology (X rays), nuclear medicine, and radiation therapy. However, X rays are invaluable diagnostic aids and can reveal the need for lifesaving interventions. Mammography (X-ray exam-

TIPS ON AVOIDING SUN EXPOSURE

- Avoid sunbathing between the hours of 10 A.M. and 3 P.M., when the sun's rays are strongest.
- Wear protective clothing, such as a hat and long-sleeved shirt.
- Use a sun-blocking agent, or sunscreen, such as PABA (para-aminobenzoic acid). It should have an SPF (sun-protector factor) rating of 15 or higher. Sunscreen should be applied one hour before going out in the sun, and reapplied after swimming or perspiring heavily.

ination of the breast), for example, can detect very early a tumor that is too small to be identified during a physical examination. Computerized tomography helps locate brain tumors. For this reason, no one should refuse any necessary X-ray procedure recommended by a physician. But in response to the overall increase in use and types of diagnostic radiology, guidelines have been developed.

Nuclear medicine, which uses radioactive chemicals to diagnose abnormalities in organs and tissues, exposes the whole body to short-term radiation and should be used only when it is essential to the diagnosis. To avoid unnecessary exposure to X rays, follow these steps:

- □ If abdominal or intestinal X rays are needed, the sexual organs should be shielded whenever possible.
- □ The X-ray film should not be larger than the area to be examined, and the beam should fall only on the film.
- □ Dental X rays should be done only as needed, and the patient always should wear a protective lead shield. The dentist or dental technician should also follow protective techniques.
- □ Many patients view an X ray as the first step in a diagnosis. But often diagnoses are made using a patient history, physical exam, or blood test. Let the physician decide whether an X ray is appropriate, rather than requesting one yourself.
- □ Keep a record of when and where X rays were taken as well as the purpose.
- □ If you live in a state where X-ray records are destroyed after seven years, be sure to request that the X rays or reports be sent to your home. If you have a new physician, make sure your previous doctor releases the records to the new one.
- □ Fluoroscopy, in which a contrast material is used to provide a clearer outline of selected areas, delivers a larger dose of radiation than X-ray film

does. Alternate means should be considered unless this test is an essential part of a procedure, such as in an upper GI series or barium enema.

- X rays should be taken only by an accredited X-ray technician or a radiologist.

OCCUPATIONAL CARCINOGENIC HAZARDS

Awareness and caution are the keys to limiting risk from occupational exposure to carcinogens. The federal Occupational Safety and Health Administration (OSHA) issues and enforces workplace standards, conducts on-site inspections, and deals with complaints about violations from workers.

Employees have an obligation to become familiar with the safety standards of their company and to comply with all health and safety rules. Workers must also be careful not to carry hazardous materials home on their clothing or body. Protective clothing worn in the workplace should not be brought home to be washed.

Any possible violations or health hazards should be reported to a supervisor and/or to OSHA. Questions about the safety of a particular chemical may be directed to OSHA. To further ensure employee safety, many states now have "right to know" laws that require the employer to divulge the makeup of chemicals used in the workplace upon an employee's request. If there is a question about the safety of a chemical, contact OSHA.

HEREDITY

In addition to age and environmental hazards, heredity can influence a person's cancer risk quotient. Again, if a person's family history places him or her in a high-risk category, it is simply another reason for increased vigilance, not panic. A person with a family history of cancer has even more reason to take steps to avoid known cancer-causing substances, such as tobacco, and to arrange with a physician for special cancer screening.

Certain cancers seem to show more of a hereditary connection than others: cancer of the breast, colon and rectum, endometrium, lung, prostate, stomach, and possibly the ovaries. Hereditary risk increases with the number of close relatives a person has who developed cancer. Some studies have shown that a woman whose mother or sister had cancer in both breasts has a much greater risk of developing cancer than if the relative had cancer in only one breast. Recent research suggests that people may inherit a susceptibility to certain cancer-causing agents.

There are some cancers for which a clear genetic tendency has been identified: retinoblastoma, a rare cancer of the eye thought to be due to an absence of two protective genes; and medullary carcinoma, a rare cancer of the thyroid. Familial polyposis, also rare, is a condition that predisposes people to develop polyps in the colon and eventually to develop colon cancer. Hereditary malignant melanoma is signaled by the development of moles on the body. People at risk must routinely scrutinize any moles and report any change in color or size immediately to a physician.

The importance of individual responsibility borne by a person with a known genetic tendency to develop cancer is illustrated by the risk for lung cancer in those with a family history of the disease. The risk for such an individual—one whose parent, sibling, or child has had lung cancer—is approximately three times more than that of the general population. If that person also smokes cigarettes, however, his or her risk may be 15 times greater than that of the general population.

The influence of heredity makes an accurate medical and family history extremely important. With this information in hand, the physician and patient can investigate life-style changes that may reduce the risk of cancer and initiate screening programs that will help detect cancer in the early stages. A woman whose mother or sister has had breast cancer, for instance, should have more frequent mammograms than a woman who has no such history. She should also have her breasts examined twice yearly by a physician, in addition to a careful monthly self-examination.

All of the above factors—personal habits, heredity, environmental influences—affect a person's individual tendency to get cancer; therefore, anything that falls into the risk category, such as smoking or heavy drinking, should be made known to the physician. Early detection of cancer is a joint project between physician and patient, but the success of such a project rests heavily on the patient.

DIET AND CANCER

The precise role of diet in cancer is unknown, but the American Cancer Society states that it plays a significant causal role in 10 types of cancer: lung, colon/rectum, breast, prostate, pancreas, stomach, ovary, bladder, and liver. Both the American Cancer Society and the National Cancer Institute have proposed dietary guidelines aimed at lowering cancer risk. These guidelines are very similar to the dietary recommendations of the American Heart Association and also are in line with what is recommended for people with diabetes. The American Cancer Society emphasizes that a healthful diet is part of the primary defense against cancer and so encourages people to modify their diets, thus converting the dietary factor from adversary to potential ally against cancer. The recommended diet is based on abundant evidence that the normal American diet is not optimal. In addition to avoiding obesity, dietary guidelines recommended by the American Cancer Society include:

- *Reduce total fat intake.* A diet high in fat may be a factor in the development of certain cancers, particularly of the breast, colon, and prostate.
- *Eat more high-fiber foods.* In the past, some people have interpreted this as a call to add large amounts of bran to food. This should be avoided;

recent studies indicate that an excess of bran may actually promote rather than prevent colon cancer. A balanced consumption of whole-grain cereals and breads, fruits, and vegetables will provide a variety of fiber as well as essential vitamins and minerals.

- *Include foods rich in vitamins A and C in the diet.* Dark green and deep yellow vegetables and yellow fruits are rich in beta carotene, a form of vitamin A. Studies indicate that this may be protective against cancer of the larynx, esophagus, and lung. People who consume adequate vitamin C (ascorbic acid) have a lower incidence of stomach and esophageal cancers. Ascorbic acid blocks production of nitrosamines, which are carcinogenic. A word of warning, however: These vitamins should come from the diet instead of from high-dose supplements. Megadoses of vitamin A can be highly toxic; excessive vitamin C may increase the risk of urinary irritation.
- *Include cruciferous vegetables in the diet.* These are members of the mustard family and include broccoli, brussels sprouts, kohlrabi, and cauliflower. These foods are believed to lower the risk of cancers of the gastrointestinal and respiratory tracts.
- *Be moderate in consumption of alcoholic beverages.* Heavy drinkers, especially those who also smoke, are at high risk of developing cancers of the mouth, larynx, and esophagus. Alcoholism is also associated with an increased risk of liver cancer as well as of cirrhosis and other liver diseases.
- *Be moderate in consumption of salt.* Cured, smoked, or nitrate-cured foods, such as hams, bacon, or smoked fish, absorb some of the tars that result from incomplete burning during smoking. The tars are similar to those found in cigarettes. Charcoal broiling deposits cancer-causing substances, such as benzopyrene, on the surface of foods. Cooking with charcoal therefore should be done in moderation.

Recent Research. One dietary agent, a chemical called sulforaphane, was reported in 1992 by a Johns Hopkins University research group to be a powerful anticancer compound. Sulforaphane, found in broccoli, brussels sprouts, and other related vegetables, seems to act as a catalyst for cell enzymes that help protect against tumor development. Experts warn, however, that continued research is necessary to properly assess its benefits and discover its possible uses. Other nutrients, vitamins, and fiber in green leafy vegetables make them healthful choices in any diet.

Several other nutrients have been linked to a possible lowered risk of cancer, but not enough evidence is available to say for certain that they are beneficial. For example, vitamin E blocks the production of cancer-causing nitrosamines and also provides other necessary functions. A Johns Hopkins study published in 1992 found lower levels of vitamin E, selenium, and, particularly, beta-carotene—all natural antioxidants—in those subjects who had cancer than among those who didn't. Study continues to confirm the possibility that they may inhibit tumor production, particularly in chemically induced cancers. Many health-food stores and faddists urge that people take supplements, but a well-balanced diet contains abundant sources of selenium and beta-carotene, and taking large amounts of any vitamin or mineral can be hazardous.

Although there is no indication that high iron intake has a preventive effect against cancer (and, in fact, may be a risk factor in heart disease), iron deficiency has been associated with cancer of the upper alimentary tract and possibly cancer of the gastric glands. Since iron is important to overall health, the diet should provide adequate sources of this mineral.

Alcohol intake should be limited not only because it interferes with proper nutrition but also because its heavy usage may contribute to development of oral cancers and cancers of the larynx, throat, esophagus, and liver. This is especially true when it is accompanied by cigarette smoking or chewing tobacco.

THE ROLE OF FAT AND OBESITY

A high fat intake appears to be the dietary factor with the strongest established association with cancer as well as with heart disease. Diets high in animal fats or saturated fats are associated with an increased risk of cancers of the heart, prostate, large bowel, and colon. Even corn oil, high in omega-6 unsaturated fatty acid, has been shown to promote the growth of tumors. Some laboratory studies indicate that total caloric intake may be at least as important as the amount of fat, and restricting calories may inhibit tumor growth.

The link between fat intake and colon cancer has been the most definitive. A high-fat diet also may increase the risks of developing cancers of the breast and prostate.

Obesity increases the risk of developing many health problems, including cancer. Cancers of the colon, rectum, and prostate are more common in obese men, and cancers of the gallbladder, bile passages, breast, cervix, ovaries, and uterus are more common in obese women. Some studies indicate that the location of fat may be more significant than its quantity: Fat centered around the waist, abdomen and upper body appears to present greater health risks than fat in the hips or thighs. Fat in the abdomen area is believed to be more "mobile"—it is more readily broken down—and also contributes more to high serum cholesterol than fat located elsewhere in the body.

DETECTION AND SCREENING

The older person should regard his or her increased risk of cancer not as a reason for fatalism or an excuse to let nature take its course, but instead as an incentive to be particularly alert and responsible regarding health maintenance. Early detection is the next best thing to prevention. The long-term survival rates for patients with localized cancer are dramatically higher than in those with regional spread, a testimony to the effectiveness of early detection.

As a rule, patients with widespread cancer have the lowest chances of survival. Although the nature of the specific cancer also affects how fast it spreads, most adult tumors are slow-growing. Therefore, delay in seeking diagnosis or treatment must be singled out as the major obstacle to early detection and a contributing factor to mortality.

Early detection affects not only the cure rate for cancer but can also have an impact on the treatment. Depending on the stage (extent) of the cancer, treatment may be either short-term and relatively nonintrusive, or radical and intrusive.

Two components in a successful early detection program are the individual's self-monitoring program and the periodic cancer screening undertaken by health professionals as part of a regular health maintenance regimen. Everyone should be familiar with the warning signs publicized by the American Cancer Society:

- **C**hange in bowel or bladder habits
- **A** sore that does not heal
- **U**nusual bleeding or discharge
- **T**hickening or lump in breast or elsewhere
- **I**ndigestion or difficulty in swallowing
- **O**bvious change in wart or mole
- **N**agging cough or hoarseness

If any of these symptoms are present, medical attention should be sought immediately. Delay or denial can greatly increase risk of death if cancer is present, and it can cause needless apprehension if the symptom does not turn out to signal cancer. However, these symptoms are not necessarily signs of an early stage of cancer. Eighty percent of breast lumps detected by women during self-examination, for instance, are noncancerous.

CANCER STAGES

An essential part of the diagnostic process involves determining how far the cancer has spread into regional tissues or distant organs. This so-called "staging" is a factor in deciding which type of treatment is most appropriate. Surgical removal is generally considered curative for a localized tumor, for instance, but chemotherapy is the preferred alternative for widespread cancer cells. Staging also helps predict the future course of the disease. In the past, patients with a certain type of cancer may have been diagnosed at a specific point in the disease where there may have been undetectable metastases. Therapy to attack such residual cancer cells will now be automatically prescribed for new patients with the same stage of cancer. Diagnostic procedures that help identify the stage may include X rays, computerized tomography, biopsy, and laboratory tests.

DIAGNOSTIC IMAGING

Magnetic resonance imaging (MRI) is one of the high-technology diagnostic tools that have replaced exploratory surgery for some cancer patients. MRI can detect hidden tumors by outlining on a computer screen atom vibrations that result from exposure to an enormous electromagnet. Computerized tomography (CT) scanning, another method, uses X rays. The resulting cross-sectional pictures not only show the tumor's location, but also its shape, much more accurately than do conventional X rays. Both these tests are noninvasive and painless.

CANCER THERAPIES

Three major types of treatment for cancer exist, all of which may be used singly or in combination. The nature of the cancer, the stage at which it is discovered, the likelihood of spread, and a person's age and degree of risk all influence the treatment approach.

SURGERY

Surgery is considered the most effective treatment when the cancer is localized and there is a possibility of completely removing the tumor. Surgery may also be used to reduce the size of a tumor so that it will respond more effectively to radiation and chemotherapy. Advances in surgical techniques have led not only to an improved cure rate for some types of cancer, but have made some cancer surgery less disfiguring and traumatic than it once was. The therapy is not appropriate for widespread cancer or for cancers involving vital organs, such as the liver, although it may be used in advanced cancer to reduce the size of a tumor and relieve symptoms rather than to cure the cancer.

Depending on the location and extent of the cancer, the consequences of surgery may require major accommodations from the patient. Before the operation the physician should thoroughly explain what the results of the surgery will be and any adjustments the patient will have to make. For instance, if the bladder, colon, or rectum is involved, an ileal conduit (an opening in the abdomen for urine) or a colostomy (an opening for feces) may be required. If a mastectomy is performed for breast cancer, a prosthesis or breast reconstruction is often considered. The patient should make sure he or she understands what is involved in the procedure and why it is necessary. The physician should also inform the patient of the availability of any support groups responding to his or her particular type of cancer, and describe fully the anticipated treatment.

RADIATION

Although it has been known for some time that radiation can kill cancer cells, refinements in technique have made this method more effective and have reduced the side effects. Radiation therapy may be delivered in the form of beams of X rays from a machine directed at the tumor or as implants of radioactive substances placed into a body cavity or tumor, either permanently or temporarily. Radiation therapy destroys the cancer cell's ability to reproduce. Some cancers, such as that of the lymph nodes, are more responsive than others to radiation therapy.

Although this treatment is sometimes the sole therapy, it is most often used in conjunction with surgery and/or chemotherapy. Surgery, for instance, is often used to remove a large cancerous mass and followed with radiation treatments to destroy the individual cancer cells left behind. Radiation is also used when the tumor cannot be removed surgically because it is too large or has involved vital organs. Preoperative radiation is used sometimes to reduce the chance that cancer cells will spread through the bloodstream during or after surgery.

The goal of treatment is to deliver the largest amount of radiation to the tumor while causing minimal damage to normal tissue. To do this, the beam is directed at the cancer itself in divided doses administered over several sessions rather than in one large dose, which would cause lethal damage to the whole body. Computerized tomography (CT, formerly called CAT scan) and ultrasound help the therapist to verify the exact location of the tumor, thus providing a more precise target for radiation and reducing unnecessary exposure of other tissues. Lead shields are also used whenever possible to protect surrounding tissues.

Some people fear cancer treatment such as radiation as much as they do the disease itself. The complications and discomfort one experiences, however, have been blown out of proportion. Over the years, improved techniques in cancer treatment have minimized side effects, and strategies have been developed to deal with those that do occur.

CHEMOTHERAPY

Chemotherapy is the use of anticancer drugs, usually in combination, to kill cancer cells throughout the body. It is given orally in pill or liquid form or intravenously. It may be used alone—for instance, in the treatment of leukemia—or in combination with surgery and/or radiation to treat other cancers. Different anticancer drugs disrupt cell function in different ways:

- *Alkylating agents.* Interfere with cell division by damaging the genetic material in the cell.

- *Antimetabolites.* A substitute for various substances required for cell growth, they impair the cancer cell's ability to divide.
- *Antibiotics.* Disrupt cancer cell function by altering the manufacture or repair of genetic material. Antibiotics used in cancer treatment are highly toxic and are not given to fight bacterial infections.
- *Plant alkaloids.* Derived mainly from periwinkle plants, they prevent cell division by inhibiting the formation of proteins necessary for reproduction.

These agents are used together to increase the overall effectiveness of the attack on cancer cells and to reduce the chance that cancer cells will be resistant in some stage of their development to a specific class of drugs. Combining the drugs also helps balance out the toxicity of individual agents.

Since chemotherapy attacks rapidly growing cancer cells during the cell division process, it is most effective against small, fast-growing tumors. Large tumors, which have more resting or nondividing cells, may be resistant to this treatment. Chemotherapy is also sometimes used in cases of advanced cancer, not as a curative therapy but rather to relieve discomfort and symptoms.

Adjuvant chemotherapy, given after surgery, for example, is used as a precautionary measure taken when it is unclear whether or not the cancer may have spread. Especially in the case of breast cancer, it has proven to be a lifesaving treatment.

Common Side Effects. Today researchers have learned that different ways of administering chemotherapy may reduce the toxic side effects of certain drugs. One antibiotic, doxorubicin (Adriamycin), used in treating a number of cancers, is far less damaging to the heart muscle when given very slowly over a longer period of time than when given faster over a shorter period. However, most anticancer drugs commonly have adverse side effects regardless of the way they are administered. For example, most cause nausea and vomiting, although this tends to be temporary and can be controlled in most patients. New antinausea drugs may offer hope for future chemotherapy recipients.

Bone marrow normally produces white blood cells to fight infection, red blood cells, and platelets; these functions are hindered after chemotherapy. Bone marrow suppression usually begins immediately and builds over a period of days or weeks. A person with bone marrow suppression is at high risk for infection, anemia, and possibly serious bleeding. A second course of chemotherapy is generally not given until the blood count—an indication of bone marrow function—returns to normal.

Many patients find that hair loss, although temporary, is one of the most personally devastating effects of cancer therapy, and it may occur with both radiation treatments and chemotherapy. The rapidly growing hair cells are a natural target for the chemotherapeutic agents. Patients will experience different degrees of hair loss, from a

SOME STRATEGIES TO OVERCOME NAUSEA DURING CANCER CHEMOTHERAPY

- Use antinausea drugs.
- Practice self-hypnosis.
- Practice relaxation techniques.
- Take small, frequent feedings rather than regular meals.
- Schedule the chemotherapy at night rather than during the day.
- Avoid preparing food yourself.
- Eat food that is cool or at room temperature, in order to minimize food odors.

slight thinning to complete loss of hair. Hair usually begins to grow back within just a few weeks after the last course of chemotherapy. With radiation, however, the loss of hair roots in the radiated area may be permanent. Some new techniques may minimize hair loss, depending on the drugs being used and the type of cancer: A cold compress, or "ice turban," restricts circulation to the head and will help keep the drugs from reaching hair follicles in the scalp. Scalp tourniquets have also been used during chemotherapy.

When chemotherapy is ongoing but is halted temporarily, hair usually starts to grow back. Measures can be taken to protect and encourage new growth:

- Have your hair cut in an easy-to-manage style.
- Use a mild, protein-based shampoo, cream rinse, and conditioner every four to seven days.
- Avoid using electric hair dryers, or use them only at the coolest setting.
- Avoid electric curlers, curling irons, hair clips, elastic bands, hair or bobby pins, hair spray, or dye.
- Avoid excessive brushing and combing, since they put stress on the hair.

HORMONAL THERAPY

High doses of natural and synthetic steroid hormones may be used to treat cancers such as lymphomas, certain breast cancers, and some leukemias. They may also be used to relieve symptoms of other cancers due to swelling of tissues. Alternatively, hormone-blocking drugs may be used to treat cancers that are dependent on hormones for growth, or that occur in hormone-producing glands. Side effects of steroid hormones include increased blood sugar, hypertension, swelling of the face and extremities, easy skin bruising, loss of bone density, and increased susceptibility to infection.

NEW DIRECTIONS AND TRENDS

Current cancer research branches out into several directions—prevention, efforts to improve cure rates (including techniques for early detection), and efforts to improve the quality of life for cancer patients (including the development of effective but less mutilating surgical procedures, more potent pain control methods, and techniques for reducing the side effects of treatments). A variety of techniques and substances now being studied in the research phase are showing promise for future effectiveness.

IMMUNOTHERAPY

Research in this area focuses on ways to activate the body's own ability to fight off and control malignant cells without damaging normal cells, either by strengthening the body's immune system or by developing vaccines to the same end.

Interferon comes under the category of immunotherapy. Composed of naturally occurring body proteins that aid in resisting viral infection, interferon also has a regulatory effect on the growth of cells, called an antiproliferative effect. There is some evidence that this twofold ability to confer immunity and control cell growth may make interferon an effective cancer therapy. Interferon has been approved by the Food and Drug Administration (FDA) for the treatment of a rare blood cancer of older Americans, hairy-cell leukemia. Previously very expensive and in short supply, interferon is now produced through genetic engineering. Despite the heavy media attention this potential therapy has received, it is important to realize it is still under study. Evidence to support its efficacy is promising in some areas and disappointing in others. Interleukin-2, a growth factor that stimulates immune-system cells to fight cancer directly, and other biological response modifiers are also under study. In the treatment of kidney cancer and melanoma, interleukin-2 is undergoing active research.

HYPERTHERMIA

Research has shown that cancer cells are more susceptible to the effects of changes in temperature than are normal cells. Hyperthermia therapy is the use of heat to kill malignant cells. The use of total body hyperthermia is limited because extreme heat may also injure normal cells—although not at the same rate as cancer cells—and because it is extremely uncomfortable for the patient. The effect of heat in combination with chemotherapy and radiation is also under investigation.

Localized hyperthermia directs heat to a specific area using techniques such as diathermy, ultrasound, radio waves, and microwaves. By confining the heat to the tumor area, many of the negative side effects of whole-body hyperthermia can be avoided. Both methods are still considered experimental, but they look promising for the future.

MONOCLONAL ANTIBODIES

One experimental therapy that seems to hold out hope of the broadest potential for use in cancer management is monoclonal antibody technology. These laboratory-developed antibodies combine a normal antibody-producing cell, known as a plasma cell, with a cancerous cell. The resulting hybridoma, as it is called, seeks out specific targets in cancer cells. When successful, hybridomas will produce large quantities of site-specific antibodies (depending on the initial antibody used) for a long period of time. Most hybridomas today are produced from antibodies found in mice.

Monoclonal antibodies have potential in both the diagnosis and treatment of cancer. Specific antibodies for a certain type of cancer can be made with a radioactive iodine that is injected into a patient's bloodstream. The antibodies should attach themselves to the cancer cells and thus reveal the location of the cancer when X-rayed.

Treatment possibilities include using monoclonal antibodies to destroy or damage cancer cells, to deliver anticancer drugs directly to cancer cells, and to deactivate the growth substance secreted by cancer cells.

There are still many unanswered questions in monoclonal antibody research. For one thing, most monoclonal antibodies have been derived from mice and could cause serious side effects or death if injected into humans. Researchers are working on producing human hybridomas, but many problems have yet to be resolved. Nevertheless, this field, which is under very active investigation, offers many far-reaching possibilities.

BONE MARROW TRANSPLANTATION

Transplanting bone marrow has become an important treatment for selected patients with leukemia, and its potential role in the treatment of other cancers is under study. Autologous bone marrow transplants, in which a portion of a person's own marrow is removed before treatment, then saved and later restored, may help deal with the disruption of bone marrow function that is a side effect of many cancer treatments. Having the bone marrow on hand and thereby eliminating the problems of finding a donor may make the process more routine. This might make it possible for the patient to tolerate larger doses of anticancer drugs or radiation therapy.

OTHER ADVANCES

Cancer researchers are exploring numerous other areas that promise improvements in diagnosis and treatment in the next few years. These include:

- □ Determining the importance of oncogenes, the genes found in tumor cells. Analysis of the various products of these oncogenes may help predict which tumors are likely to recur after surgery and identify family members at risk.
- □ Research into interrupting the two-stage process of cancer development
- □ Study of the causes of pain in cancer patients and the options for controlling it
- □ Use of growth factors that stimulate bone marrow cells to withstand very high doses of chemotherapeutic drugs
- □ Adjuvant and neoadjuvant chemotherapy, giving chemotherapy before and after surgery; identification of HTLV (human T-cell leukemia virus) and research into a vaccine to prevent this type of cancer
- □ More refined techniques for early detection of certain cancers. For instance, prostatic ultrasound may provide a means to detect previously unsuspected prostate cancer.
- □ Investigating new combinations of drug therapy, combinations of drugs, and combination of treatments, such as chemotherapy and radiation or surgery
- □ More conservative management of certain cancers, for instance, fewer colostomies for colorectal cancer, or allowing patients to retain the larynx and voice in cancer of the larynx

QUESTIONABLE THERAPIES

Over the years claims of cancer "cures" have been made for a variety of substances ranging from apricot pits to carrot juice and for techniques ranging from relaxation and imagery exercises to the Orgone Energy Accelerator. Even otherwise harmless claims are dangerous in the long run if people refuse traditional, proven treatment in favor of the unproven and thus give the cancer adequate time to spread unchecked. Moreover, many of these alternative cancer treatments are offered in settings or in forms that free them from institutionalized consumer protection regulations, leaving the consumer open to exploitation and experimentation. Many alleged cancer preventives and/or cures are marketed in ways that, while in accordance with the letter of the law, contradict its spirit. For instance, it is illegal for unproven claims to appear on a product. As a result, in many "alternative" stores, pamphlets promoting certain substances are found on shelves in one part of the store and the corresponding products are displayed in another part. The American Cancer Society reviews unproven methods of cancer treatment and will make its evaluation of the method available to you on request. Check with your local chapter.

Laetrile therapy has received much public attention. Made from the extract of apricot pits, laetrile contains cyanide and is supposed to "kill" cancer cells. A national clinical trial conducted by the National Cancer Institute offered no support for this theory. In fact, some individuals who have gone the laetrile route have shown signs of cyanide poisoning.

Nutritional gimmickry seems to provide the richest source for these "instant cures." Many health-food stores or mail-order houses package a specific nutrient as a cancer cure, for instance, vitamins A and C. The problem is that the research indicating possible health benefits from these sources is usually based on studies using sensible portions of foods containing the nutrients; the findings are perverted by the mail-order house to suggest that concentrated megadoses of the vitamin are even more helpful. On the contrary, such "therapy" may be toxic.

EVALUATING CLAIMS FOR UNKNOWN THERAPIES

Dr. Victor Herbert, a noted nutritionist, hematologist, and authority on medical fraud, suggests asking the following questions to determine whether an unconventional cancer treatment is legitimate:

- Is the therapy based on personal observation or can it withstand examination by other scientists?
- Was it tested in controlled studies against a placebo to rule out patient suggestibility? Could the "effect" be attributed simply to the expected course of the disorder or to the fact that the patient really did not have cancer?
- Has its safety been tested? Is the risk-to-benefit ratio worthwhile?
- Has research on the therapy been published in scientific journals and reviewed and verified by professional peers?

Some suggested therapies do no damage in themselves and may indeed be helpful with certain aspects of cancer management, particularly the psychological stress associated with the disease and some treatments. The Simonton technique, for example, is of the "mind over matter" variety and consists of a series of mental exercises that will supposedly help the patient control his or her cancer. Although patients who have a fighting attitude toward their disease seem, in some studies, better able to cope, there is no current conclusive evidence that the immune system responds to "positive thinking." Relaxation and visual imagery techniques, when used in conjunction with standard cancer treatments, may be helpful in controlling the psychological distress and even some of the physiological side effects, such as nausea. On the other hand, people should not accept the idea that they have had some part in causing their cancer because of some personality trait or pattern of thinking.

Your physician, your local branch of the American Cancer Society, the National Cancer Institute, and the FDA are all good sources of information regarding unfamiliar treatments. Your next-door neighbor, a clerk at the health-food store, and magazine advertisements are not.

LIVING WITH CANCER

One of the effects of improved treatment methods and higher cancer survival rates is that more attention is finally being paid to a significant aspect of cancer that was often ignored or underemphasized in the past—the psychosocial aspect of living with a cancer diagnosis, either one's own or a family member's. With increasing frequency, health-care professionals and patients themselves are redefining cancer care as something more than the medical management of the disease. Since cancer can now be considered more as a chronic illness than a death sentence, its impact on the daily routine of living, on the patient's interactions with family and friends, on work, and on future plans must now be considered an important part of cancer management. A person with cancer now often has to deal with the disease and the stresses of treatment while maintaining as normal a life-style as possible. Techniques for coping, support services, counseling, and attention to financial and social concerns are now a major part of cancer therapy.

Fear and anxiety are normal responses to any illness but especially to cancer when, at first, the outcome is uncertain. It is hoped that this fear will motivate the patient to seek out and follow through on medical advice. Sometimes, however, excessive fear can lead to denial of the disease or rejection of needed treatment. Information and open communication are the keys to dispelling unwarranted fears about cancer and to developing constructive coping strategies. The patient's health-care team is a primary source of information: The patient should openly express any fears, concerns, or questions to the physician, nurse, or hospital social worker. Some physicians prefer to discuss aspects of the patient's condition and treatment with a family member present to encourage discussion and prevent misunderstandings.

The patient with cancer should also look to family members for support and discuss his or her concerns and expectations with them honestly, as well as listen to theirs. If family members have moved away or died, close friends can provide the needed communication network. People from work and social, community, or church groups may turn out to provide unexpected support.

Numerous organizations will provide information and counseling to cancer patients as well as help with transportation and financial advice. (See Appendix A, "Sources of Help.") Many of them will put the cancer patient in touch with someone who has already experienced what the patient is going through. Facts and perspective ring truer when they come from someone who has personal experience with the disease. Also, it may be easier to discuss certain concerns with objective, sympathetic outsiders than with family members or friends.

WHEN THE DIAGNOSIS COMES

The diagnosis of cancer is a difficult one to absorb at any age, but for middle-aged or older adults, there are some additional burdens to contend with. Adults in mid-life are already dealing with major life changes—changes in physical appearance, the empty-nest syndrome, the death of parents and/or peers. The older person may be coping with the stresses of retirement and a changing societal and self-image, and he or she is dealing with aging as well as changes in body image. When a diagnosis of cancer comes at this time of life, it adds to the stresses already present and brings new concerns about financial security and maintaining independence. Those who have successfully adjusted to the changes of middle or old age will be in a better position to deal with a diagnosis of cancer. If, however, they are still in the process of, or have not been able to face up to, these adjustments, coping with cancer will be an especially difficult task.

People react to a diagnosis of cancer in different ways. Some may want all the information they can get, others may refuse to accept the truth, and still others may be able to absorb only small amounts of information at a time. Doctors need to be honest in telling the patient what to expect, but they also need to tailor what they have to say according to the individual's readiness to hear it.

Periods of denial, anger, or depression are normal responses to a cancer diagnosis. Counseling and mild tranquilizers may be necessary to help the patient through this initial adjustment period.

It is important to note that no one can accurately predict how long a particular patient will live with cancer. Patients will often react to a time limit—for example, "you have six months to live"—as if it were a sentence of death. Doctors should therefore avoid making such statements, and patients and family members should refrain from pressing for a time limit. There are numerous cases in which a person given six months or a year to live is doing well long after that period of time has passed.

FEAR OF PAIN

Many people believe that cancer will always bring severe pain. Studies have found that, overall, about 30 to 40 percent of patients have pain, but that this is almost always controlled by readily available medications. Patients with terminal cancer are more likely to experience severe pain than are others.

For most effective pain control, medication should be given on a round-the-clock basis rather than allowing pain to become intense. Due to individual differences, some people metabolize drugs faster than others and may require more frequent medication to keep pain from building up.

Patient-controlled analgesia (PCA) is frequently an option. PCA pumps, which are filled with a prescribed intravenous pain medication, allow the patient to administer, at the push of a button, preset doses at proper intervals. This has led to more individual pain control. It also provides cancer patients with control of their own medication.

Sometimes cancer patients hesitate to ask for pain control drugs because they are afraid of becoming addicted, or because they feel they would be "giving in" to the pain, or even because they are afraid that if the pain medication works now it will be ineffective should the pain worsen later. Although patients can develop tolerance to a drug and require ever larger doses for the same relief, they do not have the underlying psychological dependence that characterizes addiction. Tolerance can be overcome by switching to another medication from the wide range of available drugs. Besides medication, nerve-blocking measures—injections of local anesthetic, alcohol, or severing the nerve—may also be appropriate. The patient and his or her physician should discuss pain control options just as they discussed treatment options. In that way, they can come up with a plan that meets the patient's physical and psychological needs. A number of medical centers now have specialized pain clinics to help people with intractable pain. Consult your doctor or major medical center in your area for information (or see Appendix A). Taking medication for mild pain is not "giving in," but can be an important part of coping with cancer. A person who is not in pain will eat better, be more active, and generally will have a better outlook, which can all contribute to a positive outcome. For terminally ill patients with severe pain, relief usually can be obtained while still leaving the individual alert for long periods of time and in contact with others.

REHABILITATION

Rehabilitation after cancer treatment must be both psychological and physical. A short period of "mourning" or depression is normal following any kind of surgery that has changed a person's physical appearance or ability to function. A cancer patient needs some time to reflect on what has happened and incorporate it into his or her life. But if this phase persists, counseling should be sought. The cancer patient needs to begin making the transition back to a normal, active life. Former cancer patients can be of valuable service at this point, offering practical tips on day-to-day living and an understanding ear for the patient's concerns.

Fear of cancer recurring after successful treatment is not uncommon. The patient should not hesitate to call the physician or other support service if he or she has any questions or simply needs reassurance. This anxiety is normal and will gradually diminish if family and health-care staff respond to the patient's concerns at this time.

Research indicates that patients who struggle to survive, who cooperate and participate in their treatment, and who focus on maintaining a normal existence deal better with cancer. A good attitude and the use of available support services are important.

MAJOR TYPES OF CANCER

BREAST CANCER

Until recently breast cancer was the major cancer killer among women. (Lung cancer now claims that distinction.) The breast is still the most common site of cancer in women. It is estimated that one out of nine women will develop breast cancer at some time, and women over 50 are at particular risk.

FACTORS THAT INCREASE THE RISK OF BREAST CANCER

- Mother or sister has had breast cancer
- No completed pregnancy
- Had first baby after age 30
- Obesity
- High waist-to-hip fat ratio in postmenopausal women
- Previous breast cancer
- Long menstrual history (early menstruation with late menopause)
- Age over 50
- Possible link to DES, but not proved. (DES, or diethylstilbestrol, was prescribed from the late 1940s to the 1960s to prevent miscarriage.) Possible link to oral contraceptives containing estrogen.

Like many other cancers, the cure rate for breast cancer is directly linked to early detection. The American Cancer Society guidelines for breast cancer screening in asymptomatic, normal-risk women is as follows:

- □ monthly breast self-examination (see Figures 12.1–12.3)
- □ annual breast exam by physician for women over 40
- □ screening mammogram (X-ray examination of breast) by age 40 and another mammogram every one to two years until age 50
- □ annual mammogram for asymptomatic women over the age of 50

Most breast cancer begins in the milk ducts or in the milk-secreting glands known as lobules. Cancer confined to the inside of the duct or lobule is almost 100 percent curable by surgery. The cancer may remain dormant in this stage for years before spreading through the lymph ducts and nodes or through the bloodstream.

DIET

A high-fat diet and excess pounds have been linked to an increase in a woman's risk of developing breast cancer. The largest U.S. study, involving 89,538 nurses, found that both total fat and unsaturated fat intake pose a significant risk to postmenopausal women. Obesity is also a risk factor for breast cancer in older women. Another study of 37,105 women between 55 and 69 reported in 1992 that the distribution of fat is also important. Older women with a high waist-to-hip fat ratio seem to be at increased risk, especially if they have a family history of the disease. The general dietary guidelines

BREAST SELF-EXAMINATION

All women should examine their breasts each month. For menstruating women, this should be a week after the start of a period; postmenopausal women can select any easy-to-remember date.

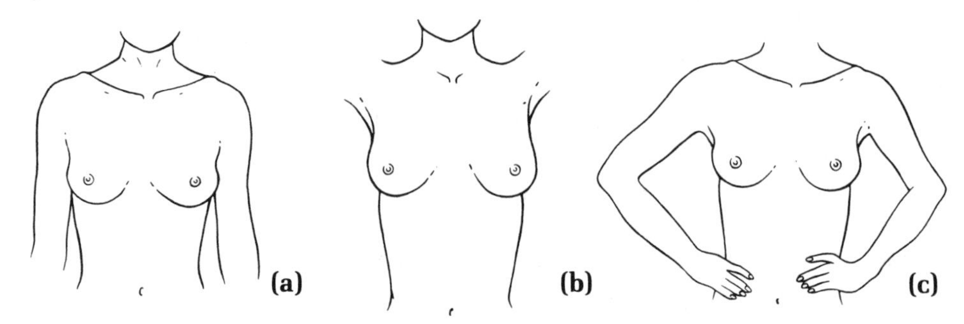

Figure 12.1
Start by standing in front of a mirror with arms at your sides. Look for any changes such as puckering of the skin. Do the same with arms raised overhead, and then finally with hands on the hips and chest muscles tensed.

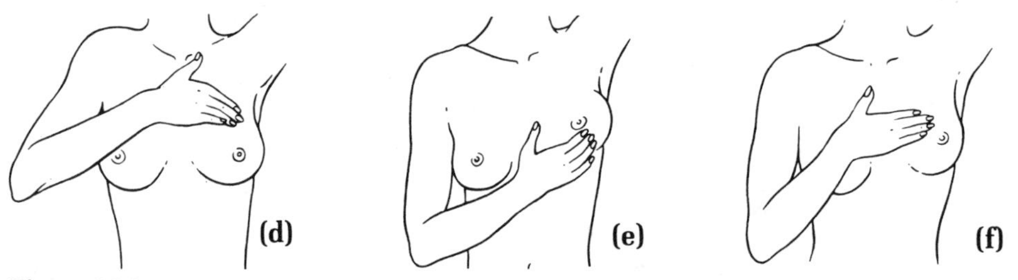

Figure 12.2
Next, lift one arm up behind your head and, using the other hand, examine the entire breast, moving counterclockwise and from the outer portion toward the nipple. (Alternatively, the breast can be examined in horizontal strips.) Repeat this procedure on the second breast, raising the opposite arm over your head. Feel for any unusual lump or thickening.

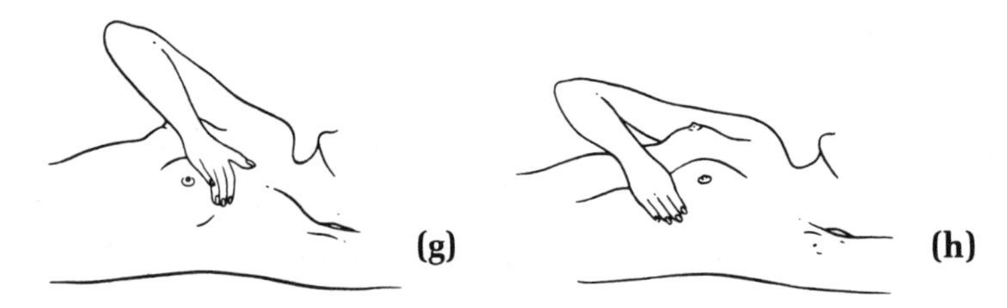

Figure 12.3
Then lie down and place one arm under your head and, using the other hand, examine the entire breast, moving clockwise and from the outer portion toward the nipple. Repeat this procedure on the second breast, placing the opposite arm under your head. Make sure to cover the entire area from under the armpit across to the breastbone and up to the collarbone.

Finally, squeeze each nipple to check for discharge. Any lump, change, discharge, or other unusual finding should be checked promptly by a doctor.

recommended by the American Cancer Society are designed to reduce the amount of fat in the diet and provide a good basic plan to follow.

DIAGNOSIS

If any of the following warning signs are present, see your physician immediately:

- a lump that does not go away
- thickening of tissue
- dimpling or peeling of skin
- change in breast or nipple shape or contour
- nipple discharge
- retraction or scaliness of nipple
- pain or tenderness

If you or your doctor note any of the above symptoms, or if a mass shows up in a routine mammogram, a biopsy is the next step. Suspected cancer can be confirmed only with a biopsy.

A needle biopsy done under local anesthetic is often the first step. In this procedure, a hollow needle is inserted into the lump to withdraw fluid or tissue and is sent for laboratory analysis. If fluid is withdrawn and the lump disappears or collapses, it is probably a benign cyst. If no abnormal cells are found on analysis, no further tests will be needed. This technique is inexpensive, relatively painless, and has a low risk of infection.

However, if fluid was not withdrawn or if the lab report is positive, a surgical biopsy will be necessary. Women with large breasts who have a small lump near the chest wall, or those whose mammograms indicate a possible lump that cannot be felt, will have to have a surgical, or excisional, biopsy in which the lump is removed for laboratory analysis. An estrogen-receptor test should be done at the same time to see if the tumor is stimulated by estrogen.

The vast majority of breast lumps are not cancerous. If the lab tests do indicate cancer, however, then the woman should discuss treatment options with her physician. Breast cancer is also subject to staging, which can provide a rough guideline of the advancement of the disease.

TREATMENT

In the past a one-stage approach to diagnosis and treatment of breast cancer was standard policy. The biopsy was done under general anesthesia, the tissue examined immediately, and if the results were positive, a mastectomy would be performed at that time. This approach is no longer common. Now the biopsy is done as a preliminary procedure, and the woman has the opportunity to find out the diagnosis, discuss options with her physician, and, if desired, get a second opinion on the best course to

BREAST CANCER STAGING

Stage I

Small tumor (less than 2 centimeters, or .78 inch). No spread to lymph nodes or evidence of metastases.

Stage II

Tumor between 2 and 5 centimeters, with no spread to lymph nodes or metastases, *or*

Tumor smaller than 5 centimeters across, with spread to lymph nodes but no metastases.

Stage III

Tumor larger than 5 centimeters, *or*

Any tumor seen with invasion of skin or wall of the chest or other grave signs, *or*

Tumor with spread to lymph nodes of collarbone, but no distant sites.

Stage IV

Any tumor with distant metastases, whether or not lymph nodes are involved.

take. The time between diagnosis and treatment can provide a valuable adjustment period and give the woman the opportunity to look into available resource groups that can provide information and support during this stressful period.

Currently physicians may differ on how to treat breast cancer, as new techniques and modified approaches are constantly evolving. Surgery is still the most common treatment, but there are various techniques within this realm. The traditional Halsted radical mastectomy removes the breast, underlying muscle, and axillary lymph nodes. The *modified* radical mastectomy removes the breast and axillary lymph nodes. *Simple* mastectomy involves removing only the breast. Surgeons differ in their opinions on which method offers the best chance of cure, and the extent of the disease often determines which surgical procedure is appropriate (see Figure 12.4). Simple mastectomy is usually used for Stage I or II disease. A study supported by the National Cancer Institute indicated that simple mastectomy is as effective as radical mastectomy in most cases.

TYPES OF MASTECTOMIES

Shaded areas indicate what is removed in each procedure. The cancer is designated by the blackened lump.

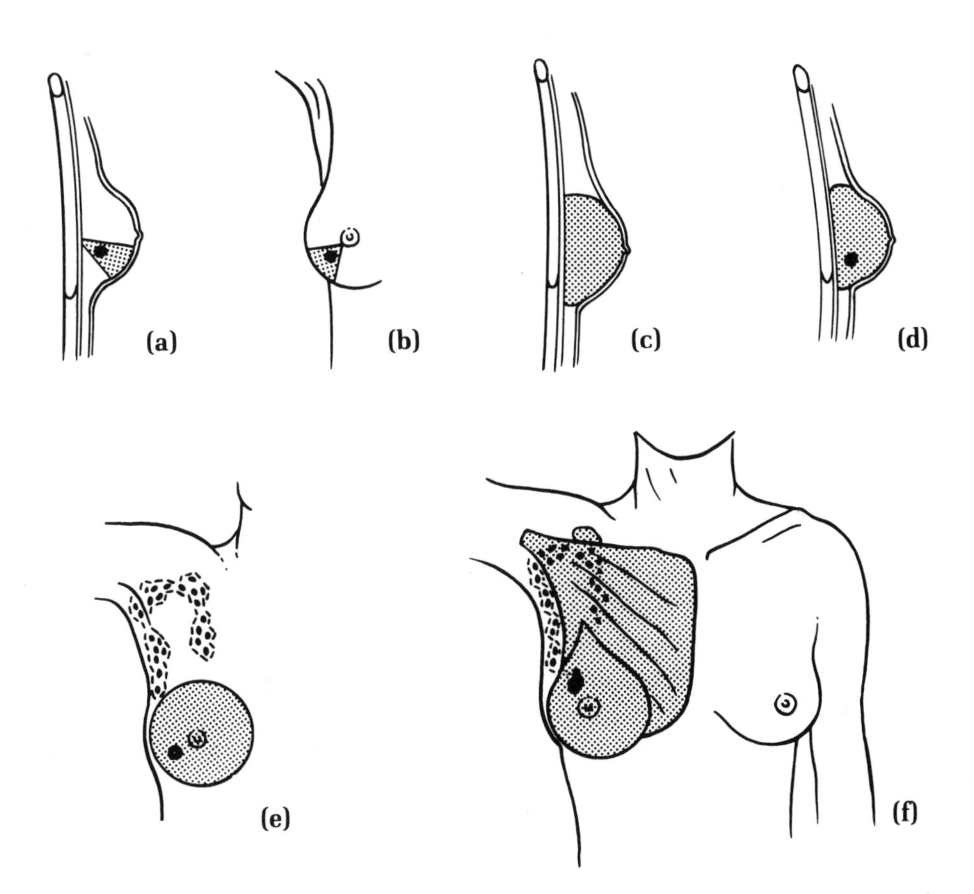

Figure 12.4

(a, b) Lumpectomy or segmental mastectomy, showing removal of the cancer and surrounding tissue.

(c) Subcutaneous mastectomy, showing removal of breast but not the nipple and skin. (Because this procedure is usually done as a preventive measure, no tumor is shown.)

(d) Simple mastectomy, showing removal of breast, nipple, and skin but not lymph nodes or muscle.

(e) Modified radical mastectomy, showing removal of breast, lymph nodes, and surrounding tissue but not the underlying muscle.

(f) Radical mastectomy, showing removal of breast, lymph nodes, and surrounding muscle.

In this study, lymph nodes were removed or irradiated after simple mastectomy if they were found to be cancerous, and no difference was found in survival rates between those receiving radical mastectomy and those receiving simple mastectomy and follow-up radiation treatment.

Another encouraging finding of a study supported by the National Cancer Institute is that lumpectomy—removal of the cancer and surrounding tissue with the rest of the breast left intact, followed by radiation therapy and adjuvant chemotherapy—seems to be as effective in treating small, localized cancers as total mastectomy is.

Radiation therapy is usually used as an adjunct to surgery. Only for those patients with Stage IV cancer, for whom mastectomy would be ineffective, or for those too ill for surgery, is radiation used exclusively. Radiation is most common following a lumpectomy; it is not considered necessary, as a rule, when a mastectomy has been performed. Radiation treatments are given four or five times a week over a four- to six-week period.

Chemotherapy is also used in conjunction with surgery and/or radiation, primarily for those patients whose cancer has invaded the lymph nodes and who are therefore at risk for further spreading of the cancer. A combination of drugs is usually given over a period of a year or longer. Chemotherapy does not seem to offer any advantage if the lymph node is not involved.

Hormone therapy has been found effective in estrogen-receptor-positive tumors. The estrogen- and progesterone-receptor tests done at the time of biopsy help determine whether the cancer's growth rate is affected by these hormones. Previously, estrogen production was blocked in premenopausal women by removing the ovaries or exposing them to radiation, but the current approach uses drugs to block or halt estrogen production. Sometimes removal of the adrenal and pituitary glands is recommended. One of the adrenal glands produces androstenedione, a male hormone, which the postmenopausal woman converts to estrogen; the pituitary produces hormones that stimulate the ovaries. In postmenopausal women, estrogen levels may be reduced satisfactorily by removal of the adrenal glands alone. If the adrenal glands are removed, the woman will have to take replacement cortisone and possibly a drug to regulate salt processing; taking Pitressin, a synthetic form of the hormone vasopressin, to conserve water may also be necessary.

Alternatively, many estrogen-receptor-positive tumors in women who are five years or more beyond menopause respond to supplemental estrogen or other hormones.

THE BENEFITS OF ADJUVANT THERAPY

Encouraging results of an Oxford University study of adjuvant therapy—the use of drugs to eradicate residual cancer cells after surgery—were reported in 1992. The study involved 75,000 women with breast cancer that seemingly was confined to the breast and lymph nodes under the arms. The treatments studied were chemotherapy using three anticancer drugs (for example, cyclophosphamide, doxorubicin, and 5-fluorouracil), treatment with the estrogen-blocking drug tamoxifen, and surgery or radiation designed to stop ovarian function. These treatments, separately and in combination, seemed to provide benefits for all the women studied, regardless of their age and disease progression. Analysis showed that an additional six women out of every 100 with cancer that had spread to the nodes, and an additional 12 out of every 200 with cancer that had not spread, would survive for at least 10 years following adjuvant therapy.

Tamoxifen shows the additional benefits of preventing cancer *and* lowering cholesterol. Those taking it for two to five years decreased their chances by 39 percent of having breast cancer in the other breast. The cholesterol-lowering properties of tamoxifen may give women protection against dying of heart attack as well. For the women over 50, tamoxifen treatment for two or more years was more beneficial than a six-month chemotherapy regimen of more toxic drugs, although the combination of both treatments showed the best results. For women over 70, the use of tamoxifen alone, which has fewer side effects than many anticancer drugs, may be a preferable course when other conditions make chemotherapy an unreasonable option. More study is necessary to determine the specifics on these adjuvant treatments. Unknown factors include the time in which such therapy should begin and whether it is safe to combine it with estrogen replacement therapy.

MAKING DECISIONS

There are many variables to take into consideration when making the choice of treatment. Treatment may depend on the stage of the disease, estrogen-receptor status, whether the woman is in a risk category, whether she is pre- or postmenopausal, and the preferences of both the patient and the physician. Whatever the circumstances, the woman should make sure that she understands the rationale for the choice of some therapies or elimination of others before going ahead with a treatment. A second opinion from a well-qualified breast specialist will often be helpful in reaching a decision. This almost always can be arranged without incurring undue delay.

Not the least of these treatment decisions is the decision about where to be treated and by whom. It is perfectly acceptable to ask for past treatment statistics regarding the medical facilities and oncologists available to you.

BREAST RECONSTRUCTION

Breast reconstruction should be discussed when treatment options are investigated. Knowing beforehand about the alternatives available to a woman may help to reduce her anxiety about breast surgery. Breast reconstruction is a possibility even for those who have had a radical mastectomy.

Usually a soft silicone prosthesis is implanted under the skin or pectoral muscle (see Figure 12.5). Safety and effectiveness data supplied by manufacturers of silicone

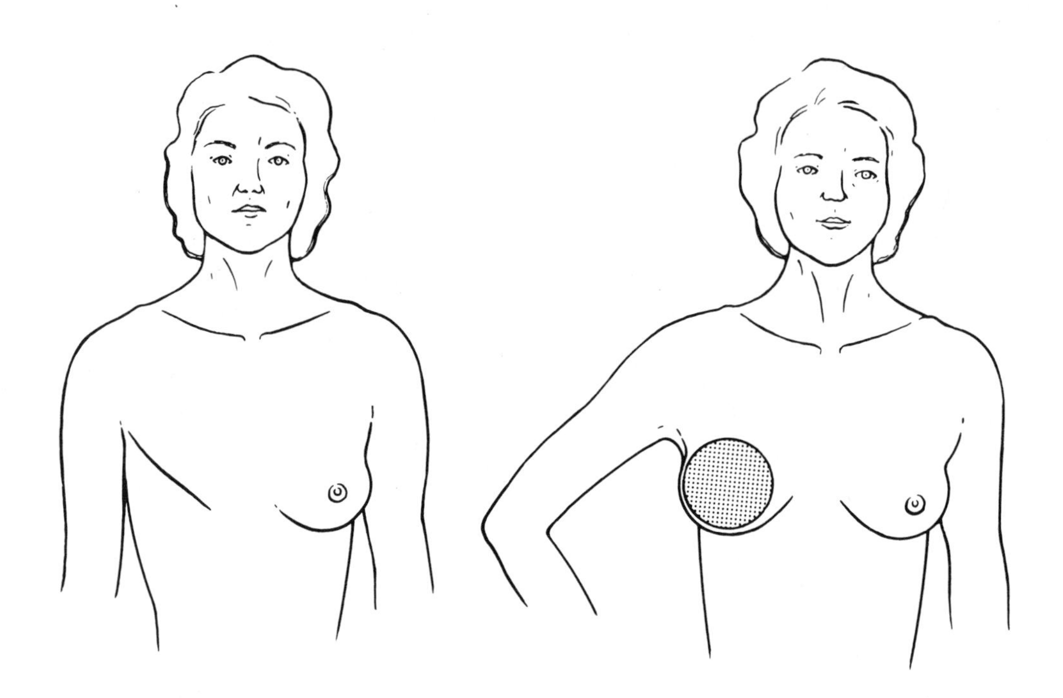

Figure 12.5 Breast Reconstruction
The shaded area shows the position of an implant after a mastectomy.

breast implants have been scrutinized by the FDA, and implant use is being regulated because of the following concerns: Hardening of the tissues surrounding the implant may occur, it may interfere with mammography screening, and it may rupture or leak. Silicone implants still are available for breast reconstruction following mastectomy, but these devices continue to be studied for the above reasons. A woman considering a silicone implant should thoroughly discuss the option with her physician, who can inform her of any new developments. An alternative breast reconstruction method involves using tissue removed from the abdomen or other part of the body to construct a breast.

LUNG CANCER

Lung cancer is responsible for more deaths in the United States than any other form of cancer. The majority of lung cancer cases, which are found in the 55- to 65-year-old group, include:

- □ cigarette smokers, especially those who have smoked for 20 years or longer
- □ those exposed to industrial carcinogens such as asbestos, especially those who are also smokers
- □ those with a history of tuberculosis
- □ possibly those whose family members or ancestors have had lung cancer, suggesting a genetic link
- □ possibly those with a dietary deficiency of vitamin E
- □ possibly those who have had long-term, intimate contact with a heavy smoker, i.e., so-called passive smokers

Lung cancer is unfortunately very difficult to diagnose in its early stages; the warning signs usually indicate a relatively advanced stage of the disease. It begins with precancerous cellular changes in the lung that produce no symptoms but gradually evolve into cancer. There is evidence that a smoker who develops these early precancerous changes can still circumvent the normal progression of the disease. If the smoker quits immediately, the damaged bronchial lining will often repair itself. The American Cancer Society estimates that cigarette smoking is responsible for 90 percent of lung cancer deaths among men and 79 percent among women.

FOUR TYPES OF LUNG CANCER

Squamous Cell Carcinoma. Squamous cell carcinoma arises in the central part of the lung, in the larger bronchi, or air passages leading to and through the lungs. This is the only type of cancer that has a detectable precancerous stage that may last for years. During this phase abnormal cells will show up in the sputum upon examination. If abnormal cells do show up, the bronchial tree can be examined with a fiber-optic bronchoscope, a flexible instrument, in an attempt to locate the source of the cells. No tumor will show up on X rays until later stages. Squamous cell cancers do not spread as rapidly as other lung cancers and thus respond to surgery and radiation treatments more suc-

WARNING SIGNS AND SYMPTOMS OF LUNG CANCER

- Persistent cough
- Blood-streaked sputum
- Chest pain
- Recurring attacks of pneumonia or bronchitis
- Wheezing that is unrelated to asthma
- Weight loss

cessfully. Squamous cell carcinoma has a better prognosis than other forms of lung cancer.

Adenocarcinoma. Adenocarcinoma refers to glandular structures composed of tumor cells ("adeno" means gland) starting in the smaller bronchi and often spreading into the pleural spaces between the lung and chest wall. The most common lung cancer in women, adenocarcinoma has a lower cure rate than does squamous cell carcinoma. Surgery, sometimes followed by radiation therapy or chemotherapy, is the standard treatment. Bronchiolalveolar carcinoma is a subtype of adenocarcinoma that is not associated with smoking and may have a better prognosis. (Squamous cell carcinomas and adenocarcinomas account for the majority of lung cancer cases.)

Small Cell, or "Oat Cell," Carcinoma. Made up of cells that resemble oat grains under the microscope, this type of cancer is the most invasive of all lung cancers. The cancer has often spread to distant parts of the body by the time of diagnosis, making surgery an ineffective form of treatment. Ten years ago, only half of those patients diagnosed with this type of cancer were given more than two months to live. Now, combination chemotherapy has enabled many patients to survive for up to two years and some are expected to reach the five-year mark. This type of cancer is responsible for approximately 20 percent of lung cancer cases.

Large-cell Lung Carcinoma. This is a rare cancer that resembles adenocarcinoma in its behavior. Treatment is also similar. There is some question about whether this is a distinct classification or a variation of squamous cell carcinoma and/or adenocarcinoma.

DIAGNOSIS

Except for squamous cell carcinoma, early diagnosis of lung cancer is difficult. The National Cancer Institute has studied the effectiveness of periodic chest X rays and sputum cell examinations for high-risk individuals—heavy smokers over 45. Although unsuccessful in early diagnosis of small-cell lung cancer, the screening programs do seem to detect a higher percentage of early squamous cell carcinomas and adenocarcinomas than is found in the general population. Thus, some experts recommend that heavy smokers over the age of 45 or 50 have periodic sputum cell analysis and chest X rays.

Although the overall outlook for lung cancer survival is poor, advances are slowly being made. Prevention, especially quitting smoking, is obviously the best measure.

COLON AND RECTUM CANCERS

Cancers of the large bowel, which includes the colon and rectum, follow cancers of the lung and breast (for women) and prostate (for men) on the list of leading cancer killers. The cure rate for this cancer is only about 50 percent, but when detected at an early stage, the cure rate can rise as high as 91 percent for colon cancer and 83 percent for rectal cancer.

The incidence of colorectal cancer increases in those over 40 but, unlike lung cancer, the cancer can be easily detected in its early stages.

Early diagnosis is a very realistic goal. However, many people, even some physicians, ignore or avoid the basic screening procedures essential for early detection. The American Cancer Society recommends:

- An annual digital rectal examination for everyone over the age of 40, whether they have symptoms or not. Many bowel cancers begin in the rectum and can easily be felt by the physician. This simple examination could save many lives.
- An annual stool guaiac test to detect occult blood for everyone over age 50. Simple, inexpensive kits available in many drugstores contain specially treated paper or slides on which the individual smears a small amount of stool. The kit is then sent to a laboratory for analysis.
- Proctosigmoidoscopy—examination of the rectum and colon with a flexible lighted tube—every three to five years after the age of 50, provided that two consecutive annual examinations were negative. Any suspicious area can be biopsied at the time of examination.

If any of these tests indicate suspicion of cancer, further examinations and tests may be needed. These include a barium enema, in which a chalky substance containing

FACTORS THAT MAY INCREASE RISK FOR COLORECTAL CANCER

- family history of the disease
- polyps in the colon
- possible link to high-fat, low-fiber diet
- ulcerative colitis and other inflammatory bowel diseases

WARNING SIGNS OF COLORECTAL CANCER

- change in bowel habits, including either diarrhea or constipation
- blood in stool
- rectal bleeding
- pain in the lower abdomen

barium to outline the colon on an X ray is infused into the rectum, and colonoscopy, which uses a long, flexible tube inserted into the colon to allow the mucous membranes to be observed. Samples can be removed for biopsy at the time of colonoscopy.

TREATMENT

If cancer is found, further tests may be done to determine if it has spread to the kidneys, ureter, bladder, or other parts of the body. Surgery is the most effective treatment. The aim is to remove the tumor and adjacent colon and lymphatic tissue. The ends of the intestine are then rejoined (an anastomosis), restoring function of the colon. Sometimes a temporary colostomy, an opening between the colon and the surface of the body, will be needed if the intestine cannot be repaired at the time of the operation. Occasionally, a permanent colostomy will be necessary in cases of rectal cancer. However, the development of more sophisticated surgical techniques has made this unnecessary for most patients. Only about 15 percent of those whose rectal cancer is detected early will need a permanent colostomy.

Radiation therapy may be used either before or after surgery in some cases, depending on the size and nature of the cancer. Adjuvant chemotherapy is sometimes recommended for those patients with very large tumors or for those whose cancer is suspected of having spread to other parts of the body.

Delay in seeking diagnosis or treatment is, as with most other cancers, a major obstacle to survival. If procedures for early detection are followed, some estimates of subsequent cure rates can go as high as 90 percent. Many people are fearful of the surgery and its consequences and wait until long after they first suspect a problem before obtaining medical advice. Frequently an early diagnosis would have resulted in less mutilating surgery and virtually no long-term aftereffects. But even if a colostomy is required, most patients are able to live full, normal lives. There is no reason to curtail work, travel, or sexual activity. As with many things, fear and the imagination can conjure up images that often are much worse than the reality.

PROSTATE CANCER

The prostate gland is about the size of a walnut and encircles the top of the urethra, which carries urine and ejaculate from the body. Cancer of the prostate is the most common cancer in men. Average age at diagnosis is 73. Since the cause of prostate cancer is unknown, there are no established guidelines for prevention, but men can greatly reduce their risk of death if they have regular examinations of the prostate.

Because early prostate cancer produces no symptoms, early detection depends on routine screening. In the past, the only recommendation was that all men have a digital rectal examination of the prostate once a year after the age of 40. Now a rectal ultrasound probe that can produce images of the prostate has proven a more accurate diagnostic tool. The ultrasonic waves can outline abnormalities before the cancer is

HIGHER-RISK INDICATORS FOR PROSTATIC CANCER

- history of venereal disease
- history of prostate infection
- age over 50
- possible link to a high-fat diet
- risk is also much higher among African-American men

suspected clinically. The best and most simple diagnostic method, however, seems to be a blood test that measures prostate-specific antigen (PSA), which is excreted by the cells lining the prostate. The PSA level is elevated in 25 to 92 percent of men with prostate cancer. In a study to determine its usefulness as a screening tool, 1,653 healthy men were tested, 112 of whom underwent biopsies. For five of the 37 men who had prostate cancer, a high level of PSA was the only suspicious finding. The blood test may be more acceptable to patients than the ultrasound method. In any case, these two screening tools, in addition to the annual rectal exam, improve the chances of early detection.

The first symptom of prostate cancer is usually difficulty in urination because the enlarged prostate can obstruct urine flow. However, this symptom does not appear until the cancer has reached an advanced stage.

Other late symptoms include pain or a burning sensation upon urination or a weak or interrupted urine flow. These symptoms may also indicate benign disorders, but they should always be evaluated. Back pain or other pain in the bones is also a common symptom because of the spread of advanced cancer to the skeleton.

If swelling or nodules are found during the rectal examination, a biopsy is done to determine whether or not cancer is present. If the biopsy is positive, further studies to determine the extent of the disease will be done, including blood tests, X rays of the skeletal system, bone marrow cell study, and a bone scan using radioactive isotopes.

TREATMENT

Treatment for prostate cancer varies depending on the extent of the cancer, the patient's general health status, and his psychosexual needs. Sometimes no treatment is considered necessary for those in whom the disease is confined to one or two microscopic areas of the gland. Surgery or radiation is the preferred treatment for those with more advanced disease, in which the cancer is confined to the prostate. Surgery, a radical prostatectomy, once frequently led to male impotence because the pelvic nerves were severed during surgery. However, improved surgical techniques have made it possible to preserve sexual function. Radioactive implants have also been used. External radiotherapy is another alternative, but it has demonstrated a lower rate of success and a higher incidence of impotence (see chapter 6).

More advanced stages of the disease are treated with radiation and hormone therapy, often to prolong life and relieve symptoms even if a cure is not possible. Another form of hormone therapy—the use of hormones to control the production of the pituitary's luteinizing hormone, which stimulates testosterone secretion—has been effective in halting testosterone production without producing the negative side effects of estrogen therapy. Anticancer drugs have also been used in the treatment of advanced stages of prostate cancer to slow tumor growth and relieve symptoms.

CERVICAL CANCER

Because the symptoms of cervical cancer are not necessarily early warning signs but may signal advanced disease, regular screening examinations that include a Pap test are essential. The Pap test is a smear or sample of epithelial, or lining, cells scraped from the cervix that are mounted on a slide, stained, and examined in a laboratory for signs of abnormal cell changes. The American Cancer Society and National Institutes of Health recommend a Pap test for women, which should be done every three years after two consecutive yearly tests have been negative. The American College of Obstetrics and Gynecology still recommends annual pelvic examinations and Pap tests. The frequency of testing should be decided by the woman and her physician, bearing in mind the risk factors involved in not periodically having the tests. Women who have had hysterectomies don't need a Pap test.

WOMEN AT RISK FOR CERVICAL CANCER

Women at risk for cervical cancer include those who have:

- intercourse at an early age
- multiple sexual partners
- family history of cervical cancer
- history of syphilis or gonorrhea
- papilloma virus (related to genital warts)

WARNING SIGNS OF CERVICAL CANCER

- intermenstrual or postmenopausal bleeding
- unusual discharge
- abdominal pain

Cervical cancer has three stages:

- *Dysplasia (abnormal growth).* Dysplasia involves changes in some cells of the cervix. This is a precancerous stage, and in many cases the cells will return to their normal state without treatment. Dysplasia can be detected by a Pap test.
- *Carcinoma in situ.* This refers to abnormal cells that do not invade neighboring tissue. This condition is considered preinvasive cervical cancer and may persist for eight to ten years. It can be detected by a Pap test, and treatment can produce a complete cure.
- *Invasive cancer.* The cancer cells have spread to surrounding tissue, lymph channels, and blood vessels, and on to lymph nodes and distant organs. Most cases of invasive cervical cancer are found in women between 45 and 55 years old. Invasive cancers are further subdivided according to the extent of the spread.

The overall five-year survival rate for cervical cancer is 66 percent. It rises to 88 percent for those patients whose cancer is diagnosed early; for carcinoma *in situ,* or localized cancer, the cure rate is virtually 100 percent.

TREATMENT

Preinvasive cervical cancer is usually treated by the following methods, which do not require extensive surgery and need not affect reproductive ability.

Conization is the removal of a cone-shaped wedge of cancerous tissue. General anesthesia and a short hospital stay are necessary. Careful follow-up, including semiannual pelvic exams and Pap tests, is recommended after conization.

Cryosurgery, which kills cancerous cells by freezing them with carbon dioxide, is used to treat dysplasia and preinvasive cancer. This procedure requires no anesthesia and may be performed in the doctor's office. Vaginal discharge lasting two to four weeks is common following treatment. Sexual intercourse should be avoided for 10 days. If abnormal cells remain or return, conization will probably be necessary. Laser therapy is an experimental therapy that may replace cryotherapy eventually.

Invasive cervical cancers are treated with surgery or radiation, or a combination of the two. Stage I cancers (confined to the cervix) are usually treated by radical hysterectomy, which involves removal of the uterus, the upper vagina, ligaments supporting the uterus, and adjacent lymph nodes. In women who are approaching or past menopause, the ovaries are sometimes removed to prevent the occurrence of ovarian cancer.

Stage II cancers (extending to the upper third of the vagina or to tissue around the uterus but not the pelvic wall) are treated with radical hysterectomy, sometimes followed by radiation therapy.

For more advanced cases, radiation is the usual therapy. Radiation is preferred over surgery for patients in whom surgery would pose a threat: the elderly, diabetics, and those debilitated by some other condition. Radiation therapy may be given in the form of X rays or radioactive implants placed in the vagina or uterus. The implants usually stay in place two to four days, during which time the woman remains hospitalized.

ENDOMETRIAL (UTERINE) CANCER

Endometrial cancer, or cancer of the lining of the uterus, usually occurs in women between the ages of 50 and 65. Over recent decades, the incidence of endometrial cancer has steadily increased. It is now more common than cervical cancer. Survival rates for endometrial cancer are quite high: 83 percent overall and 93 percent when the cancer is diagnosed early.

CONTRIBUTING FACTORS

Estrogen is known to be involved in endometrial cancer, and a number of studies have shown that postmenopausal estrogen therapy increases the risk of endometrial cancer. The degree of risk appears to be dose-related; the longer the period of medication and the higher the dose, the greater the risk. In the past, estrogen was prescribed on a daily basis. Now some doctors recommend that the smallest possible dose be given for three out of every four weeks. Hormone replacements that contain both estrogen and progesterone do not increase the risk.

Obesity's link to endometrial cancer is well established. One possible explanation is that fat cells manufacture a certain amount of estrogen, and, thus, overweight women have a natural source of excess estrogen. Women with diabetes and high blood pressure seem to have a higher incidence of this cancer. However, it is unclear whether these conditions are actually associated with the cancer, since women with these conditions are usually also overweight.

FACTORS THAT INCREASE THE RISK OF ENDOMETRIAL (UTERINE) CANCER

- history of infertility
- failure to ovulate, or other menstrual irregularities
- prolonged estrogen replacement therapy unaccompanied by progesterone
- obesity
- late menopause
- family history of endometrial cancer

DETECTION AND DIAGNOSIS

A Pap test is not highly accurate in detecting endometrial cancer. If there is reason to suspect the presence of this cancer, cells from the uterine lining will be obtained by using an aspirator. It is recommended that women at high risk have an endometrial tissue sample taken at the time of menopause. Women on estrogen therapy, which should include progesterone, need to have a pelvic examination and Pap smear every 6 or 12 months and an endometrial tissue sample taken every year or two. If the sample indicates cancer, another procedure, dilation and curettage (D&C), is done to confirm the diagnosis. During a D&C, the cervix is widened or dilated and a curette is used to scrape the lining of the uterus. This procedure requires light anesthesia and is usually performed in a hospital. An alternative procedure is an aspiration curettage, which uses a long pump to withdraw cells. This procedure can be done without anesthesia in a doctor's office.

Although the cure rate for endometrial cancer is quite high, early diagnosis and treatment are still important to prevent the cancer from spreading to other organs.

OVARIAN CANCER

This type of cancer occurs most often in women over 60. Its potential as a deadly cancer stems from its tendency to be "silent," producing few if any obvious signs or symptoms until it has become advanced. It ranks second in incidence among gynecological cancers—estimated to strike one in every 70 women—but it causes more deaths

STAGES OF ENDOMETRIAL CANCER

- Stage 0 (overgrowth or adenomatous hyperplasia of the endometrium). This is a precancerous stage that may be effectively treated with hormone therapy or a D&C. However, if the hyperplasia persists, a hysterectomy may be recommended.
- Stage I (cancer confined to the body of the uterus). This is treated with a hysterectomy and removal of tubes and ovaries. This may be the only therapy needed.
- Stage II (both the cervix and uterus are affected). This usually requires removal of the uterus, ovaries, sometimes the lymph nodes, cervix, and part of the vagina—in addition to radiation therapy.
- Stages III and IV (cancer has spread beyond reproductive organs). Treatment depends on which organs are affected. Therapy will probably include a combination of surgery and radiation, and possibly chemotherapy.

than any other cancer of the female reproductive system. One must remember, however, that it still accounts for only 4 percent of all cancers among women. In 1992, ovarian cancer was responsible for about 13,000 deaths compared to 46,000 deaths that resulted from breast cancer and the hundreds of thousands of deaths from heart disease.

A woman who has had breast cancer has double the risk of developing ovarian cancer, as do women who have never had children. Of those who have given birth, the younger they were at first pregnancy, the better. Other seemingly protective factors include use of oral contraceptives and early menopause, all resulting in a reduced number of ovulations in a woman's lifetime.

DETECTION AND DIAGNOSIS

Once again, early detection is important, but it can be difficult. The Pap smear does not reveal ovarian cancer. Complete evaluation is possible only by thorough pelvic examinations and awareness of subtle symptoms, such as enlargement of the abdomen (caused by fluid buildup), abnormal vaginal bleeding, and vague digestive disturbances for which there are no other explanations.

TREATMENT AND PROGNOSIS

Surgery combined with radiation and/or chemotherapy is the prescribed treatment. In cases when the cancer is detected early, surgical removal of the involved ovary may be all that is necessary. However, because most cases are caught later, surgical treatment usually includes removal of one or both ovaries (oophorectomy), the uterus (hysterectomy), and the fallopian tubes (salpingectomy).

A new drug called Taxol, which currently is obtained from the bark of yew trees, has been approved for the treatment of advanced ovarian cancer. Other means of producing Taxol are being investigated.

Although the overall five-year survival rate for ovarian cancer is 39 percent, the relative rate for cases that are diagnosed and treated early is 87 percent.

LEUKEMIA

Although often considered a childhood disease, leukemia actually strikes many more adults than children: The 1992 ratio was about 26,000 to about 2,500. A cancer of the blood-forming tissues, leukemia causes millions of abnormal, immature white blood cells to be released into the circulatory system, interfering with the infection-fighting normal white cells, the anemia-preventing normal red cells, and the hemorrhage-controlling platelets.

The disease does not seem to discriminate between the sexes. In most cases, there are no known causes for leukemia. Some potential links exist with those people who have Down's syndrome or other genetic abnormalities or with those who have been exposed to excessive amounts of ionizing radiation or to chemicals such as benzene, which is a toxic component of lead-free gasoline. A retrovirus, HTLV-1, is responsible for some forms of leukemia and lymphoma.

DETECTION AND DIAGNOSIS

Early symptoms are often mistaken for those of other, less serious conditions. Warning signs include fatigue, paleness, weight loss, repeated infections, bruising easily, nosebleeds, or other hemorrhages. Once a physician suspects the disease, he or she can usually make the diagnosis based on blood tests and a biopsy of the bone marrow.

TREATMENT AND PROGNOSIS

Chemotherapy, which kills the abnormal cells, is the most effective treatment, along with transfusions of compensatory blood components and antibiotics. In some cases, bone marrow transplants may be the most appropriate course of action.

There has been a dramatic improvement in cure rates for leukemias that affect children, from 4 percent to 73 percent in the last 30 years. However, the overall rate is 35 percent because of the more serious adult leukemias, called granulocytic and chronic lymphocytic. The hope is that research will continue to yield more effective drugs that will produce the same dramatic results in adults that have occurred in children.

SKIN CANCER

The vast majority of the more than 600,000 cases of skin cancer diagnosed each year, although preventable, are also highly curable basal cell or squamous cell cancers. There are about 32,000 cases of the most serious skin cancer, melanoma, included in that figure, and its incidence has increased about 4 percent each year since 1973. In combination with sun exposure, there are also the risk factors of Caucasian heritage, fair complexion, and living near the equator (see Table 12.1).

DETECTION AND DIAGNOSIS

Early detection of skin cancer is critical. Changes in the skin, such as suspicious moles or sores that do not heal, should be investigated by a physician immediately.

TABLE 12.1
Skin Cancer and Sun Exposure

Skin type	Reaction	Susceptibility
I	Always burns, never tans	Highest
II	Always burns, or tans less than average	High
III	Mild burns, and tans about average	Average
IV	No burns, and tans more than average	Low

Monthly self-examination is recommended. Growths associated with basal and squamous cell skin cancers appear as pale, waxlike, pearly nodules or as red, scaly, sharply outlined patches. Small, molelike growths that increase in size, change color, become ulcerated, and bleed easily may indicate melanoma.

MELANOMA. Melanomas may develop from moles or pigmented cells known as melanocytes. Experts recommend monthly at-home skin examinations using a good light source. A spouse or friend should check areas that cannot be seen. Any sudden appearance of a new mole or skin spot—or persistent itching, tenderness, or pain in or near a mole—should be monitored. In addition, watch for any scaling, crusting, ulceration, or bleeding of the skin. When checking for melanoma, the American Cancer Society recommends a simple ABCD rule:

A is for asymmetry.
Check to see if one half of the mole does not match the other half.

B is for border irregularity.
Check to see if the edges are ragged, notched, or blurred.

C is for color.
Check to see if the pigmentation is not uniform. Colors may vary in a single area from tan to brown or black. Red, blue, or white areas may also be present.

D is for diameter.
Check to see if the diameter is greater than 6 millimeters (about the size of a pencil eraser). In fact, any sudden or progressive increase in size of a mole or skin spot should be of special concern.

TREATMENT AND PROGNOSIS

Four methods of treatment of skin cancers currently prevail. Surgery is used in 90 percent of all cases. Radiation therapy, electrodesiccation (destroying the diseased tissue with heat), and cryosurgery (destroying the diseased tissue by freezing it) are alternatives. In cases of malignant melanoma, it may be necessary to excise nearby lymph nodes in addition to the primary growth.

For all skin cancers, cure is highly likely if they are detected and treated early. However, malignant melanoma spreads quickly to other parts of the body. Of the estimated 8,800 deaths that occur each year from skin cancer, 6,700 are from malignant melanoma.

13

Arthritis

Arthritis is a general term that applies to any disorder involving inflammation of the joints and surrounding tissue. In its various forms, arthritis is one of the most common disorders in the United States, and it is also the disease most frequently associated with old age in the public's mind. In fact, more than 37 million people (one in seven) in this country have some type of arthritis, according to the Arthritis Foundation. Most kinds of arthritis can occur at any age. However, since many kinds of arthritis are chronic and progressive in nature, older people frequently suffer from joint disorders. (For an illustration of what a normal joint looks like, see Figure 13.1.)

Many types of arthritis have no cure, although most can be managed sufficiently to minimize pain and prevent major disabilities. Early diagnosis and appropriate treatment are keys to how well a person will do in living with arthritis. The person most likely to have long pain-free periods or to be able to maintain an acceptable level of activity despite chronic symptoms is the one who consulted a physician early and then cooperated fully in the recommended plan of care. Procrastination not only permits symptoms of pain and discomfort to persist, it can result in permanent joint damage that can hinder a person's mobility, comfort, and quality of life. The precise cause of many kinds of arthritis is unknown, but a number of contributing factors have been established. These include:

- *Wear and tear on the joints.* The most common manifestation of this is osteoarthritis, also referred to as degenerative joint disease. Injuries or

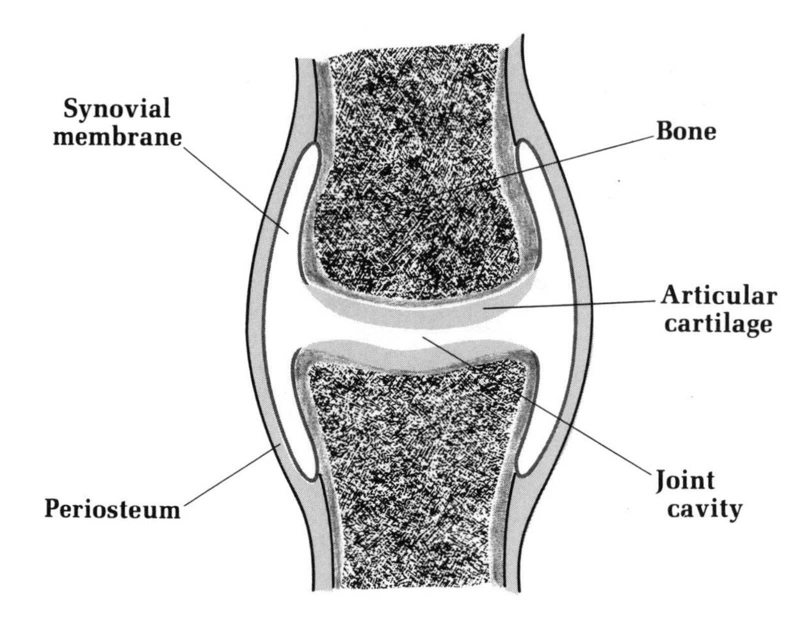

Figure 13.1 Structure of a Normal Joint

excessive stress on a joint—for example, the damage to the knees of football players and other athletes—also can lead to arthritis.

- *Genetic predisposition.* Some forms of arthritis, such as gout, rheumatoid arthritis, and osteoarthritis, appear to run in families.
- *Biochemical or metabolic abnormalities.* Gout, which is due to excessive uric acid in the blood, is a prime example.
- *Endocrine disorders.* Hormonal imbalances can result in inflammation, joint deformities, and other factors leading to arthritis. Rheumatoid arthritis, for example, invariably goes into remission during pregnancy, and recent studies have found a lower incidence among women who take postmenopausal estrogen replacement.
- *Infection.* Both viral and bacterial infections may play a role in arthritis. Untreated gonorrhea, for example, can lead to a painful form of arthritis that clears up with antibiotic treatment.
- *Complications of other diseases.* Men with hemophilia, for example, often develop arthritis due to bleeding into the joints.

- *Drugs.* Some drugs—for example, thiazide diuretics used to treat high blood pressure—may provoke gout or other forms of arthritis characterized by biochemical imbalances.
- *Possible immune system defects.* There is growing evidence that several types of arthritis are autoimmune disorders in which the body's defense system turns on itself and destroys its own tissue.

OSTEOARTHRITIS (DEGENERATIVE JOINT DISEASE)

This is the type of arthritis most closely associated with aging. Other types may occur in earlier years, and because of their progressive nature they will grow worse as time goes by, but osteoarthritis develops primarily because of the passage of years.

Osteoarthritis is the gradual degeneration of cartilage, the shock absorber in a joint. Eventually, the cartilage may disappear completely, leaving the bone surfaces without a cushion. Inflammation, the major symptom in most other kinds of arthritis, is at worst a minor problem in most osteoarthritis. Although this condition can be caused by overuse of a joint or repeated injury to a joint—dancers' ankles, for instance, or pitchers' shoulders are often affected—it is generally the result of the repetitive use of joints over time. Therefore, just about everyone will eventually develop some degree of osteoarthritis with age, although it will not usually be severe enough to cause any noticeable symptoms or discomfort. This degenerative disease may be present in its early stages in people in their twenties or thirties, but it does not usually produce any symptoms until people reach their fifties. There are exceptions, however. Some people are stricken early in life, while others may not be affected until old age.

Although repetitive use of the joints and aging contribute to development of osteoarthritis, it is also possible that people may be born with a predisposition to the disease. Researchers believe that some people may have defective cartilage or that their joints may not fit together correctly. These abnormalities would not cause any apparent defects but might eventually contribute to degeneration of the joints.

The joints most commonly affected by osteoarthritis are those of the fingers, vertebrae, knees, hips, and neck. Symptoms usually entail discomfort in and around the joint, as well as stiffness. Typically, the pain and stiffness are absent or relatively mild in the morning and progress as the day wears on. Hot, swollen joints, characteristic of other forms of arthritis, usually do not occur in osteoarthritis.

As a rule, osteoarthritis does not affect the whole body; instead, it is usually found in one or two specific joints alone. Usually only when the spine or weight-bearing joints such as the hip or knee are affected is there any severe pain or incapacity. The hands are the most frequent site of osteoarthritis, with the ends of the fingers and base of the thumb being involved the most often. Osteoarthritis typically produces bony spurs—new bone growth—in the joints. When these are confined to the ends of the fingers (Heberden's nodes), they rarely cause pain or interfere with use of the hands, although they may make the hands somewhat unsightly.

In the spine, bony spurs can cause considerable pain because they exert pressure on sensitive nerves, producing symptoms similar to those of a ruptured disk. Therefore, even though the effect on the joints themselves is not that serious, osteoarthritis of the spine can be severely painful and incapacitating.

TREATMENT

There is no single treatment for osteoarthritis; an individual patient's regimen will depend upon the severity of the disease and the joints affected. To minimize the effects of osteoarthritis on weight-bearing joints, a person should maintain ideal weight; obesity puts extra stress on the joints and can hasten their degeneration. Exercise is also vital. Stretching and range-of-motion exercises help maintain mobility, but activities that put excessive stress on joints (for example, jogging, if you have bad knees) should be avoided. Good posture is important, as is wearing properly fitted shoes. Many people have one leg slightly longer than the other without ever knowing it; this can lead to osteoarthritis of the hips and knees. Wearing a properly fitted shoe lift to even out the leg lengths can prevent further damage.

Particular attention should be paid to protecting the vulnerable joints. Strategies range from simple, commonsense ones such as warming up before exercise, using a long-handled mop to wash the floor instead of scrubbing on hands and knees, and avoiding activities that will put pressure on joints, to more specific and sophisticated ones that require the recommendation and supervision of a physician or physical therapist. And, of course, controlling weight is one of the most effective ways to relieve stress on joints.

In some instances, canes, walkers, or other aids may be needed to reduce pressure on the joints. Many self-help devices are available that can make daily functioning easier. The *Self-Help Manual for Arthritis Patients,* available from your local chapter of the Arthritis Foundation, is a catalog of such devices and includes many useful tips.

DRUGS AND OTHER TREATMENTS

The goal of drug therapy in arthritis is to reduce pain and control inflammation. Although inflammation is generally a part of the body's healing process, in arthritis it is part of a destructive process. Thus the major drugs used are anti-inflammatory agents (namely aspirin), nonsteroidal anti-inflammatory drugs (NSAIDs), or antiprostaglandins (prostaglandins are substances that increase inflammation), as well as adrenocorticoids or corticotropin. Other drugs reduce the uric acid level in the body, which at elevated levels can cause gout. Disease-modifying antirheumatic drugs are believed to actually slow down the underlying disease process, although the way they do this is unclear. These drugs take several months to work, and they must be carefully monitored because they are powerful compounds. Acetaminophen (Tylenol) and other aspirin substitutes can relieve the pain of osteoarthritis, especially for people who have an intolerance for aspirin and other pain relievers (see Table 13.1).

TABLE 13.1
Drugs to Treat Arthritis

Action/disorder	Drugs	More common side effects
Antigout (relieve pain, reduce inflammation, reduce uric acid, and/or suppress prostaglandins)	allopurinol (Lopurin, Zyloprim)	Skin rash or sores, hives, or itching
	colchicine	Diarrhea; nausea or vomiting; stomach pain
	NSAIDs (nonsteroidal anti-inflammatory drugs) fenoprofen (Nalfon) ibuprofen (Advil, Medipren, Motrin, Nuprin, Rufen) indomethacin (Indameth, Indocin) ketoprofen (Orudis) naproxen (Anaprox, Naprosyn) phenylbutazone (Butatab, Butazone, Butazolidin) piroxicam (Feldene) sulindac (Clinoril)	Skin rash; abdominal or stomach cramps, pain or discomfort (mild to moderate); diarrhea; dizziness, drowsiness, or light-headedness; headache (mild to moderate); heartburn, indigestion, nausea, or vomiting; for phenylbutazone only: swelling of face, hands, feet, or lower legs, rapid weight gain; for indomethacin only: severe headache, especially in the morning
	probenecid (Benemid, Parbenem, Probalan) probenecid and colchicine (Colabid, ColBenemid, Col-Probenecid, Proben-C)	Diarrhea (mild); headache; loss of appetite; nausea or vomiting (mild); stomach pain
	sulfinpyrazone (Anturane)	Nausea and vomiting; stomach pain
Antirheumatic, disease-modifying (reduce inflammation and/or may induce remission)	azathioprine (Immuran)	Unusual tiredness or weakness; loss of appetite; nausea or vomiting
	antimalarials chloroquine (Aralen) hydroxycholoroquine (Plaquenil)	Diarrhea; difficulty in seeing to read; headache; itching (more common in African-American patients); loss of appetite; nausea or vomiting; stomach cramps or pain
	gold compounds auranofin (Ridaura) aurothioglucose (Solganal) gold sodium thiomalate (Myochrysine)	Skin rash or itching; ulcers, sores, or white spots on lips or in mouth or throat; for auranofin only: abdominal or stomach cramps or pain (mild or moderate); bloated feeling, gas, or indigestion; decrease or loss of appetite; diarrhea or loose stools; nausea or vomiting; for aurothioglucose and gold sodium thiomalate only: irritation or soreness of tongue; metallic taste; redness, soreness, swelling, or bleeding of gums
	methotrexate (Folex, Mexate, Rheumatrex)	Less common or rare for treatment of noncancerous conditions: diarrhea; reddening of skin sores in mouth and on lips; stomach pain; acne; boils; loss of appetite; nausea or vomiting; pale skin; skin rash or itching

TABLE 13.1
Drugs to Treat Arthritis (*cont'd*)

Action/disorder	Drugs	More common side effects
	penicillamine (Cuprimine, Depen)	Fever; joint pain; skin rash, hives or itching; swollen and/or painful glands; ulcers, sores, or white spots on lips or in mouth; diarrhea; lessening or loss of taste sense; loss of appetite; nausea or vomiting; stomach pain (mild)
	sulfasalazine (Azulfidine)	Aching of joints and muscles; headache (continuing); itching; skin rash; increased sensitivity of skin to sunlight
Antirheumatic, nonsteroidal anti-inflammatory (relieve pain, reduce inflammation, and/or suppress prostaglandins)	aspirin compounds (Bayer, Easprin, Ecotrin, Empirin, Norwich, St. Joseph, ZORprin, and others) choline salicylates (Arthropan) magnesium salicylates (Doan's, Magan, Mobidin) choline and magnesium salicylates (Trilisate) salsalate (Amigesic, Diagen, Disalcid, Mono-Gesic, Salicylic Acid, Salflex, Salgesic, Salsitab) sodium salicylate (Uracel)	Abdominal or stomach cramps, pain, or discomfort (mild to moderate); heartburn or indigestion; nausea or vomiting
	NSAIDs diclofenac (Voltaren) diflunisal (Dolobid) fenoprofen (Nalfon) flurbiprofen (Ansaid) ibuprofen (Advil, Medipren, Motrin, Nuprin, Rufen) indomethacin (Indameth, Indocin) ketoprofen (Orudis) meclofenamate (Meclofen, Meclomen) naproxen (Anaprox, Naprosyn) phenylbutazone (Butatab, Butazolidin, Butazone) piroxicam (Feldene) sulindac (Clinoril) tiaprofenic acid (Surgam) tolmetin (Tolectin)	Skin rash; abdominal or stomach cramps, pain or discomfort (mild to moderate); diarrhea; dizziness, drowsiness or light-headedness; headache (mild to moderate); heartburn, indigestion, nausea, or vomiting; for phenylbutazone only: swelling of face, hands, feet, or lower legs, rapid weight gain; for indomethacin only: severe headache, especially in the morning

Immunosuppressants (reduce inflammation)	azathioprine (Immuran)	Unusual tiredness or weakness; loss of appetite; nausea or vomiting
	adrenocorticoids/corticotropin betamethasone (Celeston, Selestoject) corticotropin (Acthar, Cortrophin-Zinc) cortisone (Cortone) dexamethasone (Decadron and others) hydrocortisone (Cortef, Hydrocortone and others) methylprednisolone (Depo-Medrol, Medrol, Solu-Medrol and others) paramethasone (Haldrone) prednisone (Deltasone and others) triamcinolone (Amcort, Kenalog, Trilone and others)	Increased appetite; indigestion; nervousness or restlessness; trouble in sleeping; for triamcinolone only: loss of appetite. (Many other side effects may occur if you take this medicine for a long period of time. Check with your pharmacist or physician for more details.)
	chlorambucil (Leukeran)	*Less common:* Black, tarry stools; blood in urine or stools; cough or hoarseness; fever or chills; lower back or side pain; painful or difficult urination; pinpoint red spots on skin; sores in mouth and on lips; unusual bleeding or bruising; joint pain; skin rash; swelling of feet or lower legs; changes in menstrual period; itching of skin; nausea and vomiting
	cyclophosphamide (Cytoxan, Neosar)	Dizziness, confusion or agitation; missing menstrual periods; unusual tiredness or weakness; darkening of skin and fingernails; loss of appetite; nausea or vomiting
	methotrexate (Folex, Mexate, Rheumatrex)	*Less common or rare for treatment of noncancerous conditions:* diarrhea; reddening of skin sores in mouth and on lips; stomach pain; acne; boils; loss of appetite; nausea or vomiting; pale skin; skin rash or itching
Others (reduce pain of osteoarthritis)	acetaminophen (Tylenol and others) sometimes combined with codeine or other prescription narcotic drugs	Side effects are rare, making acetaminophen a good choice for people with osteoarthritis who cannot tolerate other medications.

Source: Consumer Reports Books, *The Complete Drug Reference*, 1992 edition, © The U.S. Pharmacopeial Convention, Inc. Permission granted.

HEAT AND COLD

Dressing warmly and applying heat packs, or swimming in heated pools, will help relieve pain. Many people find that paraffin baths, in which a painful hand is placed in warm, melted paraffin, is helpful. Extreme cold seems to aggravate pain.

REST

Although many people with osteoarthritis experience pain and stiffness when they first get up, after moving around a bit this usually subsides. However, pain and stiffness often seem to get worse as the day wears on, especially if the joints are being used a good deal. Occasional rest periods will help relieve the pain. It is, therefore, important to have a schedule that incorporates planned rest periods throughout the day. When nerves in the cervical or neck area are affected, bed rest and traction may be needed. A cervical collar can help reduce strain on the neck.

SURGERY

Hip joint replacement surgery is often successful for those whose disease has progressed to an advanced stage. The surgery does restore function but is considered only for those whose movement is severely restricted by the disease, since the artificial joint may eventually wear out and have to be replaced.

Several knee operations may help osteoarthritis patients. The insertion of an arthroscope (a hollow instrument with viewing devices) into the knee joint, and microsurgery to remove particles that are damaging the cartilage, is a procedure that has gained popularity over older surgical methods. In recent years improved artificial knee joints have been developed, and knee replacement is becoming increasingly popular.

Other joints that are candidates for repair or replacement include the fingers and shoulders. There are also new procedures using cartilage transplants, but these are still experimental and reserved for very severe cases. Still another new procedure entails withdrawing some of the joint fluid when it is found to contain tiny crystals that are shed from the bone. These crystals can cause irritation and inflammation; removal of the joint fluid, followed by an injection of cortisone into the cavity, can provide marked relief.

OUTLOOK

Most people with osteoarthritis do very well. There may be periods when the joint pain flares up, but these generally do not last long and can be relieved with drugs, rest, and heat.

RHEUMATOID ARTHRITIS

Rheumatoid arthritis is one of the more disabling forms of the disease. In this country it afflicts more than 7 million people, making it the most common form of disabling arthritis. Although rheumatoid arthritis may occur at any age, it usually first appears in the thirties and forties. It is three times more common in women than in men.

Rheumatoid arthritis is a systemic disease that may affect many organs in addition to the joints. It is usually bilateral; if one knee or finger joint is affected, for example, the same joint on the opposite side usually will be similarly attacked. The most frequent sites are the knees, hands, feet, neck, and ankles, although the disease can attack any joint. The initial symptoms include:

- swelling in one or more joints
- early-morning stiffness
- recurring pain or tenderness in any joint
- inability to move a joint normally
- obvious redness and warmth in a joint
- unexplained weight loss, fever, or weakness combined with joint pain

PREDISPOSING FACTORS

The cause or causes of rheumatoid arthritis are unknown, but certain factors suggest a pattern of development and predisposing factors. These include:

Autoimmune Disorder. The first symptoms of rheumatoid arthritis often follow a viral infection, which may suggest that an immune response has been triggered by the infection. This response may promote the inflammation of the joint lining and lead to rheumatoid arthritis.

Rheumatoid Factor. This is a gamma globulin or antibody that is present in the blood and joint fluid of the majority of patients with rheumatoid arthritis. It acts against a person's normal gamma globulin, in effect making the body allergic to itself. Rheumatoid factor is manufactured by synovial cells and released directly into the joint cavity. When it comes into contact with the normal gamma globulin, an immune complex is formed. In the body's attempt to protect itself, a substance called complement attracts inflammatory cells to destroy the immune complexes. Inflammation is the body's natural protective reaction to injury or the presence of viruses or bacteria. Normally, after the immune system attacks and repairs the problem, the inflammation subsides. But in arthritis the protective mechanism seems to backfire, and the inflammation response releases enzymes that can destroy joint tissue. A circular process results: Inflammation, the body's response to the damage caused by the enzymes, produces more destructive substances, leading to more damage and then to another inflammatory reaction.

Various theories about what causes the rheumatoid factor to develop include infection or a viral agent. Research continues on possible links with parvoviruses, the Epstein-Barr virus, or mycobacteria. No definite explanation has been established. It is also possible that the immune complexes are only one part of the disease process of rheumatoid arthritis and not an initiating cause.

Genetic Predisposition. Obviously not everyone who has an infection, virus, or unknown triggering agent develops rheumatoid arthritis. One theory is that some people have a genetic tendency to develop rheumatoid arthritis. This theory has been bolstered by discovery of a genetic marker, HLA-DR4, a tissue type that is similar to a blood type. A person with the HLA-DR4 tissue type is at higher risk for developing rheumatoid arthritis.

HOW THE DISEASE PROGRESSES

Since rheumatoid arthritis is a systemic disease, it can produce symptoms throughout the body. In the early stages people may feel tired, feverish, or weak. Lack of appetite and weight loss are common. In addition to joint symptoms, a person may complain of inflamed eyes, pleurisy, and a generalized inflammation of heart muscle, blood vessels, and other tissues. Rheumatoid nodules, which are lumps under the skin, may form, but they usually do not cause any major problem. Some people have an initial severe attack of rheumatoid arthritis and then have no symptoms for a prolonged period. However, the symptoms usually do reappear eventually, and flare-up periods followed by remission are a major characteristic of rheumatoid arthritis, a lifelong disease.

Initially inflammation is confined to the joint lining, the synovium (see Figure 13.2). As the synovium becomes enlarged and thickened, it attacks the articular cartilage, leading to possible deformity of the joint. Fluid accumulates in the joint cavity. Both the inflammation of the joint lining and the fluid accumulation produce pain. In response to the pain, the body attempts to rest the joint, producing muscle spasm or stiffness. The stiffness makes movement of the joint even more difficult and painful. If the disease progresses unchecked, the articular cartilage may be destroyed and, with the cartilage, the edges of the bones may fuse together. Although the inflammation process—and therefore the pain—will stop, the fusion results in a loss of joint function.

DIAGNOSIS

Early diagnosis and treatment can make a significant difference in the long-term outcome of rheumatoid arthritis. The Arthritis Foundation estimates that, on average, people wait four years after symptoms first appear to seek medical advice. Because arthritis is progressive, the longer it goes untreated, the greater the damage it can do. Medication, exercise, and other treatments can go a long way toward maintaining joint mobility, but if too much time has elapsed, surgery and joint replacement may become the only effective treatment.

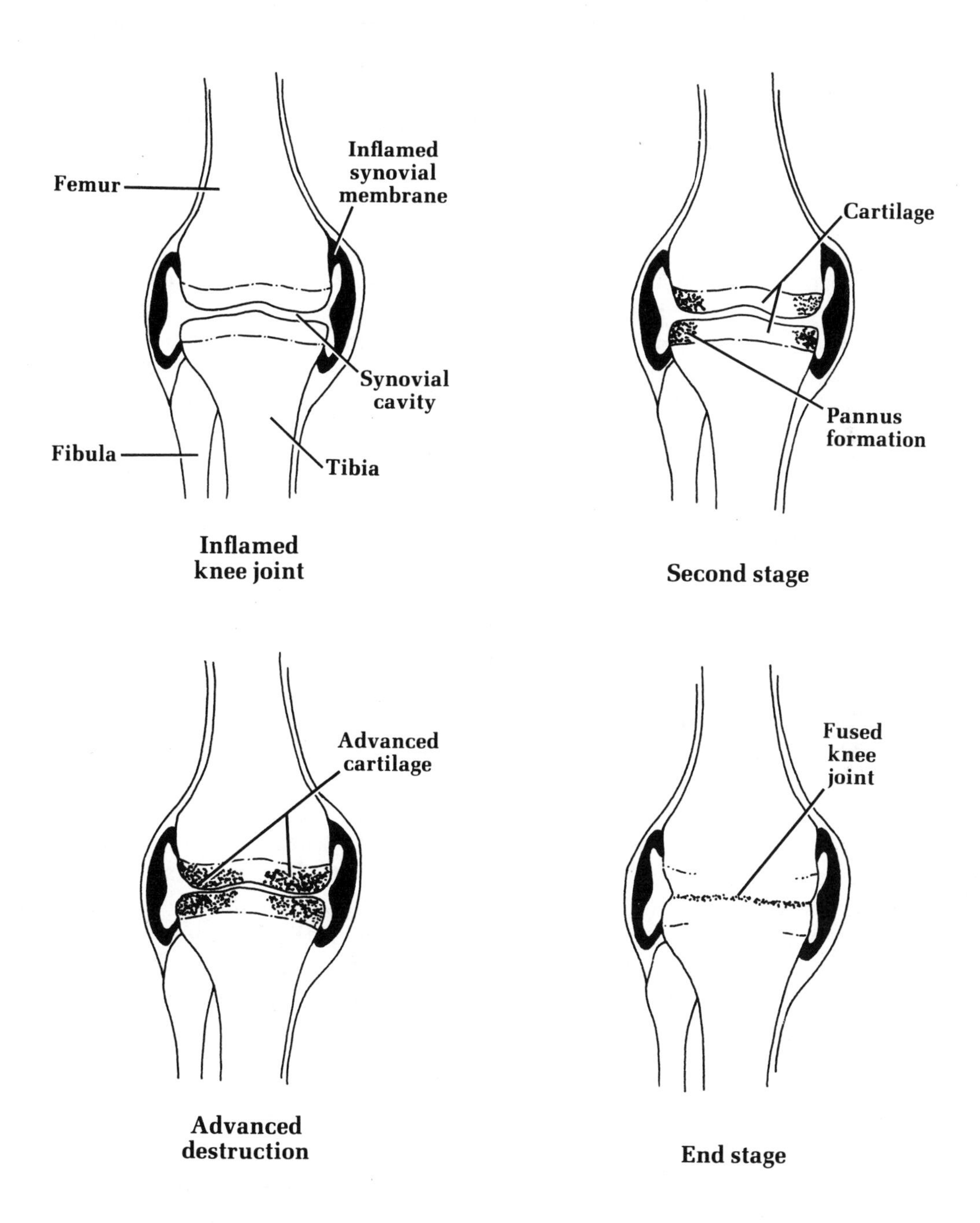

Figure 13.2 Progression of Rheumatoid Arthritis

A diagnosis of rheumatoid arthritis is based on the person's medical history, a physical examination, the presence of characteristic symptoms, and certain laboratory tests. Often the doctor will request a sedimentation rate test, which measures the rate at which red blood cells fall within one hour. An elevated rate indicates inflammation somewhere in the body. Blood tests to detect anemia and the presence of rheumatoid factor may also be made. X rays may be taken to determine changes in the joints.

TREATMENT

Many people with rheumatoid arthritis have only mild symptoms that do not interfere with daily functioning in any significant way. Others may have occasional severe attacks with long symptom-free periods. For a minority of those with rheumatoid arthritis, however, the disease becomes progressively more severe and the periods between attacks shorter. Whatever the degree of the disease, however, various methods of treatment can prevent or delay serious damage to the joints. Appropriate treatment will depend on the degree of joint pain and damage and the other systemic symptoms. As a rule, a combination of treatments is recommended that can offer relief from pain and increase mobility.

DRUG THERAPY

Aspirin is the mainstay of treatments for rheumatoid arthritis. Its anti-inflammatory effect is important in controlling the disease. A much higher dose of aspirin is needed to activate the anti-inflammatory property than is needed for ordinary pain control. The recommended dosage for headache pain—two regular tablets (5 grains, or 325 milligrams) of aspirin every four hours—will not suffice for control of the inflammation of arthritis. Instead, the dose may be anywhere from 16 to 24 tablets per day.

Many people think that because aspirin is used for so many relatively minor aches and pains and is a nonprescription medication, it is not effective against a disease as serious as rheumatoid arthritis. Or alternatively, they may think that it is harmless and resort to self-medication without supervision of a physician. Both of these attitudes contain basic flaws: Although it is true that aspirin is taken for just about any kind of minor ailment, it is also one of the most effective, safest, and cheapest arthritis medications available. Still, it is not without potential side effects. The dosage and length of therapy also can determine how successful aspirin is in controlling inflammation. It is therefore essential that a physician monitor the effectiveness and progress of therapy.

If side effects do occur, they should be brought to the attention of the physician without delay. High doses of aspirin can cause stomach irritation, gastrointestinal bleeding, nausea, ringing in the ears, and thinning of the blood. A number of different aspirin products are available, but these tend to be much more expensive than regular aspirin and are not any more effective. Buffered aspirin, for example, also contains an

TABLE 13.2
Tips on Taking Aspirin

Side effects	Action
Ringing in the ears	Reduce dosage slightly
Nausea, vomiting, and gastrointestinal irritation	Try taking more frequent but smaller doses. Take aspirin with milk, antacid, or food, such as crackers and milk. Drink a glass of water after each dose. Try taking aspirin in suspension by dissolving tablets in half a glass of milk or water, followed by another half glass. Avoid taking aspirin with orange juice or other acidic foods, which increase irritation.
Bleeding	Do not take aspirin with other drugs that thin the blood. Decrease the dosage. Avoid alcohol use while taking aspirin.

antacid. The same effect can be obtained by taking regular aspirin with an antacid or glass of milk. Coated and time-release aspirin products also are available to reduce stomach irritation, but these products may not be absorbed as efficiently as plain aspirin. High-strength aspirin preparations for arthritis may be more convenient for some people but are usually more expensive; the same effect can be achieved simply by taking three regular aspirin.

Aspirin compounds, except those for buffered aspirin, are generally not appropriate to arthritis treatment. This is especially true of compounds that contain caffeine or phenacetin. Aspirin substitutes such as acetaminophen (Tylenol, etc.) may relieve arthritis pain, but they do not have the needed anti-inflammatory action to qualify as adequate for the treatment of rheumatoid arthritis.

OTHER ANTIARTHRITIS DRUGS

Although aspirin is the main drug used in treating rheumatoid arthritis, a number of other medications are available and may be prescribed when aspirin is ineffective or when a patient cannot tolerate it. These drugs include:

NONSTEROIDAL ANTI-INFLAMMATORY DRUGS (NSAIDs). These relatively new medications are often prescribed as alternatives to aspirin. The most popular, now sold over the counter after years of being prescribed for everything from back pain to arthritis, is ibuprofen (Advil and others). These drugs are highly effective against inflammation, and some are believed to have other beneficial effects, such as inducing a remission. NSAIDs interfere with the production of prostaglandins, hormonelike substances that contribute to the inflammation process. Although all NSAIDs are chemically similar, their effect varies with the individual. It is sometimes necessary to try several NSAIDs before finding the one that works. Generally, a week or 10 days of therapy is necessary before it is clear whether the drug is effective or not. If a particular NSAID becomes ineffective after long-term use, another can usually be substituted. NSAIDs should be taken only under the supervision of a physician, and any adverse effects should be reported promptly.

Adrenocorticoids/Corticotropin. When it was discovered in the 1950s that cortisone could produce dramatic relief of arthritis pain and inflammation, it was hailed as a new miracle cure for the disease. The miracle proved to be very short-lived, however.

Although adrenocorticoids, also known as corticosteroids, can produce a dramatic reduction in inflammation, the effect is temporary, and the accompanying side effects of prolonged use of steroids can be severe. These include lowered resistance to infection because steroids interfere with the immune system response (immunosuppression). Other side effects include thinning of the bones and gastrointestinal problems. Generally, these drugs are used only if pain or inflammation cannot be controlled by aspirin or other drugs, and then only for short periods. Some of the systemic side effects can be avoided by injecting the steroid directly into the joint, but this cannot be done repeatedly because it may actually cause joint damage.

Other Immunosuppressive Drugs. These drugs act by slowing down cell division. The cells involved in the inflammation process divide and multiply more rapidly than normal cells. Thus, this medication interferes with the immune system response by slowing down its activity. Close monitoring by a physician is necessary because the activity of normal healing cells may also be affected, causing increased susceptibility to infection.

One drug that interferes with the growth of certain cells by blocking an enzyme that sustains cell life is methotrexate (Folex, Mexate, Rheumatrex). Belonging to a group of medicines known as antimetabolites, it is used in the treatment of cancer, psoriasis, and rheumatoid arthritis. Although its use for arthritis has increased, methotrexate is a very powerful drug that must be supervised closely.

Gold Compounds. When the symptoms of rheumatoid arthritis are severe and do not seem to respond to aspirin or other treatments, injection of gold salts is sometimes effective. Gold therapy is slow-acting: It may be several months after therapy is initiated before any benefits are felt. Previously, there were often serious side effects from gold therapy; however, with time and experience has come a better understanding of proper dosage, and the incidence of side effects has declined. It is not known exactly why gold works, but when it is effective it reduces early-morning stiffness and swelling and increases strength and mobility. The benefits of gold therapy may gradually disappear over time, and since it is impossible to know beforehand if the treatment will work, it is not recommended except in cases where other treatments have been unsuccessful. Oral gold preparations reduce the side effects somewhat, but they may not be as effective as the injections.

Penicillamine. Like gold, penicillamine (Cuprimine, Depen) is used only when other standard treatments have failed to bring relief. Penicillamine is a chelating agent, a substance that removes excess lead, copper, or other "heavy" metals from the body. It requires several months to take effect, but when it works the results can be dramatic. Penicillamine does have potentially serious side effects and must be used only under the close supervision of a physician.

Antimalarial Agents. Chloroquine (Aralen) and hydroxychloroquine (Plaquenil), drugs normally used to treat malaria, also control inflammation. Like gold and penicillamine, these drugs are slow-acting but are usually well tolerated. Anyone taking one of these drugs should have regular eye examinations, because serious damage to the retina is a possible side effect.

Gold, penicillamine, and antimalarial agents are usually taken in combination with another anti-inflammatory (either aspirin or an NSAID) to achieve an additive effect, and to produce relief while waiting for the slower-acting medications to work.

NONDRUG TREATMENTS

Rest and Exercise. Although most people don't think of rest and exercise as being specific treatments, they are very important in the overall management of rheumatoid arthritis. Both are necessary to maintain mobility, but neither must be taken to excess. Since fatigue is a common component of rheumatoid arthritis, specific rest periods are all the more essential so the patient will be able to carry out normal activities. Daily exercise is vital to maintain joint mobility and function, but too much activity can backfire, increasing pain and joint inflammation.

The arthritis patient should learn to organize daily schedules to provide rest periods that will relieve stress on joints but also time them so that they will not interfere too much with normal activities. Caffeine or other drugs that may interfere with sleep patterns should be reduced. If fatigue is persistent, anemia may be responsible. In this case, the treatment should be aimed at the disease, not the fatigue.

Remember, too, that arthritis is a disease with ups and downs; there are days when you feel terrific with nary a twinge, and other times when it takes real effort just to get out of bed in the morning. As much as possible, try to keep your schedule flexible enough to take advantage of good periods and to pamper yourself during flare-ups. This does not mean letting the disease rule your life, however; common sense should be the rule. Some days you just may need to force yourself to get out of bed, move around, and seek symptom relief.

Exercise helps keep joints flexible and muscles toned, providing more support for joints; it is also good for morale and promotes enhanced feelings of well-being. Exercise that puts gradual pressure on the joint helps nourish the cartilage by stimulating lubrication of the joint. Although there may be some pain at the beginning of the exercise program, exercise is probably the most effective way to avoid severe, long-term pain. Many people have found that with regular exercise their pain diminishes to the extent that they can cut down on medication.

Since pain is a warning signal sent by the body, it is important not to exercise shortly after taking painkillers; you may exercise to excess because you simply won't feel the masked warning messages from the body. Gentle stretching or range-of-motion exercise, however, can be done even when painkillers are being taken. An exercise program tailored to your specific needs should be developed in cooperation with your physician and possibly a physical therapist.

The exercises that are most helpful for people with arthritis are those that help maintain the joints' full range of motion and apply gradual pressure to the joints rather than sudden stress. Swimming, especially in a heated pool, is one of the most effective

HOW TO PREPARE FOR EXERCISING

1. A nice, slow, general stretch lying in bed is a good way to begin the day. Stretch like a cat getting up. Stretch one arm up, then the other, pull knees up, then do a few bicycle turns in the air. Stretch legs out straight, roll to the side, swing the legs off the edge of the bed, and use the momentum to help you sit up.
2. To maintain function, each joint in the body must be put through its full range of motion each day. Remember, stiff, painful joints did not develop overnight, and relief will not come quickly either.
3. If no exercise-induced pain lasts for more than two hours, then exercise time and activity can be increased.
4. Applying heat, taking a warm bath, or soaking stiff joints all can aid in relaxing joints and muscles prior to exercise.
5. Experiment with different activities. Every exercise doesn't work for every person. Give an activity two weeks to a month for first results, then choose another exercise if results are not forthcoming.
6. Exercise daily unless you are having a flare-up with hot, painful joints. Some arthritis symptoms may be due to stiff, unused muscles. It is important to keep muscles in strong, supple condition. Muscle strength will help keep joints stable.

therapies. Warm-water exercise programs are available at some local chapters of the Arthritis Foundation, and many hospitals have special arthritis clinics where information on exercise programs may be obtained.

The key to benefiting from exercise is frequent repetition: Ten- or 15-minute sessions performed three or four times a day are best. Exercising aggressively for one hour is not only ineffective but may be counterproductive, causing even more joint damage. Exercising when the joint is inflamed can aggravate the inflammation. It is best to rest to reduce inflammation and then to exercise. Even when inflammation is a problem, some sort of exercise program, such as simple stretching or range-of-motion exercises, should be followed.

Heat and Cold. Heat treatment can help relax muscles and relieve pain and stiffness. Many people find that a warm bath or shower helps reduce early-morning stiffness. Heat, whether in the form of a warm shower, heat pack, or heat lamp, can also be helpful after exercise. Paraffin baths—in which a painful hand, for example, is immersed in melted wax—relieve pain for many patients. Care should be taken that the wax is not scalding hot. Warm compresses that are changed frequently can have a similar effect.

Cold packs applied directly to the painful area can numb the area and relieve pain. Cold can also inhibit transmission of pain impulses to the brain and cool down "hot" joints.

Joint Protection. Canes and walkers can reduce stress on joints, and a physical therapist can teach methods of using your joints with the least possible strain. For instance, use your hands with the fingers extended whenever possible. Close doors with the whole hand rather than with the fingertips. Splints to hold joints in proper position may be recommended for use either at night or during the day. Typically made of light-

Table 13.3
Exercises Appropriate for Arthritis Patients

Recommended	Not recommended
Swimming	Running
Cycling (use caution if knees are affected)	Skiing
Isometrics, which increase muscle tone without putting stress on joints	Jumping rope
Moderate weight lifting	Jogging
Yoga	Tennis
Walking	Racquetball
Stretching	

weight plastic with foam padding, splints allow joints to rest and help keep surrounding muscles and ligaments limber.

SURGERY. In cases of advanced disease, surgical repair of joints may be advised. In some of these procedures, diseased synovium is removed and the joints are realigned. Both large and small joints are now being repaired using these techniques. Removal of the diseased synovial membrane also reduces the pain of the synovitis, but it is usually done only when drug therapy has been unsuccessful or when one joint is significantly more inflamed than others.

Increasingly, joint replacement surgery is being used to restore function for people who are severely handicapped. Joints that are candidates for replacement include the hips, fingers, and knees. In considering joint surgery, make sure that the surgeon is experienced in repairing or replacing the joints in question. A skilled hand surgeon may not be the best choice to operate on the knees or hips, and vice versa. When in doubt about the need for surgery, the type of operation, or the best surgeon, a second opinion can be helpful.

LIVING WITH RHEUMATOID ARTHRITIS

It would be folly to imply that people with rheumatoid arthritis can go about their daily lives giving little or no consideration to the disease. Even though in most instances the disease can be controlled and its victims lead rewarding, productive lives, adjustments and compromises are often needed. Chronic diseases are by nature difficult, particularly those that are both painful and disabling.

Many people make the mistake of thinking that a stiff upper lip is all that is needed. Determination is important, but in dealing with arthritis, common sense is perhaps even more essential. Sometimes simple household or personal tasks, such as opening a jar, putting on panty hose, or getting up off a low toilet seat, can be very difficult if not impossible. A variety of gadgets are available that make it easier to perform ordinary tasks. Surgical supply houses or arthritis specialists usually have catalogs. Physical and occupational therapy also are valuable in learning new skills.

Arthritis also takes its toll on family members and personal relationships. For example, many arthritis patients find they avoid sexual relations because at the end of the day they are fatigued, or they fear anything that may produce more pain. While sexual intimacy may not be the most important factor in a relationship, it certainly is an important one, and there is no reason the arthritis patient should be denied a warm and loving association. Often, simply timing sexual activity to coincide with the "best" part of the day—perhaps in the morning after a shower to get limbered up, or after an afternoon nap—solves the problem. Experimenting to find positions that are comfortable and do not put stress on painful joints also helps.

People with chronic diseases often resort to becoming manipulative and complaining. It is understandable, but it does not make life pleasant for those who live with the patient. The person with arthritis should not hesitate to ask for help when it is needed and to accept offers of help. But this is quite different from becoming overly demanding or dependent. Take time to assess what is really important and, if need be, reorder your priorities. A homemaker may want a spotless house, but does it really matter that every speck of dust is removed from hard-to-reach places? Instead of wearing yourself out doing massive cleaning and then spending a couple of days in bed, it is far better to do a little each day and to encourage (not nag) other family members to do their share.

In recent years, there have been major advances in the long-term management of rheumatoid arthritis. It is now rare for a person to become severely crippled from the disease, and even those with considerable disability can learn to be self-sufficient.

THE ARTHRITIS SELF-HELP COURSE

Anyone who suffers from chronic arthritis can benefit from the Arthritis Self-Help Course, a program developed in 1978 at Stanford University.

In six two-hour-weekly sessions, participants are taught about the different kinds of arthritis. They learn how to design their own exercise program; manage pain with techniques like relaxation; improve their nutrition; and fight depression and fatigue. They also learn ways to solve the problems posed by their disease and to communicate more effectively with their physicians.

On average, participants report their pain is reduced by 15 to 20 percent. Those who were depressed when they started the program are less so when they finish. They see the doctor less often and in general lead more active lives, going out more often and spending more time with friends and family.

Follow-up studies have shown that the factor most closely linked to improvement in pain, depression, and activity level is a positive adjustment in attitude. Graduates of the course have higher levels of *self-efficacy*—the confidence that they are able to deal with their disease.

The Arthritis Self-Help Course is available throughout the United States and in Canada, Australia, and South Africa. In this country, the course is given through the Arthritis Foundation—at 792 locations in 1991—at an average cost of $20. For more information, contact the Arthritis Foundation headquarters at 1314 Spring Street NW, Atlanta, GA 30309, telephone (404) 872-7100.

GOUT

Gout, also called crystal arthritis, is one form of arthritis that almost always can be kept under control to avoid periodic flare-ups. It is also the one form of arthritis for which the cause is well established. People with gout have an inborn metabolic error that causes crystals from excessive uric acid in the blood to form and settle in the joint space, resulting in inflammation and severe pain.

We often associate gout with the gluttony of King Henry VIII—but there is nothing that predisposes a person to gout. The disease almost always occurs in men, with the first attack usually coming in middle age. Typically, an attack comes on without warning. A big toe is the favored site; within hours the joint will be red, swollen, and inflamed, as well as extraordinarily painful. Gout sufferers describe the pain of an attack as much worse than the most severe toothache. Even the slightest touch or the weight of a bed sheet will send waves of extreme pain through the foot and leg. If untreated, an attack usually lasts for several days, and then the sufferer may not have another episode for several months. As time goes by, the attacks usually become more frequent, and more joints—usually those of the elbow, ankles, knees, or fingers—may be affected. It is understandable that, in times past, gout sufferers became preoccupied with their disease and lived in dread of the next attack.

Fortunately, times have changed. The vast majority of gout patients can now live without attacks; several drugs can eliminate the cause—namely, excessive uric acid in the blood. Uric acid is normally filtered from the blood through the kidneys. The conditions that lead to gout arise when there is an overproduction of uric acid or when, for some reason, the kidneys cannot eliminate uric acid adequately. As a result, uric acid crystals form in the joint spaces, irritating the joint lining and causing a severe inflammatory reaction. The inflammation affects the nerve endings in the joint, which accounts for the severe pain.

Sometimes people with high uric acid will have large deposits of crystals, or tophi, in soft tissues (such as the outer ear) without having the usual symptoms of gout. Many will also develop urate kidney stones, which are made up of uric acid. In such instances, the first indication of high uric acid may be the development of a kidney stone. Hyperuricemia (excess uric acid) in itself does not need to be treated if it causes no symptoms, but people with elevated uric acid levels should be tested regularly for signs of kidney damage. People with high uric acid also tend to have an increased incidence of heart attacks, but it is not known if there is a relationship between the uric acid and heart disease or if other common characteristics of gout patients, such as being overweight, account for the rise.

Gout appears to be linked to a genetic factor: Some people have a predisposition to develop hyperuricemia. In addition, diet, infections, and certain drugs—especially diuretics used to treat high blood pressure—can precipitate gout. In susceptible people, frequent aspirin use also can cause hyperuricemia.

TREATMENT

Gout is one of the most successfully managed forms of arthritis. If the treatment regimen is followed carefully, it can almost always be kept under control. It is also one of the few forms of arthritis for which aspirin is not appropriate. Drug therapy for gout is twofold: (1) an analgesic other than aspirin, such as acetaminophen (Tylenol) or codeine, for the pain; and (2) an anti-inflammatory drug to control the inflammation. Colchicine is the traditional drug used during the acute phase.

Colchicine is an ancient drug derived from the autumn crocus or meadow saffron, a plant that has been used in folk medicine to treat gout since the sixth century. Benjamin Franklin is reputed to have been treated with colchicine during his European travels and is said to have introduced the drug to American physicians. Colchicine has remarkable anti-inflammatory action, but it seems to work only for gout and not for other forms of arthritis. The major problem with colchicine is its extreme toxicity. Indeed, the ancients recognized it as a poison and hesitated to give it to humans as medicine. Today a gout patient will be instructed to take a 1-milligram tablet of colchicine at the first sign of an attack, and 0.5 milligram every two or three hours until the pain abates, or until diarrhea, nausea, vomiting, or abdominal cramps develop. This is a sign that a toxic level has been reached and that the patient should take no more of the drug. If the colchicine is continued, severe diarrhea and intestinal hemorrhaging may occur. As little as 7 milligrams of colchicine may be fatal, so it is very important that the patient recognize when it is time to stop the drug. Why is such a toxic medication prescribed? Mainly because even a small dose produces dramatic relief: A person who is writhing in pain and unable to bear even the slightest touch to an inflamed joint may be up and walking about, free of pain, within a few hours.

Patients who cannot tolerate colchicine may be given potent nonsteroidal anti-inflammatory drugs (NSAIDs) as an alternative. The two used most often are phenylbutazone (Butazolidin and others) or indomethacin (Indameth, Indocin). Phenylbutazone is perhaps the more effective of the NSAIDs, but it also has a long list of potentially serious side effects, including serious blood disorders, liver damage, nausea, vomiting, gastrointestinal bleeding, and kidney damage. It is generally prescribed for only a short time, and the patient should have frequent ongoing blood tests. Indomethacin is less likely to cause severe blood disorders and is also effective in treating acute gout. Both drugs take longer than colchicine to end an attack, but most patients will still experience relief within a couple of days.

After the acute phase of the gout attack has passed, the physician will look into the underlying cause. If medications, such as diuretics, are responsible, alternative drugs may be prescribed. If there does not appear to be a secondary cause, treatment depends on how frequent and intense subsequent attacks are. For chronic gout, where the attacks are frequent, colchicine is sometimes given in low doses as a preventive. If the side effects of colchicine, even in low doses, are too severe or if the attacks persist, a uricosuric agent—one that lowers the level of uric acid by blocking its reabsorption as it filters through the kidney—may be tried. Probenecid (Benemid and others) or sulfinpyrazone (Anturane) works in this manner. Alternatively, a drug that blocks production of uric acid, such as allopurinol (Lopurin, Zyloprim), may be prescribed. Allopurinol also may be given in combination with either probenecid or sulfinpyrazone. These drugs are never administered during an acute attack of gout; they may, in fact, make the attack worse. They are given only to prevent attacks of gout by altering the conditions that can lead to it.

NONDRUG THERAPY

DIET. It has long been known that certain foods can precipitate an attack of gout. These include foods rich in purine—organ meats, sardines, anchovies, dried peas and legumes—which can increase the level of uric acid. Wine, beer, and sometimes other alcoholic beverages also can bring on an attack of gout. Patients with mild gout or elevated uric acid are often advised to avoid these foods and beverages. Ironically, many gout patients develop strong cravings for the very foods that are responsible for their disease.

WEIGHT REDUCTION. Obesity not only puts a strain on the affected joint, producing more pain, it can also be responsible for the hyperuricemia. Therefore, weight reduction is sometimes the only treatment needed for gout. It is important, however, to follow a sensible weight-loss plan that produces a gradual reduction, because a sudden dramatic drop in calories can actually cause an attack.

Gout patients should make sure they drink lots of nonalcoholic fluids to increase urine output and flush out the excessive uric acid. Since even the slightest pressure during an attack of gout is so very painful, using a bed frame to keep sheets and blankets off an affected foot may help. Most gout patients cannot tolerate wearing regular shoes. For this reason, sandals or roomy soft shoes, such as sneakers, may be more tolerable.

PSEUDOGOUT

Pseudogout is caused by crystals of calcium pyrophosphate dihyrate (CPPD) in the joint space. Pseudogout is more common in men than in women, and its incidence increases with age. The knee, rather than the toe (as in primary gout), is the most frequent site, although the fingers, toes, hips, shoulders, elbows, and ankles may be affected. Sometimes there are no acute attacks, as in true gout, but the disease may result in chronic inflammation and calcification of joint cartilage. In this stage, pseudogout may be confused with rheumatoid arthritis or inflammatory osteoarthritis.

Pseudogout usually can be treated effectively with nonsteroidal anti-inflammatory drugs. Cortisone injected directly into the joint may be used for acute attacks.

INFECTIOUS ARTHRITIS

Sometimes arthritis may be a complication of another disease caused by a virus, bacterium, or fungus. Microorganisms enter the joint and cause infection and inflammation. Infectious arthritis is the only arthritis for which there is really a complete cure, provided the infection is diagnosed in time and treated with the appropriate antibiotic. If the infection is not treated promptly, however, the joint may be permanently damaged and chronic arthritis may develop. People who have used steroids for long periods or who have a lowered resistance to infection for some other reason may be at risk for infectious arthritis. In addition, those with rheumatoid arthritis seem to be at risk for bacterial arthritis. If a person with rheumatoid arthritis is persistently bothered by pain in one joint, even when the disease is in remission elsewhere, bacterial arthritis should be suspected.

Staph infections, gonorrhea, tuberculosis, rheumatic fever, osteomyelitis (bone infection), and a variety of viral and fungal infections all can cause infectious arthritis. In all cases of infectious arthritis, treatment involves identifying the causative agent and then prescribing the appropriate antibiotic or antifungal drug.

LYME DISEASE ARTHRITIS

A good deal of publicity has been given to Lyme arthritis, a disease carried by deer ticks and named for the Connecticut town in which it was discovered. When the ticks bite, they leave a coil-shaped bacterium called a spirochete, which sometimes causes a rash that spreads out in a circular fashion around the bite. The bite may not be noticeable, and a rash may not occur. Nevertheless, more serious flulike symptoms—aches and pains, fever, chills, lethargy, fatigue—may follow days or weeks later. Joint pain is common. The heart and nervous system may become affected later in the disease process. Very painful Lyme arthritis can persist in some people for years following infection.

Avoiding tick-infested areas is the best way to avoid Lyme disease. However, paranoia about walking through wooded areas can cause you to miss out on the pleasures of nature. Simply using common sense is a better alternative. Liberally apply an insect repellant that contains deet to skin and clothing (after you have spot-tested it for an allergy). Also, when walking through tall grass or brush, wear boots, pants that can be tucked into your socks, and light-colored clothing that makes it easier to find any ticks. Also, put flea and tick collars on your pets to protect them and keep them from bringing ticks into the house. Replace the collars at regular intervals. And most important, whenever you or your pets come indoors after a day of romping through the woods, check your skin and theirs for any unwelcome hangers-on.

If you find a tick attached to the skin, pull it out with tweezers or small forceps. Wash the bite wound with soap and water, and disinfect it with rubbing alcohol. If you experience a rash, see a physician immediately. Early diagnosis and treatment with high doses of antibiotics that kill the bacteria may prevent long-term complications such as arthritis.

SOFT-TISSUE RHEUMATISM

A number of conditions affect the muscles, tendons, ligaments, or tissue surrounding joints that may cause pain and stiffness. Although some people may misinterpret the symptoms as arthritis, such disorders actually fall into another category of rheumatic disease: soft-tissue rheumatism. Treatment for some of these conditions may be similar to treatment for arthritis, but a specific diagnosis will lead to the best course of therapy. Not all of these disorders are chronic in the same sense that arthritis is, but recurrence may be a problem with some.

Disorders classified as soft-tissue rheumatism may be either localized, confined to a specific joint or two, or diffuse.

Some of the more common localized conditions include:

Bursitis. Inflammation of the bursae, small fluid-filled sacs around the joint space. It occurs most commonly in the shoulder, hip, knee, and elbow. Pain is localized and the area may be hot and red. It frequently follows an injury to the area or the excessive use of the joint; tennis players, for example, often develop bursitis in their shoulders.

Capsulitis. Inflammation of the joint capsule, most commonly the shoulder.

Costochondritis. Inflammation of cartilage outside the joint. The ribs are commonly affected.

Fasciitis. Inflammation of the membrane covering the muscles, the fascia. Plantar fasciitis occurs in the heel. Other sites include the neck, back, thighs, hands, and feet.

Ligamentitis. Inflammation of ligaments, the bands of fibrous tissue that connect bones. This may be caused by improper joint motion, particularly in the knee and ankle.

Nerve-entrapment Syndrome. A condition caused by swelling of a ligament that puts pressure on an adjacent nerve. Carpal tunnel syndrome, for example, causes hand and wrist pain because of pressure on the nerve that passes through the carpal tunnel in the wrist.

Tendinitis. Inflammation of the tendons, the tissue that connects muscle to bone, and their sheaths, often caused by overuse or injury. Tennis elbow is a form of tendinitis. Shoulders, wrists, hips, knees, ankles, and fingers, as well as elbows, may be affected.

Diffuse conditions include:

Fibrositis. Symptoms include pain in muscles, ligaments, and tendons, difficulty in sleeping, and local tenderness in any of several trigger points, primarily in the shoulders, back, or hips. Tingling, numbness, fatigue, and anxiety are common. Since X rays reveal no changes in muscles or other tissues, in the past the person suffering from fibrositis was often misdiagnosed or the symptoms were dismissed as psychological. Now the characteristics of the condition are more widely recognized.

Giant-cell Arthritis. A rare disorder involving inflammation of the blood cells that can lead to severe headache, fever, weight loss, anemia, and blindness.

Polymyalgia Rheumatica. Characterized by stiffening in the shoulder and hip area. It affects older people primarily. Treatment usually involves a combination of rest, exercise, and drug therapy.

Arthritis may also be associated with other diseases. For example, people with psoriasis often develop psoriatic arthritis, and ulcerative colitis may also be accompanied by arthritis.

14

Maturity-onset Diabetes

Of the 14 million Americans with diabetes, 90 to 95 percent suffer from maturity-onset diabetes, the most common form of this endocrine disorder. Maturity-onset diabetes, also known as Type 2 or non-insulin-dependent diabetes, comes on gradually and is most common after the age of 40 and among people who are overweight. Type 2 diabetes usually can be controlled by diet, in contrast to juvenile diabetes, referred to as Type 1 or insulin-dependent diabetes, which requires insulin injections. (For the sake of consistency, we will use the terms Type 1 and Type 2 diabetes.) Some people with Type 2 diabetes may eventually require insulin shots; also, some adults develop Type 1 diabetes, characterized by a failure of the pancreas to produce insulin.

Diabetes is a widespread and serious health problem, but it is manageable. According to the American Diabetes Association, almost 750,000 people are diagnosed with diabetes each year, and 150,000 die. But through early diagnosis and careful attention to diet, and with medication regimens and other methods of self-care, people with diabetes can greatly reduce the chances of disability and life-threatening illness.

Type 2 diabetes arises when the body is unable to make effective use of insulin, a hormone produced by special islet cells located in the pancreas. Among other functions, insulin is essential to the body's metabolism. Without sufficient insulin, the body is unable to utilize blood sugar, or glucose, its major fuel. Carbohydrates are the major source of glucose, so insulin is essential in the metabolism of carbohydrates. It is also important in the metabolism of proteins and fats, and performs other vital functions.

In contrast to Type 1 diabetes, in which the pancreas secretes little or no insulin, patients with Type 2 diabetes often have normal or even high levels of the hormone, but for some reason the body is unable to use it. This may be due to a larger amount of insulin-resistant fat tissue (about 80 percent of Type 2 diabetics are overweight), a reduced number of receptors that enable insulin to enter the cell, abnormal receptors, or other factors. Resistance may also occur because of a defect in which the body's immune system perceives its own insulin as "foreign" and attacks it. Current research on drugs that suppress selected parts of the immune system, correcting the defect while allowing the rest of the system to carry out defensive functions, may someday be used in the treatment of Type 2 diabetes.

Being overweight is not the only risk factor for diabetes; having a close relative with the disease greatly increases the risk in adults age 40 and older. Certain drugs, disorders of the pancreas and endocrine system, and stress also may produce diabetes, usually Type 1.

SYMPTOMS AND DIAGNOSIS

Regular physical examinations that include blood and urine testing are important in detecting Type 2 diabetes, which does not always produce symptoms in its early stages. In fact, about half of all people with diabetes are not aware that they have the disease. Older adults who are either overweight or have a family history of the disease, or both, should see a physician if they have any of the following symptoms:

- extreme hunger or thirst
- frequent need to urinate
- marked weight loss
- nausea and vomiting
- fatigue or drowsiness
- blurred vision
- impotence in men
- frequent vaginal infections in women
- irritability and mood swings
- itching
- frequent infection of small skin abrasions, which heal slowly
- numbness, tingling, or pins-and-needles sensations in the hands or feet
- slow-to-heal cuts, particularly on the feet

Diabetes is characterized by high levels of blood glucose because the body is unable to use it for fuel. Eventually some of the excessive glucose will be secreted by the kidneys in the urine. Detecting glucose in the urine is a warning sign of diabetes, but since other factors can produce this symptom, blood tests to measure the level of glucose are a more accurate diagnostic tool.

THE AMERICAN DIABETES ASSOCIATION TEST FOR DIABETES RISK

Write in the points next to each statement that is *true* for you. If a statement is *not true* for you, mark it with a zero. Add up your total score, and read the instructions that follow the test.

1. I have been experiencing one or more of the following symptoms on a regular basis		
▪ excessive thirst	Yes 3	______
▪ frequent urination	Yes 3	______
▪ extreme fatigue	Yes 1	______
▪ unexplained weight loss	Yes 3	______
▪ blurry vision from time to time	Yes 2	______
2. I am over 30 years old.	Yes 1	______
3. My weight is equal to or above that listed in the chart at the end of this test.	Yes 2	______
4. I am a woman who has had more than one baby who weighed more than 9 pounds at birth.	Yes 2	______
5. I am of American Indian descent.	Yes 1	______
6. I am of Hispanic or African-American descent.	Yes 1	______
7. I have a parent with diabetes.	Yes 1	______
8. I have a brother or sister with diabetes.	Yes 2	______
	Total	______

If your score is 3–5 points:
You probably are at low risk for diabetes. But don't just forget about it, especially if you're over 30, overweight, or of African-American, Hispanic, or American Indian descent.

What to do about it:
Be sure you know the symptoms of diabetes. If you experience any of them, contact your doctor for further testing.

If your score is over 5 points:
You may be at high risk for diabetes. You even may already have diabetes.

What to do about it:
See your doctor promptly to find out if you have diabetes. Even if you don't have diabetes, know the symptoms. If you experience any of them in the future, you should see your doctor immediately.

The American Diabetes Association urges all pregnant women to be tested for diabetes between the twenty-fourth and twenty-eighth week of pregnancy.

Note: This test is meant to educate and make you aware of the serious risks of diabetes. Only a medical doctor can determine if you do have diabetes.

To diagnose diabetes, blood sugar is measured in the morning following an overnight fast. Two separate readings of more than 140 milligrams of glucose per deciliter of blood are generally considered indicative of diabetes. If the blood sugar is only slightly elevated, the physician may order an oral glucose tolerance test (OGTT). In preparation, the individual must eat sufficient carbohydrates (100 to 150 grams per day) for three days preceding the test and then fast the night before. He or she is then given a sugar drink, and blood samples are taken every 30 minutes for two to three hours afterward. In nondiabetic people, blood sugar rises for as long as one hour after the drink and then gradually drops. Those with diabetes will show higher blood sugar at the one-hour point, without the expected drop. The results of these tests can be thrown off by many factors, including alcohol abuse, liver disease, prior gastrointestinal surgery, and decreased activity levels. Many medications, including antidepressants, steroids or certain other hormones, thiazide diuretics, and the anticonvulsant drug phenytoin (Dilantin) may also either raise or lower blood glucose.

CONTROLLING TYPE 2 DIABETES

Numerous studies have demonstrated that most cases of Type 2 diabetes can be successfully controlled by maintaining proper weight through diet and exercise. In fact, there is strong evidence that these factors alone may prevent Type 2 diabetes and its complications. However, anyone who has tried to lose weight knows only too well that cutting down on calories is difficult. For diabetic patients especially, reducing calories may be even harder because they often feel hungry most of the time. The person may be overweight and have high levels of blood glucose, but the body is unable to make proper use of this fuel. The brain especially requires a steady supply of glucose; if the supply is not forthcoming, the brain will send out powerful hunger signals. This explains why extreme hunger is one of the major symptoms of diabetes: The brain is being deprived and is trying to protect itself by signaling that it needs more food. Therefore, diabetics need even greater willpower to lose the excess weight; if this can be achieved, however, the body is able to make better use of its insulin, and the feeling of hunger will then abate.

WEIGHT CHART

(shows 20 percent over maximum recommended weights)

Height (without shoes)		Weight in pounds (without clothing)	
Feet	Inches	Women	Men
4	9	127	
4	10	131	
4	11	134	
5	0	138	
5	1	142	146
5	2	146	151
5	3	151	155
5	4	157	158
5	5	162	163
5	6	167	168
5	7	172	174
5	8	176	179
5	9	181	184
5	10	186	190
5	11		196
6	0		202
6	1		208
6	2		214
6	3		220

This chart shows weights that are 20 percent heavier than the maximum recommended for both men and women with a medium frame. If your weight is at or above the amount listed for your height, you may be at risk for developing diabetes.

A specific diet plan can also help maintain a more healthy balance of glucose and insulin in the bloodstream. A reduction in dietary fat and simple sugars and an emphasis on complex carbohydrates and fiber is recommended. Consult a physician trained in nutrition, a registered dietitian, or a certified nutritionist for an individual dietary plan. And remember that when weight control is the goal, exercise is just as important a component as a dietary plan.

Of course, not all people with Type 2 diabetes are overweight, and there are instances in which weight loss alone is not sufficient to control the diabetes. If blood sugar still remains high in such patients, or in overweight diabetic patients who cannot lose weight, medication may be prescribed. This usually entails taking pills from a family of drugs known as oral hypoglycemics. For some patients, however, insulin injections may be needed. (Insulin cannot be taken orally because it is a protein hormone and would be rendered useless by the digestive process.)

DIET

Maintaining normal weight will usually control Type 2 diabetes, but it is not a cure; if the lost weight is regained, chances are the blood sugar will rise and any previous symptoms may recur. To prevent complications, normal weight must be maintained for life. To plan for safe weight loss, the patient should work with a dietitian to come up with a satisfactory eating plan—one that the patient can live with and that still controls the level of blood sugar in the body.

Older individuals who have a lifetime of bad eating habits may need much support in changing them. Additionally, being diagnosed with an incurable chronic disease often leads to anger or denial of the illness and results in self-destructive behavior patterns. These include gorging on forbidden foods. Joining groups such as Weight Watchers and Overeaters Anonymous and utilizing techniques such as hypnosis and behavior modification may facilitate weight loss. Individual counseling or a diabetes support group may help the newly diagnosed diabetic cope with his or her disease.

EXERCISE

Regular exercise and cutting calories offer a faster and less painful way of losing weight than does dieting alone. Aerobic activities, such as brisk walking, jogging, swimming, and cycling, are most important. These activities exercise the large muscles, which in turn reduces insulin resistance and rapidly burns glucose. This form of brisk, prolonged activity also helps condition the cardiovascular system, increasing the heart's efficiency and reducing the risk of coronary artery disease and heart attacks, which are associated with both Type 1 and Type 2 diabetes. Aerobic exercise also helps reduce stress, and it will lower cholesterol and possibly hypertension. All of these are major risk factors in the development of heart disease.

Older adults—in fact, anyone over age 35—who have not practiced regular, vigorous exercise should consult a physician before embarking on such a program. Heart disease, even a previous heart attack, is not a contraindication for strenuous exercise, so long as the program is properly tailored to match the individual's health status.

To design a safe yet effective regimen, the physician may recommend a stress test that measures how the heart performs during vigorous exercise. In this procedure, pulse, blood pressure, and a continuous electrocardiogram are taken while the individual rides an exercise bicycle or walks a treadmill. Test results are then read by a physician.

Anyone starting an exercise program should begin gradually and work up to a heart-conditioning level. The routine should be done at least three or four times a week (see chapter 2).

MEDICATIONS

Even though most people with Type 2 diabetes can be treated by weight loss alone, in practice many end up taking an oral hypoglycemic medication. These drugs are also called sulfonylureas because they are related to the sulfa drugs. They lower blood sugar by stimulating the pancreas to produce more insulin and possibly decreasing insulin resistance. Although these drugs all belong to the same family, they have somewhat different actions; some may be either short- or long-acting, with different times of peak action and various dosage schedules (see Table 14.1).

Although people who take oral medications do not have the same risk of developing excessively low blood sugar as those taking too much insulin, this reaction can

TABLE 14.1
Drugs Used to Treat Type 2 Diabetes

Generic name	Brand name	Daily dosage range	Time of peak action
acetohexamide	Dymelor	250 mg to 2 g	4 to 5 hours after taking
chlorpropamide	Diabinese Glucamide	100 mg to 500 mg	3 to 6 hours after taking
glipizide	Glucotrol	5 mg to 40 mg	1 to 3 hours after taking
glyburide	DiaBeta Micronase	1.25 mg to 20 mg	4 hours after taking
tolazamide	Tolamide Tolinase	100 mg to 1 g	3 to 4 hours after taking
tolbutamide	Oramide Orinase	500 mg to 3 g	3 to 4 hours after taking

occur. Skipping a meal or not eating enough, consuming alcohol, taking certain drugs concurrently, and overexercising may bring on excessive low blood sugar, or hypoglycemia. Persons with adrenal insufficiency (Addison's disease) or liver, kidney, or pituitary gland disorders, as well as elderly people, may require careful dose adjustments to prevent hypoglycemia.

If hypoglycemic symptoms occur, the individual should immediately take a quick source of sugar—for example, a glass of orange juice—followed by a protein source for sustained glucose release. Diabetic patients should always carry hard candies for a quick sugar source when away from home.

Although a controversial study has shown that oral hypoglycemic drugs may carry some increased risk of death from heart disease, complications of uncontrolled diabetes are usually considered a much higher risk overall.

COMPLICATIONS OF DIABETES

Diabetes can affect many organ systems through changes in the blood vessels, nerves, and other less clearly understood mechanisms. Although complications are somewhat more common in Type 1 diabetes and are usually related to poorly controlled blood sugar and/or the duration of the disease, those who control their diabetes

SYMPTOMS OF HYPOGLYCEMIA

- Headache
- Extreme fatigue
- Sudden drowsiness or change in alertness
- Nervousness or tremulousness
- Confusion or personality change
- Hunger
- Profuse perspiration
- Cold feeling
- Clammy skin
- Pallor
- Blurred or double vision
- Rapid pulse or palpitations
- Numbness or tingling in lips, nose, or fingers

Note: The drug propranolol (Inderal) may mask symptoms of hypoglycemia.

well may also suffer these effects. And those with long-standing diabetes actually may be spared complications. Even with this somewhat unpredictable outcome, strict control of blood sugar and regular medical follow-up of any early signs of concurrent disease are vital to minimize the risk of complications.

LOSS OF VISION

Diabetes is the chief cause of new cases of blindness in adults, according to the American Diabetes Association. Most commonly, diabetes affects the retina and lens of the eye. Diabetics with hypertension are especially at risk, since high blood pressure can cause hemorrhaging and other abnormal changes in the retina and optic nerve.

The retina, which lies at the back of the eyeball, contains the color- and light-sensitive cells that transmit electrical impulses to the brain, resulting in visual perception. In diabetic retinopathy, the walls of the capillaries nourishing the retina weaken and burst or become constricted and die. The resulting small hemorrhages and decreased supply of oxygen and other nutrients to the retina can result in visual impairment.

More seriously, fragile new blood vessels can develop in the retina, leaking blood into the jellylike vitreous humor that fills the eyeball. The bleeding can initially cause temporary dimming of vision or blindness; eventually fibrous scar tissue forms, leading to permanent vision loss and retinal detachment that can result in blindness. Advances in laser surgery and microsurgery, used to destroy weakened or excess blood vessels and repair a detached retina, now reduce the chance of permanent damage. Patients who suffer loss of sight resulting from bleeding into the vitreous humor may be helped by having this substance replaced by an artificial solution.

Diabetic patients are also sometimes subject to an early and rapidly developing form of cataracts that closely resembles that often found in elderly people. Research suggests that the lens may become clouded because glucose combines with lens proteins or because enzymatic changes related to high blood sugar occur. Treatment is the same as for other types of cataracts: removal of the lens, the prescription of special glasses or contact lenses, or the surgical insertion of an intraocular lens to restore vision.

People with diabetes should promptly report blurred vision, evidence of bleeding, or other visual changes to an ophthalmologist. In addition, regular eye examinations (every six months to one year, or more often) are vital to prevent or minimize loss of sight.

HEART DISEASE

Multiple changes in the cardiovascular system put diabetic patients at an increased risk for diseases affecting the blood vessels and heart. People with diabetes are more likely to develop arteriosclerosis (hardening of the arteries) and atherosclerosis (fatty buildup in the arteries) earlier and at a faster rate than the general population. High blood pressure and increased blood cholesterol and triglyceride levels—major risk factors for stroke and heart attack—are also more common. The characteristic thickening of capillary membranes that results in impaired blood flow to the heart also affects the limbs, particularly the lower legs and feet. As a result, diabetics are vulnerable to skin ulcers, infection, and gangrene. In fact, diabetes is the leading cause of nontraumatic lower limb amputation in this country.

In addition to changes in both large and small blood vessels, people with poorly controlled diabetes have an abnormal type of hemoglobin as well as the normal type. Excess sugar in the blood attaches to hemoglobin and results in a combined molecule that carries less oxygen to the tissues.

The increased risk of heart disease may also be due to the attraction of platelets—blood particles responsible for normal clotting—to the walls of arteries that have been injured by diabetes-related factors. When platelets accumulate and clump together, they can trap other cells as well as the LDL cholesterol that forms fatty plaque to clog blood vessels. This will result in decreased circulation. (Aspirin taken daily in small doses has been shown to reduce clumping of platelets.) The high but ineffective levels of insulin found in many people with Type 2 diabetes may also increase the risk of atherosclerosis by promoting fat synthesis and rapid cell growth within the artery walls. (However, insulin injections needed by Type 1 and some Type 2 diabetics have not been shown to increase this risk.)

To minimize the chance of developing cardiovascular disease, people with diabetes should reduce or eliminate the following risk factors:

Smoking. Nicotine stimulates the release of substances that increase blood pressure, constrict the blood vessels, and, in general, make the heart work harder. Toxic gases in cigarettes decrease the amount of hemoglobin available to carry oxygen and may increase formation of fatty plaques.

Obesity. In addition to making cells resistant to insulin, being overweight is associated with high blood cholesterol, triglycerides, and hypertension. Weight loss has the added advantage of reducing or eliminating the need for medication in many Type 2 diabetics.

Hypertension. Diabetic patients should closely observe any restrictions on salt and calories, as well as medication schedules. Although relatively easy to control, hypertension is dangerous because there are often no symptoms or feelings of being ill. Since there are no symptoms, many patients do not think they have a serious disease and stop taking their medication to lower blood pressure.

Impaired circulation joins with two other complications of diabetes—nerve damage and susceptibility to infection—to vastly increase the risk of gangrene. Cold feet,

FOOT CARE FOR PEOPLE WITH DIABETES

1. Inspect your feet daily, watching for the following potential danger signs:
   - redness or discoloration, especially near corns, calluses, or at pressure points (heel, big toe, ball of foot)
   - cracked, peeling, or dry skin
   - swelling, tenderness, warmth, or other signs of infection
   - thickening or discoloration of toenails
   - ingrown toenails
2. Wash your feet daily in warm, not hot, water. If you are unable to test water temperature with your feet because of impaired sensation, use your elbow or a thermometer. Use a gentle soap and a soft brush, sponge, or fine pumice stone to remove dead skin. Avoid alcohol, coarse pumice stones, and other agents that may damage skin. To avoid drying out the skin, limit soaking time to 10 to 12 minutes. Dry your feet and surfaces between toes thoroughly with a soft towel. Use a lanolin-based or other lubricating lotion to soften dry skin.
3. Protect your feet from injury by always wearing shoes, slippers, or, when in the water, swim sandals. If you are wearing soft or open-toe shoes, watch where you step to avoid stones and other sharp objects.
4. Buy comfortable, well-fitting shoes. If you have a foot deformity that cannot be accommodated in a ready-made shoe, it is wise to invest in a custom-made one. (In some states, Medicaid may cover orthopedic shoes ordered on a doctor's prescription form.) Avoid very high heels, sharply pointed toes, and constricting boots. Choose shoes made of materials that let the feet "breathe." Have at least two pairs, and alternate them so each has the chance to dry out. Break in new shoes gradually, and be on the alert for signs of irritation during this period.
5. Wear cotton socks or stockings and change them daily—more often if your feet are sweating. Do not wear garters or socks with tight elastic bands, which can reduce circulation to the feet.
6. Do not self-treat corns, calluses, or fungal infections such as athlete's foot. If a corn or callus is developing, soak the foot in warm water for 10 minutes and scrub gently with a soft brush. Apply a lubricating lotion to the area when dry. Check your shoes to see what part may be rubbing or putting pressure on the area. Switch to another pair, or protect your foot by using a piece of lamb's wool or moleskin over the affected area. Any redness or discoloration around a corn or callus should be brought to the attention of a podiatrist. All corn removal products contain harsh substances that can contribute to skin breakdown; corns and calluses should be removed by a podiatrist or other foot specialist.

7. Trim your toenails regularly. File them or use nail clippers (not scissors) straight across the top, being careful not to damage underlying tissue. Do not cut into the corners as this can cause ingrown toenails. Moisten the cuticles with oil and gently nudge them back with a cuticle stick. People who have poor vision or limited hand flexibility should have their toenails trimmed by someone experienced in foot care for diabetics.
8. Promote good circulation. If you must sit with your legs crossed, cross them at the ankle rather than at the knee. Keep your feet raised when sitting to avoid pooling of blood. Flex your feet or shift your weight from one foot to the other to increase circulation when sitting or standing for long periods.

numbness, or tingling in the toes; leg cramps when walking or climbing stairs; dry or shiny skin; and loss of hair from the feet and toes are all symptoms of circulatory/nerve damage and may indicate poor control of blood sugar. Diabetic patients should practice meticulous foot care to avoid serious foot infections, ulcers, and perhaps eventual amputation.

NERVE DAMAGE

High blood sugar is thought to cause damage to a variety of nerves affecting many parts of the body. For example, injury to peripheral sensory nerves—those nerves that carry impulses from the skin to the brain and spinal cord—can result in the altered sensations described earlier. Injury to peripheral motor nerves—those that carry impulses from the brain and spinal cord to muscles and glands—can cause muscular deterioration and weakness. Damage to the autonomic nervous system—nerves that affect smooth muscle, the heart, and glands—can result in impotence, gastrointestinal and urinary tract problems, dizziness on standing (orthostatic hypotension), and irregular heartbeats.

Widespread nerve damage, or neuropathy, may cause few symptoms in some people while producing disabling problems in others. It may begin early in the course of the disease, long before any symptoms appear. Nerve damage often produces some form of pain, ranging from mild discomfort to severe stabbing or aching sensations. Although many parts of the nervous system may be affected, often it is the legs and feet that show the most obvious damage.

Some diabetic patients are troubled by dizziness or fainting when they suddenly change position, as when getting out of bed in the morning or when rising from a chair. This is caused by orthostatic hypotension, a temporary drop in blood pressure that occurs when going from a lying or sitting position to an erect one. The problem usually can be controlled by avoiding sudden changes in position: for example, sitting up for a minute or so before getting out of bed in the morning. Wearing elastic stockings may also help to reduce the pooling of blood in the legs that contributes to the drop in blood pressure. Weakness or other functional impairment in the arms and legs may be compensated for by braces or other assisting devices.

Research indicates that keeping blood sugar in the normal range while observing meticulous skin care can prevent or minimize neuropathy and the risk of gangrene. Patients who experience pain should consult their physician for appropriate pain medication.

IMPOTENCE

For some men, impotence is one of the first signs of diabetes. The problem is caused by nerve damage, which makes it impossible to achieve an erection. The problem usually cannot be cured, but new techniques using special penile prostheses can restore sexual function. Some of the devices have balloonlike structures that are inflatable; others are more rigid and hold the penis in a more or less permanently erect position (see chapter 6). Diabetic men troubled by impotence should consult a urologist who can determine the most appropriate type of prosthesis.

KIDNEY PROBLEMS

Diabetes is one of the most common causes of kidney failure in the United States. The kidneys serve, among other functions, as a filter for wastes carried in the blood. Exposure to high glucose levels causes the membranes of blood vessels supplying the kidneys and other organs to thicken and lose the ability to filter waste. Arteriosclerotic changes in the capillaries result in partial blockage, further contributing to kidney damage and perhaps eventual kidney failure. Increased susceptibility to infection adds to the potential for damage.

Although the kidneys have vast reserve capacity—the body can function successfully with only one—diabetes damages both organs. Dialysis and kidney transplants may add years to the lives of those whose kidneys have failed; however, dialysis is expensive and time-consuming, and kidneys for transplant are in short supply. In addition, research indicates that healthy kidneys often develop symptoms of disease when transplanted into diabetic patients.

Once again, good control of blood glucose is essential to prevent or reduce damage to the kidneys. Studies have shown that reducing blood sugar to normal levels may even reverse kidney damage if started early on. Moreover, diabetic patients should seek medical attention at the first sign of a urinary tract infection. Symptoms include pain or burning on urination; frequency, urgency, or difficulty in voiding; and cloudy, blood-tinged, or foul-smelling urine.

INFECTION

People with diabetes are susceptible to infection from many sources—the common cold, bacteria that invade a simple cut, or normally harmless microorganisms that live in the mouth. Infections and colds tend to last longer in diabetics and require antibiotic therapy. And infection upsets the body's hormonal and metabolic balance, resulting in increased resistance to insulin. Women with diabetes may be particularly susceptible to vaginal yeast infections.

Diabetes somehow hampers the ability of the immune system to combat infection, possibly by interfering with white blood cell function. People with this disease should avoid coming into contact with those who might transmit an infectious illness. When this is not possible, good hygiene, particularly frequent handwashing, may prevent the spread of bacteria. Diabetic patients should also be immunized against pneumonia; they should get yearly inoculations against influenza and a tetanus booster shot every 10 years.

People with diabetes should promptly seek medical attention when infection does set in so that prompt treatment can be started to shorten the duration of illness and bring blood sugar back to normal.

MONITORING BLOOD SUGAR

Traditionally, urine testing has been the only way diabetic patients could monitor their disease at home. Urine testing still has its place, but in addition, diabetic patients are now taught to do home blood sugar measurements. Although some physicians have not felt this necessary for patients with Type 2 diabetes, anyone who wants to ensure good control of blood glucose should learn this simple test. Blood glucose testing can also serve as a positive reinforcement for the majority of Type 2 diabetic patients who are overweight; as weight loss is achieved, lower blood sugar levels become evident. There are now a number of highly accurate, relatively inexpensive machines that patients can use for home glucose testing. Patients should ask their doctor to show them how to use a home machine. By keeping daily records of blood sugar measurements, both the patient and physician can quickly spot patterns of poor control of diabetes and take steps to correct them.

THE LONG-TERM OUTLOOK

A diagnosis of diabetes often comes as a shock, and since most people know that it is a potentially life-threatening disease, it is understandable that the news can be depressing. There is a bright side, however. Type 2 diabetes is much less threatening than Type 1, and with proper diet, exercise, and medication, if needed, blood sugar can be brought back into the normal range. This greatly reduces the chances of serious complications, and many experts believe that so long as blood sugar is kept within a normal range, a person with diabetes should expect to live a full, productive life.

HOW TO DO HOME BLOOD GLUCOSE TESTING

There are two methods for home glucose testing:

1. *Visual strip method.* A drop of blood is placed on a chemically treated strip and compared against a color chart representing different sugar levels.
2. *Glucose meter method.* A drop of blood is placed on a chemically treated strip, which is inserted in an electronic glucose meter that analyzes reflected light from the strip. The blood sugar level is indicated in a digital reading.

The visual method is the less expensive of the two, but it is also less reliable. For example, it may be difficult to accurately judge the color that appears, especially for those with vision problems. Glucose meters are available for under $150 and may be covered by insurance if the physician certifies the need for testing.

Check with your doctor as to when and how often to test your blood sugar. The normal range for blood glucose in a fasting state and before meals is lower than that obtained one to two hours after meals. Below are the basic steps for monitoring blood glucose using an electronic meter. Ask your physician to teach you how to use your particular device and then double-check your technique.

1. Calibrate the machine according to the manufacturer's instructions.
2. Wash your finger with soap and water, and dry it thoroughly.
3. Squeeze the finger for several seconds to stimulate blood flow.
4. Prick the side of the fingertip with sterile lancet and wipe the first drop of blood onto a gauze pad.
5. Apply a second drop to test strip.
6. Observe any time interval specified by the manufacturer and then blot the strip onto specially supplied blotter paper.
7. Insert the strip into slot on the meter, read glucose level from digital readout, and record it in a notebook.

The development of computerized insulin pumps that are implanted in the abdomen and programmed to deliver insulin as needed offer hope for better control and management of Type 1 diabetes. In the treatment of Type 2 diabetes, there are several promising new oral drugs. Researchers also are working on techniques to take islet cells from dead fetuses and transplant the cells under the skin of Type 1 diabetics. The cells would start producing insulin as though they were in the pancreas. However, research using fetal tissue is still a controversial issue and is under strict federal guidelines.

On these and other fronts there is increasing hope for better control of diabetes. In fact, the American Diabetes Association states that diabetes research has been responsible for the better, healthier lives of 11 million Americans.

15

Chronic Lung Diseases

Breathing is the most essential function of the body. Deprived of oxygen, the body will die within 5 to 10 minutes. The respiratory (pulmonary) system, responsible for the vital transportation of air into the lungs, also filters out infectious agents and provides the air necessary for speech. Air pollution, noxious fumes, smoking, and overcrowded living conditions where infections are easily spread all take a heavy toll on the body's breathing mechanism. Every day the average person inhales about 3,000 gallons of air that may be contaminated with poisons, irritants, and toxins.

HOW THE PULMONARY SYSTEM WORKS

Air, breathed in through the nose or mouth, passes through the windpipe (trachea) to the bronchial tubes, which divide into smaller branches called the bronchioles. From there it enters the lungs and the thin membranes of the alveoli, or air sacs. Here, inhaled oxygen, vital to nourishing all tissues, is exchanged for waste carbon dioxide that is then expelled by the lungs (see Figure 15.1). The chest muscles, together with the diaphragm, act as a bellows, expanding to allow the lungs to inflate and pull in air, and contracting to expel the stale air.

The lower respiratory tract (composed of the bronchial tubes, their branches, and the lungs) is protected by a variety of defenses from invasion by foreign bodies. Filtering hairs that are in the nose and continue into the upper part of a muscular tube known as the pharynx collect impurities. The next line of defense is the epiglottis. It is the flap

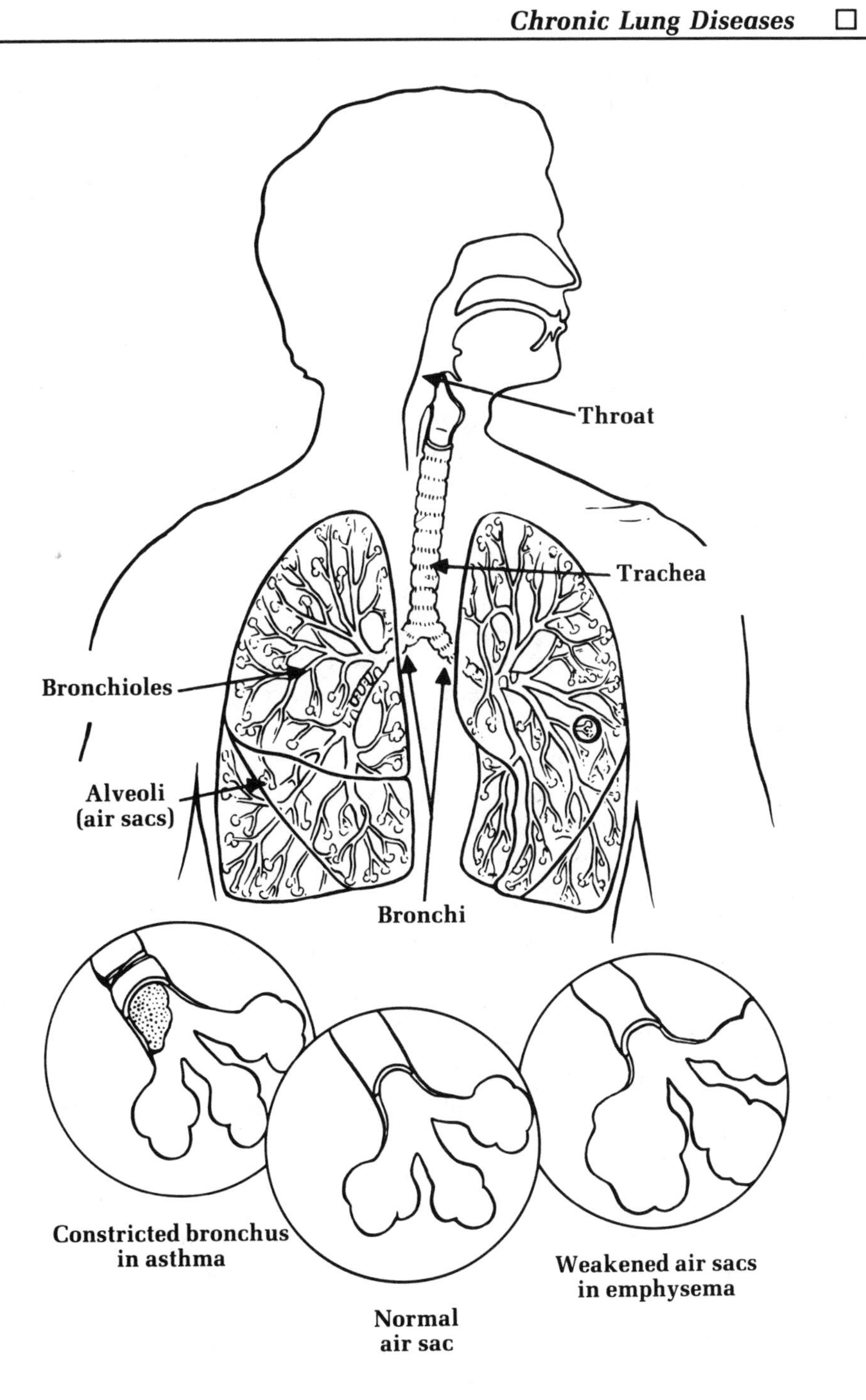

Figure 15.1 The Pulmonary Tree

of skin that covers the larynx, or voice box, when you swallow to prevent food or other foreign particles from entering the trachea, or windpipe.

The next barriers are the mucous secretions and cilia, minute hairs on the cells lining the respiratory tract. Together they trap microorganisms and sweep them back up into the throat. Coughing helps to expel intruders from the bronchial tubes. The last in the line of defense are macrophages, white blood cells in the alveoli that destroy foreign invaders.

Assaults on the respiratory system can weaken these defenses: Viral and bacterial infections can carry diseases into the lungs; cigarette smoking and upper respiratory infections can partially paralyze the cilia, clogging the air passages with debris and causing further irritation; heavy alcohol intake, surgical anesthesia, prolonged bed rest, and large doses of barbiturates or immune suppressants can also hinder respiratory controls and reduce the lung's ability to take in air. Chronic asthma may also eventually cause lung damage.

When the respiratory system is impaired, the oxygen supply to the organs is diminished. The heart overextends itself as it compensates for the oxygen deficiency by pumping more blood, and it may become enlarged.

Severe oxygen depletion can lead to cyanosis, a slightly blue skin discoloration. Always a serious symptom, cyanosis frequently accompanies certain cardiac conditions and sometimes pneumonia and chronic bronchitis.

The state of the lungs is one good indication of general health. Anyone troubled by coughing, wheezing, shortness of breath, or who is prone to constant respiratory infections and other lung disorders, needs to know the cause of the breathing difficulty and how to increase maximum oxygen intake and decrease respiratory irritants.

CHRONIC OBSTRUCTIVE PULMONARY DISEASE

Chronic bronchitis and emphysema are banded together under the term *chronic obstructive pulmonary disease,* which doctors often refer to simply as COPD. Its incidence has increased dramatically, rising by 87.5 percent between 1970 and 1987. The American Lung Association estimates that 14.8 million people in the United States suffer from these conditions.

During air pollution disasters, increased mortality occurs largely among elderly individuals suffering from these diseases. Although much is known about the causes of chronic obstructive pulmonary disease, no cure has been found. Depending on whether emphysema or bronchitis is more prevalent, symptoms may include: excessive mucus, impaired clearance of mucus; chronic cough; increased susceptibility to respiratory infections; obstruction of the smaller airways; swelling and rupture of the lung's alveoli, resulting in difficult breathing; insufficient oxygen in the blood; and easy tiring.

Those who smoke half a pack of cigarettes a day are five times as likely to die of chronic obstructive pulmonary disease as are nonsmokers, while those who smoke two packs a day are 20 times as likely to succumb to the disease.

HOW TO CHECK YOUR LUNG FUNCTION

The Match Test

- Be sure the room is draft-free.
- Light a match from a matchbook and let it burn halfway down.
- Hold it 6 inches from your mouth and try to blow it out *with your mouth wide open.*

If you cannot extinguish the match, it usually indicates your lungs are not in the best of condition, possibly as the result of a lung disorder.

Chest Expansion

- Take your chest measurement. (Men should measure around the nipples; women just under the breast.)
- Take a full breath and measure again.

The second measurement should be at least 1.5 inches greater than the first, with variations according to gender and size. Expansion that is less than 1.5 inches, regardless of gender or size, suggests weak lungs. A medical checkup would be worthwhile.

Timed Exhalation

- Take a deep breath.
- Time yourself while you exhale as rapidly as possible. Time only the exhalation.

If it takes you 3 to 4 seconds or less to exhale a normal amount, your lungs are healthy. If it takes longer, this may indicate the possibility of emphysema or another lung disorder.

Although quitting smoking will not reverse lung damage, it will usually reduce the frequency of symptoms, particularly the phlegm-producing cough. While most authorities agree that the risk of bronchitis and emphysema is greater from cigarette smoking than from environmental pollution, the risk from environmental factors still exists.

Prolonged inactivity also leads to excessive disability in patients with chronic obstructive pulmonary disease. As long as there is no severe cardiac disease, there should be a regular exercise program prescribed by a physician. If the patient is severely disabled, the program should be supervised by a physical therapist. Breathing exercises may be helpful for anxious patients who develop an excessively rapid breathing rate during exertion.

The severity of the disease increases with age, and varies with the individual and his or her place of residence, heredity, and innate resistance. Environmental pollution can be controlled only minimally by an individual patient through such means as the use of air filters to clean the air in the home, but most air pollution problems will have to be addressed on a national or global scale.

EMPHYSEMA

Emphysema is a pulmonary disease in which progressive damage to the millions of tiny alveoli (air sacs) in the lungs causes difficulty in exhaling, a fatiguing cough, breathlessness from slight exertion, and sometimes a barrel-shaped chest as the lungs try to compensate.

In more than 80 percent of all cases, emphysema, commonly called air hunger, is a direct consequence of smoking. Presently, men with emphysema outnumber women by 64 percent, but with more women smoking, the ratio will likely change. The disease usually appears between the ages of 50 and 60. In the United States, half of those afflicted are over 65, while nearly all the rest are over 45.

During the respiratory process, the alveoli expand and contract in unison as air is inhaled and exhaled. As emphysema develops, the tiny grapelike clusters of alveoli lose their elasticity, become distended, and eventually rupture.

Under normal conditions there is an efficient exchange of oxygen and carbon dioxide in the alveoli. When the chambers become damaged, carbon dioxide cannot be expelled completely and stagnant air accumulates. As breathing becomes shallower and requires more effort, the muscles of the neck, chest, and diaphragm work harder to get enough oxygen into the bloodstream, and respiration increases to 25 inhalations a minute instead of the normal 15.

CAUSES

Advancing age, heavy smoking, or hereditary predisposition can promote the disease. The leading cause is cigarette smoking, particularly over a long period. The risk for heavy smokers exposed to pollutants on the job and elsewhere is very high. However, even light smokers can sustain tissue damage; studies show emphysema is not uncommon among them as well.

DIAGNOSIS

In its early stages emphysema cannot be detected by X ray, but airway function can be measured by a test done in the doctor's office with a spirometer, which measures the amount of air that can be expelled from the lungs with maximum effort. When measurements detect residues of carbon dioxide remaining in the lungs, there is reason to believe that the cause is impairment of the alveoli. Lung scans using radioactive isotopes are also useful in diagnosing and evaluating the extent of lung damage.

TREATMENT

To stop progression of the disease, it is mandatory that all patients quit smoking. If environmental pollutants are the cause, a change of job or early retirement with compensation for the disability should be strongly considered.

The patient should avoid exposure to wet and windy weather and respiratory infections, have flu shots and a pneumonia immunization, and, if necessary, lose weight. Drinking plenty of liquids to keep sputum loose, and using prescribed antibiotics at the first sign of bronchitis or other upper respiratory infections (including colds), may also help. Breathing exercises to strengthen breathing muscles, and the use of drugs that dilate the bronchial passages, may make breathing easier. For people who have an inherited form of emphysema (they were born with a deficiency of a protein known as alpha 1-antitrypsin, or AAT), treatment with alpha 1-proteinase inhibitor (Prolastin) is the proper course of action. In severe cases, oxygen therapy may be needed. Reports on lung transplants have been encouraging, but experience is limited.

TIPS ON BREATHING MORE EFFICIENTLY

Deep breathing—that is, moving the diaphragm rather than the upper chest—can help people with chronic obstructive pulmonary disease take in more oxygen and reduce breathlessness. The American Lung Association suggests the following steps be practiced often throughout the day to make diaphragmatic breathing "second nature."

- Relax your upper body, letting neck and shoulders droop.
- Place both hands on your abdomen above the waist, and breathe in through your nose. If you are breathing through the diaphragm, your hands will move outward as the abdomen expands.
- Exhale slowly through pursed lips and repeat the entire procedure. If you feel dizzy, take a few breaths using the upper chest and then try going back to breathing through the diaphragm.

ACUTE BRONCHITIS

Bronchitis, generally a self-limiting disease, is an inflammation of the bronchial tree. It is caused by a virus, a bacterium, or the inhalation of chemical pollutants or cigarette smoke. The microorganism or irritation causes a heavier secretion of mucus that, in turn, causes the characteristic phlegm cough. While complete healing and return of lung function is possible, bronchitis can be serious in debilitated patients and the elderly if it is prolonged and develops into chronic bronchitis and possibly pneumonia.

CHRONIC BRONCHITIS

Chronic bronchitis is a degenerative disease in which the walls of the bronchial tubes become thickened, inelastic, and constricted, and the respiratory cilia are irreparably damaged. The mucous membranes of the bronchi are permanently inflamed, and the airways become filled with sticky mucus. There is a chronic or recurrent mucus-producing cough that lasts three or more months and recurs year after year. Chronic bronchopulmonary diseases impair the mucus-clearing ability of the lungs.

Chronic bronchitis may result from a series of attacks of acute bronchitis, or it may evolve gradually due to heavy smoking or the inhalation of air contaminated with other pollutants in the environment. Airway obstruction can result from the buildup of

GETTING THE MOST FROM YOUR COUGH

Buildup of mucus in the airways can stimulate the urge to cough so that it can be expelled. But with chronic obstructive pulmonary disease, the individual may not be able to generate enough force to bring up the mucus, the so-called productive cough. The result is an unproductive, hacking cough or coughing spell that leaves the person fatigued, frightened, and short of breath. Cough medicines should not be used unless allowed by the physician. The American Lung Association suggests the following steps for making a cough productive:

- Sit with your feet on the floor and head bent slightly forward.
- Breathe in deeply.
- Hold your breath for a few seconds.
- Cough twice; first to loosen the mucus, then a second time to bring it up.
- Breathe in by sniffing gently.
- Spit out the mucus; swallowing it can upset your stomach.

mucus, thickening and narrowing of the bronchial walls resulting from frequent respiratory infections, and, in some cases, spasms of the bronchial muscles. Coughing, though distressing, is essential to the elimination of bronchial secretions and to clear the airways.

TREATMENT

Removal of the bronchial irritants is essential in treating chronic bronchitis. Smoking must be stopped, and the patient should avoid any environment in which irritants or noxious fumes are present. Antibiotics are recommended when there is pus in the sputum or when high fever persists, and some pulmonary specialists advise that antibiotics be taken prophylactically at the first sign of cold or upper respiratory infection. Carbon dioxide retention and cyanosis may require the use of oxygen therapy.

Slight-to-moderate breathlessness may be helped by breathing exercises. Drinking plenty of liquids, remaining indoors, and using nebulizers and vaporizers may also be helpful. You can make your lungs more efficient by incorporating the following steps into your daily therapy:

- Practice "pursed-lip breathing"—exhaling slowly while keeping your lips in a whistling position—to relieve breathlessness.
- Do exercises that strengthen the diaphragm and abdominal muscles.
- Organize your time to allow rest periods between activities requiring exertion.
- Clear the lungs of excess mucus by lying in special positions that help mucus drain from the lungs. This is known as *postural drainage.* If your physician approves, have a physical therapist or visiting nurse teach a family member how to "clap" on your chest to further loosen mucus.
- Build strength by taking a short walk every day.
- Use appropriate combinations of medicines, breathing aids, and life-style changes to make life more comfortable.

THE FACTS ABOUT SMOKING

A smoker faces a risk of death from chronic bronchitis that is four to 25 times greater than a nonsmoker's. As a result of quitting, the cough and sputum may disappear within a few weeks, lung functions can improve, and deterioration of the respiratory tract will be slowed (see chapter 3).

If you smoke, consider these facts:

- Heated smoke dries and irritates the airway lining.
- Tobacco irritants paralyze the cilia, tiny hairlike sweepers that help clean out dirt and mucus.

- □ Excess secretion of mucus clogs the airways and provides a fertile ground for infection-causing microorganisms.
- □ Carbon monoxide, present in cigarette smoke, is poisonous and robs your blood of oxygen, making you tired and short of breath.
- □ Irritation from tobacco smoke allows certain enzymes to flourish and inflame the air alveoli, or sacs, leading to their destruction. As more alveoli break, your lungs are unable to transmit inhaled oxygen into your blood.

When you stop smoking, consider these facts:

- □ Your body immediately begins repairing the damage to your airways.
- □ Your cough will diminish or disappear after anywhere from a few days to several weeks of coughing up excess mucus.
- □ With your airways less constricted, you will breathe easier and have more energy.
- □ Your lungs will be better able to defend themselves against infection.
- □ Your blood circulation and sense of taste and smell will improve.

ASTHMA

Asthma is the cause of breathing problems in about 10 million people. Its prevalence has increased in every age and racial group, in both men and women. Between 1980 and 1987, the number of people reporting asthma increased by nearly 30 percent, according to the American Lung Association.

Characterized by an oversensitivity of the bronchi, asthma is a chronic, often disabling disease that affects adults as well as children. Attacks can be provoked by numerous factors, including exposure to allergy-producing substances and irritants such as dust, tobacco smoke, or other pollutants. They can also be the result of vigorous exercise, infection, and stress.

Frequently a person who has suffered childhood asthma will notice it disappear, seeming to have outgrown it during adolescence, only to have it return in adulthood. The attacks may be precipitated by an infection or by exposures to a triggering factor, such as cigarette smoke or an allergen.

During an asthma attack, both large and small airways become narrowed because of inflammation and spasm of the bronchial muscles. Thick mucus further blocks the airways, leading to wheezing, coughing, and difficulty in breathing. Attacks vary widely in duration, intensity, and frequency.

The causes for the recent increase in the prevalence of asthma are not entirely clear. Environmental factors, such as increased air pollution, have been suggested as asthma triggers. Also, the lack of ongoing treatment for asthma sufferers increases the likelihood of attack.

ASTHMA TRIGGERS

Air Pollution

- Auto exhaust
- Cigarette smoke
- Ozone
- Sulfur dioxide

Allergic Reactions

- Animals
- Feathers
- House dust
- Molds
- Some foods

Cold Air

Drugs

- Aspirin
- Some heart medications

Emotional Stress and Excitement

Household Products

- Cleaners
- Paint
- Some sprays

Infections

- Common cold
- Influenza

Occupational Dusts and Vapors

- Some grains
- Some metals
- Some plastics
- Wood

Sleep (Nocturnal Asthma)

Vigorous Exercise

TREATMENT

Because asthma frequently leads to life-threatening emergencies or permanent lung damage, it is important to learn how to control the disease. People whose asthma is brought on by a particular allergen should avoid that source wherever possible. Sometimes desensitization shots are available for such offenders as molds, pollen, and certain grasses. Exposure to cigarette smoke, environmental pollutants, and household dust should be avoided. Most people with asthma are advised not to keep cats or dogs; even if the pets do not seem to provoke attacks, their dander is an irritant that increases vulnerability to bronchospasms.

A report released in 1992 by the International Asthma Management Project, a group of 18 physicians and scientists assembled by the National Heart, Lung, and Blood

Institute, recommended sweeping reforms of current asthma treatment. Treatment has always centered around the actual asthmatic attack, but treating the inflammation that is the core of the disease is now suggested. For people who suffer from anything more than occasional mild asthma, this means treatment with anti-inflammatory drugs, namely inhalants such as adrenocorticoids (beclomethasone, dexamethasone, flunisolide, and triamcinolone), cromolyn sodium, or nedocromil sodium (a potent anti-inflammatory agent).

These drugs may prevent asthma attacks, but they do not offer symptom relief once an attack is in progress. Inhaled bronchodilators, such as albuterol, epinephrine, or metaproterenol, open up the air passages and therefore usually bring relief. They are also recommended for use before exercise, an activity that can provoke an asthma attack. For people with mild asthma, periodic use of these bronchodilators during flare-ups may control the condition. With the exception of some epinephrine inhalers, these drugs are available only by prescription.

You should follow your doctor's advice before using inhalants and other medications in the treatment of asthma. If your physician does not have specific experience in pulmonary medicine, ask him or her to help you arrange a consultation with a specialist. It is important that asthma patients learn the correct way to take their medication. To relieve an attack, the smallest of airways must be opened. To this end, the inhalant medications should be diluted and inhaled very slowly to enable the particles to penetrate deeper into the lungs and open the tiny passages (see Figure 15.2).

HOW TO BREATHE MORE EASILY WITH ASTHMA

Learning to relax while breathing can help prevent the nervousness and anxiety that compound breathlessness and trap more air in the lungs. The American Lung Association suggests practicing the following technique for five minutes twice a day and when you feel yourself becoming short of breath.

- Sit up straight in a chair with your arms dangling at your sides.
- Breathe deeply, slowly, and evenly all through the following steps.
- Tense your upper torso by simultaneously clenching your fists, shrugging your shoulders, and tightening your arms. Hold the tension while counting to 2.
- Release tension, letting your shoulders drop, hands open, and arms hang relaxed. Count to 4.
- Tighten your legs and feet. Count to 2.
- Relax your legs and feet, keeping your upper body relaxed at the same time. Count to 4.

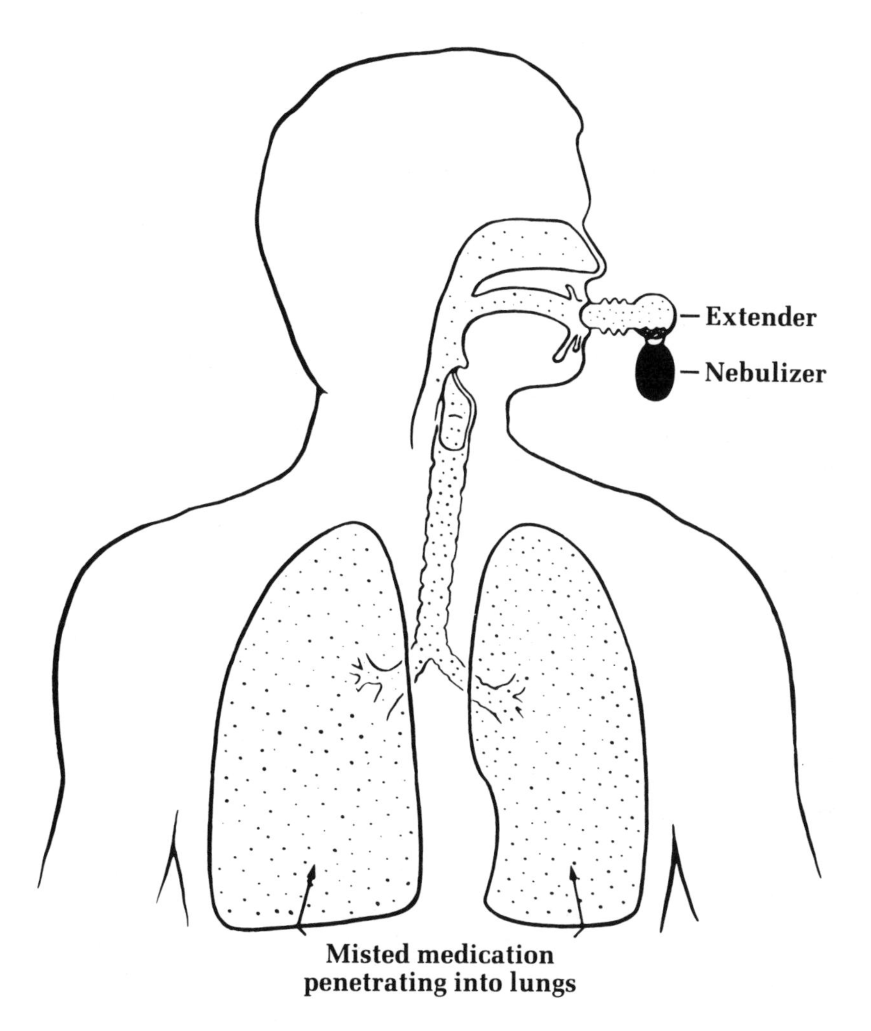

Figure 15.2 How to Use a Nebulizer
Nebulizers deliver tiny droplets of medicine deeply within the lungs. The smaller the particles of medicine, the deeper they will penetrate into the small airways, opening them up. To use a nebulizer properly, the medication should be diluted and an extender, or flextube, added to the end of the nebulizer. This helps break the droplets into a fine mist.

To inhale the medicine, take the biggest breath possible to ensure that the medication will penetrate as deeply into the lungs as possible. Breathe slowly, as if you were sipping hot soup, which also helps the medication get to where it is needed most. Be sure to "trigger" or squeeze the nebulizer just *after* you begin breathing in, not before you take your deep breath.

Severe or prolonged asthma attacks require prompt medical attention in addition to the use of a bronchodilator. The individual should try to remain as calm as possible at the start of an attack, something that is often easier said than done. Sitting down and leaning forward, with elbows or arms resting on a table, may be the most comfortable position.

COMPLICATIONS AND PRECAUTIONS

Chronic, poorly controlled asthma can lead to emphysema. During attacks, continued stretching of the alveoli by accumulations of stale air can cause them to eventually lose their elasticity and cease to function. As stated previously, the rate of asthma-related deaths has been increasing by about 6 percent each year. It is highest for people over 65 and for African-Americans.

The reasons for the prevalence and relative severity of asthma in older people is probably due to the other diseases that are more common in that age group, such as cardiovascular problems and the fact that medications for some other illnesses may exacerbate the condition. For instance, arthritis patients may find that aspirin and other medications cause attacks. Continued research should bring more information about the success of newer federal guidelines for the treatment of this serious disease.

OCCUPATIONAL LUNG DISORDERS

Respiratory diseases are widespread and figure among the most serious health problems originating in the workplace. Each year about 65,000 Americans develop some respiratory disease related to their work environment, and 25,000 die from it. Since these diseases may take 20 or more years to develop, it can be difficult to trace their original cause.

The common factor in a variety of occupational lung disabilities is long-term exposure to microscopic and submicroscopic dusts, from inorganic sources (minerals and metals) or from organic ones (cotton, moldy hay, mushroom spores).

Although some occupational lung disorders may take the form of chronic bronchitis, emphysema, or cancer, most are now grouped under the single heading of dust disease—*pneumoconiosis,* or "dusty lung." These include black lung disease (officially known as coal worker's pneumoconiosis), brown lung (also called byssinosis and caused by an allergylike response to inhaled dusts from cotton, hemp, or flax), farmer's lung (caused by inhalation of organic dusts), and asbestosis and asbestos-induced cancers.

Symptoms of these disorders are shortness of breath, abnormal fibrous tissue in the lungs, wheezing, and coughing with or without phlegm (if serious, the phlegm will be bloody). All of these diseases can eventually lead to pneumonia, tuberculosis, and lung cancer, and they can increase the risk of developing tuberculosis.

TREATMENT

Treatment for pneumoconiosis can only relieve symptoms. The unhealthy environment that caused the condition should be avoided, and smokers should quit the habit.

In addition to the harm smokers do themselves, there is growing evidence that passive smoking also is harmful, especially to people with chronic lung disorders. Tremendous numbers of people are sensitive or allergic to tobacco smoke and the invisible particles that contain irritating substances. The lung responds to irritating smoke with chronic secretion of mucus and coughing, both common symptoms in smokers. Nonsmokers who are prone to respiratory infections are particularly sensitive to secondhand smoke.

PNEUMONIA

Pneumonia is not a single disease but a group of diseases. They are caused by different bacterial or viral infections, irritation of delicate lung tissue by the inhalation of poisonous liquid or gas (e.g., chlorine), or the blockage of a section of the lung caused by inhaling a tiny bit of food or vomit. The general term *pneumonia* refers to infection and resulting inflammation of lung tissues and alveoli. Treatment varies with the cause of the infection.

If pneumonia is not treated, it can be fatal. But even with treatment, mortality runs from 5 to 10 percent, with most deaths occurring in the over-50 age group. Among people over 65, it is one of the five leading causes of death. Those whose lungs have been weakened as a result of being bedridden for long periods for other ailments are also vulnerable. The course of the disease in older persons does not follow the same pattern as in younger age groups, with one difference being that there is less response to medication in older patients.

The number of pneumonia cases and deaths reaches a peak in the months between December and March. In closed rooms, viral infections that weaken the respiratory tract's normal defense system are spread easily from one person to another. Pneumonia often accompanies flu and bronchitis attacks. In 73 percent of flu patients age 70 and over, pneumonia will develop; in 36 percent of such patients between the ages of 60 to 69, pneumonia and bronchitis develop simultaneously.

SYMPTOMS

Pneumonia either begins as, or is preceded by, an upper respiratory infection like a cold, and is accompanied by fever and a cough, often with pus-filled sputum.

Sweating, sharp pain in the chest, difficulty breathing, and cyanosis may also be present. The patient feels weak, has muscle aches, and loss of appetite often accompanied by stomach distress. As the illness progresses, an initially dry cough may produce sputum, ranging from green to yellow or rusty in color (which indicates bleeding). Not all of these symptoms appear in everyone, but the presence of a number of them should always serve as a danger sign.

If left untreated, certain microorganisms responsible for pneumonia may spread to other parts of the body and cause infection in the lining of the heart (endocarditis) or the membranes of the brain (meningitis).

TREATMENT

Once a diagnosis is confirmed by chest X ray and blood and sputum cultures, the physician will prescribe an antibiotic if the pneumonia is due to a bacterium. For viral pneumonias, treatment is intended to relieve symptoms. Cough medicines and mild painkillers may be used to relieve a cough or chest pain. To help reduce fever, aspirin and lukewarm sponge baths may be recommended. In severely debilitated patients, certain cases of pneumonia may require hospitalization.

PREVENTION

Nutrition and exercise, especially aerobic exercise, are important to maintain general health and a strong respiratory system resistant to viral infections. Lung irritants and tobacco smoke should be avoided. Prompt treatment of any upper respiratory infection can help prevent pneumonia. Additionally, a vaccine against pneumococcal pneumonia is usually recommended for all persons over 65 and for younger people with diabetes or chronic heart or lung diseases. Those who have had a pneumococcal polysaccharide vaccine should not receive a second one. Individuals whose immune systems are weakened, such as those with AIDS, and who are being treated with immunosuppressive drugs, are vulnerable to other forms of pneumonia, such as *Pneumocystis carinii,* and should take particular care to avoid outside sources of infection.

LEGIONNAIRES' DISEASE

Legionnaires' disease, another form of pneumonia, is caused by the *Legionella pneumophila* bacterium present in contaminated humidifiers and air-conditioning systems. The disease was first recognized after a group of American Legion members meeting in Philadelphia in 1976 became ill; however, research indicates that the bacterium has caused disease outbreaks since 1965.

The disease affects men more than women, and their average age is 56. After an incubation period of two to 10 days, the victim (who often has a history of other debilitating lung and heart diseases) develops fever, generalized weakness and loss of appetite, chills, diarrhea, dry cough, sore throat, and sometimes headaches and confusion. Fever rises over several days and hospitalization is necessary.

Treatment with antibiotics cures Legionnaires' disease; however, patients with compromised immune systems who are not placed on antibiotics have a high mortality rate.

INFLUENZA

Three different classes of influenza viruses—types A, B, and C—are responsible for flu. Flu, also called the grippe, tends to come in epidemics and, periodically, in worldwide pandemics. Type A flu occurs most commonly in widespread epidemics about every three years. Outbreaks of Type B flu occur every five years or so, whereas Type C viruses are localized and cause only minor sporadic outbreaks of mild illness.

Older people who have the flu have a greater tendency to develop a more serious illness and/or pneumonia. If fever, cough, and sore throat continue for more than four days, pneumonia should be suspected, especially if there is shortness of breath, spitting up of blood, a second rise in temperature, or a relapse in which the cough intensifies. Because of the possibility of developing pneumonia as a secondary infection, flu is especially serious for people already in a weakened state.

SYMPTOMS

The effects of flu infection can differ from person to person. Sometimes flu will cause obvious symptoms. Often, however, the patient will feel weak and will develop a cough, headache, and a sudden rise in temperature. Other symptoms include aching muscles, chills, and red, watery eyes.

Because the elderly are prone to develop pneumonia along with the flu, doctors recommend a flu shot for everyone over 65 and anyone with chronic heart and respiratory disorders, cancer, diabetes, kidney disease, anemia, or conditions that affect immunity. The flu vaccine, usually given in early autumn, carries a low risk of side effects. However, people who are allergic to eggs or who are chronically ill should not take the shot. Also, those who are acutely ill should wait until they are better before taking a flu shot.

PLEURISY

Pleurisy is an inflammation of the pleura, the two-layered membrane that encases the lungs and the rib cage. It is caused by any disease that also inflames the lung, such as pneumonia, tuberculosis, or a tumor, and can be triggered by flu, a severe cold, rheumatic fever, bronchitis, or kidney disease.

Pleurisy in its early stages may be fibrous or dry, with inflamed membrane surfaces rubbing against each other. Often, however, the inflammation leads to a seepage of fluids between the membranes, a condition known as pleural effusion. In dry pleurisy, the symptoms are either mild or sharp chest pains aggravated by coughing and pains in the abdomen, neck, and shoulders. There may also be a crackling or harsh grating sound during breathing. In a pleural effusion, pain subsides or disappears completely, but breathing becomes difficult.

TREATMENT

Treatment for pleurisy consists of finding the underlying cause and resolving it. Aspirin may be recommended to relieve pain. To prevent pneumonia from developing, it is important to try to cough up secretions that may accumulate. To minimize pain, the doctor may suggest that the patient hold a pillow against the chest while attempting to cough.

COMPLICATIONS

Empyema, or the buildup of purulent fluid in the pleura, is the most serious complication, but it responds well to antibiotic treatment and careful surgical drainage of the fluid.

PULMONARY TUBERCULOSIS

The number of tuberculosis cases in the United States had declined from more than 84,000 cases annually in 1953 to about 23,000 cases very recently. However, the decline has stopped, and more cases are occurring in many groups—primarily children and young adults, especially among minorities in inner cities. Infection in people with the AIDS virus accounts for some of this increase. Other people with impaired immune systems are at risk as well. This includes people who are being treated with steroids or cancer chemotherapy drugs that suppress the immune system. Prevention must be taken seriously by those at risk, particularly now that a new strain of tuberculosis has emerged that does not respond to the antibiotic treatment that cures the typical disease. The much-publicized strain has caused deaths in urban areas such as New York City. Research that had been halted, for the most part, because of success in treatment and decline of the disease is now resuming in response to this deadly turn in tuberculosis infection.

However, in the United States tuberculosis still usually occurs among elderly, impoverished, and malnourished individuals who are homeless or living in unsanitary housing and among malnourished persons such as alcoholics. And tuberculosis continues to be a major world health problem. There are an estimated 8 million cases and 3 million deaths each year worldwide. The influx of immigrants from areas such as Southeast Asia, Mexico, and Central and South America, where tuberculosis is common, may also be a factor in the increase in new cases in the United States.

DIAGNOSIS AND TREATMENT

An estimated 10 million Americans are infected with tuberculosis bacteria, but many of these people are not treated because they do not know they have been exposed. In adults, early signs of the disease may be totally absent or symptoms resemble those of the flu. Gradually, weight loss, fatigue, and a slight fever develop. A cough may be dry at first but then produces increasingly large amounts of yellow or green sputum that may contain blood. Difficulty breathing, pleural chest pains, and night sweats may also accompany tuberculosis.

Anyone at high risk for tuberculosis or who has these symptoms should get a tuberculin skin test to check for infection and, if the test is positive, a follow-up chest X ray and sputum culture to check for damage.

The typical disease can be treated on an outpatient basis with a combination of drugs, which may include isoniazid (in conjunction with vitamin B_6), streptomycin, ethambutol, and rifampin. Rest and a nutritious diet are vital to recovery. Antituberculosis drugs may be required for one to two years *after* the person has recovered to prevent a recurrence or complications. (Many patients stop taking the drugs too soon, especially if they are feeling well.) Regular checkups for at least two years after recovery are also recommended.

Since tuberculosis remains a serious and highly infectious disease, and now includes a new drug-resistant strain, anyone living with a patient should be examined for infection as soon as possible. Older persons with lung disorders who live with young children should also have themselves thoroughly checked.

PULMONARY EDEMA

This swelling of the lungs due to fluid accumulation is a life-threatening symptom of heart failure. Inefficient pumping by the left ventricle of the heart results in a backup of blood in the vessels, increased pressure, and rapid filling of the alveoli with plasma, the liquid part of the blood.

Symptoms include extreme difficulty breathing, cyanosis, anxiety accompanied by a feeling of suffocation, a dry or sputum- or blood-filled cough, pallor, and sweating. The person should be taken immediately to the nearest hospital emergency room.

HIGH-ALTITUDE PULMONARY EDEMA

This form of pulmonary edema occurs when a person suddenly travels to an area of oxygen-deficient high altitude and the body cannot adjust to it. Heavy exertion before the event increases the risk, as does chronic lung disease and age. The symptoms, which appear within 24 to 72 hours after arriving in a locality above 10,000 feet, include shortness of breath, rapid heartbeat, slight fever, a cough that may become bloody, and cyanosis. Oxygen should be administered at once and the patient brought to a lower altitude. The best prevention is a gradual ascent to a high altitude and moderated physical activity during the adjustment period.

CHRONIC COUGH

Although a cough can free the respiratory tract from harmful secretions and foreign matter in the bronchial tubes, it can also be a symptom of a serious pulmonary problem. Coughing up bloody phlegm, with or without chest pain, can indicate pneumonia, tuberculosis, pulmonary edema, a blood clot in the lungs, or cancer in the respiratory tract. If the bloody cough is accompanied by pain in the lungs, it could signal pneumonia, pulmonary tuberculosis, lung abscess, or lung cancer. A cough that appears for the first time in the middle-aged individual who smokes could be a sign of lung cancer. Persistent coughs accompanied by purulent sputum, chest pain, or blood should be evaluated by a doctor.

AIRWAY OBSTRUCTION

In adults, the inhaling of foreign objects most often occurs while eating, while under the influence of alcohol, or while holding objects such as screws or nails in the mouth. First-aid measures are necessary only if the person is unable to clear the object by coughing and if the airway is severely obstructed. If the individual can speak or cough effectively, he or she should be left to clear the object without assistance. If the person cannot talk or is turning blue, the Heimlich maneuver should be applied.

Foreign bodies that cannot be cleared spontaneously or with the Heimlich maneuver must be promptly removed by a physician. People who have been revived by the Heimlich maneuver should also be seen by a physician to check for the possibility of damage to internal organs from the abdominal thrusts.

HOW TO DO THE HEIMLICH MANEUVER

First, encircle the person's waist from behind. Then, make a fist with one hand and position it, thumb side toward the victim and slightly above his or her navel. With your other hand, grasp the fist and thrust it into the abdomen, inward and upward deliberately and forcefully, to dislodge the blockage. Try it again if necessary.

BREATHING AIDS

People with chronic lung diseases sometimes require specialized equipment to deliver medications, oxygen, or moist air deep into the lungs to help clear mucus out of the airways or to ensure a sufficient supply of oxygen in the blood. If your physician orders a breathing aid, a respiratory therapist, technician, or community health nurse can demonstrate its use.

NEBULIZERS

Nebulizers produce a fine spray of medicine that is breathed deeply into the lungs. Some nebulizers require the user to squeeze a bulb to power the spray; others plug into electric outlets and operate with compressed air or oxygen. In a metered-dose nebulizer, the medication is prepackaged in a spray container. Nebulizers can be used before or after postural drainage.

IPPB MACHINES

Intermittent positive pressure breathing (IPPB) machines use pressure to push additional air into the lungs when the individual inhales. During exhalation, there is no pressure and the individual breathes out normally. A physician must specify that the patient needs IPPB, which is meant only for intermittent use. *The Merck Manual,* a reference text for physicians, states that although the machines are widely used, they have not been shown to help raise secretions of mucus or improve the overall condition of those patients with chronic obstructive pulmonary disease who are able to remain somewhat active.

OXYGEN

The physician may prescribe home oxygen therapy for patients who have chronically low levels of oxygen in the blood, or for those whose levels drop when they begin an exercise program. Oxygen is prescribed at a specific rate of flow per minute that should not be changed by the patient; too much oxygen can damage the lungs and interfere with the body's mechanism for ridding the blood of carbon dioxide.

A respiratory therapist, technician, or community health nurse will instruct the patient on how to set the flow rate, when and for how long to use oxygen, and necessary procedures for reordering supplies.

For safe use, *never* smoke in a room where oxygen is being used. The American Lung Association recommends that the oxygen tank should be at least 10 feet from open flame, gas stoves, pilot lights in water heaters or furnaces, and electrical equipment that may spark.

HUMIDIFIERS AND VAPORIZERS

Inadequate fluid intake and a dry room environment can make mucus more viscous and harder to cough up. A humidifier, vaporizer, or even a pan filled with water can add moisture to the air, which helps soften and loosen the mucus so it can be coughed up. As with other breathing aids, humidifiers and vaporizers must be cleaned carefully, according to the manufacturer's instructions, to avoid spreading infections.

Those living in areas with poor air quality, or who have allergies in addition to lung disease, might consider an air filter or air purifier. Devices that produce ozone gas should be avoided.

TRAVELING

Millions of people with breathing disabilities travel in spite of their condition. With some precautions and planning, there is no reason why an older person with a chronic lung disorder can't have an enjoyable trip. The amount of preplanning necessary depends on the specific condition, medications, and any need for equipment.

Since flying involves many stresses that affect the respiratory system, individuals suffering from an upper respiratory infection should delay their departure until they are well, and those suffering from asthma or emphysema should seek medical advice before getting on an airplane. Major airlines may supply oxygen equipment if the passenger is preapproved by the airline's medical department and has a note from his or her physician. Arrangements should be made well in advance of the trip.

RECOMMENDED ADULT IMMUNIZATIONS

Older people often think that immunizations are for the young and neglect this aspect of illness prevention. On the contrary, immunizations against certain diseases are a vital part of staying healthy for people of all ages. Immunizations for the following are recommended:

Influenza. Immunization is recommended for all persons over 65; for adults of any age who have diabetes, chronic heart or lung disease, kidney failure, or other chronic diseases; for nursing-home residents; and for certain health-care workers. Should be avoided by people who are hypersensitive to eggs. Should be given annually.

Pneumococcal Pneumonia. Immunization is recommended for all persons over 65 and for people at risk of complications of pneumonia—for example, people with diabetes or chronic heart or lung diseases. People who have had any type of pneumococcal polysaccharide vaccine should not receive a second immunization against pneumonia.

TIPS FOR TRAVELERS WITH LUNG DISEASE

Before you leave on a trip, you might consider these suggestions:

- Get extra medicines and prescriptions to carry with you. Keep some of your medicines in carry-on baggage in case your luggage is lost.
- Write out your daily schedule for taking medicines and treatments; it's easy to forget old routines in new surroundings.
- Ask your physician for the name of a doctor in the areas you will be visiting. If you will be traveling to a non-English-speaking country, a number of organizations have physician referral lists, often at a reasonable charge.
- If you'll need oxygen, arrange in advance with your airline. Airlines won't allow you to use your own oxygen equipment, but they will supply oxygen to selected patients for a fee. (Take your own equipment with you in your baggage.)
- If you will be traveling to a country with a different voltage system, buy adapters (available in radio electronics stores) that will allow you to plug any electric machines into foreign outlets.
- Check with your local health department for any forecasts of potential flu epidemics in the areas you plan to visit.
- Plan a realistic schedule and be sure your traveling companion is prepared to go at your pace.
- In cities or areas with high pollution, travel at night or early in the morning, if possible, when emissions are likely to be lower.
- Those with allergies should check their rooms and accommodations for potential problem substances, such as feather pillows.

Measles and Rubella (German Measles). Immunization is recommended for all adults who lack documentation of having received measles or rubella live-virus vaccines or whose blood tests fail to show immunity against the diseases. Not recommended for people with immunodeficiency or a history of hypersensitivity to neomycin.

Tetanus/Diphtheria. Immunization is recommended for all adults who have not been immunized previously. Two doses of the combined vaccine should be given four weeks apart, with a third dose given six to 12 months after the second one. A booster should be given every 10 years. In addition, tetanus immune globulin should be given to people with large cuts, punctures, or other wounds that may be contaminated by dirt; to people who are uncertain whether they have received their full tetanus/diphtheria immunization; or who have not received a booster in the last 10 years. Tetanus/diphtheria vaccine should be avoided by people who have had a hypersensitive reaction to a previous dose.

Hepatitis B. Immunization recommended for all adults at risk of developing the disease. This includes health-care workers, hemophiliacs, or others exposed to large amounts of transfusions and other blood products; family members or sexual partners of people with hepatitis B infection; or male homosexuals with a high risk of hepatitis exposure.

OTHER POSSIBLE VACCINES

Mumps. Most adults are probably immune to mumps, but anyone thought to be susceptible to the disease can be immunized. Not recommended for people with immunodeficiency or a history of hypersensitivity to eggs or neomycin.

Polio. Vaccination is recommended for adults who have not previously received a complete series of either killed- or live-virus polio vaccines. Vaccines are especially important for people traveling to areas where polio is endemic and for incompletely immunized adults in households where children are to be immunized. The live-virus (oral) vaccine should be avoided by people with immunodeficiency.

Rabies. Vaccination is recommended for veterinarians, animal handlers, certain laboratory workers, and travelers to countries where rabies is common.

Miscellaneous. Vaccines against cholera, meningitis, plague, and yellow fever are recommended for travelers to areas where the diseases are common and for people who are at special risk of exposure.

16

Mental Functioning in Aging

All too many people still view senility as an inevitable component of old age. Contrary to this popular, albeit mistaken belief, the vast majority of people retain their intellectual faculties well into the later years and, indeed, to the end of their lives. There are examples of accomplishments of famous and not-so-famous people in their seventies, eighties, and even older. If an individual has positive expectations about remaining intellectually fit, and there are no mentally disabling diseases present, he or she can remain intellectually alert and productive into the later years.

There are, however, certain disorders that do affect mental function and are more commonly associated with aging. Most of these respond to treatment once the underlying cause is discovered. However, some researchers believe that nearly a third of the people diagnosed with dementia—the irreversible deterioration of mental function—have other, more treatable conditions. This is why it is imperative to make absolutely sure that the diagnosis is accurate before assuming that a person has Alzheimer's disease or some other disabling brain disorder. There are numerous examples of older people who have been institutionalized with what was thought to be an irreversible brain disease, only to be diagnosed later with malnutrition, depression, or some other treatable disorder.

DEPRESSION

Many people think of depression as simply being gloomy or sad, and that a depressed person can "snap out of it" if he or she will only try to be a bit more cheerful.

All of us feel a bit melancholy from time to time, and we may even describe ourselves as being depressed. In reality, however, true clinical depression—or affective disorder, to use its medical name—is an organic illness involving biochemical changes in the body.

According to the National Institute of Mental Health, approximately 10 to 15 percent of older Americans suffer from significant depression—that is, depression severe enough to require treatment. Some experts, however, think that even this is a low estimate. Dr. Barry Gurland, a Columbia University authority on mental health in the aged, has found that 26 percent of persons over age 65 who seek medical attention suffer from a treatable clinical depression.

Often, depression will produce different symptoms in an older person than in a younger man or woman. For example, a younger person may complain of a variety of physical symptoms, while in an older person depression may mimic symptoms of senility—memory loss, confusion, or disorientation and inattention to personal needs. Delusions and other signs of intellectual impairment are relatively common. This form

TABLE 16.1
Major Differences Between Depression and Dementia

Depression	Dementia
Comes on in a short period of time with full-blown symptoms. Medical attention is sought soon after onset.	Usually comes on gradually, and patient and family may not be aware of symptoms or seek help until later.
Patient can describe decline in function in great detail; may state how bad memory is or how confused he or she feels.	Patient is vague in describing symptoms; denies problems with memory or feelings of confusion.
Patient shows little motivation in completing tasks on performance tests; however, objective performance is better than own accounts of decline.	Patient tries hard to complete task, at least in early stages; objective performance is worse than own accounts of decline.
Ability to attend to tasks and concentrate is generally good.	Ability to attend to tasks and concentrate is generally poor.
Prior history of depressive episodes in patient or family.	No prior history of depressive episodes.
Patient appears depressed.	Patient has mood swings, shows little emotion, or may be depressed.
Variable performance on test items of similar difficulty. Impaired social relations early in course of illness; insecure around others.	Consistent performance on test items of similar difficulty. Impaired social relations later in course of illness; demanding around others.
Patient able to answer most questions of orientation and general knowledge—e.g., age, date, address, current President's name.	Patient cannot answer most questions regarding orientation or general knowledge.
Able to cook for self, dress, do household chores. Able to find way home.	Unable to perform activities of daily living without difficulty. Gets lost in own community or neighborhood.

of depression, called depressive pseudodementia, is thought to account for about 15 percent of the depression that occurs among elderly people. The mental deterioration found in pseudodementia, as well as the forgetfulness and inability to concentrate characteristic of more typical depression, disappears when properly treated. But since this disorder can mimic dementia, it is important to know how the two differ.

The cause of clinical depression is often unknown. We tend to think of depression as an emotional response to a misfortune or sad event, and occasionally this type of normal sadness or grief may trigger clinical depression. More often, however, there is no identifiable cause of the depression, although research indicates that a biomedical imbalance is a likely possibility. Some researchers hypothesize that suppressed anger may in some way upset the brain's biochemistry and lead to the depression.

Anyone showing signs of persistent mental impairment should be seen by a physician. If depression is suspected, the doctor may order psychological testing either to help confirm the diagnosis or point to another cause. Depression is often difficult to diagnose since there is no simple blood test or foolproof examination that pinpoints the disease. Frequently the diagnosis is based on a constellation of symptoms.

DIAGNOSTIC CRITERIA

During an episode of depression, at least three of the following symptoms are present according to diagnostic standards set by the American Psychiatric Association.

1. Insomnia or excessive sleepiness
2. Loss of appetite, weight loss, or excessive eating and weight gain
3. Loss of libido
4. Low energy level or chronic tiredness
5. Feelings of inadequacy, loss of self-esteem, or self-depreciation
6. Decreased effectiveness or productivity at school, at work, or at home
7. Decreased attention, concentration, or ability to think clearly
8. Social withdrawal
9. Loss of interest in or enjoyment of pleasurable activities
10. Irritability or excessive anger
11. Inability to respond with apparent pleasure to praise or rewards
12. Less active or talkative than usual, or feeling slowed down or restless
13. Pessimistic attitude about the future, brooding about past events, or feeling sorry for oneself
14. Tearfulness or crying
15. Recurrent thoughts of death or suicide

TREATMENT

Sometimes depression will end spontaneously without treatment, but this may take six months or more. If left untreated, especially in an older person, the condition may progress to such a state of hopelessness that the victim is totally unable to function or may even attempt suicide.

Depression is commonly treated with a combination of drugs and psychotherapy. Recent studies have found that, in some cases of depression, psychotherapy may be just as effective as drug therapy, but drugs may produce quicker results. The most-used drugs are called tricyclic antidepressants, so named because of their three-ring chemical structure. The drugs are believed to work by increasing the activity of the brain's catecholamine neurotransmitters, thereby restoring normal chemical balance.

Drugs. The choice of antidepressant drug depends upon the type of symptoms. Some, such as amitriptyline (Elavil and others) or doxepin (Adapin or Sinequan), are sedatives and may be the best choices for people who suffer from anxiety or sleeping problems in addition to the depression. Imipramine (Tofranil and others) and desipramine (Norpramin and others) are not as sedating and may be better choices for people who are excessively sleepy. Other tricyclic antidepressants are amoxapine (Ascendin), clomipramine (Anafranil), nortriptyline (Aventyl or Pamelor), protriptyline (Vivactil), and trimipramine (Surmontil).

Monoamine oxidase (MAO) inhibitors—such as isocarboxizid (Marplan), phenelzine (Nardil), and tranylcypromine (Parnate)—also increase the action of the brain's catecholamine neurotransmitters, but these drugs usually are not prescribed unless the tricyclic antidepressants fail to produce an adequate response. Anyone taking an MAO inhibitor must be particularly careful about drug and food interactions that can cause a dangerous, even fatal, rise in blood pressure. Drugs that must be avoided include those that affect the sympathetic nervous system; these include amphetamines, cocaine, dopamine, epinephrine, methyldopa, or related compounds. Prohibited foods include any high-protein product that has been chemically aged, fermented, pickled, or smoked. These include cheeses, especially the aged varieties such as cheddar; pickled herring; beer; wine; liver; yeast extract; dry sausages such as Genoa, hard salami, or pepperoni; fava beans; and yogurt. Excessive caffeine and chocolate consumption should also be avoided.

A newer drug that is chemically unrelated to other available antidepressants is fluoxetine (Prozac). Although it was touted at first as a wonder drug for depression, it has been bogged down in controversy because of its connection to suicides that occurred among some of its users. Many physicians feel that fluoxetine has been misjudged as a drug whose only role was to help severely depressed and possibly suicidal patients become mobile enough to commit suicide. Regardless, fluoxetine may not be the best choice for someone who has exhibited pronounced suicidal tendencies, at least not until further information is available. It still has great value for others suffering from depression.

Lithium salts may be prescribed on a long-term basis to prevent the extreme mood swings of manic depression. However, the dosage must be very carefully adjusted to avoid a toxic overdose of lithium; elderly patients often will develop signs of lithium overdose at amounts that are normally well tolerated by a younger person.

Electroshock. Severe cases of depression may be treated by electroshock therapy. Unfortunately, such therapy is widely misunderstood by the general public, largely because of highly distorted accounts of how it is administered. Contrary to popular belief, patients undergoing modern electroshock treatments do not feel any "shock," thanks to pretreatment with muscle relaxants and sedatives. There will be a slight twitching of the eyelids or muscles in the arm, but this is the only visible sign of electrical current passing through the brain. There is a temporary loss of memory, but this quickly passes; the kind of permanent amnesia or brain injury depicted in movies and other sensationalized depictions of the therapy rarely occurs. Although electroshock treatments are reserved for severe depression, they have a distinct advantage over drug therapy in that they produce much quicker results. Antidepressant drugs may take several weeks or even months to produce results, whereas electroshock treatments work much faster. Thus, these treatments may be preferable for people who are suicidal or for whom drugs are not working quickly enough. Often a single treatment will suffice, although most patients require more.

Psychotherapy. Psychotherapy is an important component in the treatment of depression. In the early phase, psychotherapy may provide needed emotional support while the patient waits for antidepressant drugs to take effect. After the acute phase has ended, psychotherapy may be useful in helping the patient understand his or her disease and develop coping techniques to avoid future episodes.

Physical Activity. Exercise is still another important aspect of long-term treatment. Research has found that regular vigorous exercise—for example, jogging, cycling, brisk walking, and swimming—increases catecholamine activity in the brain and helps overcome or prevent depression.

OTHER CAUSES OF MENTAL IMPAIRMENT

Although depression is one of the more common causes of mental impairment among older people, there are nearly a hundred different conditions or medications that can cause depression, memory disturbance, confusion, or even psychosis. When the cause is discovered and promptly treated, the person usually regains normal mental capabilities.

CONDITIONS THAT CAUSE MENTAL IMPAIRMENT

Brain Disorders

Advanced syphilis
Brain abscess
Brain injuries
Brain swelling
Concussion/contusion and other brain injuries
Meningitis
Strokes and mini-strokes
Tumors

Cardiovascular Disorders

Congestive heart failure
Hardening of the arteries
Heart attack
Irregular heart rhythms

Miscellaneous Other Diseases

Anemia
Chronic lung disease
Disturbances in body chemistry
High blood sugar
Kidney failure
Liver failure
Low blood sugar
Low blood volume
Overactive adrenal glands (Cushing's syndrome)
Thyroid disorders
Underactive pituitary

Other Conditions

Adverse drug reactions
Alcoholism
Anesthesia or surgery
Arsenic, lead, or mercury poisoning
Carbon monoxide poisoning
Deficiency of nutrients such as vitamin B_{12}, folic acid, or niacin

Dehydration
Depression
Environmental change and isolation
Excessive drop in body temperature
Infection
Pain
Blindness or deafness

MEDICATIONS

In tracking down possible causes of mental problems in an older person, start by looking in the medicine cabinet. Drugs are among the most common causes of mental impairment among the elderly. Many people have chronic diseases requiring several medications that, alone or in combination, can have adverse effects. In addition, most drugs are broken down by the liver and eliminated by the kidneys; as we grow older, these organs cannot handle drugs and other potentially toxic substances as efficiently. The drugs may remain in the body longer and build up to toxic levels. Very often an older person will require special drug dosage adjustments, and even then his or her risk of adverse effects may be greater than in a younger person.

Very often a physician may have to try a different medication or even eliminate one or more drugs to reduce side effects. People taking drugs that have a narrow margin between a therapeutic and a toxic dose—for example, digitalis—should have periodic blood tests to measure drug levels. To reduce the chances of intellectual impairment, anyone taking multiple medications should:

- Have all prescriptions filled at the same pharmacy so that the pharmacist can be on the alert for adverse interactions. Some pharmacies have a computerized record-keeping system that makes detection easier.
- Make a list of all medications, both the generic and brand names as well as the doses, and carry it with you to all doctor's appointments. In making your list, don't overlook nonprescription drugs and any vitamin or mineral supplements you may be taking.
- Take medications only as prescribed. For example, if you are told to take a drug three times a day, do not take all three pills at once.
- Do not use alcohol in combination with drugs affecting the central nervous system—sedatives, tranquilizers, barbiturates, and others. This restriction applies to nonprescription cold pills and sleep medications as well as to prescription drugs.

- Avoid chronic use of laxatives; they can cause chemical imbalances leading to confusion.

DIET

Nutritional deficiencies are common among the elderly. Many older people, especially those who live alone, see little point in cooking for themselves and subsist on tea, toast, sweets, and the like. Others simply may not be able to afford fresh fruits and vegetables and the other essentials of a healthful diet. Lack of cooking facilities, the inability to get to a supermarket because of physical disability or fear of crime in the neighborhood, lack of teeth or poorly fitted dentures, a sluggish appetite, and alcoholism are among the myriad other factors that may contribute to malnutrition among older people. Limited fluid intake and use of diuretic medications can lead to dehydration, compounding existing deficiencies. Learning how to plan a balanced diet using inexpensive foods, and taking advantage of food-stamp programs, supermarket delivery services, and programs such as Meals on Wheels, can all help meet an older person's nutritional needs. Trying to eat at least one meal a day in a social setting—for example, a senior citizen center—helps to relieve loneliness and may stimulate appetite at the same time. Very often, once the nutritional deficiencies are corrected, the mental symptoms will abate.

ENVIRONMENTAL POLLUTION

An increasing number of people attribute mental—and physical—deficiencies to exposure to chemicals and other pollutants in their environment. It is a difficult theory to prove, although we know that noise pollution increases mental confusion, and direct exposure to certain chemicals is certain to cause loss of function. Multiple chemical sensitivity (MCS) is the name of the disorder that has been called "the twentieth-century disease" by some experts.

Discussions of the topic at the American Occupational Health Conference in 1991 gave time to physicians on both sides of the issue. One physician who dismisses MCS as a type of hysteria pointed to an example of a 30-year-old woman who claimed MCS to be a result of her work in a chemical plant, even though her job as a telephone sales operator there did not bring her into contact with any chemicals and she did not work in the buildings where laboratories were located. Another physician who is a self-described believer in MCS as an actual disease process gave an example of one university faculty member who had driven through a cloud of toxic chemicals and then complained of loss of memory, fatigue, and trouble concentrating whenever she came into contact with cigarette smoke, perfumes, and other low-level irritants.

The Occupational Safety and Health Administration (OSHA) regulates chemical exposure limits. With more evidence supporting the disease potential of multiple chemical sensitivity, the limits may be lowered. Industry resistance is unlikely to decrease otherwise. If you think you may be a victim of environmental illness, try to document your exposure to the pollutants you think may have affected your mental or physical functioning. Then consult your doctor with your evidence.

ALZHEIMER'S DISEASE

In recent years, all of us have become much more conscious of the tragedy of Alzheimer's disease. On the one hand, it is not as widespread as many people have been led to believe. There are more than 50 causes of dementia, many of which are dismissed mistakenly in favor of an Alzheimer's diagnosis. On the other hand, it is beneficial for more people to be aware of Alzheimer's disease and its impact on the victim and his or her family. Alzheimer's disease affects about 4 million Americans, and its victims may live for many years as they progressively become more ill. Meanwhile, their families must shoulder this emotional, mental, and financial burden. Add to that the fact that the older population is on the rise, and you will understand why Alzheimer's disease garners so much attention.

Although Alzheimer's disease received its name only 80 years ago, it is not a new disease. Throughout history, there have been instances of dementia and senility that undoubtedly were caused by what we now call Alzheimer's, named after the German physician who first described the disease in the medical literature.

Alzheimer's disease is responsible for at least half of all senile and presenile dementia, which is the progressive, usually irreversible deterioration of all intellectual ability. The condition usually appears after age 65, but in rare instances it has been known to develop in people as young as the mid-forties. It starts slowly, with mild memory loss and depression or moodiness. But unlike the normal mild forgetfulness that most people will experience regardless of age, in Alzheimer's disease forgetfulness progresses until the victim becomes unable to remember the most commonplace data: his or her address, birth date, or names of children and lifelong friends. Eventually, the person loses the power of speech and the ability to take care of the most basic bodily functions. Abnormalities in the cerebral cortex of the brain are responsible for loss of memory, the power to think rationally, learning ability, and the changes in personality and sense of judgment that characterize this disease.

Alzheimer's disease is a common contributing cause of death, but it usually does not kill directly. Instead, its victims die from accidents and the consequences of extreme disability, such as the total inability to eat that is found in the later stages of the disease. Older adults rarely survive more than five years beyond their diagnosis. Younger patients may live more than 20 years with the disease.

IMPORTANCE OF DIAGNOSIS

Eventually a simple diagnostic test may lead to quick diagnosis of Alzheimer's disease. At this time, however, conclusive diagnosis of Alzheimer's can be made only

MENTAL FUNCTION TESTS

Testing for progressive memory loss as well as other signs of intellectual decline should include a complete physical, psychiatric, and neurological examination. The workup may include:

Detailed medical history. This may be acquired from the patient or a family member if the patient's recall is not reliable. A family history of certain hereditary disorders or past events, such as head injuries or mini-strokes, may be responsible for current symptoms. Previous work exposure to toxic substances may also be a factor.

Laboratory tests. Blood, sputum, and urine analyses may show an imbalance of hormones, vital chemicals, toxic levels of medications, or evidence of viral or bacterial infection—all possible causes of mental symptoms.

X-ray studies. An X ray may show an infection, mass, or head injury. A CT (computerized tomography) scan may show a tumor or structural abnormalities in the brain.

Electroencephalogram. This test measures the electrical patterns in the brain and may be used to detect brain tumors, infections, stroke damage, or other brain abnormalities.

Psychological testing and mental status examination. These tests may be useful to rule out emotional disorders and to test memory and mental awareness.

through an autopsy, after the brain is examined for the changes that are indicative of the disease. Tentative diagnosis is currently based on results of psychological and mental testing, CT scanning, a patient history, and evidence of continuing mental deterioration.

Researchers believe that there is more than one type of Alzheimer's disease because certain patients seem to deteriorate more rapidly than others. Those who suffer from psychiatric symptoms such as hallucinations or delusions; slowed, rigid movements like those in Parkinson's disease; or involuntary muscle contractions known as myoclonus fall into this group.

POSSIBLE CAUSES: THE PRIME SUSPECTS

Discovering the cause and finding an effective treatment for Alzheimer's disease are among the top research priorities in the United States today. Because it is now known that the disease directly affects only a small, specific area of the brain, scientists think they are close to finding the cause or causes.

Areas of particular interest to researchers are genetics, immunology, the study of viruses, and environmental toxins. In the general population there is little evidence that Alzheimer's disease runs in families. However, in a small number of patients, genetics plays a definite role. Someone who is an identical twin, for example, has a nearly 50 percent chance of developing the disease if the other twin is affected. But having a parent, child, or sibling with Alzheimer's disease does not significantly increase the risk.

Parallels between Down's syndrome and Alzheimer's may provide insight into both of these diseases. Down's syndrome is a genetic disorder that results from the inheritance of an extra portion of chromosome 21. As Down's syndrome patients age, they exhibit the same brain abnormalities as Alzheimer's patients. By using Down's syndrome as a model, researchers may be able at least to determine the relative importance of genetics versus immunology or environmental factors.

The immune system may also be involved in the development of Alzheimer's disease. Researchers hypothesize that an immune system defect might make it easier for some form of microorganism to enter the brain, which results in the abnormal formations typical of Alzheimer's disease.

Viral suspects in Alzheimer's disease include the so-called slow viruses, which cause damage to the brain or central nervous system many years after initial infection. Creutzfeld-Jacob disease, a very rare, progressive, inevitably fatal illness that causes dementia and that strikes both men and women in their late fifties, is caused by a slow virus. However, there has been no evidence that Alzheimer's disease can be transmitted from one person to another.

Evidence has been found both for and against aluminum as a suspect in causing Alzheimer's disease. However, scientists state that using aluminum cookware poses no risk in developing the disease.

BRAIN CHANGES

Changes in the cerebral cortex, the part of the brain responsible for intellectual functions such as thought, memory, and language, cause the symptoms of Alzheimer's. Although patients eventually lose the ability to walk and talk, areas of the brain controlling these functions are not affected.

The brain of an Alzheimer's patient contains microscopic areas of degeneration known as neuritic or senile plaques and abnormal fibers called neurofibrillary tangles. Although the brains of many elderly people show some of these changes, those with Alzheimer's disease have a greater number of abnormal areas, and the amount of intellectual decline is proportional to the size of the affected area.

The chief feature of Alzheimer's disease is the deficiency of certain enzymes needed to synthesize acetylcholine, a neurotransmitter. Neurotransmitters are chemicals that carry nerve impulses across the tiny gaps between nerve cells known as synapses. This defect of the acetylcholine system is particularly evident in nerve cells in the prefrontal cortex and hippocampus, an area important in memory. People who develop this disease in their forties or fifties may have defects in other neurotransmitter systems as well as in the synthesis of acetylcholine.

CURRENT RESEARCH

Although there is no cure for Alzheimer's disease, researchers have made great strides in understanding how the brain creates and retains memory. For example, it is now known that the memory of an event is stored in more than one place in the cortex. Acting on developments in brain research, drug companies have devoted extensive resources to memory-improving drugs.

Their emphasis is on developing drugs that either mimic acetylcholine or prevent it from being destroyed. Although such drugs hold great promise, more time and research is needed before we will have agents that are both safe and effective. To date, experimental agents have helped improve memory to a modest degree on performance tests; however, test performance may not always predict everyday functioning. Effects of these drugs may be short-lived or effective only in mildly or moderately impaired patients. Some, such as physostigmine, can cause serious side effects and must be given under close medical supervision.

Other treatments have had mixed results or demonstrated only slight improvements in Alzheimer's patients. One type of drug, ergoloid mesylates (Gerimal, Hydergine, and Niloric), is available by prescription and may slightly improve mood and intellectual performance in some moderately impaired patients. One of the problems of developing drugs for brain ailments, however, is finding a way for an oral medication to cross the blood-brain barrier, a closely joined layer of capillaries and connective tissue designed to protect the brain from the penetration of foreign substances.

CARING FOR THE ALZHEIMER'S PATIENT

Until a cure for Alzheimer's disease can be discovered, there is much that family members can do to maximize the quality of life for their loved one. The patient should be seen regularly by a psychiatrist, neurologist, or family physician or internist who consults with a neurologist. Maintenance of otherwise good health will prevent additional confusion from other causes. Pick a physician who will spend time with you and answer questions.

Although the disease itself is not curable, certain conditions that may accompany it are helped by medication. Symptoms of restless, agitated behavior and paranoid delusions respond to drugs used to treat psychoses. Sleeping medications may be helpful to reduce agitation and the confusion that comes from lack of sleep. For reasons not yet understood, approximately 25 to 30 percent of Alzheimer's disease patients show signs of depression in addition to the symptoms of the disease. Although treatment with an antidepressant does not usually produce any striking improvement in intellectual function, the physician may prescribe such a drug to improve mood.

Of the two major types of medications used to treat depression, the MAO inhibitors may be more suitable for Alzheimer's patients than the tricyclic antidepressants. This may be because the elderly, and especially those with Alzheimer's, have higher levels of monoamine oxidase (MAO), an enzyme that destroys two neurotransmitters whose low levels have been associated with depression. MAO inhibitors allow these neurotransmitters to reach more normal levels. (See discussion of these drugs in the earlier section on depression.)

DAY-TO-DAY CARE

Understandably, Alzheimer's disease takes a tremendous emotional and physical toll on family members and others who are close to the patient. It is important for anyone taking care of the individual to contact local groups dealing with this disease. The Alzheimer's Disease and Related Disorders Association (ADRDA) can supply a list of local chapters that offer support groups for relatives. It can also furnish information on how to care for the patient and provide referrals to agencies offering assistance. Some communities have adult day-care centers offering programs for Alzheimer's patients.

In the early stages of the disease, both patient and family should plan how they will manage finances needed for future care. Retaining a lawyer knowledgeable in Medicare, Medicaid, and Social Security law can prove helpful in setting up joint bank accounts, power of attorney, and other ways to handle finances.

The course of Alzheimer's disease may be one of long, stable periods at progressively lower levels of functioning or one of a steady, rapid decline. Family members should assist the patient in staying as independent as possible during each period. Good nutrition, maintenance of sight and hearing, and a stable, familiar environment help the patient to cope. Above all, make it simple for the patient to understand what is being asked.

In the early stages of the disease when there is only mild memory loss, list making may be enough to assist with daily activities. If the individual takes medications, a divided pillbox labeled with the days of the week and an alarm clock set to ring at the same time each day will help jog the memory.

Encourage the person with Alzheimer's to use whatever talents or abilities remain with him or her. Someone who may no longer have the attention span to read a book, for example, may still be able to play a familiar musical instrument. Even the severely impaired person who cannot speak a coherent sentence may enjoy dancing or listening to music.

A well-balanced diet and plenty of fluids will help prevent vitamin deficiencies and dehydration. Severely impaired people may refuse to eat certain foods, and a good deal of coaxing and trial and error may be needed to provide a good diet. Avoid any alcoholic beverages, which serve only to confuse the patient.

As the disease progresses, more supervision and memory aids will be needed. Keep family photos around, and label them if the individual has trouble remembering names. A blackboard with the day of the week and date on it may help the patient become aware of his or her surroundings. The Alzheimer's Disease and Related Disorders Association suggests posting signs around the house—for example, "FLUSH" over the toilet or "TURN OFF" over water faucets. Make sure the patient can safely use the stove before letting him or her do so alone. Keep clutter to a minimum. A busy environment is confusing to the patient.

Familiar people and surroundings are important in keeping confusion to a minimum, but even so, Alzheimer's patients often wander from home and may need constant watching. Kindly but firmly insist that the patient remain inside with you until it is time to leave the house. Alert your neighbors to the individual's condition so they can report any wandering to you. People with Alzheimer's disease should wear an ID bracelet, available from Medic Alert, that indicates their diagnosis and an emergency phone number on the back. Make sure that the individual carries very little, if any, money to prevent him or her from taking a taxi or public transportation out of the immediate neighborhood.

If it is necessary for you to be away from home for several days or longer, find a relative or friend whom the patient knows well and have that person stay at your home. This is preferable to moving anyone with Alzheimer's. If the patient will be spending time in a new environment, such as an adult day-care center, a family member should accompany him or her on the first few visits to make the transition easier.

Since the Alzheimer's patient cannot retain new information, an activity in which he or she will be involved should be presented as simply as possible, and just before the event itself. For example, the Alzheimer's Disease and Related Disorders Association suggests that a family member should tell the patient of a visit to the doctor just before it is time to leave.

To allow for decision making yet minimize confusion, put the individual's clothing in a separate closet and give him or her a choice of only a few items to wear. Similarly, when planning a menu, say, "Would you like chicken or fish?" rather than, "What would you like for dinner?"

Alzheimer's patients who cannot or will not brush their teeth are at risk of cavities and/or gum disease. This is especially true if the person is taking an antidepressant, which may decrease the flow of saliva. To brush the patient's teeth, use a long-handled or angled brush or an electronic toothbrush.

Urinary incontinence is often found late in Alzheimer's disease. Make sure the patient knows how to get to the toilet; if he or she is unable to find the way, make the trip to the bathroom with the patient within an hour or two after the patient has drunk fluids.

To minimize bowel incontinence, provide a high-fiber diet and plenty of fluids. The patient should be taken to the bathroom at about the same time a bowel movement would usually occur. If these techniques are not successful, have the doctor check for hemorrhoids, blockages, or any medication that may be causing a problem.

Many Alzheimer's patients are restless and spend a lot of time pacing. If your loved one is losing sleep because of this, try darkening the room and setting an example by lying down as if to take a nap. At bedtime, warm milk may induce sleep and a night-light may reduce anxiety. If sleeplessness and agitation continue to be a problem, notify the physician, who may prescribe medication.

On the other hand, some Alzheimer's disease patients have difficulty moving about as the disease progresses. A cane or walker may help the patient to walk. Encourage exercise, even when the patient is sitting. Check with the doctor to see if any medications may be interfering with the ability to move.

Alzheimer's patients at all stages of the disease feel frustration, anger, and despair; they know that something is wrong. A friendly grasp of the shoulder or any similar affectionate physical touch helps the patient maintain contact with others, even when he or she can no longer speak.

GETTING OUTSIDE HELP

The relative of the Alzheimer's patient should get some help at home to ease the burden of care (see Appendix A, "Sources of Help"). Depending on the state where you live, Medicaid may pick up some or all of the expenses, so long as the individual meets their stringent financial guidelines. A social worker will be able to help you plan for care.

Eventually the individual with Alzheimer's disease may become too difficult to care for at home, and placement in a nursing home is necessary. Although this is often the best course for both patient and family, most people feel tremendous guilt when they come to this decision. But rather than postpone placement, the family should seek advice from the physician early in the course of the disease, since some nursing homes are reluctant to take a severely deteriorated patient who needs total care.

NORMAL MEMORY CHANGES

Many people who experience an occasional lapse in memory needlessly fear that it is a sign of Alzheimer's or an indication of some other mental deterioration. The fact is that we all forget things from time to time, and some people with perfectly normal brain capacity are more forgetful than others. In fact, studies show that it takes a 70-year-old person a quarter of a second longer, on average, than a 30-year-old person to identify a familiar object. This lag may or may not be attributable to mental deterioration, but it certainly is negligible and not worth worrying about.

As we age, changes in the brain can, but do not always, contribute to a fall-off in certain areas of recall. A decrease in the number of nerve cells and changes in some of their properties, a decrease in the flow of blood that supplies the brain with oxygen and other nutrients, and a slowing of electrical activity as measured by an electroencephalogram are some of the natural changes. Normal memory changes include:

- □ *Slowed thinking processes.* This may be particularly apparent when dealing with new problems or a problem requiring an immediate reaction.

- *Reduced attention span.* Many people find they have difficulty paying attention and ignoring distractions in the environment.
- *Decreased use of memory strategies.* Older people do not make as much use of associations and pictorial cues as younger people do, even though they may have an increased need for such cues.
- *Longer learning time.* This is especially true when an older person is confronted with new information.

Areas of memory that do *not* normally change include:

- *Immediate or short-term memory.* For example, remembering the name of someone you were just introduced to.
- *World knowledge or semantic memory.* Familiar information such as who is President, your children's birthdays, how to get to the supermarket. World knowledge is actually likely to increase with age.
- *Susceptibility to interference.* Newly learned information in a specific area competes with original information, making it hard, for example, to break old habits. This characteristic is present in both old and young people.
- *Retaining well-learned information.* The old forget no faster than the young.
- *Searching for stored information.* Older people may take longer to come up with the information, but the search technique does not change with age. Searching occurs automatically as well as with conscious effort.

Again, it should be stressed that normal changes in the brain definitely do not mean that an older person can no longer learn or retain new information. As we grow older, however, we may benefit from memory exercises and other practical means of improving recall.

17

Saving Your Eyes, Ears, and Teeth

Of all the senses, vision and hearing are probably the two that keep us most in touch with the world and consequently the two that we fear the most to lose. Many people also lose some or all of their teeth, but this usually can be forestalled by good preventive dental hygiene and regular visits to a dentist. Similarly, most people can adjust to the normal changes in vision and hearing, and proper preventive care usually can avert total loss of these senses.

VISION

NORMAL VISION CHANGES THAT COME WITH AGE

If you don't already need glasses to read this page, you probably will someday. It is a perfectly normal part of growing older, but it can be frustrating.

Often vision changes are the first sign of aging. Perhaps you have always had 20/20 vision, or maybe you have had the same corrective lens prescription since you were in your twenties. But as you enter your forties, fifties, or sixties, you notice that you have to hold the newspaper at arm's length to focus on the page or that you need to take off your glasses to see close up. You may notice that your eyes get tired or that you develop headaches after only short periods of close work.

Vision changes occur gradually and may start at different ages in different people. At first you may be able to adjust to the changes by reading in short stints or avoiding small print, but sooner or later nearly everyone needs reading glasses. The condition is called presbyopia, from the Greek word meaning "old eye." Normally long muscle fibers relax or contract to change the shape of the lens in the eye according to whether you are focusing on a near or distant object. The lens, which consists of elastic fibers, thins or flattens to see a distant object, and it becomes rounder and wider to focus on an object close up.

As a person grows older, additional fibers accumulate in the lens. Although some experts estimate that the process may start as early as age 10, when the eye reaches its full size, most people do not notice the effects until their mid-forties. The increased number of fibers gradually reduces the lens's elasticity, making adaptation for close work more difficult. It may also take more time to change focus from one object to another.

The solution is simple: corrective lenses to do the work the lens of your eye can no longer do by itself. If you have never had to wear glasses before, you may resent the imposition now. Indeed, most people put off getting glasses until they can no longer keep up day-to-day activities without them. But most everyone finds that once they get glasses, the pleasures of reading and being able to see close objects clearly again are worth the minimal trouble of toting and keeping track of the pair.

If you already have corrective lenses for another condition, bifocals or trifocals may be necessary to see both far and near without changing glasses. Some people who need glasses only for reading prefer bifocals with clear top lenses so that they can look up from their book to a distant object without taking their glasses off. Bifocals and trifocals may take some getting used to, but nearly everyone does adjust to them, given time and persistence. Since the lens fibers continue to accumulate throughout life, your corrective lens prescription may have to be increased, perhaps as often as every year.

Over-the-counter, ready-to-wear reading glasses are a viable alternative if you simply want to see the printed page more clearly. Of course, this does not negate the importance of seeing an eye doctor for other problems or for periodic checkups (see Figure 17.1).

Another normal effect of aging on vision affects the pupil. The pupil controls the aperture of the eye, growing larger in the dark to let in as much light as possible and becoming smaller in the presence of bright light in order to protect the eye. But as one grows older, the pupil is unable to open as wide or to adapt as quickly as it did before. The result is that older people need more light in order to see clearly. According to the American Optometric Association, the average 60-year-old needs seven times as much light as a 20-year-old in order to see the same object clearly. For this reason, it is inadvisable for older people to wear tinted lenses for fashion purposes or to wear sunglasses at night.

The reduced ability of the pupil to open and let light into the eye can lead to trouble distinguishing colors. If the eye is like a camera, then the retina, which lines the back of the eyeball behind the vitreous humor, is the film. The rods and cones within the

TIPS FOR WEARING MULTIFOCAL LENSES

Bifocals, trifocals, and even quadrifocals can open up fields of vision for people who need different corrective lenses for different situations. Proper placement of the lens segment is essential for comfortable and safe use of these glasses. Invisible bifocals, in which the prominent line between segments has been eliminated, may be more cosmetically appealing to some people but can cause problems for some wearers. In any case, getting used to multifocal lenses takes some time and patience. The American Optometric Association offers these tips for wearing multifocal lenses:

- Look straight ahead, not at your feet, while walking.
- Lower your eyes, not your head, to read out of the lowest part of the lens.
- Move reading material to accommodate your head, not vice versa. Folding the newspaper in halves or in quarters may be helpful. Hold reading material close to your body.
- Wear your lenses continuously for the first few weeks, even for tasks that do not require them. In this way, you get used to shifting your eyes from lens segment to lens segment.
- Keep lenses properly positioned by making sure the frames are tightened and adjusted for your face.
- Be especially careful walking down stairs when wearing new glasses or your reading glasses.

retina are the cells that perceive light and color and transmit their perceptions via a complex series of nerves to the brain, which analyzes the data.

The problem is that the cones, which perceive color, need much more light than the rods, which perceive light and dark. With the reduced amount of light that is let in by the aging pupil, it becomes progressively more difficult for older people to distinguish the subtleties of color. Blues may appear as varying shades of gray. Pastel colors are usually the most difficult to discern. The ability to distinguish bright, "warm" colors, such as red and yellow, is not usually affected to the same degree.

All of these vision changes are normal aspects of the aging process. Not everyone will experience them to the same degree, and some people may not experience them at all. Corrective lenses and the use of more light will solve most of the problems. Some ophthalmologists suggest that exercises may forestall presbyopia in some people, but glasses are the standard recommendation.

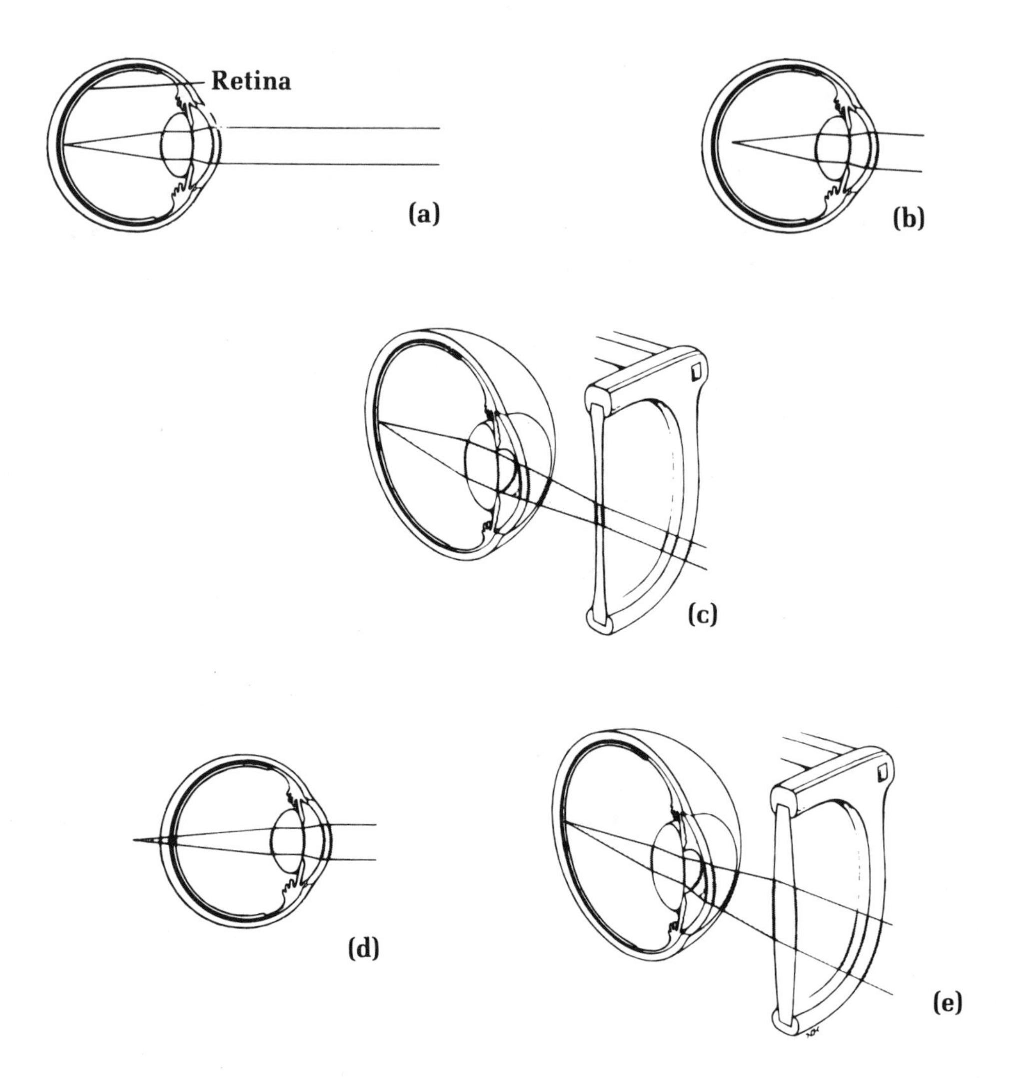

Figure 17.1 How Glasses Correct Visual Problems
Light rays entering an eye with normal vision (a) are refracted by the lens and cornea to come into focus on the retina. If the rays come into focus in front of (b) or behind (d) the retina, you will have an "astigmatism" and will be either nearsighted (b) or farsighted (d). These disorders are corrected easily with glasses that bring the light rays into focus on the proper place on the retina. Nearsightedness can be corrected by a concave glass lens (c), and farsightedness can be corrected with convex lenses (e). (Drawing courtesy Neil Hardy.)

SAFE DRIVING TIPS FOR OLDER PEOPLE

About 90 percent of the decisions made on the road are based on information received through the eyes. Therefore, any change in vision will have an effect on driving habits. Being aware of the changes that may occur with age, and taking them into account while driving, can prevent accidents. The following tips from the American Optometric Association are good, commonsense recommendations for drivers of all ages, but especially for those over 50:

- Have regular eye examinations to determine day and night vision capabilities. If corrective lenses are prescribed, be sure to choose frames that do not block peripheral vision. You may be able to pass the eye test for a driver's license without corrective lenses, but it is safer to wear them, especially for night driving. Take time to adjust to the lenses before attempting to drive while you wear them. On bright days, wear quality sunglasses; gray lenses are recommended by many optometrists.
- When possible, drive at speeds and on roads where you feel comfortable. Keep pace with the traffic flow, driving neither too fast nor too slowly. Make use of mirrors but be aware of blind spots. If you have difficulty seeing over the dashboard, sit on a pillow to raise yourself. Move your head as well as your eyes to keep sight of traffic on either side of you. Arthritis in the neck or stiff muscles that make it difficult to turn your head can combine with decreased peripheral vision to limit your line of sight. Be particularly careful when backing out. Convex mirrors placed opposite blind driveways on hills or curves are helpful in seeing oncoming traffic.
- Because adult eyes need more light to see properly, never wear sunglasses or tinted lenses while driving at night. Also, a clear windshield is preferable to a tinted one. If night vision is impaired, limit driving to well-lit, familiar roads. Make sure headlights and taillights are working correctly. Dusk and daybreak actually provide the most troublesome light conditions for driving; if possible, avoid driving at these times.
- Do not smoke or eat while driving. It can distract your attention from the road and impede vision if smoke gets into your eyes. Nicotine can also interfere with night vision. If you are taking any prescription or nonprescription medication, ask your doctor or pharmacist or read the label carefully to determine driving recommendations. And, of course, *never* drink and drive.

GLAUCOMA

The key to controlling glaucoma is early detection and treatment. Although it is estimated that 2 million Americans suffer from this disease, only half of them are aware of it. They run the risk of becoming one of the 62,000 people in this country who are legally blind due to glaucoma. Its prevalence is expected to increase as more of our population grows older.

The structures of the eye are protected from impact injury by a fluid called the aqueous humor. Normally this fluid collects in the anterior chamber between the cornea and the lens (see Figure 17.2) and is drained from the eye through Schlemm's canal. In the normal eye, fluid production and drainage maintain the correct amount of fluid.

In one type of glaucoma, Schlemm's canal becomes gradually or, less often, suddenly blocked, which traps the fluid in the anterior chamber. The intraocular pressure (pressure inside the eye) increases, and blood vessels within the eye may be pinched, cutting off the blood supply that keeps the optic nerve alive. Eventually, the nerve will be destroyed, causing loss of peripheral vision and, if untreated, blindness.

In the overwhelming majority of glaucoma cases, the buildup of pressure is gradual and insidious. In chronic open-angle glaucoma, almost no symptoms become obvious until irreparable damage has been done. The first signs of disorder may be blurred vision, colored circles around lights, or decreased peripheral vision, which may never be totally regained.

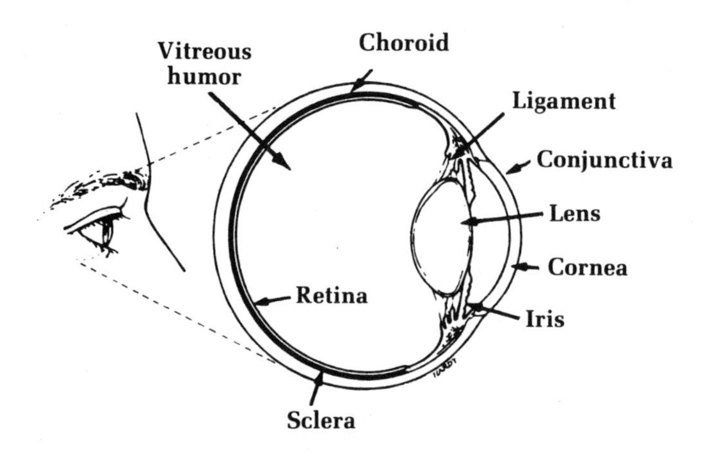

Figure 17.2 Structures of the Eye

However, if the increased pressure is detected before the nerves become choked and die, medications that lower intraocular pressure can prevent impaired vision. Taken orally or in the form of eyedrops, two types of drugs are prescribed: One reduces production of the aqueous humor, and the other facilitates the flow of the fluid out of the eye. These medications do not cure glaucoma, but they do prevent the damage to the optic nerve caused by the buildup of pressure. Treatment must be continual and lifelong in order to prevent reduced vision.

In a small number of cases, an attack of glaucoma comes on suddenly when Schlemm's canal becomes completely blocked. This blockage may be caused by injury to the eye, but more often the cause is unknown (although the disease does tend to run in families). The symptoms of closed-angle, or acute, glaucoma are a reddened, hard eyeball, vision disturbances, and pain, which may be quite severe. Acute glaucoma is a medical emergency requiring prompt attention to prevent blindness. After an initial attack, surgery may be performed that can prevent subsequent episodes.

Once the damage from glaucoma is done, it is irreparable. Thus, routine screening for early warning signs is the best preventive measure. An instrument called a tonometer is used to measure intraocular pressure. The device is placed directly onto the eyeball, which has been treated with anesthetizing drops. A type of tonometer that uses an air jet to measure pressure is widely used. Since the instrument itself does not touch the eye, no anesthesia is needed. Both methods are simple, painless, and useful in the early detection of glaucoma. A pressure reading of 14 milliliters of mercury is considered normal, well below the danger range. If a reading of 18 to 20 is obtained, follow-up examinations should be repeated every six months. A pressure reading of over 21 milliliters of mercury indicates glaucoma. People should receive their first glaucoma examination by the age of 35; those over 50 should be examined at least every two years or at every eye exam, unless previous screening indicates a high risk. Clinics and other organizations offer free testing in some neighborhoods.

Although an optometrist may perform the examination, anyone who receives a high reading should be examined by an ophthalmologist. Treatment for glaucoma must be prescribed and administered only by an ophthalmologist.

CATARACTS

The most common condition of the eye associated with growing older is cataracts, a clouding of the lens of the eye. Experts disagree as to the cause: Some say it is a normal part of the aging process for some people; others contend that overexposure to ultraviolet rays from the sun may play a prominent role. Eye injury, X rays, infrared rays, and microwaves can induce the development of cataracts. People with conditions affecting their blood sugar levels (such as diabetes) are also at a higher risk for developing cataracts. Those suffering from a chronic cancer such as leukemia may be at risk for fulminating cataracts.

A cataract is an opacity of the lens of the eye that becomes progressively worse, although at varying rates depending on the individual. As with many diseases thought to be purely a product of aging, cataracts may not necessarily result from aging per se, but from a pathological process related to another disorder. As the fibers comprising the lens become less elastic, they may also become discolored. Normally the lens is completely clear, but in a cataract the fibers may turn yellow, blocking out light and blurring vision.

The cataract may start as a small spot on the lens and then may grow until the whole lens is obscured. Left untreated, cataracts lead to blindness. This deterioration of sight may progress at varying rates in different individuals.

The usual treatment is the surgical removal of the clouded lens. Eyedrops to open (dilate) the pupil may improve vision somewhat if surgery must be delayed, but the drops will not solve the problem. Diet and exercise can do nothing to improve the condition. There is evidence that wearing sunglasses that block out ultraviolet rays may decrease the risk of developing cataracts later, but once the clouding process begins, only surgery will cure it.

It is not necessary to wait until the cataract is "ripe" to do surgery; as soon as impaired vision interferes with daily activities and the quality of life, the cataract should be removed.

The operation may be done under general or local anesthesia. Local anesthesia is preferred by some doctors because it enables surgery to be performed on even elderly patients. There are several different procedures for the operation. Your doctor should discuss with you the method that is best suited to your needs. This will depend on the location and severity of the cataract and the presence of other health problems. If both eyes are affected, the more severe cataract will be removed first, followed by a second operation to remove the other one once the first has healed.

After the lens is removed, a replacement is necessary in order for the patient to focus clearly. Plastic intraocular lens implants, inserted at the time of surgery, serve as "new" lenses. These implants are the most frequently used form of visual correction. In some cases, however, eyeglasses or contact lenses may also be necessary to provide the most accurate vision following cataract surgery. The patient may be fitted for contact lenses once healing is complete several weeks after surgery. Occasionally, the lens capsule will become opaque after the cataract is removed. A second procedure with laser surgery will correct this condition.

Overall, the outlook today for cataract patients is quite positive. At least 95 percent of patients undergoing surgery will have their vision improved as a result. The surgery is very safe and can involve a short hospital stay but may even be done on an outpatient basis. Ignorance and an irrational fear of surgery are the only obstacles to improved vision for most cataract sufferers. However, general anesthesia always involves some risk and should not be undergone unless failing eyesight has adversely affected the quality of life.

MACULAR DEGENERATION

An estimated 3,000 Americans become legally blind each year due to deterioration of the macula, a portion of the retina.

Because of the large number of rods and cones (light and color receptors) in the macula, it is the part of the retina responsible for the perception of fine details and the central field of vision. The most common cause of macular degeneration is a reduced flow of the blood that nourishes the eyes, which leads to separation of the area from the back of the eyeball. It may occur in one eye or in both eyes simultaneously.

If detected early enough, the degeneration may be repaired or arrested by laser surgery that seals the retina and reattaches it to the back of the eyeball. Surgery has the best chance for success if performed immediately after the deterioration process has begun—before symptoms become obvious to most patients.

Since immediate action is so crucial, a daily self-test is recommended for people over 50 and for those at high risk for the condition. With one eye at a time, focus on a straight line. If the line appears wavy or broken, macular damage may be indicated. See your eye doctor for a complete examination.

If degeneration is not arrested by immediate surgery, complete loss of the central field of vision may occur. Fortunately, since peripheral vision is retained, most patients are able to care for themselves. Many people learn Braille after age 65 to retain the ability to read. Special devices are being perfected that enable those with peripheral vision to read normally.

DIABETIC RETINOPATHY

Retinopathy refers to the degeneration of the retina, usually in association with poorly controlled Type 1 diabetes. Diabetes may lead to changes in the blood vessels of the retina, causing them to weaken and burst. New blood vessels also form on the retina, interfering with the transmission of light coming through the vitreous humor. These blood vessels are likely to hemorrhage and cause "spots" in the eyes. Also, without sufficient nourishment from the blood, the retina begins to detach from the back of the eyeball. If the degeneration is detected early enough, laser surgery may be used to reattach part of the retina. Patients with diabetes should therefore have their eyes examined frequently and report any vision problems immediately to an ophthalmologist (see chapter 14).

HEARING

NORMAL HEARING CHANGES THAT COME WITH AGE

Normal hearing is a complex process of chain reactions. Sound starts as a vibration—a door slamming or hands clapping. The vibration causes a disturbance of the air molecules, making them disperse in a wavelike pattern. These sound waves enter the external ear, which is specially designed to funnel and concentrate the sound waves as they enter the ear canal. When they strike the tympanic membrane, or eardrum, the membrane vibrates, setting in motion the tiny bones called ossicles—the malleus (hammer), incus (anvil), and stapes (stirrup)—within the middle ear. This process further modifies the sound so that the inner ear will perceive it more clearly. From the stapes the sound is transferred to the cochlea, a fluid-containing structure shaped like a snail's shell. Tiny hair cells inside the layers of the cochlea are set in motion by vibrations transmitted through the fluid. Hair-cell vibrations are then converted into electric nerve impulses that are conducted to the brain via the eighth (auditory) nerve (see Figure 17.3).

As we grow older, these tiny hair cells begin to deteriorate, probably because of lifelong exposure to noise, and do not conduct the sound messages as efficiently. Because such hearing loss is due to the deterioration of these hair cells and not of the structures that conduct the vibrations, it is referred to as a sensorineural (perceptive) hearing loss. This condition, sometimes call presbycusis (from the Greek word meaning

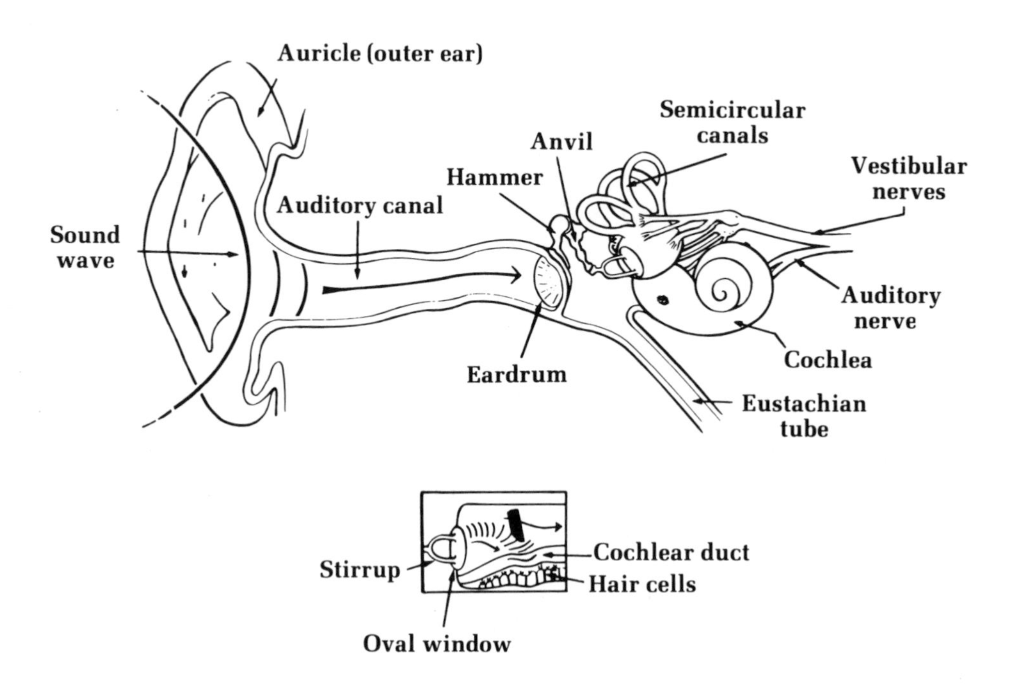

Figure 17.3 Structures of the Ear

"old hearing"), affects most people over 65 to some degree. The process of degeneration may start as early as one's middle thirties, but usually does not become noticeable until the mid-sixties. For reasons not known, men are more commonly affected than women, perhaps because men may have jobs that expose them to higher noise levels. Since women are now more likely to be employed in positions once thought of as exclusively male, we may come to see an upsurge in hearing loss in women over 65.

The first sounds to be affected by presbycusis are most commonly the higher frequencies. The frequency is determined by the rate of vibration; the quicker the vibrations, the higher the sound. In the cochlea, the hair cells that perceive sound are divided into three categories: those that perceive low-frequency sounds (located in the top region of the structure), those that perceive middle-frequency sounds (located in the center of the cochlea), and those that perceive high-frequency sounds (located at the base of the cochlea). The cilia at the base of the structure are usually the first to deteriorate to the point that sounds are not perceived correctly, and erroneous or incomplete messages are sent to the brain. As a result the person cannot correctly interpret the sound message.

Because the human voice falls within the range most often affected by presbycusis, hearing loss may take a serious emotional toll on people when socializing becomes more difficult and frustrating. The inclination to avoid such occasions and isolate oneself may be hard to resist.

Although older people are more likely to be affected by this sensorineural hearing loss, conductive problems may occur as well. The ossicles, like other bones, may become stiff and less responsive to the vibrations of the eardrum. The eardrum itself may become thicker and less flexible. A hereditary condition call otosclerosis, in which one of the ossicles, the stapes (stirrup), becomes fixed by an overgrowth of the bone, is most common in older people. This condition is usually correctable by surgery in which the overgrown stapes is removed and replaced with a metal prosthesis.

Some experts now believe that some of the hearing loss experienced by older adults may be the result of circulatory problems such as heart disease, high blood pressure, or diabetes, which diminish the supply of blood to the region. An acute infection can cause hearing loss. Certain medications such as some antibiotics, antihypertensive drugs, and large doses of aspirin are also associated with hearing loss, loss of balance, and ringing in the ears. Prolonged exposure to noise may also hasten deterioration of the hair cells in the inner ear. In some parts of the world—for example, in the African Sudan, where noise and stress levels are minimal and high blood pressure, heart disease, ulcers, and asthma are almost nonexistent—the people do not suffer from hearing loss in old age. Although definite conclusions cannot yet be drawn from this information, it seems apparent that hearing loss is not inevitable for all people and that our noisy, stressful, industrialized society predisposes us to the condition. As noise becomes more prevalent in an automated, machine-oriented world, and as more people live past 65, adult hearing loss is bound to become more of a problem.

TREATMENT OF ADULT HEARING LOSS

It is important to determine the underlying cause of hearing loss before seeking treatment. Despite all of the pathological effects that cause hearing loss, the most common reason for it is the simple accumulation of earwax. Simple, over-the-counter softening agents may be purchased to assist in removal of excess wax. If the accumulation is at all difficult to remove, see a physician for professional cleaning.

Some conditions that cause hearing loss, such as otosclerosis, are curable by surgery; others are best handled by use of a hearing aid. Still others may not improve with surgery or the use of hearing aids. People with these conditions will benefit from training in lipreading and other techniques. Before purchasing a hearing aid, therefore, it is essential to have a complete hearing examination to determine the cause and best treatment for the hearing loss.

After age 65 a hearing test should be incorporated into the yearly physical examination. If hearing loss is detected, the doctor should check to be sure that there is no medical reason for it. Ear infection is a common cause of temporary hearing loss, and hearing should return when the condition is eradicated. However, if no medical reason for the hearing loss is detected, or if after a medical condition has been successfully treated the hearing loss continues, the practitioner may make a referral for further testing. This may be done by an otologist (a physician specializing in disorders of the ears), otolaryngologist (a physician specializing in disorders of the ears, nose, and throat), or audiologist (a certified hearing specialist). Tests may include a tympanogram (to detect conductive problems in the eardrum and middle ear), acoustic reflex test (to check reaction to loud noises), audiogram (to measure the ability to hear pure tones and discriminate speech), and audiometry (to determine the ability to hear sounds at various frequencies). In certain cases, X rays and other laboratory tests may be ordered. Based on the results of these tests, recommendations will be made for the best treatment.

COMMUNICATION TIPS FOR OLDER PEOPLE WITH HEARING LOSS

When used effectively, lipreading and speechreading can help make communication with others less difficult. Lip movements, facial expressions, and gestures can all be used as visual clues to follow conversation.

One-on-one or in small groups of people:

- Be sure lighting is adequate.
- Ask people to face you when they speak and to stand about 3 feet away.
- Remind them politely if they continue to talk while looking the other way, speak to you from another room, or speak with their hands in front of their mouths.

Meetings and lectures:

- Get a good seat. (Arrive early, if necessary, so that you have more of a choice.)
- At a lecture or meeting, sit up front where you can best see and hear the main speaker.
- In smaller meetings or discussion groups, sit where you can see the most people clearly without moving your head.
- At a table, sit either at the head or the foot.
- In a living room, sit on a chair instead of a sofa.
- If possible, obtain a copy of the lecture notes or agenda beforehand. (It is easier to follow a discussion when you know what is scheduled.)
- Ask a friend to take notes for you and to let you know when the topic of discussion has changed.
- In small group discussions, ask participants to raise a finger and pause a moment before speaking. This will help you identify each speaker quickly.
- Ask speakers to use blackboards, overhead projectors, microphones, and other audiovisual aids to enhance the presentation.
- Make sure the lighting in the room illuminates the speaker's face.
- Inquire in advance about the availability of special listening devices, such as induction loops, radio-frequency hearing aids, or infrared systems. (You may want to equip a meeting room with these devices: Your audiologist should be able to provide you or your organization with information.)

At the movies, the theater, or a concert:

- Inquire whether there are devices available to amplify sound.

Noisy places:

Since hearing aids amplify background noise as well as speech, it can be difficult to understand what is being said, especially in rooms without carpeting and drapes, where there may be reverberations.

- Remove the source of the noise or move to another room. If this is not possible:
- Suggest continuing the conversation at another time (to persist when you cannot adequately concentrate may lead to misunderstandings).
- If the noise is intermittent, talk during the lulls.

HEARING AIDS

Not all hearing problems can be solved with a hearing aid; different impairments require different types of hearing devices. (People with total hearing loss due to nerve deafness will not be helped by a hearing aid.) Essentially, all hearing aids are designed to do the same thing: amplify sound. It is important to remember that a hearing aid will not restore normal hearing. These devices work best in one-on-one situations; it is difficult to localize sound in a large group of people. As the sound is amplified, it is also distorted. A consultation with an otolaryngologist or audiologist should acquaint you with the devices available and what you can expect from them. Taking some time to get used to the hearing aid will help you better judge whether it is the right solution for you.

The type of hearing aid recommended will depend on the extent of your hearing loss and any special needs. Basically all hearing aids are made up of several elements: a microphone to receive the sound; an amplifier to make it louder; a receiver that transmits the sound into the ear; a volume control to adjust sound level; and a battery, which powers the device. An ear mold is not part of the amplifying mechanism but plays an important role in the comfort and success of a hearing aid. This part should be custom-fitted to the individual ear to hold the aid in place. An improper fit may lead to improper conduction of the sound into the ear canal, whistling or squealing sounds, irritation, and even infection (see Figure 17.4).

The most common hearing aid fits behind the ear and hooks over the top of the ear structure. This model can be worn by people with a wide range of hearing impair-

BEFORE BUYING A HEARING AID

Some otolaryngologists and audiologists also sell hearing aids, eliminating the search for an independent dealer. Wherever you purchase your hearing aid you should:

1. Arrange for a brief orientation with a professional on the use and care of the device so that you will receive maximum benefit from it.
2. Make certain you can return the device within 30 days for a full refund if it does not improve your hearing sufficiently.
3. Find out about service and warranty.
4. Make an appointment for a full hearing examination within the first month to determine if the hearing aid is functioning properly.

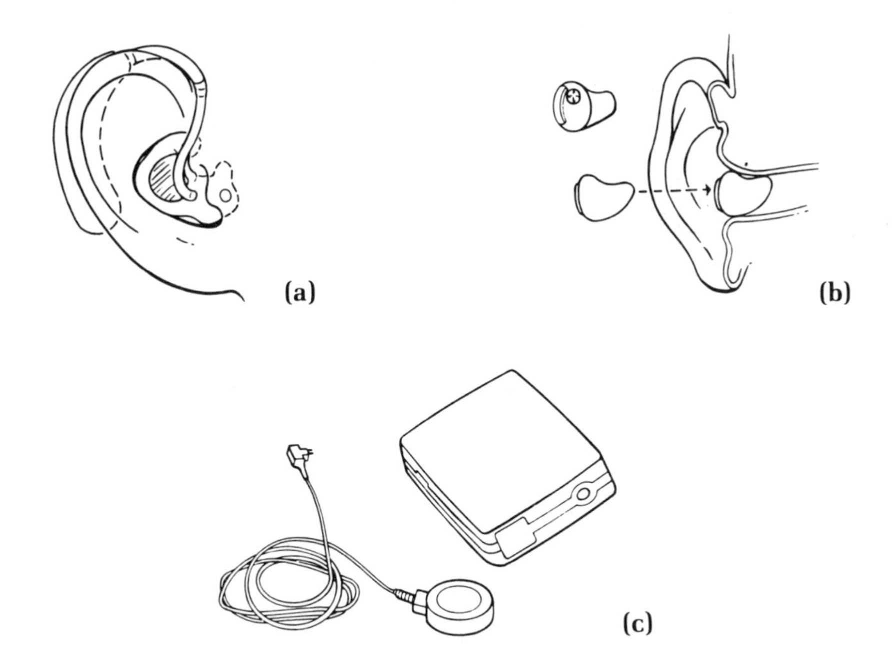

Figure 17.4 Types of Hearing Aids
The behind-the-ear model (a) is the most common hearing aid. The in-the-ear model (b) fits into the ear canal and outer ear. The body aid (c) consists of an ear mold, which is attached by a wire to a larger volume-control unit that fits easily into a pocket.

ment, from mild to severe. A canal aid that is worn completely within the ear canal is the least visible of the hearing devices. It is suitable for mild hearing loss, but those with arthritis or other trouble with their fingers may find that making the necessary, frequent volume adjustments is difficult with the tiny controls. Mild to moderate hearing loss can be improved by the in-the-ear model as well. This type is fitted into the ear canal and outer ear. It too has tiny controls that may present difficulties for those with arthritis.

People who have trouble with the miniaturized hearing aids may find a body aid easier to use. This is a larger model carried in the pocket and attached to the ear mold by a wire. Larger-capacity batteries are used, so it is not necessary to change batteries so often. This type of aid may also benefit people who have trouble with their eyes.

An alternative for patients who also wear eyeglasses is a hearing aid that fits into the eyeglass frame behind the ear and attaches to the ear mold in a way similar to the behind-the-ear model. While this model is not conspicuous, it is suitable only for those who wear eyeglasses at least 80 percent of the time. It is advisable to have an alternative for both the glasses and the hearing aid, so if something happens to one, you will not be deprived of corrected vision and hearing.

Two hearing aid features worth looking into are telecoil circuitry and tone control. When you switch the microphone control to *T*, telecoil circuitry improves the wearer's hearing over the telephone. For hearing-impaired people who hear some frequencies better than others (again, older people usually lose the ability to hear the higher frequencies first), tone control will amplify certain frequencies more than others. In-the-ear, behind-the-ear, and body aids all can be fitted with tone control.

One or both ears may be fitted for a hearing aid. If one ear tests within the normal hearing range, it will not be set up with the aid; the other ear will be fitted. If hearing in both ears is impaired, the aid is usually fitted to the better ear. In either case, this is referred to as a monaural (one ear) fitting. In other cases, a binaural (both ears) fitting is recommended. The advantage of binaural fitting is that the wearer can determine from which direction the sound is coming.

Regardless of which hearing aid you choose, you will have to take care of it to make sure it lasts as long as possible. It is a delicate piece of machinery and should be treated as such.

PROPER CARE OF YOUR HEARING AID

A hearing aid should last approximately five years. With proper care you can increase the device's longevity and decrease maintenance and repair costs. Since exposure to extreme hot or cold can damage a hearing aid, keep these two rules in mind:

- Do not wear it while you are sitting under the hair dryer or for more than a few minutes in very cold weather.
- Do not store it near a source of heat, such as a radiator.

Keep the device dry:

- Avoid wearing it in the rain or when you are perspiring profusely.
- Store it overnight in a plastic bag with silica gel to help absorb moisture inside.
- Remove the aid before using hair spray.

When not in use:

- Turn the hearing aid off, remove it, and take the battery out of the case. (If you do not turn off the aid before removing it, whistling may occur.)

Care of batteries:

- Keep spare batteries with you at all times and store others in a cool, dry place.
- Batteries should be dry and at room temperature when inserted into the aid.
- Do not buy more than a month's supply of batteries at a time.
- Clean the battery compartment and connections with a pencil eraser.

Cleaning:

- Keep the ear mold clear of earwax by cleaning periodically with soapy water.
- Never immerse the mechanical parts of the hearing aid in water.

Replacing materials:

- Replace the tubing on behind-the-ear hearing aids whenever it becomes dry or yellow.
- Replace any broken or cracked wiring on body hearing aids immediately.

OTHER AGE-RELATED EAR PROBLEMS

VERTIGO AND DIZZINESS

Besides its primary role in hearing, the ear also plays a part (along with the eyes, muscles, and brain) in maintaining balance, or equilibrium. Within the inner ear is the labyrinth, containing, among other structures, the fluid-filled semicircular canals and two chambers, the utricle and the saccule, that have hair cells embedded in a jellylike substance. Hair cells and the fluid in the semicircular canals move as the head moves, sending impulses to the brain. The brain correlates this data with information from the eyes and other sensory organs to determine the body's position and what kind of muscular reactions are needed to maintain balance.

Disorders of the inner ear and its labyrinth therefore may lead to vertigo, or extreme dizziness, accompanied by a feeling of movement or spinning and sometimes nausea and vomiting. This is caused by the contradictory information sent to the brain by the inner ear, eyes, and skin.

Although dizziness and vertigo may occur at any age (indeed, most people have had at least one episode of dizziness), older adults seem prone to attacks. Benign positional vertigo, in which a person becomes severely dizzy upon moving the head in a certain way or changing position, may be a side effect of medication, such as some antihypertensive drugs. For the most part, the cause of vertigo is unknown and the attacks subside with time. Subsequent episodes may be prevented or curtailed by antivertigo medications or by simply avoiding the troublesome position.

However, vertigo may be a symptom of an underlying condition, such as earwax accumulation, ear infection, or certain viruses. In these cases, eradication of the underlying problem usually cures the vertigo. In still other cases, a more serious disorder such as hypertension, diabetes, heart disease, anemia, or arteriosclerosis may be causing the symptoms of vertigo. Prolonged use of streptomycin may permanently destroy semicircular canal function and also cause the disorder. Any recurrent attacks of vertigo should be checked by a physician.

MÉNIÈRE'S DISEASE

Ménière's disease, which often appears at around age 50, is characterized by attacks of severe vertigo, accompanied by tinnitus (ringing in the ears), nausea and vomiting, and hearing loss. The duration of the attacks may vary from several minutes to several hours, and the frequency can be as often as once a week or as seldom as once a year, with each attack further impairing hearing.

The disease usually affects only one ear, but it can affect both. It is caused by the accumulation of fluid (endolymph) within the labyrinth of the inner ear. Alternative terms for the disease more accurately describe the disorder: hydrops labyrinthi (hydrops means "accumulation of fluid") or endolymphatic hypertension. For reasons unknown, Ménière's disease affects slightly more women than men.

The symptoms of vertigo, tinnitus, and hearing loss may occur in any order. Tinnitus may precede a full-blown attack by as much as a year. Another accompanying symptom may be *recruitment,* in which the patient becomes hypersensitive to loud noises. Ironically, recruitment often occurs in patients suffering from hearing loss.

There are several different theories concerning the treatment of Ménière's disease. Restrictions on salt, caffeine, and alcohol intake, as well as quitting smoking, do relieve symptoms in some cases. Another recommendation, a strict low-carbohydrate diet, is based on evidence that many Ménière's patients have high blood levels of insulin. Medications may offer symptomatic relief: antivertigo medications to alleviate feelings of spinning, antihistamines to drain the inner ear, and sedatives to calm the patient suffering an attack. Stress seems to play some role in the disorder; attacks often coincide with times of emotional upheaval.

In more severe cases, large doses of antibiotics may be administered to destroy the labyrinth and thereby eliminate the root of the vertigo without affecting hearing. This treatment leaves the patient dependent on the eyes and muscle reflexes for balance, and he or she is therefore unable to establish equilibrium in total darkness.

Surgical treatments include the implantation of small tubes (shunts) into the inner ear to drain the endolymphatic fluid, cutting the vestibular nerve (which relieves vertigo but preserves hearing in most cases), and removal of the labyrinth (which relieves vertigo but also destroys hearing in that ear). This last operation is done only for patients with one ear affected and for whom hearing has already been severely impaired by the disease. All surgical treatment is considered only when other, less drastic measures have failed and attacks continue to be severe and frequent. Unfortunately, in some cases tinnitus may persist even after surgery.

TINNITUS

Tinnitus, or ringing in the ears, is an annoying symptom that may be due to any one of a number of underlying conditions. Excess earwax, ear infections, and overuse of aspirin or some antibiotics are some of the simpler, treatable causes. Ménière's disease (see the previous section), nerve damage from exposure to loud noise, and even neurological disorders may also cause the problem. In many cases, however, no underlying cause can be discerned.

An abnormally open eustachian tube, which connects the middle ear to the mouth, can create a whistling noise in the ear. An aneurysm, or outpouching of a blood vessel, may cause a pulsating sound. In these two conditions, the tinnitus is called "objective," since the sound can be heard by the doctor as well. However, in most cases, the tinnitus is "subjective" and can be heard only by the patient, which contributes to his or her frustration.

There is no treatment for most cases of tinnitus, which may come and go or eventually disappear entirely. Surgery to remove the cochlea or sever the acoustic nerve sacrifices hearing and may not cure the tinnitus. Some simple, practical remedies include playing the radio softly to help block out the annoying ringing, or using tinnitus maskers. Maskers are worn like a hearing aid and continually transmit a more pleasant sound that masks the ringing. Biofeedback has also been used to teach tinnitus sufferers to relax despite the noise.

THE TEETH

Before age 35, dental caries, or cavities, are the primary cause of tooth loss. Fluoridated water supplies, toothpastes, and mouthwashes have led to a significant decrease in the number of cavities, and experts predict that dental caries will soon be a disease of the past. But the outlook may not be as positive as this prediction sounds. Although fluoride reduces the incidence of adult caries, it is of most value for teeth during their development in childhood and adolescence, the so-called cavity-prone years. The number one cause of tooth loss over age 40, periodontal disease, is unaffected by fluoride, and it is still alarmingly prevalent. However, with cavities under control, the dental profession has now concentrated its efforts on the prevention of periodontal disease, the key to keeping your teeth for a lifetime.

PERIODONTAL DISEASE

Periodontal disease is a catchall phrase for several conditions affecting the periodontium, or the structures surrounding the teeth. These structures include the gums (gingivae), the periodontal ligaments, and the alveolar bone around the teeth (see Figure 17.5).

Bacterial plaque is the culprit in all forms of periodontal disease. The most common form is gingivitis, or inflammation of the gums. Three-quarters of Americans will suffer from gingivitis at some time in their adult lives. In this condition, bacterial plaque along the gum line infects the tissue. To fight the infection, blood flow to the area is increased, producing the characteristic red and swollen gums that bleed with the slightest pressure, such as toothbrushing. Gingivitis, however, often does not cause pain and may be left untreated as a result, allowing it to progress to periodontitis.

In periodontitis, the plaque builds up in deposits just above and below the gumline, creating a "pocket" between the tooth and the gum. Inflammation of the gum in this area causes the pocket to expand, allowing it to accommodate an even greater amount of the harmful plaque. The inflammation also breaks down the periodontal ligaments and adjacent bone. Pus may collect in the pockets and ooze out (hence the

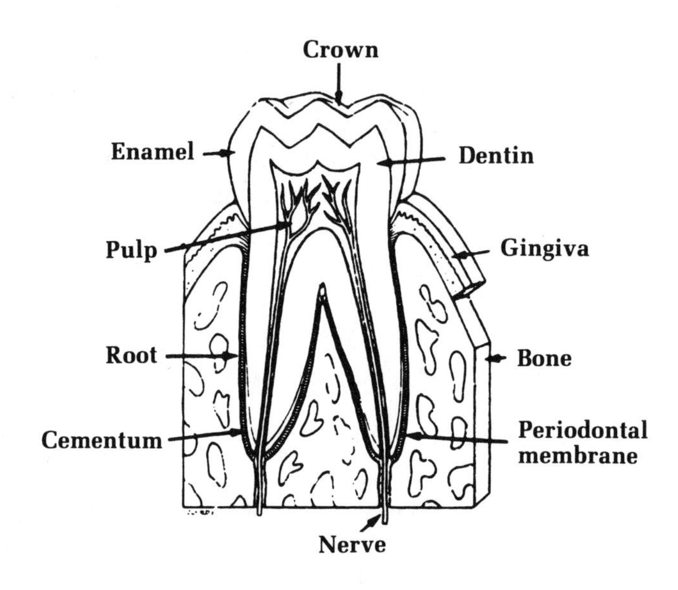

Figure 17.5 Structures of the Teeth

former name for the condition, pyorrhea, which means "flow of pus"). Even at this destructive stage, which often leads to tooth loss, periodontitis causes little if any pain.

It is estimated that 90 percent of American adults have some form of periodontal disease. Some systemic conditions, such as diabetes, parathyroid disorders, and some blood diseases, are associated with increased risk of periodontal disease. Smoking or chewing tobacco promotes gum disease. Certain medications, such as the anticonvulsant phenytoin (Dilantin), also adversely affect the gums. Deficiencies of vitamin C and perhaps folic acid may also lead to or exacerbate periodontal disease.

There also seems to be a genetic predisposition to periodontal disease. But anyone, regardless of age or coexisting condition, who has his or her natural teeth is a candidate. The disease does increase significantly with age, however, both in frequency and severity. This is not due to the aging process itself, but rather to the cumulative effects of years of poor dental hygiene—improper brushing and flossing along with a lack of professional cleaning. Fully 60 percent of people over age 45 suffer from the most severe form of periodontal disease, periodontitis, and 65 percent of those over age 65 will lose one or more teeth as a result of the disease.

Although these statistics suggest that the odds are against saving your teeth, periodontal disease and tooth loss are totally preventable.

PREVENTION AND TREATMENT

Diligent home care and regular visits to the dentist can prevent—even reverse—periodontal disease and save your teeth. Dental care professionals differ on how often one should brush and floss, but a general recommendation would be to brush within one half hour of eating and to floss once or twice a day. (Ask your dentist or hygienist for advice based on your particular condition.) Many dentists also recommend gum massage by means of an irrigating instrument (such as a WaterPik), specially designed toothpicks, or the rubber tip on some toothbrushes. A toothbrush such as the Interplak, which has electrical moving tufts, is recommended by some dentists for easier plaque removal. (Check with your dentist first before buying this dental aid. It's expensive, and it may not be suitable for your particular dental problems.) Although there are mouthwashes that are approved by both the American Dental Association and the Food and Drug Administration as adjunctive aids in the prevention of plaque buildup, there is no good long-term study to indicate the effectiveness of these plaque-fighting products.

Even with diligent home care, plaque will accumulate on the teeth. Some of this may calcify and adhere to the surface of the tooth at the gum line. The only way to remove such plaque, called tartar or calculus, is by professional cleaning. The dentist or hygienist may use a sharp, scraping instrument or an ultrasonic device to scale away the hardened material. (Toothpastes advertised as tartar-fighting have added abrasives that may prevent buildup of hardened plaque. Ask your dentist before switching, and be sure the brand you choose has fluoride.)

In most cases of periodontal disease, personal home care has been inefficient and professional dental care neglected. People who put off a visit to the dentist's office to avoid expense and pain will find they have done neither. Treatment of advanced periodontitis is considerably more expensive and can be more painful than regular visits for preventive cleaning.

The early stages of periodontal disease are treated by removing plaque and infected tissue from around the teeth and within the "pockets." When this material is removed, the gum can begin to reattach itself to the tooth. Regular personal care and repeated visits to the dentist will keep the plaque from building up again and causing a recurrence.

More advanced cases may require a minor surgical procedure. Gingivectomy involves removing the gum tissue that has been separated from the tooth. Gingivoplasty gives the tissue a new shape that not only improves the appearance of the gums but also helps make them less receptive to subsequent buildup of plaque. If the bone has broken down and eroded, it may have to be reshaped in what is called a flap procedure. In this operation, the gum line is pulled back from the teeth and bone, deceased tissue and calculus (hardened plaque) are removed, the bone is reshaped, and the gum is replaced in its proper position. In some cases, bone grafts are inserted to replace lost bone. All of these procedures are usually done under local anesthesia. After some periodontal surgery, the wound will be packed with a medicated dressing for one to three weeks to promote healing.

OTHER DENTAL CONDITIONS AND THERAPIES

DENTAL CARIES

Being over 40 does not exempt you from the fight against cavities. While older people are less likely to develop caries on the biting surfaces of teeth, the gums are likely to have receded, so such people are more susceptible to root caries. The newly exposed tooth surface does not have the protective enamel coating but rather is covered by softer cementum, which is easily broken down by bacteria. Therefore, regular brushing with fluoride toothpaste continues to be important throughout life. Rinsing with a fluoride mouthwash will also help preserve the strength of older teeth. But fluoride alone won't prevent cavities; diet can also help you save your teeth from decay.

Tooth decay is caused by the interaction of bacteria and sugar. Bacteria collect on the teeth in the form of plaque, the sticky, translucent substance that adheres to teeth. Dental work, such as crowns and fillings, indentations in tooth surfaces (pits and fissures), and the roots of teeth exposed by receding gums are particularly susceptible to plaque buildup. The source of energy for the bacteria is sugar. In the metabolization of sugar, the bacteria release acids capable of breaking down the surface of teeth. Although any kind of sugar or starch can fuel these bacteria, sucrose (such as refined white sugar) causes by far the greatest damage in the least amount of time. In fact, most of the damage is done within the first 20 minutes of eating.

Limiting sugar intake is an important first step in preventing tooth decay. But the amount of sugar may not be as important as when it is eaten and in what form. Sugar consumed as part of a complete meal or with a sufficient amount of liquid to wash out the mouth causes considerably less damage than do sweets eaten between meals. Sticky foods, such as caramels, dried fruits, and honey, are particularly detrimental because they adhere to the teeth. Replacing these "cariogenic" foods with noncariogenic or anticavity snacks will discourage tooth decay.

Certain vitamins and minerals may also help prevent tooth decay: Adequate vitamin C may help keep gums healthy and tightly fitted around the teeth; calcium may strengthen teeth; fibrous foods may help prevent caries by stimulating saliva that rinses the teeth. Calling the apple "nature's toothbrush" is not so off-the-mark after all.

The type of cavity that most often affects people over 40 can be considerably more painful than cavities affecting children. Pain and increased sensitivity to cold or to sweets are indications that you may have a root cavity and that you should visit your dentist. In order to halt cavity development in its early stages—before pain occurs—see your dentist for a regular checkup.

In most cases, treatment of dental caries involves drilling to remove the decayed portion of the tooth, then filling the resultant indentation, usually with silver amalgam in back teeth. Front teeth are filled with gold foil, or sometimes a plastic composite material that can be matched to the tooth. A tooth-colored resin filling to conceal the silver amalgam can be used for cosmetic purposes. Also, research continues on a new method of removing decay with a chemical that does not harm healthy tooth structures. If found effective, it could possibly replace a large percentage of the drilling with a painless removal of decay.

ROOT CANAL THERAPY

If tooth decay has progressed to the point where the pulp has been infected, root canal therapy may save the tooth. The pulp of the tooth contains the nerves and blood vessels and is the only living portion of the tooth structure. However, removal of the pulp does not render the tooth useless, since it gains the bulk of its nourishment from the root covering. As long as the tooth remains firmly attached to the jawbone, it will remain viable and valuable, able to chew and even to support bridgework. The object of root canal therapy, then, is to remove the infected pulp and save the tooth. The alternative is generally extraction and replacement with a denture.

In root canal therapy (also called endodontia), a hole is drilled in the tooth through which the pulp is removed. With delicate instruments, the inside of the tooth is then reamed and filed to make certain that all infected material is extracted. This also makes the root canal easier to fill. X rays are used to determine the size of the canal and

SNACK FOODS AND YOUR TEETH

Snack foods that we eat on the run, often without something to drink and without brushing afterward, generally do more damage to teeth than what we eat at meals. The following is a list of snacks to be avoided or discouraged between meals.

Cariogenic foods

In general, sticky, sugary foods are most detrimental to your teeth and should be eaten only *with* meals. Promptly brush or rinse teeth afterward. Between-meal consumption of some fruits, especially oranges, pineapples, and peaches, which are high in natural sugars, should be limited. Because acidic foods hasten the detrimental effects of sugar, avoid certain combinations, such as lemon and sugar. Examples of foods to avoid between meals are:

Candy bars
Caramels
Chewy granola bars
Dried fruits
Raisins

Noncariogenic foods

These foods are not associated with increased cavities and are recommended as snack foods, unless your diet precludes them:

Bean dips
Eggs
Meats
Milk
Nuts
Popcorn
Raw vegetables
Sugarless products

Anticavity snacks

Foods that help prevent cavities include:

Apples
Cheddar cheese (neutralizes acid)
Homemade bran muffins (fiber encourages the flow of saliva to rinse the mouth)
Sugarless soda (contains phosphates)

whether it has been adequately cleaned. Then, over a series of office visits, the canal is irrigated, dried, and sealed several times. When the tooth has been fully prepared, it is filled permanently with a sterilized material, such as gutta-percha cement. The tooth must be perfectly filled and sealed to prevent future infection.

Local anesthesia is usually adequate for all steps of root canal therapy, but occasionally general anesthesia will be used. Recent advances have made root canal therapy easier, safer, and more effective than ever before. New materials used for fillings will not cause the permanent discoloration that was earlier associated with the procedure. The tooth may darken slightly, but this is easily treatable by having the dentist bleach the tooth.

CROWNS (CAPS OR JACKETS)

In cases in which a tooth has been severely decayed or weakened by being filled for cavities too often, an artificial crown covering may be necessary. The tooth is prepared for the crown by removal of the enamel and some of the dentin. An impression is taken of the remaining structure and the surrounding teeth, and a cap is made to fit over it. For front teeth, a mixture of gold and porcelain or plastic may be used so that the cap will not be noticeable. In back teeth, the gold cap will provide a stronger biting surface.

Temporary caps are fitted onto the tooth or teeth while the patient waits for the permanent caps to be made. These do not fit as tightly but are comfortable and cosmetically acceptable for the short term. Medications may be incorporated into the temporary caps to help the teeth stay clean and healthy until the permanent caps are ready to be cemented on. These temporary caps can come off, so care is needed to avoid hard or sticky foods, such as caramels.

DENTURES

Even though tooth loss is preventable in most cases, chances are good that one or more of your teeth will need to be replaced at some point. Over half of dental patients over age 50 have at least one replacement tooth.

A missing tooth, lost due to periodontal disease, accident, or extensive decay, leaves a gap in your mouth, causing the surrounding teeth to gradually move into the gap. This may lead to bite problems, increased periodontal disease, dental caries, and greater risk of losing more teeth. Therefore, it is imperative to have any missing tooth replaced, even if it is not noticeable to others.

A broken tooth in which the root is still intact may be replaced with a pivot crown. In this procedure, the broken crown is filed down and the pulp chamber is hollowed out using techniques common to root canal therapy. The chamber is then filled with a post that sticks above the gum line and provides the anchor for a gold crown. A pivot crown that is replacing a visible tooth may be covered with porcelain or plastic.

In cases in which the root cannot be preserved, a bridge, or partial denture, is constructed to replace the tooth or teeth. A bridge can be either permanent (fixed) or removable. There are advantages and disadvantages to each type. Your dentist will discuss with you which type is best suited to your teeth and to your life-style.

Fixed Bridges. If a small space—only one or two teeth—must be filled, a fixed bridge may be recommended. In preparation for the bridge, surrounding teeth are shaved down in order to accommodate permanent artificial crowns. To these gold or stainless steel crowns, plastic or porcelain replacement teeth will be bonded, and the complete structure will be cemented to the teeth.

Fixed bridgework offers the advantage of convenience and a natural look and feel. The replacement teeth look and function just like your own, but at least one healthy tooth must be on each side to support the stress on the replacement teeth. Because fitting a fixed bridge requires precision work, it is usually considerably more expensive than a removable bridge. Repair of a fixed bridge can also be extremely expensive. If an additional tooth must be replaced, it cannot be added to the existing bridge.

Removable Bridges. For this type of partial denture, replacement teeth are attached to a metal framework designed to snap into place by means of clasps around remaining teeth. The bridges can be designed so that the metalwork is barely visible, even when smiling or laughing.

Removable bridges are generally less expensive and involve less intricate procedures (such as the capping of teeth) than do fixed ones, but they may not be as comfortable and durable. Surrounding teeth may be loosened by the constant wear and tear of supporting the bridge, though any additional lost teeth may be added to the bridge. Repair and replacement are easier and less expensive than with the fixed bridge.

Both removable and fixed bridges require special care. Food can easily lodge in the dental work, so it is important to clean the bridge carefully soon after eating. If it is not possible to brush after meals, then rinse thoroughly with plain water. Removable bridges should be taken out and thoroughly brushed at least once a day. Since food and plaque can collect under a fixed bridge as gums recede in the area, it may be necessary to floss underneath the bridge. Your dentist should inform you of any special cleaning methods your dental work requires.

Full Dentures. Saving the natural teeth, although it is sometimes more expensive, should be a dentist's first objective. However, if remaining teeth cannot be strengthened to support partial dentures, extraction and full dentures may be the only alternative. Being fitted with full dentures takes emotional as well as physical adjustment. Developments in prosthodontics have made obsolete the common associations between dentures and a loss of attractiveness or an inability to eat favorite foods.

Originally teeth were extracted and dental impressions taken for the dentures. While gums healed, the dentures were made, and for a period of weeks the patient had no teeth, natural or artificial. Without the support structure of the teeth, the facial skin could sag, creating a sunken look. All this is avoided now that dental impressions may be routinely taken *before* extraction. The dentures are made and can be inserted immediately after the extractions. In cases where a patient is unable to tolerate the extraction of all teeth at one time, back teeth are taken out first. The gums are then allowed to heal before the front teeth are extracted and the dentures immediately inserted.

The immediate insertion of dentures not only eliminates a toothless waiting period, with all its inconveniences, but also speeds recovery of the gums and allows for easier speech and eating. But since gums tend to recede after extraction, immediate insertion of dentures may necessitate more adjustments before the dentures fit perfectly.

The base of the denture is made of pink acrylic, and plastic or porcelain artificial teeth are placed on that base. The prosthodontist can give the teeth any shape and color you like—"perfect" or "imperfect," with built-in defects and discolorations. The first few weeks will require certain adjustments and allowances, and during this time, you will need to establish a routine for taking care of your dentures.

DENTAL IMPLANTS

Previously reserved for cases in which removable dentures were impossible or impractical, implants are now making permanent artificial teeth a reality for more patients.

There are two types of dental implants: In the first method, the endosteal method, the new teeth are fastened by means of thin metal blades placed directly into the jawbone. The blades have small slits through which the bone grows, forming a firm and permanent anchor for the teeth. This method may be used to replace one or all teeth, but the jawbone must be strong and healthy to accept and support implants.

For denture wearers whose jawbones have atrophied or shrunk (a common occurrence in long-time wearers of removable dentures), the subperiosteal method is used. A metal framework with posts is constructed from impressions of the jawbone or from images obtained through a computerized tomography (CT) scan. That framework is implanted within the patient's gums, and the new teeth are snapped onto posts. Both techniques of implanting permanent false teeth involve minor surgery under local anesthesia.

Implants are not for everyone. They demand a greater initial investment of time and money, and the patient must be in good health. But for many people, implants offer a whole host of advantages: Since they fit better and do not cause a change in jaw structure, they are likely to remain comfortable longer and may not need to be replaced as often. Also, because the teeth are fastened firmly to the jawbone, patients are able to eat a greater variety of foods.

ADJUSTING TO DENTURES

Because dentures play a major role in eating, talking, and supporting facial structures, they must be comfortable. Only time spent wearing them and, if necessary, minor adjustments by the dentist can achieve that comfort, but there are some tips that may make the adjustment process easier:

1. You can't expect perfect comfort right away, but don't put up with unnecessary pain. Occasionally, projecting bone or tooth chips will cause tender spots that your dentist can easily alleviate by shaving or removing.
2. New dentures should be worn 24 hours a day for two to three weeks, then removed, soaked, and cleaned for at least six hours every day (overnight is best). Scrub them thoroughly with a denture brush and denture powder or paste.
3. Practice talking by reading aloud: Your facial muscles need time to adjust to the new shape of your teeth and to hold your dentures in place. The upper denture has a greater area of contact (the roof of the mouth) for suction, but the lower denture may be somewhat slippery until your cheek and lip muscles learn how to keep it in place.
4. Eat soft foods until you get used to the way dentures feel and work. (You should eventually be able to eat most of your favorite foods.) To prevent dentures from slipping and rocking, divide food evenly on each side of your mouth. Chew slowly and evenly.
5. A poor fit can cause many problems, including mouth sores that have been associated with the development of cancer. Instead of using commercially available adhesives, see your dentist regularly for any minor adjustments necessary to maintain a comfortable, individual fit.

The significant improvement in the success rate of implants can be attributed to the use of better materials and improved surgical techniques. However, the five-year failure rate still may be as high as 25 percent overall. If you cannot tolerate the possibility that your implant may have to be replaced, you might want to choose a more time-proven option.

Part IV

Health Resources for Older People

18

The Health-care System and How to Use It

Finding your way through the maze of health-care options in the United States has become increasingly difficult. Should you choose a private doctor or a health maintenance organization (HMO)? How does a recuperating patient manage at home? What happens in the event of illness while traveling? Despite federal health insurance the elderly are now spending a larger percentage of their incomes on health care than before the inception of Medicare. As people age, the increasing frequency of chronic illness and/or disability often coupled with a fixed or decreasing income make it vital to understand how to use our intricate health-care system to meet basic as well as special needs.

CHOOSING A DOCTOR

Many people do not have a regular physician and seek care only when they are sick. This is unwise and causes a lack of continuity in care, the potential for missed diagnoses, and development of conditions that might otherwise be prevented through measures taken after regular screenings. Everyone over 65—and people of any age suffering from chronic diseases such as diabetes and hypertension—should have periodic physical examinations every one or two years, depending upon individual health. Those on medications requiring periodic blood tests to monitor drug levels may need more frequent visits. Health care for the elderly is often more complex than that for the young or middle-aged. Many bodily systems may be affected by a single ailment. For example, a diabetic patient may have high blood pressure and cataracts; a woman may have recently become a widow, feels depressed, and is not eating enough to ward off nutritional deficiencies and dehydration.

Symptoms of disease may be different in the elderly—appendicitis without pain, pneumonia without fever, or a heart attack without chest pains. The decreased efficiency of the liver and kidneys, which break down and excrete most drugs, may dictate lower doses of medications for older individuals.

These specialized needs and the discovery that symptoms once considered to be a part of "growing old" are really symptoms of treatable disease make it important to choose a physician who will pay attention to significant quality-of-life complaints. The doctor should help the individual to function as independently as possible. Competence and interest in your comfort may be even more important than having a highly qualified specialist. To find a doctor, inquire at the nearest teaching hospital, your state's Department of Aging, or your local county medical society. To find a family practitioner or internist for your general medical needs, contact these sources as well as departments of family medicine or internal medicine at a medical center. Word-of-mouth recommendations may be helpful in evaluating how a physician responds personally to the patient. The following guidelines can help you select a physician:

- **Accessibility.** The physician should be conveniently located, have regular office hours, and be available for brief telephone consultations. If you are homebound, pick a doctor who will make house calls.
- **Management of care.** The physician should coordinate care given by any required specialists and be aware of medications prescribed by other doctors.
- **Awareness and empathy.** All reasonable complaints should be listened to and investigated—never tossed off with, "What do you expect? You're getting old." The physician should not hesitate, simply because of a person's age, to suggest surgery when it is appropriate and when it will improve the quality of life. Joint replacement for severe arthritis and cataract surgery may be appropriate even for patients in their seventies and eighties if their overall health is good.
- **Openness to nondrug interventions.** Be wary of any physician whose automatic reaction to a complaint is to write a prescription. Weight loss, stress reduction, and exercise may alleviate problems such as hypertension, either eliminating or reducing the need for medication. A physician should be willing to give these methods a fair trial.
- **Thoroughness.** The physician should devote time to taking a complete medical history and performing a complete physical exam at regular intervals. The purposes, possible side effects, and other important information regarding prescribed medications should be explained by either the physician or nurse. He or she should give you sufficient opportunity to ask

questions regarding your treatment and be sensitive to your emotional and physical well-being. One researcher estimates that as many as a quarter of all elderly suffer from treatable depression.

- **Second opinions.** The doctor should be quick to respond to requests for a second opinion and not take offense at this important patient right.
- **Contingency plans.** The physician should have an associate who handles care during vacations and in the event of illness, retirement, or death.
- **Costs.** You should have a clear understanding of all costs involved in your care before they are incurred. Ask your doctor what a recommended test is expected to reveal and whether the result would affect treatment. Sometimes less-expensive yet equally effective alternatives are available—e.g., generic rather than brand-name medications. Ask your doctor what expenses are covered by your insurance.
- **Hospital affiliation.** The physician should have admitting privileges at an accredited hospital, preferably one affiliated with a medical school. If you will need major surgery, the hospital staff should have sufficient experience in performing the particular kind of operation. (See later section, "Choosing a Hospital.")
- **Concern with prevention.** Does the physician talk about your getting regular flu shots and other immunizations? Do you have time to talk about diet and drinking habits?

The above list is not all-inclusive. The most important thing to remember is that you are paying the physician and he or she is working for you. If the doctor doesn't meet these minimum requirements or is difficult to communicate with, you should change doctors. You have the right to have all your past records forwarded to the new physician. If you can do it comfortably, tell your physician why you are leaving.

HEALTH-CARE ALTERNATIVES

Until recently, most people went to a primary doctor who handled basic medical problems and who made referrals to a specialist as needed. Today, in response to pressures to cut medical costs, other options are available, such as physician partnerships and group practices. These arrangements offer lower costs to the health-care consumer while maintaining a fairly high degree of personal attention. These multi-doctor groups share office space and equipment and may practice single or diverse specialties.

Health maintenance organizations, or HMOs, offer a broad range of medical services to subscribers who prepay a set amount, whether or not they use the services provided. Part of the philosophy underlying the HMO concept is that people will make use of preventive services and avert costly treatment of illnesses that develop when periodic health screening is not available. HMOs offer lower costs in part because of outpatient rather than in-hospital testing, and because of shorter periods of hospitalization. However, the structure of some HMOs makes it difficult for patients to be seen by their own doctors in a timely fashion. Therefore, patients considering this form of health care must be able to assert their needs; it may not be appropriate for patients who tend to be passive or reluctant to fight for their rights.

In selecting an HMO, keep in mind the two types of plans: (1) prepaid group practices (PGPs), where patients may see a different doctor for nonscheduled visits; and (2) individual, or independent, practice associations (IPAs), where subscribers see the same private physician in his or her own office. For more information, contact the Office of Health Maintenance Organizations, 7799 Leesburg Pike, Suite 1100 South, Falls Church, VA 22043, or call (703) 903-7100.

Another alternative available to those affiliated with a participating employer, union, or insurance company is the preferred provider organization, or PPO. Private physicians belonging to a PPO agree to provide extremely low cost care—sometimes $5 to $10 per visit—to covered individuals. Your regular doctor may belong to a PPO or you may select one from a list of member physicians.

Nurse practitioners and physician's assistants working in association with supervising physicians can perform physical examinations, monitor chronic diseases such as diabetes and hypertension, administer routine treatments, and provide health counseling—usually at a cost lower than what a physician charges. These specially trained nurses and assistants usually have master's degrees and advanced clinical training, and work in hospitals, ambulatory care clinics, and medically underserved areas.

An increasing amount of surgery is being done on an outpatient basis in ambulatory-care surgical centers. These facilities may be freestanding or part of a hospital and offer safe, low-cost care for selected patients. Outpatient procedures now include cataract removals, uncomplicated hernia repairs, and some biopsies. Insurance coverage for ambulatory surgery varies with the procedure and type of facility. For a list of approved centers, contact the Accreditation Association for Ambulatory Health Care, Inc., 9933 Lawler Avenue, Skokie, IL 60077, or call (708) 676-9610.

A growing category among medical groups is the freestanding emergency care center, which offers care to those living at a distance from a hospital, as well as to individuals accustomed to using a hospital emergency room for minor medical needs. These centers offer a range of care, from the treatment of upper respiratory infections and cuts requiring stitches, to stabilizing a patient who has chest pains or other heart attack symptoms until he or she reaches the hospital. The centers usually have evening and weekend hours and are less expensive than an emergency room, but more costly than a typical doctor's office visit. It is advisable to check the credentials of a center's physicians and their hospital affiliations.

AVOIDING MEDICAL QUACKERY

The increase in chronic illnesses such as arthritis and certain forms of cancer for which there are no easy cures has led many older individuals to seek out practitioners who promise miracles. Here are some tips on how to spot medical quackery:

1. Watch out for phony "medical" degrees, such as Ms.D. (doctor of metaphysics) or D.N. (doctor of naturopathy). If you are in doubt as to a professional's credentials, check with your local county medical society or look up the name in the *American Medical Association Directory* or the *Directory of Medical Specialists,* both available at public libraries.
2. Beware of anyone who advocates one type of treatment for all types of cancer. Scientists now believe that cancer includes as many as a hundred different diseases, with different therapies effective for different forms.
3. If a practitioner recommends a new treatment, ask to see recent supporting evidence in medical literature of its safety and effectiveness. Some treatments that may have initially been promising are later disproved with additional research. Anecdotal accounts from persons who were "cured" of a disease are no substitute for hard scientific data.
4. Suspect any practitioner who ridicules the traditional medical establishment or says that he or she is being persecuted by other doctors.
5. Be suspicious of any treatment that is available only in a foreign country, because policies on drugs and acceptable medical practices may not be as strict there as in the United States.

CHOOSING A HOSPITAL

When choosing a doctor you should check his or her hospital affiliation, especially if your health status requires periodic hospitalization.

In this cost-conscious era, people facing hospitalization should know their rights. For example, Medicare now reimburses hospitals a flat amount per patient, depending on the diagnosis. This often allows the hospital to save money by discharging patients earlier than they would have been in the past. If you think that you are being discharged too early, you have the right to complain to the administrator on call and to take legal recourse if necessary. Do not be frightened into accepting early discharge because of some threat that you will have to pay. You do *not* have to pay unless discharge is truly medically indicated.

Patients should volunteer information that will help the hospital staff in discharge planning. For example, if you are being admitted for a cardiac problem and will have to climb three flights of stairs to your residence upon discharge, tell this to the appropriate staff person. A patient may not be discharged from a hospital if a discharge plan has not been made and presented to the patient and/or a responsible family member.

People should always carry proof of health insurance. A hospital may refuse to admit any nonemergency patient who cannot show such proof. Frail individuals who are hospitalized may benefit if an assertive relative or friend is available to see that basic care needs are being met. Many institutions today are understaffed, making it difficult for personnel to spend sufficient time with those who need to be fed or need frequent assistance with elimination.

When choosing a hospital, consider the following:

Accreditation. The Joint Commission on Accreditation of Health-Care Organizations (JCAHO) inspects hospitals every one to three years to be certain they meet standards for adequate staffing, that they monitor and control in-hospital infections and the quality of care, and that they have licensed physicians who are responsible for setting policies governing their professional staff.

The hospital should have a currently dated certificate displayed in a prominent place. To find out if a hospital is accredited, contact the JCAH at 1 Renaissance Boulevard, Oakbrook Terrace, IL 60181, or call (708) 916-5600.

Nursing Care. Good nursing care is a sign of a good hospital. Look for a facility that has a low turnover rate for its nursing staff, a low nurse-patient ratio, and a large percentage of registered nurses rather than licensed practical or vocational nurses. It is also important that nurses are on the hospital staff and have not been hired by outside agencies. Check with your local state nurses' association for hospital statistics in your area.

Experienced Staff. If you will require a highly specialized operation, choose a hospital that performs the surgery on a regular basis. The more frequently an operation is done, the more experienced the medical team is and the better chance there is for a successful outcome. Ask your physician how many of these operations were performed in the past year. A hospital doing coronary bypass surgery should do at least a hundred a year to maintain competence.

Services. Pick a hospital with a 24-hour emergency room, intensive and coronary care units, or other services to meet your specialized needs. For example, patients who may have a prolonged recuperation for a particular illness might look for a hospital with a cooperative care unit that emphasizes patient and family participation in recovery.

TYPES OF HOSPITALS

Community hospitals:

- Also known as general hospitals.
- Are the most common facilities in the United States.
- Handle the more common medical and surgical conditions.
- Operate on a profit or nonprofit basis.
- Vary in size, with the larger facilities having a greater variety of specialists and medical technology.
- Offer personalized medical care.

Teaching hospitals:

- Are large, well-equipped institutions affiliated with medical schools.
- The majority of staff physicians hold teaching and/or research positions.
- Have highly qualified medical staff who treat unusual disorders as well as common problems.

Because these facilities train medical students, patients may be frequently examined by groups of undergraduates, interns, residents, and specialists. Patients also may have to answer the same questions regarding their medical history and endure some discomfort caused by a relative lack of experience on the part of new physicians.

Public hospitals:

- Are generally large facilities.
- May or may not be affiliated with medical schools.
- Are owned and operated by the city, state, or federal government.
- May have a large percentage of low-income patients, leading to the often unjust assumption that the care is mediocre.
- Are often good medically but sparse on the amenities.

Specialized hospitals:

- Treat a single family of diseases, such as cancer or pulmonary diseases.
- Are limited to specific organizations or groups, such as Veterans Administration (VA) hospitals for former members of the armed services.

Costs. Large teaching hospitals with their sophisticated medical technology and wide variety of specialists will be more expensive than small community facilities. If you don't need the services of a large hospital, consider a smaller accredited one.

HOME CARE

With the development of sophisticated technology and pressures to reduce hospital costs, a vast array of home-care services has come into existence. Providers include hospital-based organizations, agencies run by medical supply companies, private for-profit and nonprofit companies, and public health facilities.

Hospitals, faced with threats of cutoffs in federal funding (Medicare), are sending patients home earlier—and sicker—than they did 10 years ago. Individuals recovering from hip surgery, receiving intravenous antibiotics, or suffering from chronic respiratory disease are only a few examples of those who can now be treated at home, given the physician's approval and the willingness of the patient and/or family to learn any necessary procedures.

Home-care services include visits by a registered nurse to monitor the patient's condition and instruct the patient or family in the use of medical equipment or procedures; occupational, physical, or speech therapy, if needed; and personal care by a home health aide and/or housekeeping by a homemaker. Depending on the patient's condition and the agency, it is possible that social work services, dental care, and arrangements for collecting lab specimens may be available.

Home-care services are covered to varying degrees by Medicare, Medicaid, and private insurance companies, but rarely covered unless the patient has been hospitalized. Factors important in determining eligibility for coverage are whether the patient has an acute or chronic condition (pneumonia versus a stroke) and whether the services of a registered nurse or other skilled professional are needed. Coverage provisions are complex and subject to change, so it is wise to check with the home-care agency and your insurer before being discharged from the hospital.

CHOOSING A NURSING HOME

The percentage of people over 65 who are confined to a nursing home is small, but as the population of the country ages, nursing home admissions are on the rise. If nursing home placement is a clear possibility for a family member, it is important to take a close, advance look at available facilities to ensure the best affordable care for the individual.

Facilities range from those providing minimal medical monitoring in a sheltered living environment—suitable for a relatively healthy person who cannot manage shopping, cooking, and housekeeping chores—to those with full-time staff physicians and nurses for chronically ill patients confined to a wheelchair and unable to feed them-

SELECTING A HOME-CARE AGENCY

Because of the tremendous growth in home care in recent years, the National League for Nursing, which accredits home-care agencies, has been able to assess only a minority of the 6,000 providers in this country. Lack of accreditation does not necessarily mean substandard care. When selecting an agency, keep in mind the needs of the patient and the following guidelines:

- A registered nurse rather than a licensed practical, or vocational, nurse should monitor patient condition and instruct the patient/family in procedures and use of equipment. In large urban areas, the supervising nurse should carry a beeper.
- The nurse should maintain regular contact with the physician, apprise him or her of patient progress, and relay instructions to appropriate personnel. For example, if the patient is receiving intravenous medication and the physician orders a change in dosage, the nurse should inform the pharmacist who prepares the medication.
- The agency should have a 24-hour phone number to call for emergencies or in case of equipment failure.
- Home health aides should be trained and supervised by a registered nurse. The agency should find a replacement if the aide or homemaker is not satisfactory or becomes ill.
- If the patient is homebound, check to see what arrangements can be made for lab technicians and other auxiliary services to come into the home.
- The agency should explain all charges and what will be covered by the patient's insurance. For example, dressing changes done by an R.N. may be covered, but those done by a home health aide may not be included. Many agencies will work with the patient to define those gray areas so that they are covered by the policy. If ongoing medical needs will put a strain on finances, services of a social worker would be helpful.

selves. Different states have different names for these levels of care, but facilities with the most intensive care are usually known as skilled-nursing facilities (SNFs).

The majority of nursing homes, about 75 percent, are proprietary or profit-making; the remainder are run by nonprofit organizations or the government. Recently, hospitals have been buying or building homes, or linking themselves to established facilities and functioning as a single unit. Whatever the affiliation, pick a home that is certified at least by the state and, if looking for a skilled-nursing facility, be sure it is certified by the Joint Commission on Accreditation of Hospitals (JCAH). These agencies inspect periodically to make sure that minimum health, sanitation, nutrition, safety, and other standards are met.

WHAT TO LOOK FOR IN A NURSING HOME

Because admission to a nursing home may represent a permanent move and a jolting change, it is important to visit each home prepared with a list of questions. In making your choice, consider the following guidelines:

Convenient location:

- Should be close enough for regular visits, preferably located in the same community where the person has lived.

Physical appearance:

- Should be clean, brightly lit, with minimal odors.
- Rooms should have no more than four beds, with sufficient privacy and personal storage space.

Safety:

- General construction should be sound.
- There should be rails in corridors and bathrooms, and safety rails should be raised on beds of those residents who are not fully ambulatory.
- Floors should be clean and dry to prevent falls.
- Be sure fire exits are clearly marked and sprinklers and fire extinguishers are in working order. Stop a nurse or aide and ask for the location of the nearest fire exit. Staff should be able to tell you the plan for evacuating residents in an emergency. Ask how often fire drills and fire department inspections are scheduled.

Residents' appearance:

- Residents should be clean, out of bed, and dressed unless medical indications are otherwise.
- There should be regularly scheduled age-appropriate activities. If the home is large, there should be a recreation therapy department or other staff solely devoted to activity planning.

Medical and nursing staff:

- The house physician should perform a complete physical examination before or immediately after a resident moves in.
- At least one staff physician should be present or on 24-hour call. At a skilled-nursing facility, a registered nurse should always be on duty.
- Each resident should have an up-to-date chart, noting medications, changes in medical status, and other relevant information.
- Nursing staff should be sufficient so that resident calls are answered promptly. In institutions with staff shortages, the more demanding patients are sometimes sedated beyond what is medically necessary, just to make the nurse's job easier.
- Staff should treat residents with kindness and respect.

Hospitalization:

- Find out which local hospital will be used and how the resident will be transported during a medical emergency.
- Should there be an extended stay in the hospital, find out how long the nursing home will keep the bed open.

Other services:

- If the home is large, there should be physical, occupational, and speech therapy departments to help in resident rehabilitation following stroke or hip fracture, for example. On-site clinics offering podiatry and dental services, among others, are also an advantage.

Financial:

- What services does the basic rate include?
- Does the home receive Medicaid reimbursement?
- There should be a full-time social worker to help obtain financial assistance as well as to facilitate resident adjustment and handle family concerns.

Nutrition:

- A full-time dietitian should plan tasty, nutritionally balanced meals for all residents as well as for those with special medical needs and religious preferences.

- For residents not confined to rooms, meals should be served in a communal dining room to promote socializing, with enough staff to help those who cannot feed themselves.

For more information on how to choose a good nursing home, contact the National Citizen's Coalition for Nursing Home Reform, 1224 M Street NW, Suite 301, Washington, DC 20005, or call (202) 393-2018.

HOSPICE CARE

Although many forms of cancer have a good prognosis—and this will probably increase with new treatments and positive life-style changes—others do not. For terminally ill patients who cannot benefit from acute medical intervention, a hospice is an alternative that may help both the patient and family make the most of the last months of life.

Hospices (the term is derived from the Latin word for hospitality or lodging) provide emotional support to both patient and family, and treatment of symptoms without attempting to cure or prolong life. Pain prevention or control is one of their specialties, and many hospices tailor medications and dosage schedules to make sure the patient remains pain-free and alert.

Hospice programs may care for patients at home, in regular hospitals, or in separate, freestanding buildings. Patients might be cared for at home with the assistance of the hospice team (a physician, nurse, social worker, and home health aide), or in a facility, depending on changing needs. Whenever possible, there is an emphasis on providing a homelike atmosphere; some facilities even allow pets or serve gourmet meals.

For admission to a hospice, the patient's life expectancy usually must be no longer than six months to one year. Some private insurance companies cover hospice services, and Medicare covers many facets of care. Check with your local Social Security office for Medicaid policies.

TRAVELING HEALTHY

One of the pleasures of retirement is having the time to travel. With the yen and a sufficient income, even those suffering from chronic illness or disability should feel free to travel, given some advance preparation. It is important to plan ahead and consider options in case of illness while traveling. Here are some tips to help make your trip a happy and healthy one:

□ If planning extensive travel, have a complete physical examination, including blood work, urinalysis, and an update of routine immunizations. Allow plenty of time for special immunizations recommended for specific countries.

- □ Have a sufficient reserve of medications and supplies. Know the generic names for your drugs, as brand names may vary in different countries.
- □ Get a note from your doctor stating your diagnosis. This will avoid questioning by customs authorities as to the legitimacy of medications or insulin syringes.
- □ If you are planning a cruise and have a tendency toward motion sickness, ask your doctor to recommend an appropriate medication.
- □ Check with your insurance company to see if your policy covers illness abroad, and what special forms you should bring on your trip. Some companies will reimburse you, but you must first pay for hospital costs, physicians' fees, and so forth. Medicare covers travel in United States territories such as Puerto Rico and the Virgin Islands but excludes other countries.
- □ If you have special needs or physical restrictions that make your mode of traveling or your accommodations important considerations, plan ahead and let traveling partners, tour guides, and trip operators know before the trip begins.
- □ Be prepared for health problems on the road. Traveling with people who know basic emergency measures, such as cardiopulmonary resuscitation (CPR), and knowing these techniques yourself can provide some peace of mind. Also, chances are a physician will be available no matter where you are if and when a medical crisis occurs. (See Appendix A for sources of help when traveling.)
- □ Take with you a brief medical record providing the information a physician needs to treat you safely and efficiently in case of emergency while traveling. Have your personal physician(s) help you create a form for each member in your travel party. Carry it where it can easily be found in an emergency. Take along a copy of a recent electrocardiogram, if your physician believes it might be helpful. Some of the information you should include:
    - name and address
    - birth date
    - whom to notify in case of emergency
    - medical insurance plan
    - list of chronic and/or medical ailments you are suffering from and being treated for
    - drugs you are currently taking (use the generic names)
    - drugs to which you are allergic
    - name of your family physician

- In most large cities, the drinking water is usually safe. In rural regions, however, water may easily be contaminated by disease-causing bacteria, viruses, or parasites. If chlorinated tap water is not available and/or if local hygiene and sanitation are questionable, stick to other beverages, such as carbonated drinks (canned or bottled). Beer and wine are safe. Beware of ice cubes; use them only if you're sure that they were made from boiled or otherwise purified water.
- It's always wise to be finicky about restaurants, at home as well as abroad. And in areas where hygiene and sanitation are poor, every food source is suspect. Safety lies in careful selection. Where you suspect that food handling is questionable or refrigeration lacking, avoid cold cuts of meat, potato and egg salads, and creamed foods containing milk. Whenever you order meat, poultry, fish, or shellfish, choose thoroughly cooked and preferably piping hot dishes.

If you would like more information, the U.S. Government Printing Office (GPO) publishes a pamphlet, "Health Information for International Travelers" (stock #017-023-00174-4), for $4.75 that covers vaccination recommendations, information on motion sickness and traveler's diarrhea, food and drink precautions, tips for the handicapped traveler, and other facts. It is also available at GPO bookstores in major cities. Write to the United States Government Printing Office, Superintendent of Documents, Washington, DC 20402, or call (202) 783-3238.

19

Insurance and Health-care Costs

Medical insurance and the spiraling cost of health care have emerged as two of the most pressing public issues of the 1990s. An estimated 35 million Americans lack health insurance. Most of these are classified as the working poor whose employers either do not provide health insurance or who themselves cannot afford what is available.

Because of sharply rising health-care costs, most private insurance companies are becoming increasingly selective in granting medical coverage. Low-risk clients who are young and healthy have little difficulty in obtaining medical insurance, provided they can pay the premiums. The situation is much different for persons with chronic diseases, or those who fall into high-risk categories. If these people can obtain insurance at all, it is likely to be prohibitively expensive.

Increasingly, government is being asked to step in. Hawaii, for example, has enacted laws requiring employers to provide insurance coverage for employees.

The federal government has enacted Medicare fee structures and regulations aimed at reducing the cost of providing health care to older people and the disabled. As a result many physicians in high-cost areas such as New York and California have announced that they will no longer accept Medicare patients.

All this has led to increasing demands for a single-payer system of health care or other programs to guarantee affordable medical care to those who need it. In addition, both federal and state governments are rewriting regulations and proposing new programs to lower medical costs and broaden the availability of health care. In this climate of unrest and change, anything that we write today is likely to be outdated tomorrow.

The following sections describe Medicare and other insurance programs and regulations as of late 1992. This information is likely to change markedly in the next few years. To keep abreast of these changes, check with your Social Security office.

GOVERNMENT HEALTH PROGRAMS

MEDICARE

Medicare is the federal insurance program for those age 65 and over, and for persons of any age with severe kidney disease and selected chronic disabilities. If you elect early retirement benefits from Social Security, you automatically receive a Medicare card in the mail when you turn 65. If you sign up for Social Security benefits when you are 65, you receive your Medicare card at the same time. However, if you have turned 65 and want to delay your Social Security benefits, you have to apply for Medicare. Check with your local Social Security office for more details.

Medicare, which is administered by the Health Care Financing Administration of the Department of Health and Human Services, has two parts. Part A covers hospital stays and is provided without cost. It covers, to varying degrees, inpatient hospital care (excluding doctors' services), skilled-nursing facilities, home health agencies, and hospices. As of 1993 there is a $676 deductible per hospital admission—thus, the patient (or a supplemental insurance policy) is responsible for the first $676 of covered medical costs per admission.

Part B provides general medical insurance, for which Medicare recipients pay a monthly premium. If you do not take Part B when you first become eligible for Medicare, you can enroll during the first three months of subsequent years. But for each year you delay, your premium will increase by 10 percent. (If you have been enrolled in a private health-care plan or under a spouse's plan during the interim, this penalty can be decreased or waived.)

Part B covers physicians' charges and other approved medical costs after the patient meets the $100 yearly deductible. In general, once the deductible is met, Medicare pays 80 percent of the approved amount, and the patient is responsible for the remaining 20 percent, a payment referred to as coinsurance. It is important to keep track of your claims and the amount you have paid toward the deductible. Medicare claims are processed and paid by insurance companies that are designated Medicare carriers.

Sometimes a doctor's fees are much higher than those approved by Medicare. However, many physicians agree to accept assignment of Medicare claims, meaning that they will accept the Medicare-approved charge as payment in full. They are paid directly by the Medicare carrier for their 80 percent, with the patient paying the remaining 20 percent coinsurance.

Some physicians who do not participate in Medicare will still accept assignment on a case-by-case basis, so you should always ask in advance whether a doctor or supplier will accept Medicare for your particular case. Even if physicians will not accept Medicare assignment, they are limited in what they can charge above the approved Medicare fee. As of 1993, a physician's excess charge cannot exceed 15 percent of Medicare's allowed charge.

FILING AN APPEAL

Medicare claims are processed and paid by insurance companies that are designated Medicare carriers. If a Medicare carrier denies all or part of a claim, you can appeal the decision. Here's how:

1. *Determine why the claim was denied.*
   Sometimes the denial is based on a simple mathematical error or failure to include an itemized bill or code number. In such instances, provide the additional information and ask the carrier to review the claim.
2. *Ask for a hearing.*
   If the carrier refuses to adjust your claim and the amount is more than $100, you can request a hearing with a special officer. This hearing must be requested within six months of the denial. Hearings are usually held at your local Social Security office, although you can request that the hearing officer come to your home. If the amount of the claim is $500 or less, the officer's decision is final. In general, about 45 percent of hearings result in total or partial recovery for the person filing the claim.
3. *Request a hearing before an administrative law judge.*
   If the claim is rejected by a hearing officer and the amount is more than $500, you can request a hearing before an administrative law judge from the Social Security Administration (SSA). To do so, you must fill out a Request for Hearing form, which is available at Social Security offices.
4. *Appeal to the Social Security Appeals Council.*
   If you disagree with the judge's decision, you can make another appeal by filling out a Request for Appeals Council Review of Hearing Decision form and sending it to your local Social Security office. This must be done within 60 days of the judge's decision.
5. *File a lawsuit.*
   If the appeals council rejects your claim and you still feel that you are entitled to payment, you can file a lawsuit in federal court. To do this, you should engage an attorney.

MEDIGAP AND OTHER PRIVATE INSURANCE PLANS

There are a number of private insurance policies available to help pay for medical costs that are not covered by Medicare. For example, some employers provide group insurance for their retirees. Most people, however, must enroll in their own supplemental, or Medigap, insurance programs. These policies are designed to supplement Medicare benefits, and all states have adopted the federal government's standards for these policies. In general, Medigap policies pay:

- some or all of the Medicare deductibles and coinsurance
- certain health services that are not covered by Medicare

In addition, there are policies that cover nursing-home or long-term care as well as specified disease coverage, such as cancer. Still another alternative involves enrolling in a coordinated care plan, such as a health maintenance organization (HMO). To avoid duplicating coverage, contact your Social Security office for a copy of the pamphlet "Guide to Health Insurance for People with Medicare."

Your Medicare/Medical Insurance Claims Record

Note: You can use the "other remarks" column to keep track of your medical insurance deductible until it's met, or for notes about appeals or private supplementary insurance.

Date you mailed claim	Date of service or supply	Doctor or supplier who provided service or supply	Service or supply you received	Charge for service or supply	Date and amount of Medicare payment	Other remarks

MEDICAID

Many middle-aged people cannot envision being poverty-stricken in their later years. However, loss of job income coupled with chronic illness or the need for nursing-home care can deplete even a substantial nest egg. For the newly poor elderly, as well as for the chronically needy, state-sponsored Medicaid health insurance steps in.

Medicaid programs are administered by state social service departments and vary greatly as to income eligibility requirements and benefits provided. In general, Medicaid covers a broader range of services and for a longer period than does Medicare. Depending on the state, Medicaid may cover long-term nursing-home care, many prescription drugs, and foot care. Medicaid currently covers about half of all nursing-home stays. It has no deductible to be met and may pay the total amount for services rather than the 80 percent covered by Medicare.

Applying for Medicaid can be a grueling process, and it is wise to take along a friend or relative when going in for the interview. (Many communities have senior centers or religious organizations that help with the application process.) Your state may require you to bring many documents—rent receipts, bankbooks, utility bills—to prove financial need. Make sure you understand exactly what is required before you go, thus avoiding a second trip. For example, you may have memorized your Social Security number years ago, but you may still need to bring your card as proof. Contact your state social service department for any guides to documentation or filling out the application.

Medicaid recipients may be sent a monthly card that they must present when going for medical services. The individual or facility providing care is reimbursed directly by the state, and you will not receive a bill for any covered service. Certain expensive medical supplies or services, such as a wheelchair or private-duty nursing, must have advance approval for reimbursement. Your physician should complete the required form and send it to Medicaid or the appropriate vendor for processing.

If your present doctor will not accept Medicaid, the social service department can supply a list of physicians who do. If your doctor is willing to make an exception and take you as a Medicaid patient, check to see how he or she can join the program.

Be sure to deal promptly with any Medicaid requests for recertification information so as not to let your eligibility lapse. You must also let Medicaid know if your address, size of household, or financial status changes.

SPENDING DOWN. Many people who enter a nursing home begin by paying the bills themselves. But if their stay is prolonged, they quickly exhaust their resources and are able to meet their states' income and asset test for Medicaid.

The process by which you reach the point where Medicaid pays your nursing home bills is called a *spend-down.* When you have spent enough of your assets to reach your state's Medicaid limits, and your income is not too high, Medicaid begins to pay your bills. You also have to turn over all your monthly income (except for a personal-needs allowance) to the nursing home.

For many families, a spend-down once meant poverty for the spouse who remained at home, since all the family's assets went toward nursing-home care for the other spouse. However, Congress has passed legislation that makes it easier for spouses to maintain a more comfortable standard of living. Each state determines how much of a couple's assets remain with the spouse living at home. Check with your state's Department of Health regarding their spend-down rules and regulations.

PRIVATE INSURANCE

If you are currently employed, you may already have an insurance policy that meets your needs. However, if your coverage is through your job and will end upon retirement, or if you are in the market for a better policy, you should know what types of policies are available and what will best meet your needs.

Although costs and coverage differ from company to company, in general, group insurance offers the lowest cost protection. If you have a group policy at work, see if you can continue it after you retire. Group coverage may also be available through a union, fraternal organization, or professional society.

TYPES OF COVERAGE

Hospital-Surgical. These policies cover hospital room and board, often for a specified number of days; treatment in intensive-care and outpatient facilities; medical supplies; surgeon's fees; diagnostic tests relating to an operation; some radiation and chemotherapy; and sometimes second opinions. But they cover almost no expenses incurred outside a hospital, including a doctor's office visits and house calls. And most of these policies don't cover prescription drugs that you may need outside a hospital.

Basic Medical/Surgical. This pays for physician services related to hospitalization and surgery. It usually will not fully cover doctors' office visits and house calls.

Major Medical. This covers long-term and major, "catastrophic" medical costs beyond those paid by basic hospital/surgical insurance. Some policies will not cover any preexisting health problems until a certain time period has elapsed. Private-duty nursing and rehabilitation services may fall under this type of coverage.

Major medical policies cover between 75 and 80 percent of expenses. The deductible ranges between $1,000 and $5,000; in general, the higher the deductible, the lower the policy cost. Many plans feature a desirable "stop-loss" provision, which totally covers expenses incurred beyond a specified annual amount, up to the limit of your policy.

Long-term Health Care. Nearly 70 insurance companies now offer long-term health-care insurance that covers varying amounts of nursing-home expenses for time periods of two to ten years and sometimes home-care expenses as well. Premiums are expensive—from $500 to over $3,000 per year—but are usually guaranteed renewable. You should also expect premiums to increase over time. The younger a person is when he or she enrolls, the lower the premium. Thus, if you enroll for a long-term policy at age 55, your premium may be $600 a year compared to $3,000 or more if you sign up at age 75. Preexisting medical conditions are covered after a waiting period of usually six months. But if you have a chronic condition, such as Parkinson's disease or Alzheimer's disease, the company will not issue you a policy.

The consumer should check to see if the policy covers the services of nonskilled employees (nurse's aides often give much of the direct patient care in a nursing home), as well as skilled professionals, such as doctors, nurses, and physical therapists.

Disability Income. This coverage provides cash to an individual who is unable to work because of injury or illness. Policies vary as to definitions of disability, length of coverage, and dates when benefits begin. The maximum benefit provided is two-thirds of the gross salary. You should choose a policy that provides income if you are unable to resume work in your regular occupation. For example, a mail carrier with a leg injury might not be able to deliver mail but could work in a job that did not require a great deal of walking. With an own-occupation policy, the mail carrier could collect income rather than have to look for a position for which he or she has no experience.

The best and most expensive policies are noncancelable and guaranteed renewable. However, policy costs can be reduced if you can afford to wait awhile before coverage begins and if your pension plan covers disability after retirement, enabling you to discontinue the insurance.

PLANNING AHEAD

Well before retiring, you should assess your present insurance coverage and make plans for any transition in coverage after retirement. For example, if you are covered by an employer's group policy, find out what if any coverage continues following your retirement, how this coordinates with Medicare, and whether you are expected to pay for this coverage.

If you or a spouse will be under the age of 65 when you retire, find out whether coverage will continue until you or your dependent is eligible for Medicare. Since it is vital to avoid breaks in insurance coverage if at all possible, find out if you can extend the group coverage at your own expense. Most group plans can be extended for at least 18 months, provided you pay the premiums, which are generally much less than for an individual policy. At the end of the 18-month period, you may then be able to convert to an individual policy; the premiums will be significantly higher than under the group rate, but you do have the advantage of not having to pass a medical test or waiting period for preexisting conditions.

INSURANCE PITFALLS

Many older people fall victim to insurance fraud. There are numerous reports of older people carrying a dozen or more duplicate policies at a tremendous cost, and other reports of people whose policies fail to cover expenses as promised by unscrupulous agents.

Be wary of any insurance agent who shows up on your doorstep or tries to sell a policy over the telephone. Some disreputable agents use excessive pressure or scare tactics; others rely on personal charm or attention to persuade an older person to buy a policy. A reputable agent should carefully outline the policy's terms and coverage, and leave behind a printed brochure and business card. Never use cash to pay for insurance. All checks should be made out to the insurance company, not the agent.

When buying insurance, shop around. If you find the language confusing, ask your attorney or other knowledgeable person to review the policy to make sure that it does indeed provide the coverage you want.

Some insurance companies sell by mail, newspaper advertisement, or other direct-marketing techniques, thereby eliminating the need for an agent. These policies may offer cost savings, but caution is still needed to avoid misleading advertising or promotional claims.

After buying a policy, examine it right away to make sure that it provides what has been promised. Most states provide a 30-day cancellation period during which you can notify the insurance company that you want to cancel the policy and receive a full refund. The cancellation letter should be sent by certified mail, and be sure you keep a copy of it.

Part V

Death

20

Coming to Terms with Mortality

The attitude we have toward death—our own and that of close friends or family—depends to a great extent on how we live. Those who remain active, are curious about the world around them, maintain close relationships with family and friends, and continue to be challenged by new interests are most apt to view death as nothing more than the natural phenomenon it is.

But a positive attitude should not be equated with pretending the event will not take place. Indeed, those who are able to accept death as a part of their life are most likely to continue cultivating activities that will sustain them when, for instance, a spouse dies. They will also be able to make practical plans for their family in the event of their own death. This is especially important, for many of the fears associated with dying involve not making adequate provisions for those we love and for whom we feel responsible.

Studies show that fear of death is greatest during a person's forties, when people typically have a lot of responsibilities, are involved in many activities, and may have dependent children. But older people seem to have less fear of death. It is possible that a life review, or reminiscing, helps older people come to terms with their past and prepare for what is to come.

CHANGING ATTITUDES

This century has witnessed a dramatic reduction in the death rate of young and middle-aged persons from acute diseases and other environmental factors. According to statistics from the U.S. Bureau of the Census, three-quarters of all deaths now occur in the 65-years-and-older population group. Most deaths now result from a chronic, perhaps prolonged illness in old age, rather than from an acute illness or accident.

It was not long ago that most people died at home surrounded by friends and family who, because they cared for the person and were often present at the moment of death, did not view the event as mysterious or frightening. From early childhood onward, people came into contact with death. Today, with death occurring primarily in the elderly population, a person may not experience the death of someone close until late middle age or early old age, when a parent dies in a hospital. As late as 1949, only about 40 percent of deaths took place in a hospital, but that figure had already risen to 70 percent by the 1970s. The hospital atmosphere may create more distance between the survivors and the loved ones.

Unfortunately, the shift from home to hospital has affected many people's attitudes and much of society's approach toward death. Dr. Elisabeth Kübler-Ross, a pioneer in working with the dying, attributes much of the difficulty modern society has in accepting death to our unfamiliarity with it. And because unfamiliarity often breeds fear, it is important to understand the psychological stages you—or those close to you—will go through when confronted with death.

STAGES OF GRIEF

Researchers have found that both those who are faced with their own death and those who are faced with the death of a loved one will go through one or all of the same stages of grief, although not necessarily at the same time or in the same order. Here are the five stages of grief Dr. Kübler-Ross has identified.

Denial. Typically, this is a person's first reaction to being told of a terminal illness or the imminent death of a loved one, and may be expressed as shock or disbelief. Denial initially serves a valuable function by allowing us to distance ourselves temporarily from the reality of the issue, providing time to marshal the strength and resources to deal with illness and death. A person in the denial stage may insist on seeking several other medical opinions or investigating alternative therapies, or may refuse to make necessary changes in daily routine. A relative of a dying person may refuse to discuss any practical issues relating to the death, or may persist in discussing plans for the future. Denial can be a refusal to acknowledge the diagnosis. It is a natural and necessary reaction that cushions the blow at first, but if it is carried too far, it can be a barrier to honest communication and to real preparation for death.

Anger. Anger over the news of a terminal disease may be directed at health-care personnel, who are blamed for being incompetent or uncaring; at loved ones; at God; or at oneself. Anger is a normal and justifiable reaction that should not be suppressed or disguised. Lingering in the anger stage, however, can keep a person from accepting reality, can alienate those most important to have around at this time, and may even make hospital staff reluctant to deal with the patient. It is important for those in close contact with a dying person, such as hospital staff and relatives, to recognize that expressions of anger fill an important need for the patient and that they are often cries for help.

Bargaining. At first, a dying person may try to "bargain"—with God, or with the medical establishment—for a cure. As the person moves closer to accepting death, this bargaining will become (or at least seem) more realistic. The person may hope to survive until a certain anniversary, such as a birthday, a grandchild's commencement, or even until the beginning of the next month.

Depression. This stage is characterized by a sense of helplessness and hopelessness. Death has been accepted as a reality but has not been adjusted to in a positive way. During this stage, dying patients will often be uncommunicative and want to be left alone. For the grieving person who has lost a spouse or a close relative, temporary depression is a common reaction and should not be interpreted as a sign of mental illness. Basically, the grieving person should know that this stage will pass. Making conscious efforts to do something, to take care of small matters, can help.

Acceptance. The dying person has learned to await death without anger, and with peace and personal satisfaction with his or her life. The person may begin a process of disengagement from most people, wanting only to be with close friends and family. For the person who mourns a death, the stage of acceptance is characterized by the ability to remember the loved one without strong feelings of pain or sadness and to begin to make new emotional attachments.

It is also not unusual for someone to reach one stage and then "regress" to a previous stage. Although this is often a normal part of the person's grief, it can also be caused by medical personnel who insist on engaging in heroic measures to revive the patient after he or she has already accepted death; it can come from family who may not be able to accept the person's leaving them and who therefore make the patient feel guilty or depressed. The dying person and his or her relatives will often be in different stages at different times.

LIVING WILLS AND HEALTH-CARE PROXIES

Some of the most often debated medical ethics issues of our time surround the life-and-death decisions of people with terminal illnesses or other debilitating conditions and their family members. A number of life-sustaining medical procedures have been embraced by the medical community because, after all, its job is to save lives. But some of these procedures have incited mixed reactions from the terminally ill, many of whom just a decade ago would not have had to confront them. Right-to-die cases have received much public attention and have brought these issues into public and legal arenas.

In a 1990 Gallup poll, 84 percent of Americans said they would want treatment withheld if they were on life-support systems and had no hope of recovering. And 66 percent said they believed that people experiencing great pain with no hope of improvement had the moral right to commit suicide. Although the moral and legal ethics of euthanasia may always be a controversial topic, it is clear that more choices are given to patients these days. Several recent court cases, in which family members tried to make decisions without formal and prior directives from the patients, have highlighted the importance of written legal documentation such as the "living will."

A living will is a statement by which the signer expresses his or her refusal to undergo invasive measures or to be subjected to artificial life-support systems in case of terminal illness or natural death after an accident. The legality of a living will varies from state to state and still is subject to frequent reinterpretations.

Although the living will may not be accepted as legally valid, it can often be used in court as proof of the signer's intent and wishes. A living will should be treated as any other legal document: It should be witnessed and filed with other important papers. Family members should be aware of the existence of the will so that they will know of the signer's wishes if a relevant situation arises. If the family knows and supports what the person wants, the difficult decision to stop life-support systems will be much easier to make. Information on and forms for a living will are available from Choice in Dying, 200 Varick Street, 10th Floor, New York, NY 10014, or call (212) 366-5540.

ADVANCE DIRECTIVE

Living Will and Health Care Proxy

Death is a part of life. It is a reality like birth, growth and aging. I am using this advance directive to convey my wishes about medical care to my doctors and other people looking after me at the end of my life. It is called an advance directive because it gives instructions in advance about what I want to happen to me in the future. It expresses my wishes about medical treatment that might keep me alive. I want this to be legally binding.

If I cannot make or communicate decisions about my medical care, those around me should rely on this document for instructions about measures that could keep me alive.

I do not want medical treatment (including feeding and water by tube) that will keep me alive if:

- I am unconscious and there is no reasonable prospect that I will ever be conscious again (even if I am not going to die soon in my medical condition), *or*

- I am near death from an illness or injury with no reasonable prospect of recovery.

I do want medicine and other care to make me more comfortable and to take care of pain and suffering. I want this even if the pain medicine makes me die sooner.

I want to give some extra instructions: [*Here list any special instructions, e.g., some people fear being kept alive after a debilitating stroke. If you have wishes about this, or any other conditions, please write them here.*]

The legal language in the box that follows is a health care proxy. It gives another person the power to make medical decisions for me.

I name ______________________, who lives at ______________

______________________, phone number ______________,

to make medical decisions for me if I cannot make them myself. This person is called a health care "surrogate," "agent," "proxy," or "attorney in fact." This power of attorney shall become effective when I become incapable of making or communicating decisions about my medical care. This means that this document stays legal when and if I lose the power to speak for myself, for instance, if I am in a coma or have Alzheimer's disease.

My health care proxy has power to tell others what my advance directive means. This person also has power to make decisions for me, based either on what I would have wanted, or, if this is not known, on what he or she thinks is best for me.

If my first choice health care proxy cannot or decides not to act for me, I name

____,

address ______________________________________,

phone number ______________________, as my second choice.

I have discussed my wishes with my health care proxy, and with my second choice if I have chosen to appoint a second person. My proxy(ies) has(have) agreed to act for me.

I have thought about this advance directive carefully. I know what it means and want to sign it. I have chosen two witnesses, neither of whom is a member of my family, nor will inherit from me when I die. My witnesses are not the same people as those I named as my health care proxies. I understand that this form should be notarized if I use the box to name (a) health care proxy(ies).

Signature ______________________________

Date ______________________________

Address ______________________________

Witness' signature ______________________________

Witness' printed name ______________________________

Address ______________________________

Witness' signature ______________________________

Witness' printed name ______________________________

Address ______________________________

Notary [to be used if proxy is appointed] ______________________________

A health-care proxy, often included in a living will, assigns decisions involving health-care matters to a friend or family member. Once again, it should be treated as a legal document. Its power, however, may be limited and specific. For instance, it may cover only terminal illness. For something more inclusive, look into a durable power of attorney for health care, which gives your agent the power to make decisions under circumstances you may not have anticipated.

Despite a federal law (the Patient Self-Determination Act) that went into effect at the end of 1992 and required Medicare- or Medicaid-participating hospitals to ask adult inpatients if they have completed "advance directives," assertion of such decisions will most likely remain the patient's responsibility. Medic Alert bracelets that say "Living Will/Do Not Resuscitate" are available to those who want to make their choice immediately clear. Such a measure should not be necessary, however, if proper legal documentation and family support are in place. Also, discussing your wishes with your physician can simplify matters. After all, he or she may be the one in charge of giving the DNR—Do Not Resuscitate—order if and when the time comes.

ORGAN DONATION

Many people ensure that a part of them will continue into the future by donating their body or organs for medical research or therapy. As medical skill in the area of transplantation has become more sophisticated, it has become possible to transplant more organs; success rates for transplantation operations have increased substantially. Organ donation is indeed a gift of life—at no cost to the giver.

Nevertheless, health-care personnel are often hesitant to ask survivors to allow such a gift to be made after a loved one's death, even though the majority of states require it by law. Family members may be hesitant to allow donation because they are afraid the body will be too mutilated for a proper funeral. This fear is unfounded: Doctors can remove organs and prepare the body so that it is suitable for any type of funeral service. After an individual has signed a uniform donor card (often a part of a driver's license), he or she should inform family members to be assured the wishes will be carried out. Uniform donor cards are available from the regional transplant program listed in the telephone directory or from organizations such as the following:

American Medical Association
515 North State Street
Chicago, IL 60610
(312) 464-5000

National Kidney Foundation
30 East 33rd Street
New York, NY 10016
(212) 889-2210

Medic Alert Foundation International
P.O. Box 1009
Turlock, CA 95381-1009
(800) 344-3226

The Uniform Anatomical Gift Act allows people to make a gift of their body or parts for medical purposes to hospitals, medical and dental schools, or institutions involved in medical research or storage of organs. Anatomical gift cards are available from any local medical school or research hospital.

PREPARING FOR DEATH

A written description of the type of funeral or memorial service a person wants can eliminate disagreement among family members after the death of the person. These instructions should be kept with other important papers. In fact, it is highly recommended that you keep pertinent records in a file at home or at your lawyer's office (but *not* in a bank safety deposit box). They should be updated periodically. Family members, an attorney, or a close friend should know where the file is kept. Important items for this file include the following:

- a written description of the type of funeral or memorial service desired
- copies of all insurance policies
- Social Security card
- marriage certificate
- deeds and mortgages
- safe deposit box number
- veteran's discharge papers
- birth certificates of family members
- W-2 form
- names of attorney, insurance agent, stockbroker, and union official
- living will
- indication of uniform donor card

If there is a joint will, both spouses should examine it to be sure it is up-to-date and the provisions are as they wish. Insurance policies should also be checked to make certain that the beneficiaries are correct. Any company- or union-held policies need to be double-checked as well. When a person knows that he or she is going to die, it is often a good idea to transfer property held only in one name into the spouse's name.

LAST RITES

The funeral may hold several meanings for the survivors: It can be seen as the last opportunity to say good-bye, as a means of showing respect for the deceased, and as a way of affirming his or her place in the family and community.

Ideally, a funeral director should be able to accommodate the type of services the bereaved wish and help them in the initial acceptance of the death. However, some people in the funeral industry in the United States take advantage of survivors during this time, encouraging them to plan extravagant funerals and perhaps making them feel guilty if they want to keep things simple. The best way to prevent this is for an individual

MAKING ARRANGEMENTS

A number of concerns must be addressed in making plans for death:

- living will
- organ donation
- disposition of estate
- type of medical insurance

If you become seriously ill, what kind of care do you want?

- hospital
- nursing home
- hospice

What kind of death arrangements?

- burial
- cremation
- religious service
- memorial service
- donation of body

to put his or her wishes in writing, preferably years before it is needed. By doing this, survivors need not feel pressured into having anything other than what the deceased wanted.

In addition to outlining in advance what kind of funeral one would like, an individual should also try to make financial arrangements for it. According to the Continental Association of Funeral and Memorial Societies, the average cost of a funeral in the United States, not including cemetery costs, runs about $3,500. Providing for the costs of a funeral ahead of time helps the surviving spouse not only financially, but psychologically, by relieving him or her of making decisions under stress. Insurance may be purchased to pay for a funeral and/or a burial plot, a savings account that is earmarked for that purpose may be opened, or provisions can be made in the will.

MEMORIAL SOCIETIES

One way to get accurate information about costs and options for funerals, and perhaps to be eligible for a discount, is to join a memorial society. Memorial societies grew out of the consumer movement that arose to protest the high cost of funerals. They are nonprofit organizations that keep up-to-date information on low-cost funerals, cremation, organ and body donations, and other details. Many are affiliated with churches or civic organizations, although it is not usually necessary to be a member of these to join the memorial society.

There is a one-time fee to become a member. Funeral costs are not paid to the memorial society but directly to the funeral director. Some memorial societies have formal contracts with one or more local funeral directors who agree to provide set types of funeral services to members at a discount rate. Others simply provide information about available services and costs. A local memorial society can be found by looking in the yellow pages of the telephone directory under "Associations." It might be listed in the white pages as well, usually under "Memorial Society of . . ."

The Continental Association of Funeral and Memorial Societies is an umbrella organization that acts as a clearinghouse for information about memorial societies. It also works with government agencies on matters that affect funeral arrangements. For information contact:

The Continental Association of Funeral and Memorial Societies
6900 Lost Lake Road
Egg Harbor, WI 54209
(800) 458-5563

Information about funeral arrangements is also available from the state board of undertakers and embalmers or the office of the state attorney general.

AN ALTERNATIVE TO HOSPITAL CARE: THE HOSPICE

Hospitals are cure-oriented, not care-oriented. Because physicians and other health-care professionals are trained to cure their patients, they are often uneasy when nothing can be done to prevent death.

But just because the dying are not in need of the interventions of modern medicine does not mean that they do not need care; it's just a different type of care. A dying person and his or her loved ones need an all-inclusive holistic sort of care that attends to their emotional, psychological, and physical needs. The dying person and spouse or relatives need to know that the patient will be kept as free of pain as possible and will not be subjected to any unnecessary procedures. But aside from that, the dying patient needs the time and opportunity to discuss his or her feelings. Studies have shown that the majority of patients with a terminal illness want to know it—and that once they know, they eventually want to be able to discuss their death in an open and honest manner. A hospice environment is helpful and comforting for these people.

The hospice movement grew out of the desire to provide dying patients with both the physical and psychological care that they need in a humane setting capable of integrating family and friends. Although still not the standard practice in this country, the availability of hospice care has increased and is advocated by many physicians, including Dr. Kübler-Ross.

The hospice philosophy is to keep patients free of pain while providing them and their families with as much emotional support as possible and the opportunity to talk about their concerns with someone who has experience with the dying. Hospice workers generally will not perform the dramatic resuscitation attempts that medical personnel might in a hospital setting, although they will make every effort to see that the patient is comfortable and attend to nutritional and other needs. The hospice is meant to be a place where a person can die with dignity. There is no pretense of a "cure." In fact, in many cases the hospice may insist that the patients acknowledge that they are dying before they will be accepted.

The forms of hospice care can include a separate institution, a separate wing of beds in a hospital, or a section of beds in a nursing home. Most often, however, care takes place in the patient's home, with the help of visiting nurses, social workers, and other hospice staff. The spouse or other close relative or friend is the primary caregiver. Even in a hospice in a separate setting, the relative or friend may be responsible for much of the care. Hospice staff are available to help, but they do not attempt to intrude on the relationship between the dying person and the loved one. Hospices offer care and counseling to the caregiver as well as to the dying person. Many hospices continue to offer counseling and support to family members after the death of the patient.

Home nursing care is available through most hospices or through the Visiting Nurse Association. Caring for a dying person can be exhausting, both physically and emotionally, and this assistance can relieve some of the burden. An invaluable service is respite care—someone to come in periodically and take over all the care so that the caregiver can get away—whether for a few hours or a couple of days. If several days off are needed, readmission to a hospital is usually an option. The hospice can also be helpful in providing or locating equipment that may be needed for the care of the dying person, such as oxygen, feeding tubes, etc. For information on respite care, contact the local chapter of the American Cancer Society, the local Visiting Nurse Association, or the Older Women's League.

Financing Care. Some private insurers will cover hospice costs to some degree, but it is not standard coverage, so each policy must be looked at carefully. Medicare will pay for nearly all expenses for up to 210 days of hospice care, requiring no deductible, if the following requirements are met:

- A doctor must certify that you are terminally ill.
- You must choose to receive care from a hospice program instead of your regular Medicare benefits for the terminal illness. This means stopping curative treatment.
- A Medicare-certified hospice program must provide the care.

Patient responsibilities include payment of $5 or 5 percent of the cost of outpatient drugs (whichever is less) *and* 5 percent of the Medicare-approved rate for inpatient respite care.

The publication "Hospice Benefits Under Medicare" (Pub. No. HCFA 02154) is available from the local Social Security office or the Health Care Financing Administration, 6325 Security Boulevard, Baltimore, MD 21207, (410) 966-3000.

Types of Care. Surveys have shown that the main concerns of a patient with a terminal illness are being a burden to others, separation from loved ones and concern about their welfare, and painful death. Although hospice care does place a great responsibility on the caregiver, there are resources available to help alleviate the burden. An honest discussion of this concern can help the dying person and his or her family decide whether hospital care or hospice care is best. The options of home nursing, respite care, or even occasional readmission to a hospital may help allay the dying person's fears about being a burden. However, some couples may find that they are fully insured for hospital care but not for hospice care, and this may influence the decision.

Since the focus of hospice care is on making the patient as comfortable as possible, pain relief is a priority. Hospice staff are less likely than hospital staff to insist on a set schedule of pain medication; instead, they will administer medication to prevent pain instead of waiting until the patient is already suffering. Of course, attitudes and procedures in hospitals regarding dying patients are slowly changing, and the final decision may depend on what is available in the specific community. Patient-controlled analgesia, in which the patient is equipped with a pump that delivers a preset dose of medication at preset intervals, has become an option for many patients.

COPING WITH THE DEATH OF A SPOUSE

The loss of a spouse or life partner in old age can sometimes mean a complete restructuring of life, and there is no way to assign a timetable or a set of rules to that process. The bereaved go through the same stages of grief as do the dying. It's helpful to remember that grief is a process, a period of transition that involves a gradual letting go of the old and a creation of new networks, identities, and roles.

It is not unusual to have mixed feelings at first when a spouse dies after a long illness, especially if there has been prolonged suffering or severe deterioration. The surviving spouse has probably gone through some anticipatory grieving, although opinions vary on whether this speeds up the grieving process or creates additional stress.

Sudden or unexpected deaths do not seem to be accompanied by longer or more intense grieving, although the survivor may remain longer in the initial stage of shock or denial. In this case, viewing the body is important because it helps establish the reality of the death. The survivor also may have to cope with the need for an autopsy in many cases. Later, if no planning was done, the survivor must deal with the practical and financial affairs.

The death of a spouse may constitute a serious threat to a person's sense of self, especially if his or her role was largely defined by the spouse. In the elderly, when a family is reduced to a couple, the spouse may be the only significant presence in a person's life.

Grief is often referred to in physical terms—as a blow, for instance. In time, the impact will lessen, but many people going through this difficult period may fear that they are not "normal" or that they will never recover. Immediately after the death, the survivor is usually surrounded by relatives and friends, but afterward he or she may be left to deal with the unfamiliar and often frightening effects of grief.

GRIEVING

Being aware of what is normal in a state of grief will not relieve mourning, but it may reduce anxiety in the person who is experiencing volatile changes in behavior and emotions.

In the early stages of grief, emotions may be intense and difficult to control. Outbursts of crying and even anger are common. The newly bereaved may find that he or she cries unexpectedly in public. Preoccupation or even obsession with the deceased is also common, and it is not unusual to see visions of the deceased and to search in

HELPING THE BEREAVED

- Initially, friends and neighbors can help with practical details and responsibilities.
- Later they should encourage the survivor to take on responsibility.
- Visits after the funeral will help make the survivor feel less alone.
- Visitors should accept emotional outbursts as normal and not show surprise or uneasiness.
- Friends and relatives should not avoid discussing the deceased or the facts of the survivor's situation. They should be willing to listen to what the bereaved has to say and not insist on talking about trivial matters.
- Conversation is not always necessary. Sometimes just the presence of someone who cares will be genuinely appreciated.
- Written expressions of sympathy are helpful.
- After making initial contact with the bereaved after the death of the loved one, friends should make the effort to stay in touch. Later they should include the widow/widower in activities and treat him or her as a normal person.

crowds or familiar places for the loved one. These are natural reactions to loss and will gradually lessen in intensity.

The bereaved often will idealize the spouse or the marital relationship. This, too, is a natural reaction. But if it goes on too long, it can inhibit the grieving process because it makes it difficult for the survivor to remember the spouse realistically and put their relationship and the death into perspective. Also, idealization can increase the survivor's guilt and make it difficult to form new relationships. The survivor may feel disloyal to the spouse or may feel that no one can measure up to him or her.

Many grieving people increase their use of alcohol, drugs, or cigarettes at first to deaden their intense anxiety or sadness, but they should gradually return to the normal level of use as they begin to learn to cope.

STRATEGIES FOR COPING AFTER THE DEATH OF A SPOUSE

There are some steps the survivor can take to better cope during this time:

- At first, concentrate on handling practical matters that demand attention. Do not make any major decisions about changes.
- Ask for help when you need it—from family, friends, clergy, or counselors—whether it's someone to come over and stay with you or to help fix your car. Don't expect people to guess what you need, and don't ignore your own needs.
- Look for community programs or groups of people who are going through what you are experiencing. Sharing similar experiences with others helps you work through your feelings and reassures you of the normalcy of your emotions. If you do not seem to be able to cope or to move on at all, seek professional help from a grief counselor.
- When you feel ready, go through the deceased's belongings yourself or ask a friend to help you. Do not let someone else dispose of the spouse's possessions without consulting you.
- Don't sell the house or move to a new city right away. Not only is this a way of avoiding the situation, but it will add even more stress at a difficult time.
- Look for new avenues of interest and new sources of friends. It may not be possible—or best—to involve yourself in an outside activity at first, but it is a good idea to gradually explore potential new activities.

Gradually the symptoms of grief subside. Depression will be less intense, and as the habits that were previously connected with the deceased are altered, the daily routines of life will not automatically remind the survivor of the loved one. Health will improve and energy will begin to return to normal as the survivor passes from intense grieving into the stage where he or she can put together the pieces of a new life.

References

CHAPTER 1. NUTRITION IN THE LATER YEARS

Denton, Derek. *The Hunger for Salt.* New York: Springer-Verlag, 1982.

Herbert, Victor, M.D., and Genell Subak-Sharpe, M.S. *The Mount Sinai School of Medicine Complete Book of Nutrition* New York: St. Martin's, 1990.

Margen, Sheldon, M.D., and the Editors of the University of California at Berkeley *Wellness Letter. The Wellness Encyclopedia of Food and Nutrition.* New York: Health Letter Associates, 1992.

Starke, Rodman D., M.D., and Mary Winston, Ed.D., R.D. *American Association Low-Salt Cookbook.* New York: Times Books, 1990.

CHAPTER 4. COPING WITH STRESS

Benson, Herbert, and Miriam Z. Kipper. *The Relaxation Response.* New York: Avon Books, 1976.

Cramer, Kathryne D. *Staying on Top When Your World Turns Upside Down.* New York: Viking Penguin, 1991.

Goleman, Daniel, Ph.D., and Joel Gurin, eds. *Mind/Body Medicine.* Yonkers, NY: Consumer Reports Books, 1993.

Locke, Steven, and Douglas Colligan. *The Healer Within: The New Medicine of Mind and Body.* New York: E. P. Dutton, 1987.

Margolis, Harold J. *Stress: A Mind-Body Approach to Understanding and Overcoming Stress.* New York: Irvington, 1990.

McQuade, Walter, and Ann Aikman. *Stress: What It Is, What It Can Do to Your Health, How to Fight Back.* New York: Bantam, 1975.

Wright, H. Norman. *Beating the Blues: Overcoming Depression and Stress.* New York: Regal, 1988.

CHAPTER 6. MID-LIFE CRISIS: MEN

Levinson, Daniel J. *The Seasons of a Man's Life.* New York: Ballantine, 1986.

CHAPTER 7. MID-LIFE CRISIS: WOMEN

Gray, Mary Jane, M.D., and Florence Haseltine, M.D. *The Woman's Guide to Good Health.* Yonkers, NY: Consumer Reports Books, 1991.

CHAPTER 8. CHANGING RELATIONSHIPS

Adams, Frida C., et al. *Caring for Your Elderly at Home: How to Give Good Health Care.* New York: Wasa-Trends Publishing, 1990.

Baldwin, Donna R., and Jaqueline C. Gardner. *Grandma's Coming Home! A Guide to Establishing and Operating a Health Care Environment at Home.* New York: Doebear Publications, 1990.

MacLean, Helene. *Caring for Your Parents: A Source of Options and Solutions for Both Generations.* New York: Doubleday, 1987.

CHAPTER 9. LIFELONG LEARNING—THE KEY TO MENTAL FITNESS

Comfort, Alex. *A Good Age.* New York: Crown, 1976.

Montagu, Ashley. *Growing Young.* New York: Greenwood, 1988.

West, Robin. *Memory—Fitness Over 40.* Gainesville, FL: Triad, 1985.

CHAPTER 10. PLANNING FOR RETIREMENT

Bolles, Richard. *The Three Boxes of Life: And How to Get Out of Them.* Berkeley, Calif.: Ten Speed Press, 1981.

Dickman, Barry, and Trudy Lieberman. *How to Plan for a Secure Retirement.* Yonkers, NY: Consumer Reports Books, 1992.

CHAPTER 12. CANCER

Mullan, Fitzhugh, M.D., and Barbara Hoffman, J.D., eds. *Charting the Journey.* Yonkers, NY: Consumer Reports Books, 1990.

CHAPTER 13. ARTHRITIS

Sayce, Valerie, and Ian Fraser. *Exercise for Arthritis.* Yonkers, NY: Consumer Reports Books, 1989.

CHAPTER 14. MATURITY-ONSET DIABETES

Aloin, John F., Patricia Donohue-Porter, and Laurie Schlussel. *Diabetes, the Comprehensive Self-Management Handbook.* Garden City, NY: Doubleday, 1984.

Biermann, June. *The Diabetic's Book.* Los Angeles: J.P. Tarcher, 1990.

Colwell, Arthur R. *Understanding Your Diabetes.* Springfield, IL: Thomas, 1978.

Edelwich, Jerry. *Diabetes.* Reading, Mass.: Addison-Wesley, 1986.

Mirsky, Stanley, and Joan Rattner Heilman. *Controlling Diabetes the Easy Way.* New York: Random House, 1985.

Subak-Sharpe, Genell J. *Living with Diabetes.* New York: Doubleday, 1985.

CHAPTER 16. MENTAL FUNCTIONING IN AGING

Corbin, Juliet M., and Anselm Strauss. *Unending Work and Care: Managing Chronic Illness at Home.* New York: Jossey-Bass, 1988.

Heston, Leonard L., and June A. White. *The Vanishing Mind: A Practical Guide to Alzheimer's Disease and Other Dementias.* New York: W.H. Freeman and Company, 1991.

Mace, Nancy L., and Peter V. Rabins. *The 36-Hour Day: A Family Guide to Caring for Persons with Alzheimer's, Related Dementing Illnesses, and Memory Loss in Later Life.* Baltimore: Johns Hopkins University Press, 1991.

CHAPTER 18. THE HEALTH-CARE SYSTEM AND HOW TO USE IT

Baulch, Evelyn. *Extended Health Care at Home.* Berkeley, CA: Celestial Arts, 1988.

Buckingham, Robert W. *The Complete Book of Home Health Care.* New York: Continuum, 1984.

———. *The Complete Hospice Guide.* New York: Harper & Row, 1983.

Friedman, Jo-Ann. *Home Health Care: A Guide for Patients and Their Families.* New York: W.W. Norton, 1986.

Hamilton, Michael P., and Helen F. Reid. *A Hospice Handbook.* Grand Rapids, MI: Eerdmans, 1980.

Kohut, Jeraldine Joanne. *Hospice: Caring for the Terminally Ill.* Springfield, IL: C.C. Thomas, 1984.

Nassif, Janet Z. *The Home Health Care Solution: A Complete Consumer Guide.* New York: Harper & Row, 1985.

National Consumer's League. *A Consumer's Guide to Hospice Care.* Available through the NCL, 815 15th Street NW, Suite 928, Washington, DC 20005, or call (202) 639-8140.

Stoddard, Sandol. *The Hospice Movement.* New York: Vintage Books, 1992.

CHAPTER 19. INSURANCE AND HEALTH-CARE COSTS

Oshiro, Carl, Harry Snyder, and the Editors of Consumer Reports Books. *Medicare/Medigap.* Yonkers, NY: Consumer Reports Books, 1990.

Appendix A: Sources of Help

SOURCES OF HELP

CHAPTER 3. BREAKING BAD HABITS

Sources of Help for Alcoholism and Drug Abuse

Adult Children of Alcoholics (ACA)
P.O. Box 3216
Torrance, CA 90510
(310) 534-1815

Al-Anon Family Group Headquarters
Alateen
P.O. Box 862
Midtown Station
New York, NY 10018-0862
(800) 356-9996
(212) 302-7240

Alcoholics Anonymous
General Service Office
P.O. Box 459
Grand Central Station
New York, NY 10163
(212) 870-3400

American Council on Alcohol Problems, Inc.
3426 Bridgeland Drive
Bridgeton, MO 63044
(314) 739-5944

Association of Halfway House Alcoholism Programs of North America
23610 94th Avenue S.
Kent, WA 98031
(206) 859-0409

Betty Ford Foundation
39000 Bob Hope Drive
Rancho Mirage, CA 92270
(619) 340-3911

Center for Alcohol and Addiction Studies
Box G-BH, Brown University
Providence, RI 02912
(401) 863-1109

The Christopher D. Smithers Foundation
P.O. Box 67
Mill Neck, NY 11765
(516) 676-0067

Hazelden Foundation
P.O. Box 176
Center City, MN 55012
(800) 328-9000

Johnson Institute
7205 Ohms Lane
Minneapolis, MN 55439
(612) 944-0511

Mothers Against Drunk Driving (MADD)
511 East John Carpenter Freeway
Suite 700
Irving, TX 75062
(214) 263-0683

National Association for Children of Alcoholics, Inc.
11426 Rockville Pike
Suite 100
Rockville, MD 20852
(301) 468-0985

National Clearinghouse for Alcohol and Drug Information
P.O. Box 2345
Rockville, MD 20847-2345
(800) 729-6686
(301) 468-2600

National Council on Alcoholism and Drug Dependence, Inc.
12 West 21st Street, 8th Floor
New York, NY 10010
(800) 622-2255
(212) 206-6770

National Institute on Alcohol Abuse and Alcoholism
Parklawn Building
5600 Fishers Lane
Rockville, MD 20857
(301) 443-3860
(800) 729-6686

Rational Recovery
P.O. Box 800
Lotus, CA 95651-0800
(916) 621-4374

Secular Organizations for Sobriety (SOS)
Box 5
Buffalo, NY 14215-0005
(716) 834-2922

Women for Sobriety
P.O. Box 618
Quakertown, PA 18951-0618
(800) 333-1606

Stop-Smoking Groups

The following organizations can provide information about smoking-cessation groups. Check your telephone white pages for listings of local chapters.

American Cancer Society
National Office
1599 Clifton Road NE
Atlanta, GA 30329
(404) 320-3333
Ask for information about its Fresh Start quit-smoking program and its brochure "Seven-day Plan to Help You Stop Smoking Cigarettes."

American Heart Association
National Center
7320 Greenville Avenue
Dallas, TX 75231
(214) 373-6300
Distributes stop-smoking literature, including "Calling It Quits."

American Lung Association
1740 Broadway, 14th Floor
New York, NY 10019
(212) 315-8700
Write for its brochures "Freedom from Smoking in 20 Days" and "A Lifetime of Freedom from Smoking."

National Cancer Institute
Office of Cancer Communications
Building 31, Room 10A-24
Bethesda, MD 20892
(800) 4-CANCER
Write for its "Helping Smokers Quit Kit" and "Clearing the Air: A Guide to Quitting Smoking."

CHAPTER 6. MID-LIFE CRISIS: MEN

Sources of Help for Impotence

The Impotence Center
1104 Spring Street
Silver Spring, MD 20910
(301) 565-2718

Accredited Sex Therapists

The American Association of Sex Educators, Counselors, and Therapists
435 North Michigan, Suite 1717
Chicago, IL 60611
(312) 644-0828
Membership list is available for $5.

CHAPTER 8. CHANGING RELATIONSHIPS

Resources for Women

National Displaced Homemakers Network
1625 K Street NW, Suite 300
Washington, DC 20006
(202) 467-6346
Offers retraining programs and services to help older women reenter the job market.

Older Women's League
666 11th Street NW, Suite 700
Washington, DC 20001
(202) 783-6686
Provides variety of information and services.

Resources for Both Men and Women

ACTION
1100 Vermont Avenue NW
6th Floor
Washington, DC 20525
(202) 606-4853
Independent government agency that provides centralized coordination and administration of volunteer and other programs for older people.

American Association of Retired Persons (AARP)
601 E Street NW
Washington, DC 20049
(202) 434-2277
Provides information, insurance, and services for older people.

Legal Services for the Elderly Poor
130 West 42nd Street, 17th Floor
New York, NY 10036
(212) 391-0120

National Council of Senior Citizens
1331 F Street NW
Washington, DC 20036
(202) 347-8800

YMCAs and YWCAs
Department of Aging
Small Business Administration
Social Security Administration
Call your local chapter or office.

Resources for Caregivers
Organizations

Children of Aging Parents
1609 Woodbourne Road
Suite 302A
Levittown, PA 19057
(215) 945-6900

Choice in Dying
200 Varick Street
New York, NY 10014
(212) 366-5540
Information about living wills and state legislation covering their use.

Kansas Self-Help Network
Wichita State University
1845 Fairmount
Campus Box 34
Wichita, KS 67208-1595
(316) 689-3843
(800) 445-0116

The National Association for Home Care
519 C Street NE
Washington, DC 20002
(202) 547-7424
Information and resources for home care.

The National Self-Help Clearinghouse
City University of New York Graduate Center
25 West 43rd Street, Room 620
New York, NY 10036
Helps establish local self-help groups, maintains a referral service, etc.

Southern Tri-City Regional Self-Help Center
5839 Green Valley Circle, Suite 100
Culver City, CA 90230
(310) 645-9890

CHAPTER 9. LIFELONG LEARNING—THE KEY TO MENTAL FITNESS

Resources for Adult Learning

Administration on Aging
U.S. Department of Health and Human Services
330 Independence Avenue SW
Washington, DC 20201
(202) 619-0556

American Association for Adult and Continuing Education
2101 Wilson Boulevard
Suite 925
Arlington, VA 22201
(703) 522-2234

American Association of Community and Junior Colleges
One Dupont Circle NW
Suite 410
Washington, DC 20036
(202) 728-0200

American Association of Museums
1225 I Street NW
Washington, DC 20005
(202) 289-1818

American Association of University Women
1111 16th Street NW
Washington, DC 20036
(202) 785-7700

College Board ATP
P.O. Box 6200
Princeton, NJ 08541-6200
(609) 771-7600

Elderhostel
75 Federal Street
Boston, MA 02110-1941

The Extension Service
National Gallery of Art
4th and Constitution Avenue
Washington, DC 20565
(202) 842-6273

Gray Panthers
15 West 65th Street
New York, NY 10023
(212) 799-7572

Higher Education Program
Office of Post-Secondary Education
3012 ROB #3
U.S. Department of Education
Washington, DC 20202

Institute of Lifetime Learning
American Association of Retired Persons
601 E Street NW
Washington, DC 20049
(202) 434-2277

National Alliance of Senior Citizens
1700 18th Street NW
Suite 401
Washington, DC 20009
(202) 986-0117

National Association for Human Development
1424 16th Street NW
Suite 102
Washington, DC 20036
(202) 328-2192

National Council on the Aging, Inc.
409 3rd Street SW, Suite 200
Washington, DC 20024
(202) 479-1200

The National Home Study Council
1601 18th Street NW
Washington, DC 20009
(202) 234-5100
Provides information on correspondence courses.

National Senior Citizens Education and Research Center, Inc.
1331 F Street NW
Washington, DC 20004
(202) 347-8800

CHAPTER 10. PLANNING FOR RETIREMENT

Resources for Retirement

ACTION-RSVP
1100 Vermont Avenue NW
6th Floor
Washington, DC 20525
(202) 606-4853

American Association of Retired Persons (AARP)
National Headquarters
601 E Street NW
Washington, DC 20049
(202) 434-2277

Better Business Bureau
1012 14th Street NW
Washington, DC 20005
(202) 393-8000

National Council on Aging (NCOA)
409 3rd Street SW
Suite 200
Washington, DC 20024
(202) 479-1200

Small Business Administration—SCORE
26 Federal Plaza
New York, NY 10278
(212) 264-4507

CHAPTER 12. CANCER

Sources of Help

American Cancer Society, Inc.
National Headquarters
1599 Clifton Road NE
Atlanta, GA 30329
(404) 320-3333

Local chapters are listed in the white pages of the telephone directory. The following organizations, all sponsored by the society, can be contacted by calling your local ACS chapter. For those organizations with national headquarters, the addresses listed here can be helpful.

American Society of Clinical Hypnosis
2200 East Devon Avenue
Suite 291
Des Plaines, IL 60018
(708) 297-3317

Can supply the name of trained clinical hypnotists in your area (psychiatrists, psychologists, and social workers).

The American Society of Plastic and Reconstructive Surgeons
444 East Algonquin Road
Arlington Heights, IL 60005
(708) 228-9900

Provides a patient-referral service for those considering reconstructive surgery following cancer or other potentially disfiguring surgery.

Cancer Care, Inc.
National Cancer Foundation
1180 Avenue of the Americas
New York, NY 10036
(212) 221-3300

Provides counseling on physical and emotional effects of cancer on patients and families.

Cancer Information Service
Boy Scout Building, Room 340
9000 Rockville Pike
Bethesda, MD 20892
(800) 422-6237

The Candlelighters Childhood Cancer Foundation
Suite 460
7910 Woodmont Avenue
Bethesda, MD 20814
(301) 657-8401

An international organization of self-help groups for parents of children and adolescents with cancer. To locate a group near you, call or write the national office.

CanSurmount
c/o American Cancer Society

Uses volunteers to provide patients and families with current information.

Corporate Angel Network
Westchester County Airport, Building One
White Plains, NY 10604
(914) 328-1313 (nationwide)

Provides free air transportation to and from treatment centers for cancer patients and for an accompanying family member on private corporate airplanes. (For patients capable of walking without assistance only. Subject to availability.)

YWCA National Board
Attn.: Encore
726 Broadway
New York, NY 10003
(212) 755-4500

A nationwide program sponsored by the YWCA for women who have had breast-cancer surgery. Volunteers provide information, peer support groups, and postsurgery exercise programs.

I Can Cope
c/o American Cancer Society
Educates patients and families about cancer and how to deal with psychological stresses.

International Association of Laryngectomees
c/o American Cancer Society
Information on resources. Members visit hospitalized patients.

Leukemia Society of America, Inc.
733 Third Avenue
New York, NY 10017
(212) 573-8484
Provides financial assistance and consultation service.

National Cancer Institute
Office of Cancer Communications
Building 31, Room 10A16
Bethesda, MD 20892
(301) 496-4000
Information about the disease, treatment, and local resources. Toll-free number for questions about cancer operated by National Cancer Institute: 1-800-4-CANCER.

Reach to Recovery
c/o American Cancer Society
Volunteer organization staffed by former breast-cancer patients. Volunteers make in-hospital and home visits to women who have had mastectomies, and they provide both emotional support and practical information on breast reconstruction and other aspects of rehabilitation.

Ronald McDonald Houses
1 Croc Drive
Oakbrook, IL 60521
(312) 826-7129
Provides a place for children and/or their parents to stay during a child's treatment. To locate one near you, call or write A. L. Bud Jones, International Coordinator, at the address above.

Organizations That Specialize in Pain Control

American Chronic Pain Association
P.O. Box 850
Rocklin, CA 95677
(916) 632-0922

American Pain Society
5700 Old Orchard Road, 1st Floor
Skokie, IL 60077-1024
(708) 966-5595

International Association for the Study of Pain
909 N.E. 43rd Street
Suite 306
Seattle, WA 98105
(206) 547-6409

National Chronic Pain Outreach Association
7979 Old Georgetown Road
Suite 100
Bethesda, MD 20814-2429
(301) 652-4948

National Hospice Organization
1901 North Moore Street, Suite 901
Arlington, VA 22209
(800) 658-8898

CHAPTER 14. MATURITY-ONSET DIABETES

Resources

The American Diabetes Association
1660 Duke Street
Alexandria, VA 22314
(800) 232-3472
(703) 549-1500 (Virginia residents)
Organization with many local offices nationwide. Specializes in patient education, increasing public awareness of diabetes and funding diabetes research. Publishes literature on all aspects of diabetes, much of which is available at little or no cost.

Home Glucose Monitoring
LifeScan, Inc.
1000 Gibraltar Drive
Milpitas, CA 95035-6314
(800) 227-8862

CHAPTER 16. MENTAL FUNCTIONING IN AGING

Sources of Help for Alzheimer's Disease

Alzheimer's Disease and Related Disorders Association, Inc.
919 North Michigan Avenue, Suite 1000
Chicago, IL 60611
(800) 272-3900

Alzheimer's Disease Education and Referral Center (ADEAR)
P.O. Box 8250
Silver Spring, MD 20907-8250
(301) 495-3311
(800) 438-4380

Medic Alert Foundation International
P.O. Box 1009
Turlock, CA 95381-1009
(209) 668-3333

CHAPTER 18. THE HEALTH-CARE SYSTEM AND HOW TO USE IT

Home-Care Resources
Organizations

Home Health Services and Staffing Association
115D South Saint Asaph
Alexandria, VA 22314
(703) 836-9863, 9864
Provides members of home-care service agencies legislative and regulatory information on the state and federal level.

The National League for Nursing
350 Hudson Street
New York, NY 10014
Hotline: (800) 669-1656
Call for information on accreditation and to register complaints about an agency.

Hospice Information and Referral Services

The American Cancer Society
19 West 56th Street
New York, NY 10019
(212) 586-8700

Cancer Care, Inc.
1180 Avenue of the Americas
New York, NY 10036
(212) 221-3300

The National Hospice Organization
1901 North Moore, Suite 901
Arlington, VA 22209
(703) 243-5900

Visiting Nurse Association
See your local phone book.

Medical Insurance for Travelers

American Association of Retired Persons (AARP)
(202) 434-2277
(800) 523-5800 (customer service)
Offers a supplemental policy to Medicare that covers overseas medical expenses. Plans vary by state.

American Express
(212) 640-2000
Offers information, referral services, and financial assistance to cardholders under the Global Assist program. Members may borrow up to $5,000 for hospitalization at no interest if fully repaid within a month after receiving the bill.

Healthcare Abroad
P.O. Box 480
Middleburg, VA 22117
(800) 237-6615
(703) 687-3166
Offers a comprehensive insurance plan for $3 per day that includes $100,000 accident and sickness coverage and medical evacuation.

Resources for the Handicapped Traveler

Flying Wheels Travel
143 West Bridge
Owatonna, MN 55060
(800) 533-0363, (800) 535-6790
Specializes in independent and group travel for those confined to a wheelchair. Also offers tours, cruises, and independent vacation plans for the physically challenged.

Journeys on Dialysis
65 East India Row
22G
Boston, MA 02110
(800) 554-2637 (Massachusetts residents)
Fax: (617) 523-7970
Fax: (617) 523-0446 (for Massachusetts residents)
Arranges for dialysis on board selected cruise ships.

Society for the Advancement of Travel for the Handicapped
347 Fifth Avenue, Suite 610
New York, NY 10016
(212) 447-7284
Free referral service to a travel agency or tour operator, depending on the particular need.

Finding a Doctor Abroad

The International Association for Medical Assistance to Travelers (IAMAT)
417 Center Street
Lewiston, NY 14092
(716) 754-4883
Publishes a list of English-speaking doctors in 120 foreign countries. This list is available at no charge.

International SOS Assistance
P.O. Box 11568
Philadelphia, PA 19116
(800) 523-8930
(215) 244-1500 (Pennsylvania residents)
Offers a variety of services covering travel 100 miles away from home as well as overseas. Services include an international physician-referral network, free evacuation to adequate medical care if none exists in the country where you are vacationing, and a cash advance against your credit card to cover hospitalization and medical supplies ordered by a physician (except for first aid). Cost is $40 for up to two weeks, $80 per month, or $340 per year. (Frequent travelers may pay $275 per year.)

CHAPTER 20. COMING TO TERMS WITH MORTALITY

Sources of Support

Parents Without Partners
8807 Colesville Road
Silver Spring, MD 20910
(301) 588-9354

Widowed Persons Service
601 E Street NW
Washington, DC 20049
(202) 434-2277

Appendix B: Agencies on Aging

AGENCIES ON AGING

The offices listed in this section are responsible for coordinating services for older Americans.

Alabama
Commission on Aging
770 Washington Avenue
RSA Plaza
Suite 470
Montgomery, AL 36130
(800) 243-5463 (Alabama residents)
(205) 242-5743

Alaska
Older Alaskans Commission
P.O. Box 110209
Juneau, AK 99811-0209
(907) 465-3250

American Samoa
Territorial Administration on Aging
Government of American Samoa
Pago Pago, AS 96799
(684) 633-1251

Arizona
Department of Economic Security
Aging and Adult Administration
1789 W. Jefferson
Phoenix, AZ 85007
(602) 542-4446

Arkansas
Division of Aging and Adult Services
1417 Donaghey Plaza South
P.O. Box 1437/Slot 1412
Little Rock, AR 72203-1437
(501) 682-2441

California
Department of Aging
1600 K Street
Sacramento, CA 95814
(916) 322-3887

Colorado
Aging and Adult Services
Department of Social Services
1575 Sherman Street, 4th Floor
Denver, CO 80203-1714
(303) 866-3851

Commonwealth of the Northern Mariana Islands
Department of Community and Cultural Affairs
Civic Center
Commonwealth of the Northern Mariana Islands
Saipan, CM 96950
(607) 234-6011

Connecticut
Department on Aging
175 Main Street
Hartford, CT 06106
(800) 443-9946 (Connecticut residents)
(203) 566-7772

Delaware
Division of Aging
Department of Health and Social Services
1901 N. DuPont Highway
New Castle, DE 19720
(800) 223-9074 (Delaware residents)
(302) 577-4791

District of Columbia
Office on Aging
1424 K Street NW, 2nd Floor
Washington, DC 20005
(202) 724-5626
(202) 724-5622

Federated States of Micronesia
State Agency on Aging
Office of Health Services
Federated States of Micronesia
Ponape, ECI 96941

Florida
Office of Aging and Adult Services
1317 Winewood Boulevard, Building 2, Room 323
Tallahassee, FL 32399-0700
(904) 488-8922

Georgia
Office of Aging
Department of Human Resources
878 Peachtree Street NE, Room 632
Atlanta, GA 30309
(404) 894-5333

Guam
Division of Senior Citizens
Department of Public Health and Social Services
P.O. Box 2816
Agana, GU 96910
(671) 734-2942

Hawaii
Executive Office on Aging
335 Merchant Street
Room 241
Honolulu, HI 96813
(808) 586-0100

Idaho
Office on Aging
Statehouse, Room 108
Boise, ID 83720
(208) 334-3833

Illinois
Department on Aging
421 E. Capitol Avenue
Springfield, IL 62701
(217) 785-2870

Indiana
Department of Human Services
402 West Washington
Room E 431
Indianapolis, IN 46207-7083
(317) 232-7020

Iowa
Department of Elder Affairs
Suite 236, Jewett Building
914 Grand Avenue
Des Moines, IA 50309
(515) 281-5187

Kansas
Department on Aging
122-S Docking State Office Building
915 SW Harrison
Topeka, KS 66612-1500
(913) 296-4986

Kentucky
Division for Aging Services
Department for Social Services
275 E. Main Street
Frankfort, KY 40621
(502) 564-6930

Louisiana
Governor's Office of Elderly Affairs
P.O. Box 80374
Baton Rouge, LA 70898-0374
(504) 925-1700

Maine
Bureau of Elder and Adult Services
State House, Station 11
Augusta, ME 04333
(207) 289-3658

Maryland
State Agency on Aging
301 W. Preston Street
Baltimore, MD 21201
(301) 225-1102

Massachusetts
Executive Office of Elder Affairs
McCormick Bldg., 5th Floor
1 Ashburton Place
Boston, MA 02108
(800) 882-2003 (Massachusetts residents)
(617) 727-7750

Michigan
Office of Services to the Aging
P.O. Box 30026
Lansing, MI 48909
(517) 373-8230

Minnesota
Minnesota Board on Aging
444 Lafayette Road
St. Paul, MN 55155-3843
(612) 296-2770

Mississippi
Council on Aging
421 Pascagoula
Jackson, MS 39203
(601) 949-2070

Missouri
Division of Insurance
Truman Building 630 N.
P.O. Box 690
Jefferson City, MO 65102-0690
(800) 726-7390 (Missouri residents)
(314) 751-4126

Montana
Department of Family Services
P.O. Box 8005
Helena, MT 59604
(406) 444-5900

Nebraska
Department on Aging
Legal Services Developer
State Office Building
301 Centennial Mall South
Lincoln, NE 68509
(402) 471-2306

Nevada
Department of Human Resources
Division for Aging Services
1665 Hot Springs Road
Suite 158
Carson City, NV 89710
(702) 687-4210

New Hampshire
Department of Health and Human Services
Division of Elderly and Adult Services
6 Hazen Drive
Concord, NH 03301
(603) 271-4394

New Jersey
Department of Community Affairs
Division on Aging
S. Broad and Front Streets
CN 807
Trenton, NJ 08625-0807
(609) 292-0920

New Mexico
Agency on Aging
La Villa Rivera Building
Ground Floor
224 E. Palace Avenue
Santa Fe, NM 87501
(800) 432-2080 (New Mexico residents)
(505) 827-7640

New York
State Office for the Aging
Agency Building
2 Empire State Plaza
Albany, NY 12223-0001
(800) 342-9871 (New York residents)
(518) 474-5731

North Carolina
Department of Human Resources
Division of Aging
693 Palmer Drive
Raleigh, NC 27603
(919) 733-3983

North Dakota
Department of Human Services
Aging Services Division
1929 N. Washington
Bismarck, ND 58501
(701) 224-2577
Mailing Address: P.O. Box 7070
Bismarck, ND 58507-7070

Ohio
Department of Aging
50 W. Broad Street
8th Floor
Columbus, OH 43266-0501
(614) 466-1221

Oklahoma
Department of Human Services
Aging Services Division
P.O. Box 25352
Oklahoma City, OK 73125
(405) 521-2327

Oregon
Department of Human Resources
Senior Services Division
313 Public Service Building
Salem, OR 97310
(800) 232-3020 (Oregon residents)
(503) 378-3751

Pennsylvania
Department of Aging
Barto Building
231 State Street
Harrisburg, PA 17101
(717) 783-1550

Puerto Rico
Governors Office of Elderly Affairs
Gericulture Commission
P.O. Box 11398
Santurce, PR 00910
(809) 722-2429

Republic of the Marshall Islands
State Agency on Aging
Department of Social Services
Republic of the Marshall Islands
Marjuro, Marshall Islands 96960

Republic of Palau
State Agency on Aging
Department of Social Services

Republic of Palau
Koror, Palau 96940

Rhode Island
Department of Elderly Affairs
160 Pine Street
Providence, RI 02903
(401) 277-2880

South Carolina
Commission on Aging
400 Arbor Lake Drive
Suite B-500
Columbia, SC 29223
(803) 735-0210

South Dakota
Agency on Aging
Adult Services and Aging
Richard F. Kneip Building
700 Governors Drive
Pierre, SD 57501-2291
(605) 773-3656

Tennessee
Commission on Aging
706 Church Street
Suite 201
Nashville, TN 37243-0860
(615) 741-2056

Texas
Department on Aging
P.O. Box 12786
Capitol Station
Austin, TX 78711
(512) 444-2727

Utah
Division of Aging and Adult Services
120 North 200 West
P.O. Box 45500
Salt Lake City, UT 84145-0500
(801) 538-3910

Vermont
Office on Aging
Waterbury Complex
103 S. Main Street
Waterbury, VT 05676
(802) 241-2400

Virgin Islands
Department of Human Services
Barbel Plaza South
Charlotte Amalie
St. Thomas, VI 00802
(809) 774-0930

Virginia
Department for the Aging
700 Centre, 10th Floor
700 E. Franklin Street
Richmond, VA 23219-2327
(800) 552-4464 or (800) 522-3402
(Virginia residents)
(804) 225-2271

Washington
Aging & Adult Services Administration
Department of Social and Health Services
P.O. Box 45050
Olympia, WA 98504-5050
(206) 586-3768

West Virginia
Commission on Aging
1900 Kanawha Boulevard E.
Holly Grove
Charleston, WV 25305-0160
(304) 558-3317

Wisconsin
Bureau on Aging
Department of Health and Social Services
P.O. Box 7851
Madison, WI 53707
(608) 266-2536

Wyoming
Commission on Aging
Hathaway Building
First Floor
Cheyenne, WY 82002
(800) 442-2766 (Wyoming residents)
(307) 777-7986

Appendix C: State Insurance Departments

STATE INSURANCE DEPARTMENTS

Each state has its own laws and regulations governing all types of insurance. The offices listed in this section are responsible for enforcing these laws, as well as providing the public with information about insurance.

Alabama
Alabama Insurance Department
135 South Union Street
Montgomery, AL 36130-3401
(205) 269-3550

Alaska
Alaska Insurance Department
800 E. Dimond Boulevard
Suite 560
Anchorage, AK 99515
(907) 349-1230

American Samoa
American Samoa Insurance Department
Office of the Governor
Pago Pago, AS 96799
011-684/633-4116

Arizona
Arizona Insurance Department
Consumer Affairs and Investigation Division
3030 N. Third Street
Phoenix, AZ 85012
(602) 255-4783

Arkansas
Arkansas Insurance Department
Consumer Service Division
400 University Tower Building
1123 S. University Street
Little Rock, AR 72204
(501) 686-2945

California
California Insurance Department
Consumer Services Division

3450 Wilshire Boulevard
Los Angeles, CA 90010
(800) 233-9045

Colorado
Colorado Insurance Division
1560 Broadway
Suite 850
Denver, CO 80202
(303) 894-7499

Connecticut
Connecticut Insurance Department
153 Market Street
Hartford, CT 06103
(203) 297-3800

Delaware
Delaware Insurance Department
841 Silver Lake Boulevard
Dover, DE 19901
(302) 739-4251

District of Columbia
District of Columbia Insurance
613 G Street NW
Room 619
Washington, DC 20001
(202) 727-8017

Florida
Florida Department of Insurance
State Capitol
Plaza Level Eleven
Tallahassee, FL 32399-0300
(800) 342-2762 (Florida residents)
(904) 922-3100

Georgia
Georgia Insurance Department
Room 716 West Tower
2 Martin L. King, Jr., Drive
Atlanta, GA 30334
(404) 656-2056

Guam
Guam Insurance Department
855 W. Marine Drive
P.O. Box 2796
Agana, GU 96910
011-671/477-1040

Hawaii
Hawaii Department of Commerce and Consumer Affairs Insurance Division
P.O. Box 3614
Honolulu, HI 96811
(808) 586-2790

Idaho
Idaho Insurance Department
Public Service Department
500 South 10th Street
Boise, ID 83720
(208) 334-4320

Illinois
Illinois Insurance Department
320 West Washington Street
4th Floor
Springfield, IL 62767
(217) 782-4515

Indiana
Indiana Insurance Department
311 West Washington Street
Suite 300
Indianapolis, IN 46204
(800) 622-4461 (Indiana residents)
(317) 232-2395

Iowa
Iowa Insurance Division
Lucas State Office Bldg.
E. 12th & Grand Streets
6th Floor
Des Moines, IA 50319
(515) 281-5705

Kansas
Kansas Insurance Department
420 S.W. 9th Street
Topeka, KS 66612
(913) 296-3071

Kentucky
Kentucky Insurance Department
229 West Main Street
P.O. Box 517
Frankfort, KY 40602
(502) 564-3630

Louisiana
Louisiana Insurance Department
P.O. Box 94214
Baton Rouge, LA 70804-9214
(504) 342-5900

Maine
Maine Bureau of Insurance
Consumer Division
State House, Station 34
Augusta, ME 04333
(207) 582-8707

Maryland
Maryland Insurance Department
Complaints and Investigation Unit
501 St. Paul Place
Baltimore, MD 21202-2272
(301) 333-6300

Massachusetts
Massachusetts Division of Insurance
Consumer Services Section
280 Friend Street
Boston, MA 02114
(617) 727-7189

Michigan
Michigan Insurance Bureau
P.O. Box 30220
Lansing, MI 48909
(517) 373-0220

Minnesota
Minnesota Enforcement Division
Department of Commerce
133 E. 7th Street
St. Paul, MN 55101
(612) 296-4026

Mississippi
Mississippi Insurance Department
Consumer Assistance Division
P.O. Box 79
Jackson, MS 39205
(601) 359-3569

Missouri
Missouri Division of Insurance
Consumer Services Section
P.O. Box 690
Jefferson City, MO 65102-0690
(800) 726-7390 (Missouri residents)
(314) 751-2640

Montana
Montana Insurance Department
126 N. Sanders
Mitchell Building
P.O. Box 4009, Room 270
Helena, MT 59604
(800) 332-6148 (Montana residents)
(406) 444-2040

Nebraska
Nebraska Insurance Department
Terminal Building
941 O Street, Suite 400
Lincoln, NE 68508
(402) 471-2201

Nevada
Nevada Department of Insurance
Insurance Division
Consumer Section
1665 Hot Springs Road, Suite 152
Capitol Complex
Carson City, NV 89701
(702) 687-4270

New Hampshire
New Hampshire Insurance Department
Life and Health Division
169 Manchester Street
Concord, NH 03301
(603) 271-2261

New Jersey
New Jersey Insurance Department
Roebling Building
20 West State Street, CN 325
Trenton, NJ 08625
(609) 292-4757

New Mexico
New Mexico Insurance Department
P.O. Box 1269
Santa Fe, NM 87504-1269
(505) 827-4500

New York
New York Insurance Department
Empire State Plaza
Albany, NY 12257
(800) 342-3736 (New York State residents)
(212) 602-0203 (New York City residents)

North Carolina
North Carolina Insurance Department
Consumer Services
Dobbs Building
P.O. Box 26387
Raleigh, NC 27611
(919) 733-2004

North Dakota
North Dakota Insurance Department
Capitol Building
5th Floor
600 E. Boulevard Avenue
Bismarck, ND 58505
(800) 247-0560 (North Dakota residents)
(701) 224-2440

Ohio
Ohio Insurance Department
Consumer Services Division
2100 Stella Court
Columbus, OH 43266-0566
(614) 644-2673

Oklahoma
Oklahoma Insurance Department
P.O. Box 53408
Oklahoma City, OK 73152-3408
(405) 521-2828

Oregon
Oregon Department of Insurance
440 Labor and Industry Building
Salem, OR 97310
(503) 378-4484

Pennsylvania
Pennsylvania Department of Insurance
Consumer Services Bureau
Strawberry Square, 13th Floor
Harrisburg, PA 17120
(717) 787-2317

Puerto Rico
Puerto Rico Insurance Department
Fernandez Juncos Station
P.O. Box 8330
Santurce, PR 00910
(809) 722-8686

Rhode Island
Rhode Island Insurance Division
233 Richmond Street
Suite 233
Providence, RI 02903-4233
(401) 277-2223

South Carolina
South Carolina Insurance Department
Consumer Assistance Section
P.O. Box 100105
Columbia, SC 29202-3105
(803) 737-6140

South Dakota
South Dakota Division of Insurance
Enforcement
500 E. Capitol
Pierre, SD 57501-3940
(605) 773-3563

Tennessee
Tennessee Department of Commerce and
Insurance

Policyholders Service Section
4th Floor
500 James Robertson Parkway
Nashville, TN 37243-0582
(800) 342-4029 (Tennessee residents)
(615) 741-4955

Texas
Texas Department of Insurance
Consumer Services 111-1A
P.O. Box 149091
Austin, TX 78714
(512) 463-6169

Utah
Utah Insurance Department
Consumer Services
State Office Building, Room 3110
Salt Lake City, UT 84114
(801) 538-3800

Vermont
Vermont Department of Banking and Insurance
Consumer Complaint Division
120 State Street
Montpelier, VT 05602
(802) 828-3301

Virgin Islands
Virgin Islands Insurance Department
Kongens Garde No. 18
St. Thomas, VI 00802
(809) 774-2991

Virginia
Virginia Insurance Department
Consumer Services Division
700 Jefferson Building
P.O. Box 1157
Richmond, VA 23209
(804) 786-7691

Washington
Washington Insurance Department
Eastside Professional Building
924 East 7th
P.O. Box 40256
Olympia, WA 98504
(800) 562-6900 (Washington residents)
(206) 753-3613

West Virginia
West Virginia Insurance Department
2019 Washington Street, E
P.O. Box 50540
Charleston, WV 25305-0540
(304) 558-3386

Wisconsin
Wisconsin Insurance Department
Complaints Department
P.O. Box 7873
Madison, WI 53707
(608) 266-0103

Wyoming
Wyoming Insurance Department
Herschler Building
122 W. 25th Street
Cheyenne, WY 82002
(307) 777-7401

Index